Human Resource Management in Local Government

An Essential Guide

2nd Edition

Edited by Siegrun Fox Freyss

International
City/County
ICMA
Management
Association
icma.org

Textbooks of the International City/County Management Association

Advanced Supervisory Practices

Budgeting: A Guide for Local Governments

Capital Budgeting and Finance: A Guide for Local Governments

Economic Development: Strategies for State and Local Practice

Effective Communication

The Effective Local Government Manager

Effective Supervisory Practices

Emergency Management

The Future of Local Government Administration: The Hansell Symposium

Human Resource Management in Local Government: An Essential Guide

Local Government Police Management

Management Policies in Local Government Finance

Managing Fire and Rescue Services

Managing Human Resources: Local Government Cases

Managing Local Economic Development: Cases in Decision Making

Managing Local Government: Cases in Decision Making

Managing Local Government Finance: Cases in Decision Making

Managing Small Cities and Counties

The Practice of Local Government Planning

The Practice of State and Regional Planning

Service Contracting: A Local Government Guide

Library of Congress Cataloging-in-Publication Data

Human resource management in local government : an essential guide / edited by
Siegrun Fox Freyss.— 2nd ed.

   p. cm.

  Includes bibliographical references and index.

  ISBN 0-87326-144-5

1. Local officials and employees—United States.   2. Personnel management—
United States.   3. Local government—United States.   I. International City/
County Management Association.   II. Freyss, Siegrun Fox.

  JS331.H86 2004

  352.6'214'0973—dc22

                                2004015529

Printed in the United States of America.

08 07 06 05 04

5 4 3 2 1

04-241

About ICMA

The International City/County Management Association (ICMA) is the professional and educational organization for appointed managers and administrators serving cities, towns, counties, regional entities, and other local governments throughout the world. The mission of ICMA is to create excellence in local government by developing and fostering professional local government management and leadership worldwide. To further this mission, ICMA develops and disseminates new approaches to management and leadership through training programs, information services, and publications.

Local government managers and administrators—carrying a wide range of titles—serve at the direction of elected councils and governing boards. ICMA serves these managers and local governments through many programs that aim at improving the manager's professional competence and strengthening the quality of local governments. While ICMA recognizes professional management in all forms of local government, ICMA's origins lie in the council-manager form of local government, which combines the strong professional experience of an appointed local government manager or administrator with the strong political leadership of elected officials in the form of a council, board of selectmen, or other governing body.

ICMA was founded in 1914, adopted its Code of Ethics in 1924, and established its Institute for Training in Municipal Administration in 1934. The Institute provided the basis for the Municipal Management Series, popularly known as the "ICMA Green Books." By 1994, the institute had evolved into the ICMA University, which provides professional development resources for members and other local government employees.

ICMA's programs and activities include providing professional development; establishing guidelines for voluntary credentialing and standards of ethics for members; managing a comprehensive information clearinghouse; conducting local government research and data collection and dissemination; providing technical assistance; and producing a wide array of publications focused on local government management issues, including *Public Management* magazine, newsletters, management reports, and texts. ICMA's efforts toward the improvement of local government—as represented by this book—are offered for all local governments and educational institutions.

Contents

Preface   vii

1   Planning and Paying for Work Done   1
Internal Strategic Planning   1
The Personnel Function and the Budget   4
Organization of the Personnel Function   6
Classification and Compensation   8
Work Teams   28

2   Recruiting for a High-Performance Workforce   33
Recruitment   33
Selection   39
Hiring   53

3   Maintaining a High-Performance Workforce   59
Evaluating Employee Performance   59
Improving Performance through Goal Setting   76
Linking Performance to Compensation: Merit, Skill-Based, and
   Competency-Based Pay   78
Linking Performance to Advancement or Desirable Assignments   81
Other Motivators   84
Managing Organizational Change   86
Downsizing the Workforce   88

4   Labor-Management Relations and Collective Bargaining   93
Historical and Legal Framework   93
Employee Organizations in State and Local Government   96
Collective Bargaining Process   96
Resolving Bargaining Impasses   102
Administering the Contract   105
Challenges in Local Government Labor-Management Relations   107

5   Employee Rights: Avoiding Legal Liability   109
Employee Contracts and the Personnel Policy Manual   109
Personnel Policy Manual   110
Personnel Records   114
Discrimination   115
Sexual Harassment   126
Other Types of Prohibited Harassment   129

Family and Medical Leave Act   129

Workers' Compensation   133

Workplace Violence   137

Healthy Workplace   140

Constitutional Rights   141

6 Employee Benefits: Creating an Environment for Excellence   153

Structure of Benefit Plans   153

Delivery of Benefit Plans   161

Purchase and Design Considerations   171

Communicating the Benefits Program   172

Evaluation of Benefit Programs   173

7 Employee Responsibilities: Setting Expectations   179

Expectations of Attendance   179

Workplace Conduct   181

Interpersonal Relationships: On and Off Duty   183

Use of Public Property: Computers and the Internet   186

Confidentiality   189

Political Activity   189

Off-Duty Activities   190

Residency   193

Communicating Expectations and Responsibilities   194

Changing Policies   198

Conclusion   199

8 When Things Go Wrong   201

Discipline and Discharge of Employees   201

Investigating and Responding to Complaints by Employees   212

Complaints about Employees by Third Parties   218

Contested Cases in the Labor and Employment Arena   219

Alternative Dispute Resolution: Ways to Handle Things That Go Wrong—
Without Litigation   221

Civil Service Commissions or Appeals Boards   223

**9 Products and Services for Human Resource Management in Local
Government   225**

Nonprofit and Governmental Technical Assistance Providers   227

Selected Bibliography   233

List of Contributors   241

Index   245

Preface

Since the first edition of this book was published five years ago, several developments have made human resource management in local government more challenging. Fiscal stress has become a painful reality. It affects human resource management in several fundamental ways. Whether it involves position planning or recruiting, developing, or disciplining employees, cost becomes a central consideration for many personnel decisions.

Another change can be summed up under the term "globalization." Local governments, no matter what their size, are impacted by the high mobility of capital and people around the globe. More sophisticated financial markets, more international production processes, and a more diverse workforce have increased the complexity of public personnel management. Unfortunately, the global movements are not only of a peaceful, commercial nature, but have also brought terrorism to U.S. shores. The heightened insecurity requires local governments to divert scarce resources from traditional government functions to fund the increased safety needs in their jurisdictions.

A third challenge revolves around the need for employers to invest in human capital to make the best possible use of their human assets. But unlike fixed capital, people can exit when the pull by another employer becomes too strong. Investment in employees thus becomes a double-edged sword. It may build up the operational capacity of the agency, but it may also make the employees more marketable.[1]

One bright spot, however, has emerged in the information technology field, where the bursting of the high-tech bubble has made it easier to recruit top performers at the lower governmental pay rates. These new employees can help local governments select hardware and software appropriate for their operations, make effective use of the new acquisitions, and provide needed training for other employees.

Compared with the challenges caused by increased economic complexity and safety threats, changes in statutory and case law as well as new trends in best practices appear to be quite manageable. The U.S. Supreme Court has issued a few new rulings of importance to employers, and the Equal Employment Opportunity Commission has updated some regulations. Cities and counties, as well as professional organizations serving local governments, have been proactive in the area of human capital management and have become rich sources for finding exemplary or effective practices.

The second edition of the book has been thoroughly upgraded to reflect the new developments. As with the first edition, this book is intended as a reference text for local government executives seeking essential information about human resource management. The chapters systematically lay out the legal and professional principles and procedures that make up the best practices in public personnel administration at the county and municipal levels. The handbook makes accessible to the practitioner the substantial body of rules and guidelines that federal law, court rulings, state statutes, local ordinances, and the professional tradition of public administration have created.

The required or recommended principles and procedures explained in this guide cover the whole range of human capital management goals and activities:

- Linking human resource management to desired general governmental outcomes by taking stock of existing jobs, including job analysis, planning the nature and number of new positions, and determining appropriate compensation levels
- Attracting a high-performance workforce by recruiting, testing, and hiring the best possible applicants and properly orienting new employees
- Retaining and developing an excellent workforce by nurturing a high-performance work culture and providing effective evaluations, training, educational opportunities, financial incentives, and promotions
- Maintaining labor peace by working with unions during the certification process, in collective bargaining sessions, and in administering the union contract
- Avoiding legal liabilities by maintaining up-to-date personnel policy documents and respecting the rights of job applicants and employees
- Creating an environment for excellence by offering attractive benefit plans
- Strengthening a high-performance organizational culture by clearly communicating employee and employer responsibilities
- Avoiding organizational decline by dealing with problem employees in a timely manner
- Applying the best human capital management practices despite limited resources by using technical assistance services offered by public and private entities across the country.

All jurisdictions, irrespective of their size, are advised to adhere to legal and professional human resource management standards. Hiring, developing, and promoting a competent workforce creates the backbone for excellence in service to the public. Proper personnel procedures also are a form of risk management in that they can protect the employer from debilitating lawsuits.

However, many smaller jurisdictions do not have expert support staff to provide specialized managerial and legal knowledge in human resource management. The table below shows the relationship between the size of the jurisdiction and the employment of a human resource director. The International City/County Management Association's (ICMA) 2000 survey of local government personnel practices finds that as the population increases, so does the likelihood that the jurisdiction employs a full-time human resource administrator.

Percentages of Small and Medium-Size Municipalities Employing a Human Resource Director

Population of city	Percentage with human resource director
100,000–249,999	93
50,000–99,999	83
25,000–49,999	74
10,000–24,999	47

Source: 2000 ICMA Survey of Local Government Human Resource Functions.

Obviously, in places without a human resource director, human resource management is only one of several duties performed as needed by local officials responsible for other functions.

This book is intended to assist city and county executives, department heads, and other supervisory employees of relatively small jurisdictions, as well as students who will be serving in smaller local governments, in implementing sound human resource management practices. The guide covers the most common personnel procedures and puts them at the administrator's fingertips. Literature references, names and addresses of organizations, and Internet sites, listed throughout the text and in the last chapter, direct the user to more detailed information, technical assistance, and other resources.

Management trainees, including students of public administration, will also find this book relevant. Each chapter is written by a team of practitioners and academicians, some of whom are "pracademicians" who entered academia after years of practical service or, moving in the opposite direction, chose work in government after years of teaching and research. The purpose of the team arrangement is to draw on the best applied and theoretical knowledge in the human resource management field.

However, because the text is primarily intended for the general manager implementing personnel policies as needed, the details of academic criticism and the fine print in legal challenges to commonly administered personnel policies are kept to a minimum. Moreover, the book cannot do justice to the many jurisdictions around the country that are experimenting with innovative human resource management approaches.

The book acknowledges in each chapter the uncertain future and controversial nature of major personnel practices. For instance, Tompkins and Stapczynski point out in Chapter 1 that the classical model of the merit system is being questioned. Merit systems imply standardization of personnel policies, and the benefits of that are weighed against the drawbacks in the form of rule-laden rigidities and an inability to provide the flexibility needed to manage the modern and, as some would say, postmodern workplace.[2]

Affirmative action policies, covered by Witt and Patton in Chapter 2 and by DiNome and Yaklin in Chapter 5, are beset by uncertainties arising from legal and political challenges. Some opponents claim that affirmative action violates the Civil Rights Act of 1964 by practicing reverse discrimination and creating illegal preferences for women and minorities. Cases testing various applications of affirmative action programs continue to occupy state and federal courts, creating an unstable legal climate nationwide.

Performance appraisals and pay for performance are other controversial personnel tools, as shown by McCurdy and Lovrich in Chapter 3. Introduced in the 1970s and 1980s to improve work output, performance evalua-

tions were often poorly administered and brought disharmony to the workplace. More recently, proponents of team management have advocated abandoning individual performance evaluations and merit pay in favor of group rewards and constant attention to systemwide improvements. Other motivation experts argue that there is not one best way to motivate employees—that some employees respond better to individual rewards while others improve as attention is focused on team efforts and system shortcomings.

While Kearney and Feldman cover in Chapter 4 the important concepts and processes associated with traditional, adversarial union activities in local government, they also report on an emerging trend called interest-based bargaining, getting to yes, or win-win bargaining. These new approaches acknowledge the interests of both sides—management and labor—in certain collective bargaining outcomes and seek to turn the negotiations into a collaborative process.

In Chapter 5, the legal team of DiNome and Yaklin provides an inventory of the important laws regulating human resource management in local government. However, because statutory law and case law change constantly, the authors ask the public official to consult with legal counsel before making important personnel decisions. Likewise, Rosenbloom's analysis of the constitutional rights of employees, as interpreted by the courts, clarifies day-to-day situations, but one can expect ongoing court tests over the public service model, which tries to reach a balance among the interests of the public employer, the government employee, and the public.

Cost pressures and the increasingly diverse needs of the workforce have affected employment benefits, as described by Cayer and Volk in Chapter 6. To the traditional benefits of health insurance plans and pension plans, employers are adding wellness programs, employee assistance programs, and help with child and elder care. To keep costs under control, employers are increasingly offering these benefits in the form of cafeteria plans and requiring employees to share in the cost.

While work organizations are being reinvented, employers have to make it clear that certain boundaries should not be crossed. Research by Cozzetto, Pedeliski, and Tompkins in Chapter 7 finds that incivility and even violence in the workplace are increasing. Accordingly, employers have to insist that threatening behavior on the job is unacceptable and have to communicate clear standards of conduct in word and deed.

When things go wrong, as described by the Wise team in Chapter 8, the traditional method has been to punish the wrongdoer. Due process rights, however, circumscribe the disciplinary steps the employer can take, and the doctrine of just cause requires the employer to have strong evidence before dismissing an employee. Case law is continually testing and balancing the rights of employers versus the rights of employees, making it impossible to provide clear guidance for users of this handbook.

While the shifting principles and practices already create substantial ambiguity and uncertainty in human capital management, three broader developments further increase the complexity of public personnel administration:

- Demographic shifts in the workforce, as well as the need for workforce planning in general and succession planning in particular
- Ever-expanding use of high-tech equipment in public service and the resulting need for a highly trained workforce
- Introduction of new management theories and practices popularized under concepts like total quality management (TQM), high performance organization (HPO), reinventing government, team management, and balanced scorecard.[3]

HPO (a close successor to TQM) sees the work organization as an open system that can be constantly improved in its internal operations and in its interaction with the environment. One way to improve operations is by empowering employees and using their expertise more intensely. Managers are advised to consult with their employees regularly on ways to raise the quality of the work output and the service outcome. Job descriptions, testing procedures for new hires, and compensation must take into account the expanded responsibilities put on rank-and-file employees.

The reinventing government proponents borrow some ideas from TQM and other continuous-improvement strategies but add other suggestions uniquely suited to government service. In essence, reinventing government means replacing rule-bound, inward-looking public administration principles, such as the merit system, with flexible, customer-driven, and competitive market-driven management. The goals are a more satisfied citizenry and increased respect for government. Personnel policies in the area of recruitment, development, and pay have to be focused on the new outward-looking objectives.

The adaptation of local jurisdictions to the high-tech information age requires a high initial outlay in the purchase of hardware and software, in the hiring of expert staff, and in the training of employees. The need to maintain and upgrade the equipment, as well as the constant need to develop employees' proficiency in the use of the new acquisitions, creates ongoing costs. High-tech expenditures, however, are worthwhile in light of the outcomes: improved governmental service, reduced costs for businesses, and more satisfied citizens.[4] Four distinct areas are affected by improvements in information technology:

- Basic office management, such as word processing, billing, and payroll
- Executive management, in the form of management information systems and expert systems
- Professional decision making, through the availability of spatially patterned information generated by geographic information systems
- Communication with the public, in the form of public information systems such as Web sites and kiosks.[5]

In a survey of local governments in 2000, ICMA sought information on the use of computers in the management of human resources. It found that 92.0 percent of the cities participating in the survey used computers for human resource purposes. For payroll the figure was 86.5 percent, and for benefits administration it was 27.7 percent. To some extent the adoption of computers was a function of the size of the city.[6] Job vacancy information was posted on-line by 67.5 percent, and 7.0 percent of the cities had kiosks in public places. Cities in the Pacific Coast area showed higher percentages of adoption than other geographic divisions.[7] A newer ICMA survey, conducted in 2002, showed that more than half of local governments used an intranet to post job openings for internal recruitment, and one-third provided employee benefits forms on-line. Equally interesting for managers, in 2002 almost 40 percent of local governments reported using an intranet to enable project teams to collaborate, and more than 40 percent reported using an intranet to give telecommuting staff access to information and data.[8]

Finding the right hardware and software is a challenge because of the very competitive nature of the information industry and the rapid changes in the technology. A firm that appears to be the market leader one year may be teetering on bankruptcy a few years later. Flexibility and adaptability, but also continuity, are therefore important considerations in the purchase of high-tech products and services.

Demographic projections indicate slow population growth ahead, regional variations in population growth, the graying of the U.S. population, and a gradual diversification of the U.S. workforce.[9] If governments want to attract the best and the brightest from the emerging applicant pool, they have to make themselves appealing to heterogeneous job applicants. One way to do that is by not only ensuring equal employment opportunities but also practicing diversity management. This means forging a cooperative workforce among employees with different cultural traditions and personal needs. Human resource management consultants have developed workshops and training tapes to show employers how they can improve work output by using the cultural and individual uniqueness of their diverse employees.

The three new developments described above—demographic shifts, high-tech equipment, and new theories of management—increase the complexity of public personnel management but also promise to improve governmental service and raise the quality of civic life. It is therefore compelling to encourage

even smaller cities and counties to adopt these innovations. Resource scarcity is, of course, an obstacle, and to reduce it, this book lists various ways to obtain the needed technical assistance at moderate cost.

The constitutional and legal environment also creates complexities that a reference book cannot fully capture. Some employment principles are based on federal law and court rulings and have to be uniformly applied by all jurisdictions. Such principles include equal employment opportunity requirements under the Civil Rights Act of 1964 and subsequent amendments, the treatment of impaired job applicants and employees under the Americans with Disabilities Act of 1990, and the accommodation of persons requesting leave under the Family and Medical Leave Act of 1993. State law regulates other personnel standards; for example, labor relations are to a great extent codified by the states. Local ordinances bring additional variation to public personnel management. For instance, the number of job classes falling under civil service or under at-will employment is often the result of local decisions. Case law in human capital management is incremental and never covers all issues. In many personnel areas, courts seem to be waiting for managers to make mistakes before a rule will be developed. While this threat hangs over their heads, managers are also pressured to act proactively to reengineer their organizations.

Regional preferences have created organizational and political traditions that require different personnel policies to improve performance. This handbook therefore avoids prescribing one-size-fits-all human resource management procedures. Instead, users are encouraged to assess the particular political and organizational culture of their jurisdictions and adapt the personnel practices to local circumstances. For instance, an organization suffering from poorly performing patronage appointees might be advised to introduce the merit system or strengthen it if it is legally in place. On the other hand, a jurisdiction suffering from rigidities caused by a formal merit system might consider reducing that system's influence.

The presentation of the information in sidebars signals the degree to which personnel policies are settled. Well-established legal and professional standards are presented as "guiding principles" and reinforced as "tips" for the successful implementation of the policy. Conversely, clearly unprofessional or illegal personnel practices are identified as "red flags." In between these two extremes are the many gray areas, which are listed under "challenges." These are instances in which human resource researchers and consultants cannot give a definitive answer. The authors of the chapters cannot prescribe or proscribe proper or improper practices because the lines are not clearly drawn. Moreover, in some cases, two equally defensible standards are in conflict. In such circumstances, the manager is asked to exercise judgment and leadership.

In conclusion, the guide provides access to essential human resource management techniques accumulated over the past hundred years and considered the best practices in public personnel administration. In many instances, managers can use the tools to guide their personnel decisions. Where additional technical assistance is needed, the user is referred to relevant consulting services. However, human capital management is in flux because of ongoing changes in laws, court rulings, demographics, technology, practical insights, and theoretical knowledge. The guide therefore also lists organizations that track trends and help public administrators stay current and make proactive human resource management decisions.

---

[1] The summary term for the administration of the workforce has experienced a historical progression from "personnel management," to "human resource management," and now "human capital management." These changes reflect subtle differences as well as major shifts, which are associated with the reinventing-government movement and described in the first chapter. This book uses the three terms interchangeably, however. See Kay Coles James, "The HR Paradigm Shift and the Federal Human Capital Opportunity," *The Public Manager* 30, no. 4 (Winter 2001–02), 13–16.

[2] Siegrun Fox Freyss, "Local Government Operations and Human Resource Policies: Trends and Transformations," in *The 2004 Municipal Year Book* (Washington, D.C.: ICMA, 2004), 19–27.

[3] David Osborne and Ted Gaebler, *Reinventing Government: How the Entrepreneurial Spirit Is Transforming the Public Sector* (Reading, Mass.: Addison-Wesley, 1992); Robert S. Kaplan and David P. Norton, *The Balanced Scorecard: Translating Strategy into Action* (Boston: Harvard Business School Press, 1996); Steven Cohen and William Eimicke, *Tools for Innovators: Creative Strategies for Managing Public Sector Organizations* (San Francisco: Jossey-Bass, 1998).

[4] Russell L. Smith, "The 'Electronic Village': Local Governments and E-Government at the Dawn of a New Millennium," in *The 2002 Municipal Year Book* (Washington, D.C.: ICMA, 2002), 34–41; Barbara J. Wilson, *E-Government: Managing for the Future* (Fort Worth, Tex.: City of Fort Worth, 2003).

[5] Applications of high-tech innovations for local government are documented by Public Technology, Inc., in its publications and at its Web site, www.pti.org. Another information source is the magazine, *Government Technology,* and the Web site, www.govtech.net.

[6] Evelina Moulder, *Compensation and Benefits for Local Government Employees: Programs and Practices,* Special Data Issue no. 6 (2000) (Washington, D.C.: International City/County Management Association, 2001), 3.

[7] Evelina Moulder, *Recruiting and Selecting Local Government Employees: Programs and Practices,* Special Data Issue no. 5 (2000) (Washington, D.C.: International City/County Management Association, 2001), 4–6.

[8] Evelina Moulder, *Inside E-Government: Applications for Staff*, Special Data Issue no. 6 (2002) (Washington, D.C.: International City/County Management Association, 2002), Table 3.

[9] Richard W. Judy and Carol D'Amico, *Workforce 2020: Work and Workers in the 21st Century* (Indianapolis, Ind.: Hudson Institute, 1997); International Personnel Management Association, *Workforce Planning Resource Guide for Public Sector Human Resource Professionals* (Alexandria, Va.: IPMA, 2002); Robert P. Gill, "Essentials of Workforce Planning," *IPMA-HR News* (February 2004), 1, 3; William J. Rothwell, "Knowledge Transfer: 12 Strategies for Succession Management," *IPMA-HR News* (February 2004), 10–11.

CHAPTER 1

Planning and Paying for Work Done

JONATHAN TOMPKINS AND ALEKSANDRA STAPCZYNSKI

Work positions are the basic building blocks of organizational life. As we explore new and better ways of organizing people to carry out the work of government, positions still provide the foundation. Teamwork is encouraged more today than in the past, duties are often defined more broadly, managers are increasingly given more discretion in assigning work, and yet all of these changes take for granted the existence of relatively well-defined positions.

Once the duties and qualifications are determined, individuals with the required knowledge, skills, and abilities (KSAs) can be selected to fill vacant positions, new recruits can be oriented to their jobs, and their base pay can be set according to the demands their jobs place on them. How to plan, define, classify, and evaluate positions, and how to compensate employees on the basis of work performed, are the subjects of Chapter 1.

Internal Strategic Planning

Guiding Principle
Operating departments must have a clear understanding of their strategic objectives.

Challenges
- Preventing political dissension, information overload, and simple inertia from reducing productivity.
- In small jurisdictions, where chief administrative officers (CAOs) and department heads lack essential staff support, developing a results-oriented culture without using a formal planning process.

Personnel management is most effective when policies, procedures, and daily decisions are linked systematically to the organization's mission. For this reason, our discussion of personnel management begins with strategic planning, a management tool for enhancing organizational performance by keeping everyone focused on mission-oriented goals and objectives.

Strategic planning is a systematic process undertaken by governments and their operating departments to establish why they exist, where they want to go, and how they will get there. It results in a strategic plan outlining future goals and objectives and the strategies for achieving them. There are two general types of strategic planning. *External* strategic planning aims at resolving political issues in the larger community. It involves representatives from a diverse range of community groups, as well as elected and appointed officials, and it addresses such issues as growth management, downtown renewal, and waste disposal. *Internal* strategic planning, by contrast, takes an inward look at local government programs and services. Its primary purpose is to improve organizational performance. For this reason, internal planning is more likely than external planning to address issues relating to personnel management. Such issues include developing human resources, purchasing a new management information system, and rewriting administrative procedures. Although input is solicited from many stakeholders, participation is usually limited to key line and staff officers. Elected officials should be included in the process or at least given the option to participate.

In practice, internal strategic planning can vary from a formal and institutionalized annual ritual to an informal and unscheduled set of discussions about organizational priorities. Whether formal or informal, internal strategic planning typically involves the following elements:

- Defining the organization's mission
- Conducting environmental analyses
- Identifying and prioritizing critical issues
- Establishing goals, objectives, and strategies
- Assigning responsibility and monitoring progress.

Exhibit 1-1 provides examples of a mission statement and goals, objectives, and strategies as typically set forth in a strategic plan.[1]

As a management tool, internal strategic planning has much to recommend it. Personnel decisions are most effective when they are linked strategically to the organization's mission. A well-defined sense of mission, and the goals and objectives that flow from it, pro-

Exhibit 1-1   Elements of a Strategic Plan

Key Element	Example
Mission Statement	The mission of the city fire department is to ensure the safety of the community by responding to fires and other emergencies quickly, doing all it can to save lives and property, and educating the public about fire prevention.
Critical Issue	Growing population; insufficient and aging firefighting equipment
Goal	Upgrade fire department equipment and operations to meet growing fire service demand
Objective	Obtain voter approval of bond issue in November election for new fire station in recently annexed area and for new firefighting equipment for all fire stations in the city
Strategies	Collect data on current capacity and response times to support argument that a new station and equipment is in the public's best interest
	Assess and prioritize future fire station locations; identify most cost-efficient equipment available for purchase

vide a point of departure for establishing personnel policies and practices and a baseline for judging their effectiveness. In addition, strategic planning provides opportunities to adapt successfully to changing external conditions. The environment in which agencies operate is a dynamic one. For example, the economic downturn in the early years of the new millennium produced a period of declining government revenues and a series of fiscal crises that, among other things, greatly constrained the ability of local governments to attract and retain the best available workers.[2] The wise use of scarce resources is now more important today than ever before. Similarly, increased globalization means that local governments require a more sophisticated, multicultural, and better educated workforce than ever before. In short, strategic planning provides both a means of establishing the essential linkages between administrative decisions and the attainment of institutional objectives and a means of adapting successfully to a constantly changing environment.

Considerations relating to personnel management enter into the strategic planning process at two points.[3] First, current personnel capabilities must be taken into account when organizational goals and objectives and the strategies for achieving them are being identified. For example, employees may not possess the mix of KSAs required to achieve desired goals, or the state of morale may be so low that employees resist undertaking new strategic initiatives; KSAs may have to be enhanced and morale and motivation improved first.

Consequently, human capacity building may emerge during deliberations as a critical issue in its own right. Strategies for building human capacity may include targeted recruitment efforts, more attractive benefit packages, job-specific training courses, employee development and internal promotion programs, and increased opportunities for employee involvement in decision making.

Second, once the strategic plan has been approved and communicated throughout the organization, personnel policies and practices must be adjusted so that they are consistent with and contribute to strategic objectives. Many areas of personnel management are likely to be affected by strategic planning. For example, an impending labor shortage may lead administrators to identify a 20 percent reduction in turnover as a strategic objective. Administrators at all levels must then review existing personnel policies and practices and scrutinize their daily personnel decisions to ensure that they are contributing to reduced turnover. New personnel policies or programs may need to be developed; existing ones may need to be modified. Similarly, some jobs may need to be eliminated and others created or redesigned. Such changes must be adopted not because a neighboring jurisdiction is making them but because they clearly advance specific goals and objectives.

The city manager or county administrator has an important role to play at both of these points. In larger jurisdictions, the personnel director is generally responsible for offering advice during strategic deliberations, analyzing the gaps between current capabilities and projected needs, and adjusting personnel policies and practices as needed to implement the strategic plan. In smaller jurisdictions, however, the CAO and department heads have to undertake these responsibilities without the support of a personnel staff. How to do so successfully is one of the challenges of strategic planning.

Strategic planning is heavily process oriented and therefore difficult to sustain. Causes of system breakdown include political discord among participants, a sense of overload caused by tackling too many issues and collecting too much information, and the inertia that results when the process is perceived as a meaningless annual ritual. The remedy for each of these ills is sustained leadership. The CAO, department head, or someone designated as a "process champion" must have the time, energy, and will to keep the process on track. Administrators should not undertake strategic planning unless they are fully committed to its underlying purposes and prepared to exercise the necessary leadership. The latter includes a willingness to wade into the political fray to help participants reach agreement among competing priorities, restrict the goal-setting process to only a handful of issues each year, and hold designated individuals accountable for producing results.

The decision whether to engage in strategic planning is not an easy or simple one. Strategic planning is deliberately designed to produce change, and change causes disruptions and generates resistance. Once the decision is made to proceed, the planning process must be carefully managed. If too much is attempted too quickly, or if there is insufficient leadership, the process will collapse of its own weight. Internal strategic planning is often easier to sustain at the department level, where there is more likely to be a unified sense of mission, fewer players, and less discord.

Another challenge is how to obtain the advantages of strategic planning in a small jurisdiction where CAOs and department heads lack the support staff required to undertake a time-consuming and labor-intensive process. In fact, strategic planning need not entail a formal and institutionalized process at all. A formal, sequential process of the kind described in textbooks can actually drive out strategic thinking. What is important is that administrators at all levels think and act strategically by linking what they do to the results they wish to achieve. Administrators can often obtain good results simply by encouraging strategic analysis at staff meetings, over lunch, and in the hallways. In short, they can develop a results-oriented culture by challenging each organizational unit to define its mission, identify the issues affecting it, establish strategic goals and objectives, and align personnel

Tips for Successful Strategic Planning

❐ Assign a "process champion" to lead each strategic initiative.

❐ Keep the process simple by focusing on only a few critical issues at a time.

❐ Involve employees and other key stakeholders, including elected officials.

❐ Make sure the planning team has the resources it needs, including access to people and information, to develop the strategic plan.

❐ Avoid allowing the planning process to become a cold and despised annual ritual.

❐ Encourage all supervisors and managers to engage in strategic thinking, whether or not it is tied to a formal planning process.

policies and practices with those goals and objectives.[4]

The Personnel Function and the Budget

Guiding Principle

Adequate funding to attract, develop, motivate, and retain good employees is fundamental to organizational effectiveness.

Challenges

• Giving personnel-related budget requests the time, attention, and level of priority they deserve in the budgeting process.

• Finding the optimal balance between economy and effectiveness.

• Providing managers with optimal flexibility in managing their budgets.

The primary responsibility of personnel management is to attract, develop, motivate, and retain high-performing employees. How this responsibility is carried out changes continuously as administrators respond to internal needs and external opportunities and constraints. A labor shortage, for example, may indicate the need both for more aggressive recruitment efforts to attract skilled workers and for higher financial incentives to retain the best in the current workforce. Moreover, the growing complexity of employment law and labor relations increases the need to seek technical assistance from outside personnel specialists. When such demands cannot be accomplished with available resources, administrators must ask for budgetary enhancements.

Charged with balancing their budgets with limited revenues, city councils and county commissions tend to view requests for personnel-related enhancements with considerable skepticism. Since the budget allocates scarce resources to departments and programs, it is rarely possible to fund all budgetary requests. And since pay and benefits often represent more than 70 percent of the operating budget, proposed enhancements can have an enormous impact on the budget.[5] In the end, councils and commissions may opt for economy over promised gains in effectiveness. Nonetheless, because the ability to attract, develop, motivate, and retain good employees is a fundamental determinant of organizational effectiveness, local government administrators must see to it that strategic initiatives relating to personnel are given the time, attention, and level of priority they deserve during budgetary deliberations.

Three strategies are now being used by local governments to improve their ability to build an effective workforce. The greatest break from tradition is to allow managers to move funds between expense categories or line items as needed as long as their unit's overall budget allocation is not exceeded. Within that same constraint, ceilings on the number of full-time equivalent employees are also eliminated, allowing managers to spend payroll dollars as they wish. In a few jurisdictions, managers are also allowed to carry money saved into the next fiscal year. This strategy assumes that managers need greater flexibility in managing their budgets if they are to achieve their goals and that they can be trusted to use that authority responsibly. Advocates argue that the line-item budgets introduced in the early 1900s to tightly control expenditures are no longer needed because management is much more professionalized and accounting and auditing procedures are much more sophisticated.[6] Nonetheless, delegating greater spending authority to line managers is likely to remain a tough sell.

A second strategy is to encourage performance budgeting by requiring department heads to tie their budgetary requests to their strategic plans. Several state and local jurisdictions have embraced this strategy since the Government Performance and Results Act of 1993 mandated it for federal agencies.[7] In general, this strategy requires departments to adopt strategic plans that specify clear goals and objectives and the indicators to be used to measure progress in achieving them. Departmental budget requests are then justified in terms of their respective contributions to attaining performance goals. If managers are also delegated greater spending authority, they can be held accountable not simply for staying within their budgets but for producing results as well. Being able to establish linkages between expenditures and strategic goals also improves the ability of administrators to obtain approval of their budgetary requests from economy-minded councils, boards, and commissions. This strategy is still in its experimental stages, however. Some administrators remain concerned that if their performance goals are not met, their budgets may be reduced.

A third, and more modest, strategy is to search for economies within traditional line-item budgets to free up funds for other purposes. If a department can reduce its payroll costs, it can then ask for authority to spend the funds for training, pay-for-performance, or other capacity-building uses. Many jurisdictions, for example, are economizing by reducing their core complement of full-time employees and relying more on temporary, part-time, and contract employees to handle seasonal or occasional work assignments. The challenge lies in reducing the size of the permanent workforce without overburdening employees, undermining morale, or harming service delivery.

In the final analysis, a jurisdiction's budget is the clearest indicator of the government's priorities and policy objectives. Administrators who understand the centrality of employees to organizational performance must be willing to wade into the political fray to support those personnel-related requests that clearly contribute to organizational performance. They should also explore the merits of allowing managers greater flexibility in managing their budgets. For elected and appointed officials alike, the search for an optimal balance between economy and effectiveness never ends.

Organization of the Personnel Function

Guiding Principle

Human resource policies should provide a solid organizational foundation, but must also be open to new developments.

Challenges

- Establishing a proper degree of formalization and centralization while preserving needed flexibility.
- Using merit systems to enhance personnel management without paralyzing it.

The structure of the personnel system—whether it is organized on a merit or patronage basis, is highly centralized or decentralized, or is governed by detailed rules or general policies—clearly affects organizational performance. Highly rule-bound and centralized systems, for example, tend to reduce manage-

rial flexibility, protect marginal employees, and rob the organization of the ability to adapt to changing circumstances. Conversely, a jurisdiction without any system at all—without a central personnel office or a uniform set of policies and procedures—may find it very difficult to ensure that all departments are complying with employment law and managing personnel effectively. Some degree of central policy direction and staff support is desirable to create stability and ensure fairness, but not so much that line managers lose the discretion and flexibility they need to carry out their missions. The challenge for administrators is to determine the level of formalization and centralization that is most appropriate to their circumstances and strategic objectives.

Organizational charts of the individual administrative units are useful in schematically placing positions and ranking them in job classes. When the organizational practice seems to defy the neat arrangement of functions and ranking of positions, however, the need for a more consistent classification scheme may become obvious. Sometimes it may be appropriate to revise the organizational chart of the whole administration to clarify alterations in the relationship between line and staff agencies.

Although personnel systems exist theoretically to support the attainment of organizational objectives, those objectives are constantly changing while the personnel systems are often fixed in statute, charter, or ordinance and are therefore slow to change. Personnel systems are also designed to achieve values other than organizational effectiveness. These include due process, equal opportunity, and the elimination of patronage. In many locales, centralized merit systems continue to constrain managerial discretion long after the need for them has passed. Only recently have they begun to give way to organizational structures designed to empower managers rather than control them. While administrators in small cities and counties are probably not subject to the constraints of highly centralized merit systems, understanding their characteristics is useful for those wishing to design a personnel system that enhances performance while simultaneously protecting due process, equal opportunity, and merit.

The Civil Service System

A civil service system consists of a body of rules and regulations governing non-elected employees, including the methods of selecting, promoting, rewarding, and disciplining. Most of these rules and regulations pertain to the *career service,* those employees who competed for positions with the intent of making the civil service their career. A few rules and regulations pertain to other employees who may be dismissed at will.

The term *merit system* refers to any civil service system organized specifically to protect and promote merit principles. These principles include

- Competition for government jobs that is open to everyone
- Selection of civil servants based on their qualifications for office
- Protection of civil servants from partisan coercion
- Protection of civil servants from arbitrary treatment in all personnel actions.

These principles apply to employees in the career service but not to political appointees.

For nearly one hundred years the federal Civil Service Act of 1883 provided the model for state and local governments in establishing merit systems. The structural characteristics of the classic merit system are as follows:

A Semi-Independent Commission with Policy-Making, Administrative, and Adjudicatory Powers. The first merit systems placed control of the personnel system outside of the executive chain of command because reformers feared that CAOs would not be able to resist pressures to award jobs on the basis of patronage. Although the scope of a commission's authority varies from one jurisdiction to the next, commissions are generally responsible for establishing personnel policies, administering employment examinations, and enforcing and adjudicating merit rules.

Centralized Testing. The primary task of traditional civil service commissions is to develop competitive exams for each major occupational category, administer and score exams, and rank eligible applicants in order of their scores. The purpose is to remove all but the final hiring decision from the hands of line managers so that civil servants cannot be appointed on the basis of patronage, nepotism, or other forms of favoritism. Although commissions today often share personnel duties with administrators, centralized testing remains a key feature of formal merit systems.

A High Degree of Formalization. Formalization refers to the written rules, regulations, and procedures that characterize organizational life. In traditional merit systems, personnel decisions are governed by highly detailed rules and regulations, complex administrative procedures, and seemingly endless paperwork. These are viewed as necessary to guard against every possible abuse of authority as well as to promote values such as pay equity, administrative efficiency, equal opportunity, and due process. Emphasis in formal merit systems is placed on regulating compliance with rules rather than on facilitating organizational performance.

Once viewed as a solution, formal merit systems are now viewed as the problem.[8] When combined with line-item budgets and rigid position classification systems, formal merit systems prevent managers from hiring employees in a timely manner and deny them the flexibility they need to reassign duties and pay employees on the basis of their level of performance. These constraints make it difficult to fulfill the essential personnel functions of attracting, developing, motivating, and retaining highly qualified employees.

The Executive Personnel Office

The federal Civil Service Reform Act of 1978 introduced a model that had already been implemented by many local governments in the 1960s. An executive personnel office, directly accountable to the chief executive, was given the responsibility to administer personnel policies. In about half of local jurisdictions, civil service commissions have been retained in an advisory or adjudicatory capacity.[9]

Small jurisdictions do not need a separate personnel department. The CAO or department heads make most personnel decisions. Nevertheless, such jurisdictions are advised to have a centrally directed, merit-based personnel system. A uniform set of personnel policies helps to ensure that all department administrators are complying with merit principles and the requirements of employment law, that all employees are being treated fairly and consistently, and that all personnel decisions are contributing to the effective management of human resources.

Choosing the Best Approach

Because each government is unique in terms of its circumstances and strategic objectives, it is impossible to prescribe a single approach for organizing the personnel function. It is possible, however, to offer a few generalizations. First, if patronage and other forms of favoritism are clearly undermining the integrity and performance of civil servants, administrators should look for ways to institutionalize merit principles. Second, small jurisdictions without a professionally staffed personnel office and without uniform personnel policies should weigh the advantages of an organized personnel system against the costs. Third, if a decision is made to establish a personnel office, its primary mission should be defined in terms of service and technical assistance

rather than administrative control. Fourth, the personnel office should seek to guide and direct line managers through broad policy statements rather than through detailed rules and regulations.

Generally speaking, it is better to hold managers accountable for their actions after the fact than to constrain their actions in advance through narrowly defined rules. Too often the rules and regulations imposed by a central office dictate courses of action that are not fully appropriate to situations at the department level. Being closer to the situation at hand, managers are better positioned to decide how to appraise, discipline, counsel, and reward employees. Finally, CAOs should explore the potential advantages of relaxing the constraints imposed by rigid line-item budgets, personnel ceilings, classification schemes, and pay systems.

Classification and Compensation

Guiding Principles

- Employees doing similar work should receive comparable pay.
- Variations in pay must be based on significant differences in responsibilities and required KSAs, and on the salaries paid by other employers in the marketplace.
- The process for classifying and evaluating the relative worth of positions must be fair.

Challenges

- Determining whether to contract with a consultant or to develop a comprehensive classification and pay plan in-house.
- Complying with state and federal statutes concerning the design and implementation of classification and pay systems.
- Educating employees about the process and purpose of a classification and compensation study.
- Maintaining the integrity of a comprehensive classification and pay system.

Employees are a local government's most import asset and one of its most significant expenditure items. Today, local governments need to develop aggressive pay policies to compete successfully for well-qualified employees. Compensation levels must be high enough to attract a strong applicant pool and retain the best among the current employees. Morale is enhanced when workers know that their pay is keeping up with or exceeding the prevailing market rate. The adoption of a classification and compensation system is thus an essential prerequisite for a well-managed, comprehensive personnel system.

A classification and compensation system is a process for reviewing job duties, classifying positions on the basis of uniform criteria, and allocating positions to salary grades that reflect their relative worth and market value. Such a system lays the foundation for many other parts of the larger personnel system: establishing qualifications for recruitment, testing, and selection; establishing lines of authority and areas of responsibility; and providing a basis for defining standards of work performed. A classification and pay plan that is continuously maintained results in

- Fewer requests for reclassifications
- Fewer grievances arising out of disputed job requirements
- Fewer pay inequities and morale problems
- Reduced subjectivity in pay determination
- A solid basis for evaluating work performance.

An effective classification and pay system will attract, reward, and retain qualified personnel.

One of the most fundamental and difficult tasks in the management of any personnel system is determining the comparative worth of each position. Employees are acutely aware of what they are paid, how much responsibility they are assigned, and the "status" of their positions in relation to most other positions. Perceived inequities in pay or status can be a source of intense dissatisfaction, which translates into declining morale, lost productivity, absenteeism, grievances, and chronic bickering.

Because individuals are unable to judge fairly the worth of their jobs compared with higher-paying jobs, and because measuring the relative worth of different jobs is not an exact science, it is impossible to eliminate all feelings among employees that inequities exist in the pay system. However, every effort must be made to achieve fair job groupings and an equitable pay level for all positions in the workforce. (The International Public Management Association for Human Resources and other technical service providers, some of which are described in Chapter 9, conduct salary surveys to help governments determine appropriate pay levels.)

Classification and pay studies are regularly commissioned by local governments to reexamine the responsibilities and work performed by the jurisdiction's workforce. Each position is classified and assigned a pay grade according to its relative economic worth in relation to the marketplace and all other similarly classified positions within the workforce. Finally, competitive compensation schedules are developed and proposed for the positions studied.

The local government should hire an outside consultant to conduct these studies for two important reasons. First, it is imperative that the entire process not only be objective but be *perceived* as objective, and a consultant approaches the task with greater objectivity than can any member of the staff. A city manager or county administrator is inevitably perceived, especially by those not pleased with the results, as having a bias, no matter how professional the effort. Any staff member will have difficulty separating personalities from positions. But an experienced outside consultant specializing in this area comes in with little knowledge of the personalities and can better focus on the positions to be classified.

Second, developing a classification and pay system takes hundreds of hours. It is neither

practical nor cost-effective for personnel directors or administrators to undertake such studies, given all of their other responsibilities.

The initial implementation of the recommended classification and pay plan is not the
final step in achieving pay equity and creating
a motivated workforce. Rather, it establishes a
uniform point of departure from which to regularly review classification and pay decisions
and to ensure that they accurately reflect the
jurisdiction's current service needs and the
performance of employees. Each new position
added and all subsequent adjustments made to
the plan need to be consistent with the original plan to maintain its integrity and relevance.

Developing the Classification and Pay Plan

Guiding Principles

- A thorough job analysis provides the basis for
valid job descriptions, testing procedures, and
performance appraisals.
- Job descriptions must change as the specific
requirements of the job change.
- Job classifications and pay scales must be
updated regularly.

The following components represent the minimum scope of services that should be provided
by a consultant hired to do a classification and
pay plan.

Job Analysis. The initial step in the classification and pay study, job analysis is the
process of systematically gathering and analyzing information about a job. Information is
obtained about the nature of the work performed; the level of difficulty and complexity
involved; the amount of responsibility inherent in the job; the physical and mental
requirements; and the training, education,
and/or experience needed to perform the
job. Identifying the KSAs needed for a particular job is a critical element of job analysis.
Knowledge refers to the information and
concepts acquired through education and
work experience. *Skills* are the manual and
mental capabilities acquired through training and work experience. *Abilities* are the
natural talents and aptitudes possessed by
employees.

Various techniques may be used to collect
the information for a job analysis. Desk audits
can be conducted using questionnaires, interviews, work logs, or direct observation; the
nature of the job determines which method to
use. Direct observation, for instance, would be
inappropriate for mostly mental work but has
proven useful in assessing the amount of time
employees claim to need for the completion of
certain tasks.

Often, a combination of job analysis methods is used. For example, once the employee
has completed a position analysis questionnaire (see Exhibit 1-2), the immediate supervisor can review it and make appropriate
comments. Next, interviews are conducted to
clarify and augment the employee's questionnaire responses. New position descriptions
are then drafted for each position. Employees
and supervisors review the draft position
descriptions and submit written comments.
Final adjustments are then made.

Great care should be exercised in conducting a job analysis because it provides the foundation for many employment functions, such as

- Planning future personnel needs
- Restructuring positions
- Writing the job description and job announcement
- Designing the selection tests
- Determining compensation
- Evaluating performance
- Determining training needs
- Deciding on reassignments, demotions, or terminations.

To ensure their full cooperation with the job analysis, employees have to receive advance information about the techniques used and the purpose of the desk audit. Morale problems may arise if employees mistake the job evaluation for a performance evaluation.

Job Descriptions. The results of the job analysis are used to develop a job description, which is a written, summary statement of the job (see Exhibit 1-3). If job descriptions already exist, they should be reviewed and updated to ensure that they accurately describe the major tasks of the job, as well as the physical and mental requirements and the minimum qualifications needed to perform job duties. Updated job descriptions are essential to recruitment, selection, and work planning. Accurate documentation of the physical and mental requirements of the job also assists the jurisdiction in complying with the requirements of the Americans with Disabilities Act.

Job descriptions define the position, delineate levels of responsibility, and provide sufficient examples of major duties to establish the scope of the position. They are not intended to be either all-inclusive or restrictive. They do not provide a complete list of job tasks. It is neither necessary nor advisable to attempt to write an exhaustive position description; only enough examples of duties to present a clear picture of the essential work performed and the responsibilities of the position are necessary. Some jurisdictions use job descriptions that describe cross sections of responsibilities of several individuals holding similar positions and thus do not describe one position exactly. These general job descriptions can serve all the purposes of more specific descriptions.

Exhibit 1-3 reflects some subtle but important differences from earlier ones. First, the opening statement of purpose relates the job to the overall mission of government by emphasizing the importance of leadership and vision and by underscoring the job's role in supporting the efforts of all other departments. Second, Exhibit 1-3 identifies the "essential functions" of the job, thereby communicating that they must be performed by all job incumbents with or without reasonable accommodation. Last, it includes legal disclaimers at the beginning of the "Essential Functions" section and again at the end of the description to discourage employees from arguing that related work assignments are "not in my job description." For more essential functions, see Exhibit 1-4.

Position Classification. Positions, or groups of positions bearing the same job title, are next compared and contrasted with other positions in the workforce to determine their comparative worth. A standard method for evaluating job worth should be used. In point ranking, one of the most common methods, point values are assigned to key job factors. Below are some widely accepted compensable factors:

- Physical environment
- Basic knowledge, training, and education
- Intellectual skills and effort
- Physical skills and effort
- Experience
- Interaction with others
- Confidentiality
- Occupational risks
- Complexity

Exhibit 1-2.   Sample Position Analysis Information Sheet

Job Title_____ Date_____

Job Code_____ Dept._____

Superior's Title_____

Hours worked_____ AM to_____ PM

Job Analyst's Name_____

1. What is the job's overall purpose?
    _____

2. If the incumbent supervises others, list them by job title; if there is more than one employee with the same title, put the number in parentheses following the job title.
    _____
    _____
    _____

3. Check those activities that are part of the incumbent's supervisory duties.
    - Training   - Budgeting
    - Performance appraisal   - Coaching and/or counseling
    - Inspecting work
    - Other (please specify) _____

4. Describe the type and extent of supervision received by the incumbent.
    _____

5. JOB DUTIES: Describe briefly WHAT the incumbent does and, if possible, HOW he/she does it. Include duties in the following categories:

    a. Daily duties (those performed on a regular basis every day or almost every day)
        _____

    b. Periodic duties (those performed weekly, monthly, quarterly, or at other regular intervals)
        _____

    c. Duties performed at irregular intervals
        _____

6. Is the incumbent performing duties he/she considers unnecessary? If so, describe.
    _____

7. Is the incumbent performing duties not presently included in the job description? If so, describe.
    _____

8. EDUCATION: Check the box that indicates the educational requirements for the job (not the educational background of the incumbent).
    - No formal education required   - 4-year college degree (or equivalent)
    - Eighth grade education   - Graduate work or advanced degree (specify)
    - High school diploma (or equivalent) - Professional license (specify)
    - 2-year college degree (or equivalent)

9. EXPERIENCE: Check the amount of experience needed to perform the job.
   - None
   - Less than one month
   - One to six months
   - Six months to one year
   - One to three years
   - Three to five years
   - Five to ten years
   - More than ten years

10. LOCATION: Check location of job and, if necessary or appropriate, describe briefly.
    - Outdoor
    - Indoor
    - Underground
    - Pit
    - Scaffold
    - Other (specify)

11. ENVIRONMENTAL CONDITIONS: Check any objectionable conditions found on the job and note afterward how frequently each is encountered (rarely, occasionally, constantly, etc.)
    - Dirt
    - Dust
    - Heat
    - Cold
    - Noise
    - Fumes
    - Odors
    - Wetness/humidity
    - Vibration
    - Sudden temperature changes
    - Darkness or poor lighting
    - Other (specify)

12. HEALTH AND SAFETY: Check any undesirable health and safety conditions under which the incumbent must perform and note how often they are encountered.
    - Elevated workplace
    - Mechanical hazards
    - Explosives
    - Electrical hazards
    - Fire hazards
    - Radiation
    - Other (specify)

13. MACHINES, TOOLS, EQUIPMENT, AND WORK AIDS: Describe briefly what machines, tools, equipment, or work aids the incumbent works with on a regular basis:

    _____

    _____

14. Have concrete work standards been established (errors allowed, time taken for a particular task, etc.)? If so, what are they?

    _____

15. Are there any personal attributes (special aptitudes, physical characteristics, personality traits, etc.) required by the job?

    _____

16. Are there any exceptional problems the incumbent might be expected to encounter in performing the job under normal conditions? If so, describe.

    _____

17. Describe the successful completion and/or end results of the job.

    _____

18. What is the seriousness of error on this job? Who or what is affected by errors the incumbent makes?

    _____

19. To what job would a successful incumbent expect to be promoted?

Source: Human Resources Services, Inc.

Exhibit 1-3   Sample Job Description

Chief Information Officer

Position Purpose:

Provides leadership and vision to both Town and School operations in the area of information technology. Leads strategic IT planning for the Town/Schools; provides direction to officials and departments in integrating and aligning technology with plan objectives. Plans, organizes, directs and evaluates the IT Department and its operations to ensure effective support for organizational objectives and efficient and effective implementation of initiatives; guides departmental application services.

Supervision:

Supervision Scope: Performs highly technical and responsible duties requiring extensive judgment and initiative in planning for, managing, maintaining and supporting the use of information technology throughout the Town.

Supervision Received: Works independently under the broad general supervision of both the Town Manager and Superintendent of Schools.

Supervision Given: Regularly supervises and confers with direct reporting staff and contractors; reviews their work, the results achieved, and the associated programs, projects, and activities.

Job Environment:

Work is performed under typical office conditions with electro-mechanical computer- and telecommunications-related equipment; exposure to noise from printers, bursters, decollators and other computer-related equipment.

Operates enterprise-wide, departmental and PC-based computer systems, components, and other office equipment.

Has regular, daily contact with personnel and offices throughout the Town and School Department in answering questions, solving problems, providing training, implementing and supporting applications from vendors, and developing, implementing, and supporting applications authored by the Town's staff.

Has access to extensive confidential information from files in computer systems.

Errors could result in damage to or loss of information, damage to hardware or software or delay in service, possible monetary loss, or legal consequences adverse to the Town or School Department.

Essential Functions:

(The essential functions or duties listed below are intended only as illustrations of the various types of work that may be performed. The omission of specific statements of duties does not exclude them from the position if the work is similar, related, or a logical assignment to the position.)

Provides leadership to Town/School officials and department directors on alignment of technology with town initiatives, policy and strategic objectives. Makes presentations and prepares reports and plans.

Evaluates needs for information technology on an on-going basis; coordinates all services throughout the Town and School Department related to information technology; consults with users throughout the Town and School Department in order to determine how to improve the efficiency and effectiveness of the Town's or School Department's use of information technology on a continuous basis; maintains standards for hardware, software, and communications throughout the Town and School Department; has major input into the Town's and School Department's procurement of information technology.

Organizes and provides direction in the area of IT operations including the implementation and maintenance of the Town's computers, systems software, and connectivity. Provides direction in the area of IT applications, maintaining and supporting the use of enterprise software needed to meet the operational, management, and reporting requirements of the organization. Has principal responsibility for the implementation and support of packaged applications licensed from vendors.

Organizes and provides direction in the area of IT Customer Service, which includes the help desk, PCs, desktop applications, and IT training coordination.

Establishes and leads the annual decision-making process that will produce an IT financial plan, which prioritizes the IT initiatives for the Town, and incorporates them into the budget process. Prepares and administers the department's operating and capital budgets; performs long-range planning for information technology. Develops and presents funding strategies to support technology investments.

Performs needs analysis and develops, designs, and implements uses of information technology in response to needs of users in various offices throughout the Town and School Department. Reviews, analyzes, and establishes priorities among requests for services from Town and School Department offices.

Establishes and supervises the maintenance of security on all systems throughout the Town and School Department.

Recommends policies and practices to improve the use of information technology in the Town and School Department.

Performs similar or related work as required.

Recommended Minimum Qualifications:

Education, Training and Experience: Bachelor's degree in information systems, business or related field; five years of experience in information technology involving system planning, management and operations, training, programming or related skills with mid-range or client-server systems; two years of supervisory experience; three years of public-sector experience. Driver's license required.

Knowledge, Ability, and Skill:

Knowledge: Thorough knowledge of contemporary information technology; understanding of modern techniques of business-systems analysis and consultative skills. Knowledge of mid-range/server and PC-based systems. Thorough knowledge of programming methods and techniques. Knowledge of enterprise-wide telecommunications. Considerable knowledge of strategic planning, systems and project management.

Ability: Ability to establish and maintain effective communication, both written and oral, with all employees, public officials, vendors, citizen groups and committees, and others inside and outside the Town government and School Department as required. Ability to evaluate hardware and software options and plan for their future use, including procurement. Ability to work effectively with Town and School policy-makers and managerial employees, including the assessment and resolution of problems and setting of priorities. Ability to manage complex budgets and to prepare and review complex financial analysis. Ability to provide training to employees on a wide variety of computer software and hardware. Ability to effectively manage and supervise personnel and interdepartmental technology committees and work programs.

Skill: Strong conceptual, analytical, and writing skills. Good presentation skills. Computer skills that encompass effective use of word processing, spreadsheet, project management, presentation, mail, and Internet browser software.

Physical Requirements:

Minimal physical effort required to perform work under typical office conditions, with frequent moderate effort in such tasks as moving and installing computer hardware and related office equipment. Position requires the ability to operate a keyboard for extended periods of time. Position requires the ability to view computer screens for an extended period of time.

(This job description does not constitute an employment agreement between the employer and employee and is subject to change by the employer as the needs of the employer and requirements of the job change.)

Source: Human Resources Services, Inc.

Exhibit 1-4   Essential Functions of a Job

Overview

The Americans with Disabilities Act (ADA) prohibits employment discrimination against qualified individuals with disabilities. The ADA defines an "individual with a disability" as one who has a physical or mental impairment that substantially limits one or more major life activities; has a record of such an impairment; or is regarded as having such an impairment. A "qualified individual with a disability" is "an individual with a disability who meets the skill, experience, education, and other job-related requirements of a position held or desired, and who, with or without reasonable accommodation, can perform the essential functions of a job."

Many individuals with disabilities are qualified to perform all of the essential functions of jobs. However, if an individual with a disability who is otherwise qualified cannot perform one or more essential functions because of his/her disability, the supervisor must consider if there are modifications or adjustments (a "reasonable accommodation") that would help the individual to satisfactorily perform such functions.

Although it may be essential that a function be performed, it is often not essential that it be performed in a specific way. An individual with a disability may be able to satisfactorily perform an essential function if an accommodation enables him/her to use a different method and the accommodation does not impose an undue hardship for the organization. Consequently, supervisors should consider results or outcomes to be accomplished with respect to essential functions instead of the manner in which such functions are performed.

Definitions of Essential and Marginal Functions

A. *Essential Functions.* Job duties which a position incumbent must be able to satisfactorily perform, unaided or with the assistance of a reasonable accommodation.

B. *Marginal Functions.* Job duties which may be reassigned to other employees without interfering with performance of the essential functions. These functions are marginal only to individuals who are unable to perform them with or without reasonable accommodations because of a covered disability.

Steps in Identifying Essential Functions

A. Develop a preliminary list of job functions in order of importance, grouping related functions together whenever possible. Consider the following while developing this list:

- The results or outcomes to be accomplished instead of the manner in which functions are to be performed or have been performed in the past
- Avoid describing functions with verbs or adjectives which specify how they are performed.
- List processes or methods used only when critical to satisfactory job performance.
- The physical and mental demands which are required and any environmental factors which may have an impact on successful performance of the job
- List only those physical, mental, and environmental factors critical to satisfactory job performance.
- The knowledge, skills, and abilities (KSAs) critical to performance of the functions as well as specific education, training, and experience necessary for successful performance of the job

B. Review each job function with the following questions in mind. If "yes" can be answered to any of these questions, the function is essential; otherwise, the function is marginal.

- Does the position exist to perform the function?
- Would removing the function fundamentally change the job?
- Is the function critical to overall performance of the job?
- Is there a limited number of other employees available to perform the function or among whom the function may be distributed?
- Is the function highly specialized and is the position incumbent hired for special expertise or ability to perform the function?

C. A small percentage of time spent performing a specific function does not necessarily make the function marginal.

D. If unsure whether or not a job function should be considered essential, categorize the function as marginal.

E. If a position description does not distinguish between essential and marginal functions, all functions listed are considered essential.

Essential Functions Checklist

❏ Develop a preliminary list of job functions in order of importance, grouping related functions together whenever possible.

❏ Review each job function with the following questions in mind:

- Does the position exist to perform the function?
- Would removing the function fundamentally change the job?
- Is the function critical to overall performance of the job?
- Is there a limited number of other employees available to perform the function or among whom the function may be distributed?
- Is the function highly specialized and is the position incumbent hired for special expertise or ability to perform the function?

❏ If "yes" can be answered to any of these questions, include the function in the Essential Functions section of the position description; otherwise, include the function in the Marginal Functions section.

❏ Categorize a function as marginal if unsure whether or not it can be considered essential.

Source: Human Resources Services, Inc.

- Supervision received
- Supervision given
- Supervision scope
- Judgment and initiative
- Accountability

Rating scales are developed for each of these factors, and the position is assigned points according to the ratings given to it for each factor. The total accumulation of points for all 14 factors determines how each position is ranked in contrast to all others within the study.

Exhibit 1-5 presents a rating sheet for the position of assistant librarian. The rating scale for knowledge, training, and education, for example, contains six possible levels (not shown). The assistant librarian position was rated at the fifth level for this factor, a level corresponding to 75 points. In total, the posi-

tion received 374 points. Once the rating process is complete, positions can be assigned to specific pay grades according to their total scores, with higher-scoring jobs being placed in higher pay grades. With 374 points, the assistant librarian position would be assigned to Grade 7 and receive the corresponding salary. An example of a completed classification plan is shown in Exhibit 1-6. Note that this sample plan, with our assistant librarian at Grade 7, has a total of 16 grades.

Job rating or job evaluation is not the same as a performance evaluation. The position, not the incumbent, is evaluated, assigned points, and slotted into an appropriate pay grade. While much of the work involved in evaluating job worth is subjective, the point ranking process increases the uniformity and objectivity in the application of judgment about positions and the grouping of positions.

Exhibit 1-5 Position Rating Summary Sheet and Sample Grade Determination Chart

**Position Classification Title:
Assistant Librarian**

Factors	Final Ratings	Final Points	Score Range	Grade
Physical environment	1	5	200–224.	1
Knowledge, training, and education	5	75	225–249.	2
Intellectual skills and effort	5	34	250–274.	3
Physical skills and effort	2	20	275–299.	4
Experience	4	40	300–324.	5
Interactions with others	4	20	325–349.	6
Confidentiality	2	10	350–374.	7
Occupational risks	1	5	375–399.	8
Complexity	3	15	400–424.	9
Supervision received	4	30	425–449.	10
Supervision given	2	10		
Supervision scope	3	20		
Judgment and initiative	4	60		
Accountability	4	30		
Total Points		**374**		

Source: Human Resources Services, Inc.

Salary/Wage Survey. The position classification process determines the relative worth of positions on the basis of job content, without regard to the marketplace. The next step, then, is to collect and analyze salary and wage data from comparable employers to ensure that employees are offered competitive salaries and wages.

In most cases, selections of "comparable" employers are based upon

- Geographic location
- Population
- Comparative wealth factors
- Form of government
- Number of employees
- Comparability of classifications.

For some positions, it may be desirable to survey other types of organizations, such as state government, a local university, or a private company. The data collected from these surveys are then used to ensure that the compensation plan as a whole, and the pay grades within it, provide pay that is fair relative to what other employers are paying. If competitive wages and salaries are not offered, recruitment and retention problems quickly arise.

Two examples of compensation plans are provided here. The plan shown in Exhibit 1-7 identifies 10 fixed salary steps within each grade. Employees may be advanced through these salary steps on the basis of longevity, acquisition of additional knowledge and skills, job performance, or some combination of these factors. The plan shown in Exhibit 1-8 identifies only the salary range for each grade. This system allows greater flexibility in setting pay because employees are not advanced through the same set of predetermined steps. One employee might be awarded a 2 percent pay increase and a second employee a 4 percent increase, depending on their respective levels of performance or their acquisition of additional competencies.

Exhibit 1-6   Sample Classification Plan

Grades 1, 2, 3
No positions included in study

Grade 4
Council on Aging Van Driver

Grade 5
Animal Control Officer

Grade 6
Council on Aging Outreach Worker
Civilian Communications Officer

Grade 7
Assistant Librarian

Grade 8
Finance Commission Administrator
Solid Waste Coordinator/Facilities Manager

Grade 9
Assistant Recreation Director
Public Health Nurse
Youth Services Counselor

Grade 10
Assistant Town Treasurer

Grade 11
Computer Systems Analyst
Economic Development Officer
GIS Specialist

Grade 12
Council on Aging Director
Director of Youth and Family Services
Health Director
Recreation Director
Library Director
Superintendent of Wastewater Collection System
Human Resource Director
Town Planner

Grade 13
Building Commissioner
Superintendent of Highways/Cemeteries/Trees
Town Accountant

Grade 14
Deputy Fire Chief
Police Lieutenant/Administration
Police Lieutenant/Operations
Town Engineer

Grade 15
Finance Director
Chief Information Officer

Grade 16
Director of Public Works
Fire Chief
Police Chief

Source: Human Resources Services, Inc.

A more sophisticated compensation plan seeks to achieve a "best fit" between the internal worth of the job as determined through the point-ranking method, and the external worth of the job, as determined through salary and wage surveys. The pay ranges for each pay grade are established in a way that maximizes this best fit. Sometimes, however, it is necessary to place a job in a higher grade than is indicated by its internal worth. This occurs, for example, when there is a high demand for individuals trained in certain occupations and applicants can therefore command higher salaries in the marketplace. While an occasional position may fall outside the grade ranges, a compensation plan that places too many positions outside the grade ranges means that the grade structure is inappropriate. Comparisons are made among the organization's current salaries to determine whether any positions have been incorrectly assigned. These positions are further reviewed to determine whether all job factors have been evaluated appropriately.

Plan Administration. The final report provided by the consultant should include a methodology and rating manual enabling the city or county to maintain and update the classification and compensation plan. The consultant should also provide technical assistance for implementing the plan, showing, for example, how to negotiate with labor unions within the context of the study, how to develop a financial strategy for implementing the plan, and how to handle employee appeals regarding classification and reclassification decisions.

The classification plan should be reviewed as a whole every five years and continuously for individual position assignments or groups of positions when the job content changes dramatically. Reclassifying positions is done only when there is a significant change in the requirements of a position; in such cases, a new job description must be prepared. Reclassifications should not be used as a way to increase compensation when an employee has achieved the maximum step in the salary grade, nor should they be used as a way to reward an individual for special skills or length of service to the community.

Alternative Approaches to Classification and Pay

The traditional, standardized approach to classification and pay was developed in the early

---

Exhibit 1-7   Step-Based Compensation Plan

The first three grades of a step-based compensation plan are shown here; the complete plan provides for 14 grades. The percentage in the far left-hand column shows the increase in salary at Step 1 compared to Step 1 of the previous grade.

Proposed Compensation Plan FY

Base =	16,500.00
Hrs/Wk =	37.50

%	Grade		Step 1	Step 2	Step 3	Step 4	Step 5	Step 6	Step 7	Step 8	Step 9	Step 10
-	1	Hourly	8.43	8.77	9.12	9.48	9.86	10.26	10.67	11.09	11.54	12.00
		Weekly	316.09	328.74	341.89	355.56	369.78	384.57	399.96	415.96	432.59	449.90
		Annual	16,500.00	17,160.00	17,846.40	18,560.26	19,302.67	20,074.77	20,877.76	21,712.87	22,581.39	23,484.64
5	2	Hourly	8.85	9.20	9.57	9.96	10.35	10.77	11.20	11.65	12.11	12.60
		Weekly	331.90	345.17	358.98	373.34	388.27	403.80	419.96	436.75	454.22	472.39
		Annual	17,325.00	18,018.00	18,738.72	19,488.27	20,267.80	21,078.51	21,921.65	22,798.52	23,710.46	24,658.88
5	3	Hourly	9.29	9.66	10.05	10.45	10.87	11.31	11.76	12.23	12.72	13.23
		Weekly	348.49	362.43	376.93	392.01	407.69	423.99	440.95	458.59	476.93	496.01
		Annual	18,191.25	18,918.90	19,675.66	20,462.68	21,281.19	22,132.44	23,017.73	23,938.44	24,895.98	25,891.82

Exhibit 1-8   Salary Range–Based Compensation Plan

The first three grades of a salary range–based compensation plan are shown; the complete plan provides for 10 grades. The percentage in the far left-hand column shows the increase in minimum salary compared to the minimum salary of the previous grade.

PROPOSED COMPENSATION PLAN, FISCAL YEAR

% Grade			MINIMUM	midpoint	MAXIMUM
	Base =		25,000.000		
8	1	Annual	25,000.000	30,291.00	35,582.80
8	2	Annual	27,000.000	32,715.00	38,429.42
11	3	Annual	29,160.000	35,332.00	41,503.77

1900s as a control mechanism to prevent managers from arbitrarily determining the pay received by individual employees. But while this method has proven highly successful in ensuring internal and external pay equity, it has three disadvantages.

First, it creates procedural hurdles that discourage managers from attempting to reclassify those positions that truly deserve to be reclassified. Second, it discourages managers from assigning tasks involving levels of difficulty and complexity greater than those represented by the job's current pay grade assignment; this in turn prevents employees from developing their talents to the fullest extent and robs the organization of the ability to benefit from those talents. Third, it precludes managers from rewarding employees for superior levels of performance, at least where a pay-for-performance system is not built on top of the traditional pay structure.

What these disadvantages amount to are the morale problems that are created when two individuals are given equal pay for equal work without regard to their level of performance. Where managers do not have the flexibility to reward individual performance, they are tempted to reclassify positions simply to secure a pay raise for a superior employee, something that undermines the integrity of the classification and pay plan. Consequently, a few jurisdictions are now experimenting with alternatives to the traditional approach. (For more on new compensation models, see *The New Compensation Model,* IQ Report: ICMA, December 1998.)

Broadbanding. Broadbanding replaces several pay grades with a few broad salary bands. The pay range for each band is much greater than that for a traditional pay grade. For example, if the federal government adopted the framework shown in Exhibit 1-9, the pay range for an engineering position could be as broad as 10 traditional pay grades. No longer must the employee seek out a different line of work, possibly a managerial position, to secure economic advancement. Broadbanding allows employees to continue to move up in salary on the basis of higher levels of performance, competence, and training, and the supervisor is once again delegated responsibility for setting individual pay levels, at least within broad salary ranges. Emphasis is shifted from paying employees according to the jobs they hold to

Tips for Successfully Developing and Implementing a Classification and Pay System

- ❏ Hold orientation meetings with government officials and employees to explain project activities and objectives.
- ❏ If they are not already available, draw organizational charts of the whole administration and of the individual agencies.
- ❏ Determine job duties and responsibilities (essential functions) using trained observers, on-site interviews, position analysis questionnaires, or work logs.
- ❏ Develop draft and final job descriptions.
- ❏ Rate positions and assign them to pay grades on the basis of an objective evaluation system.
- ❏ Establish salary schedule(s) using comparative salary data.
- ❏ Provide guidelines for maintaining and updating the position classification and compensation plan.
- ❏ Review requests for reclassification carefully, rate positions using a standard rating system, and adjust the classification plan accordingly.
- ❏ If needed, update organizational charts to reflect changes in positions and ranks.
- ❏ Update salary schedules to reflect annual cost-of-living increases.
- ❏ Periodically collect and analyze comparable salary data to make sure positions are being paid competitively in comparison to the labor market.

paying them according to their unique abilities and contributions. The success of such systems depends, however, on the use of an objective, widely accepted method for assessing individual performance and competence.

Market-Based Pay. A few jurisdictions, especially smaller ones, are now adopting market-based pay systems. A market-based system skips the position classification step and assigns jobs to pay grades solely on the basis of marketplace comparisons. Its advantage is that the pay plan can be adjusted each year according to changes in labor supply and demand. Its disadvantage is that the pay plan may ignore significant differences in difficulty and complexity between jobs, paying them the same simply because they are paid the same in the marketplace. It may also incorporate into the pay plan racial, gender, or other biases that might be inherent in external wage and salary structures.

Pay for Performance. If the traditional classification and pay process described above is used

to determine each position's base pay, employers may construct a pay-for-performance system on top of this foundation. Such a system enables managers to compensate employees according to their individual levels of performance in addition to job content and labor market comparisons. (The issue of pay for performance is treated more fully in Chapter 3.)

Implementing the Classification and Pay Plan

Once the classification and pay plan is complete, it is up to the city or county manager to see that it is properly implemented and maintained. Successful implementation will require equitable judgments made in a consistent and objective manner.

Initial Step Placements for Current Employees. The placement of two or more positions (jobs) in a certain grade represents a judgment that those positions should be compensated comparably within the range provided for that grade. The organization can define

Exhibit 1-9   Framework for Broadbanding

					S/E		
GS-15						S/E	S/E	S/E
GS-14				S/E				
GS-13			S/E		FP	FP	FP	FP
GS-12				FP				
GS-11								
GS-10			FP					
GS-9		S/E						
GS-8					D	D	D	D
GS-7		FP	D					
GS-6	S/E							
GS-5		D		Administration/	Engineering/	Health	Law
GS-4	FP		Technical	Analysis/Other	Sciences		Enforcement
GS-3		General					
GS-2	D	Support					
GS-1	Office Services						

Single Pay Schedule   Candidates for Separate Personnel Systems

S/E = Senior/Expert   FP = Full Performance   D = Developmental

Source: National Academy of Public Administration, *Modernizing Federal Classification: An Opportunity for Excellence* (Washington, D.C.: NAPA, 1991), 45.

steps or subranges within the grade in order to distinguish among employees (not positions) on the basis of established criteria. These criteria may include job performance, special abilities, experience, and other factors determined by the organization. For example, an applicant with several years of relevant work experience may be hired at a higher salary step than an applicant with very little experience, even though both hold positions in the same grade.

Red-Circled Positions and Salaries. Sometimes a pay exception is needed to recruit employees for positions where labor demand is high. An employee compensated at a level above the grade's maximum can be held at that status in one of two ways until retirement or termination. First, a red-circled employee can be held at the current rate of pay until the pay plan is adjusted by cost-of-living increases to equal or exceed the employee's actual compensation. Alternatively, a red-circled employee may be treated like any other employee at the top of the grade. He or she may be eligible for cost-of-living adjustments (COLAs) but not step increases. It is recommended that a single administrative policy be adopted and subsequently applied in all cases.

Cost-of-Living Adjustments vs. Step Increases.

A COLA is different from a step increase. A COLA is intended to recognize a general rise in the costs for goods and services experienced by almost everyone. Each year the organization should determine an appropriate percentage COLA and apply that increase across the entire salary schedule. This raises the compensation rates for the entire salary schedule equal to changes in the cost of living. By contrast, a step increase and/or movement from minimum to maximum within the grade range recognizes factors worthy of compensation increases above the COLA. Such factors include superior performance and additional competence. This distinction between COLAs and step increases is crucial for the successful implementation of classification and compensation plans in the public sector.

Union Issues.

Public organizations should consider the implications of a current or potential unionized workforce in developing classification and pay structures. As a representative of employees, the union has a legitimate interest in the introduction of new or revised salary structures. It can also influence the implementation of the new systems either positively or negatively, depending on the degree to which it supports them. Therefore, it is highly desirable that management work with the union in the development, introduction, and administration of salary structures. Agreement on management's rights, expectations about the process, and related issues must be made clear at the outset of the negotiations.

Legislation.

Construction and application of the classification and compensation plan are also affected by both federal and state legislation, particularly the Fair Labor Standards Act (FLSA). The FLSA sets minimum wage, overtime pay, equal pay, child labor, and record-keeping requirements. The minimum wage provisions require employers to pay at least a minimum hourly rate regardless of the worth of the job. When the minimum is increased by law, the wages of those who already earn above the minimum may be adjusted accordingly.

Overtime pay is also regulated. For every nonexempt job, employers must pay one and a half times the employee's regular rate for all hours worked over 40 per week. Executive, professional, administrative, and other highly paid workers are exempt from the overtime provisions, although the burden falls on the employer to justify the exemption on the basis of the employee's actual duties, not just the job title.

FLSA requirements are highly complex and difficult to observe in practice. A thorough knowledge of the FLSA is critically important to successful pay administration.

Complying with the requirements of Title VII of the Civil Rights Act (1964, amended in 1972) and the Equal Pay Act (1963) virtually requires a well-designed, clearly nondiscriminatory classification and compensation system. The haphazard pay arrangements adopted prior to the passage of these acts usually cannot withstand legal scrutiny today. Specific application of these statutes to the job review process means that jobs involving equal duties and responsibilities must be evaluated similarly and without discrimination based on race, color, age, sex, religion, national origin, handicap, or veteran status. Under the Equal Pay Act, for example, male and female dispatchers must be paid the same if their seniority and merit match, but a female dispatcher and male firefighter could be paid different rates. However, if a jurisdiction has committed itself to a com-

Job Descriptions and the Americans with Disabilities Act

fyi

Regardless of the size or complexity of an organization, good **job descriptions** produce important benefits: Prospective and current employees better understand the expectations of the job. Supervisors have more guidance in hiring, developing, promoting, and supervising employees. Managers and other professionals have the information they need to recruit, examine, and select qualified candidates for positions.

Job descriptions can and should be used not only for recruitment and promotion, but also in the administration of local government. They help define initial expectations, further define organizational charts, and provide fundamental building blocks for administering compensation systems. Job descriptions should also be used when developing employee objectives, performance plans, and performance appraisals.

Today, job descriptions are more important than ever. One reason is the **Americans with Disabilities Act (ADA).** The underlying premise of Title I, the employment section, is that people with disabilities who are able to work should have opportunities to do so. Title I requires employers to reasonably accommodate the known physical and mental limitations of an otherwise qualified job applicant or employee unless doing so would impose an undue hardship on the employer. Providing reasonable accommodation includes such things as making workplace facilities accessible and usable, restructuring jobs and work schedules, acquiring or modifying work equipment or devices, modifying examinations and training materials, and providing qualified readers or interpreters.

According to the ADA, a qualified individual with a disability is "an individual who, with or without reasonable accommodation, can perform the essential functions of the employment position that such individual holds or desires." This means that employers must assess each person's work abilities in relation to the specific requirements and essential functions of each job. **Essential functions** are those basic duties that are central to a job and cannot normally be transferred to another position without disruption in the flow or process of work. This is where job descriptions become so important. Essential functions must be determined through job analysis and recorded in a job description. Otherwise, an employer cannot fulfill its duty of making reasonable accommodation. If the essential functions of the job can be accomplished with or without reasonable accommodation, the employer cannot use disability as a reason to preclude the applicant from an employment opportunity.

Thus, under the ADA, the job description's list of duties and responsibilities takes on new significance. In the event of an ADA challenge, employers must be able to show that employment decisions are based solely on the applicant's ability to perform the essential functions of the job. **Job analysis** must be designed and carried out to distinguish between essential and nonessential duties. A properly developed job description, prepared before advertising and interviewing, can be used as evidence of the essential functions that the employee must perform. Employers therefore should be careful to accurately identify all essential job functions in the job description. Nonessential or peripheral duties can also be listed but should be clearly distinguished from the essential duties. All job descriptions should be reviewed and updated periodically to ensure their continued accuracy.

parable worth wage policy, a dispatcher and firefighter with the same number of points under a job evaluation point system must be paid comparably, with adjustments possible for differences in seniority and merit.

Benefits. There is another side to the compensation equation. Wages and salaries in most cases count for most of the compensation package, but without other benefits, government employers would find it very difficult to attract and retain qualified personnel. The benefit survey is usually part and parcel of the pay survey; in making marketplace comparisons, analysts must calculate the cost of the total wage and benefit package. However, benefits may also be viewed as a separate function to illustrate how the various pieces of the classification and compensation subsystems interrelate.

Benefits are generally spelled out in the personnel ordinance or bylaws or in any accompanying set of personnel rules and regulations. As is the case with salary adjustments, most determinations of benefits for union employees are made at the bargaining table for each unit, often resulting in a multiplicity of personnel policies.

Among the more common benefits are holidays, vacations, sick leave and sick leave "buy backs," personal and professional leave, educational incentive pay, medical and life insurance, workers' compensation or injury leave, pensions, unemployment compensation, shift differential pay, and skill pay. Some of these are required by state statute, but most are variable and hinge upon collective bargaining agreements. They can typically add 30 to 35 percent to the employee's base wage. (See Chapter 6 for more information on benefits.)

Interns and Part-Time, Temporary, and Contract Employees

Employing civil servants on a full-time, career basis allows the local government to attract and retain individuals who are highly skilled and committed. But the benefits of a large, full-time staff to cover every possible contingency must be balanced against the need to use personnel efficiently and economically.

It is especially difficult to staff a work unit efficiently where workloads vary significantly because of seasonal fluctuations or the infrequent need for special expertise. At times a department may have more employees than it actually needs, and at other times it may have too few. To allow for greater flexibility in staffing and to hold the line on payroll costs, private firms are relying increasingly on part-time, temporary, and contract employees. Although there are greater constraints on the use of such employees in the public sector, this strategy can nonetheless produce important cost savings, especially in smaller jurisdictions. Administrators initiate this strategy by distinguishing between core jobs that departments cannot do without and contingent jobs that can be filled using part-time, temporary, and contract employees. The challenge lies in reducing the size of the permanent workforce without overburdening the remaining full-time employees, undermining morale, or harming service delivery.

Interns. Internship programs can be win-win situations in that the student gains needed work experience while the jurisdiction gets a temporary employee at more or less low cost. High school or undergraduate students often are expected to volunteer their time while graduate students usually receive a stipend. Interns can work part time during the academic year or full time during the summer break. They can be used successfully as management trainees and professional assistants or for short-term projects for which permanent staff is unavailable. However, staff time needs to be devoted to the intern's supervision and evaluation.

Part-Time Employees. A part-time job is one in which the incumbent works fewer than

35 hours a week. It is generally viewed as a permanent position, but one in which the duties do not require a full-time worker. Part-time jobs not only reduce payroll costs but also allow departments to attract qualified workers who wish to devote more time to their families or to other personal needs. It is possible, although not always easy, to fill positions at any level and in any occupation on a part-time basis. State laws and local ordinances govern the conditions of employment for part-time employees, including their benefit levels. Those part-time employees who are employed at least half time often receive the same benefits as full-time workers, except that benefits such as sick leave and vacations are prorated. Where part-time employees are entitled to full benefits, the cost savings from employing them are somewhat reduced.

Job Sharing. Two half-time jobs may be created out of one full-time position. Job sharers perform all tasks jointly or divide them between themselves according to their skills, abilities, and interests. They also divide the workweek between themselves, choosing either to work half days or to work full days on an alternating basis. Because there are no cost savings inherent in job sharing (half-time workers, for example, are often entitled to full health insurance benefits), it is usually viewed as an alternative work schedule designed to attract qualified workers who for personal reasons do not wish to work full time.

Job sharing entails some potential difficulties. Although research has shown that job-sharing arrangements can increase job satisfaction and productivity, it has also shown that job sharers need to be highly compatible so that they can work well together with no loss in continuity.[10] Additionally, supervisors must determine how to evaluate work performance and what level of benefits to provide to job sharers.

A unique kind of job sharing often used by small cities and counties is to share employees between two or more jurisdictions through a contractual agreement that establishes the duties the employee is to perform for each jurisdiction, as well as the pay and benefits to be provided by each jurisdiction. For example, public health nurses, nutritionists, inspectors, and veterinarians are often shared among counties in rural areas. It is a useful means for securing the services of skilled individuals who wish to be employed full time but without incurring the full cost of employing them.

Temporary Employees. A temporary employee is employed, generally on a full-time basis, for only a limited period of time. Substantial cost savings are possible by employing temporary employees to work on special, short-term projects or to handle workloads that are unusually high at certain times of year. Budgets often contain a line for such contingencies. Temporary employees are typically hired for low-paying, relatively unskilled positions because most people in technical, professional, and administrative career paths seek permanent positions. Although the use of temporary employees allows tax dollars to be used more efficiently, it tends to deny long-term employment opportunities to those with fewer skills. In addition, although temporary employees are easier to employ because they are not subject to the same competitive selection requirements as permanent employees, their use nonetheless entails considerable paperwork when waves of temps are constantly being hired and rehired.

A related cost-saving strategy is to hire temporary employees to fill vacant permanent positions for as long as the law allows. Money is saved because temporary employees are generally paid less, are denied COLAs, and are not entitled to insurance benefits. However, because this strategy is generally viewed as an abuse of employment authority, as well as an unjust practice from the employee's perspective, hiring temporary employees to fill permanent positions is usually regulated by state law.

Red Flag

- Be sure to ascertain what laws and ordinances govern the selection and employment of part-time, temporary, and contract employees in your jurisdiction.
- Be careful not to reduce the permanent workforce to a point where the remaining employees are burdened with excessive workloads.
- Develop expertise in contract administration before using the services of contract employees routinely.

In many states, for example, temporaries can be hired only for a limited length of time and without the possibility of being continuously rehired.

Contract Employees. A contract employee is a temporary employee who contracts to provide a specific service or product by a specified date. It is an option used when individuals with specialized skills are needed for a relatively short period of time. It is often less expensive, for example, to hire consultants to accomplish special tasks than to maintain a permanent in-house staff to perform the same duties.

However, the use of contract employees is not without its difficulties. Controlling the performance of such individuals must be accomplished through contract compliance rather than direct supervision. There is the very real possibility of fraudulent claims for expenses, abuse of authority, or nonperformance that not only undermines mission attainment but also creates unneeded political shock waves. Unless contracts are carefully written and diligently enforced, the work performed may cost the agency more in the long run than if it were performed by in-house employees.

Some local governments contract out entire functions to a private employer. Money may be saved, for example, by hiring security

guards who are paid lower salaries and benefits through a private employer. These savings may be offset, however, by a lower level of service and commitment.

Work Teams

Guiding Principles

- Work teams can improve performance when the work is complex and a variety of skills and experience is needed.
- The work to be done or the problem to be resolved determines the appropriate work team.
- Work-team leaders and members need training before and during the change to team management.
- Hiring procedures should assess an applicant's ability to work in teams.

Challenges

- Making sure that the team approach is perceived by employees as a capacity-building innovation, not a temporary fad.
- Identifying the work processes that will benefit from a team approach.
- Encouraging executive and supervisory personnel to trust their employees and to switch from a top-down management approach to a mentoring and coaching role.
- Helping employees accept the new organizational culture and increased responsibilities.
- Adjusting personnel policies to reflect and reinforce the new organizational principles.

Position-based personnel systems tend to discourage teamwork. Work is compartmentalized into sets of specialized tasks and assigned to individual workers. Each employee is held accountable for performing only those duties described in his or her position description. To early personnel theorists, this seemed highly efficient. From their perspective, the idea of assigning broad responsibilities to groups of employees invited confusion, duplication of effort, and the abdication of individual responsibility. Today, however, there are compelling reasons to encourage teamwork, and more flexible classification and pay systems may be needed to facilitate the shift toward team-based organizational structures.

Work teams are groups of employees who collaborate with one another to achieve common goals and objectives. When fully implemented, the team concept represents an alternative to the traditional top-down, hierarchical approach to decision making. In structural terms, decision making becomes much more horizontal as teams at all levels, composed of individuals from several levels and even from different units, bring their combined resources to bear on complex problems relating to core work processes. The synergy resulting from group collaboration has been shown to produce greater innovativeness, creativity, and risk taking.[11]

Establishing work teams is a deliberate strategy to increase employee involvement in decision making and problem solving. It is premised on the belief that those closest to work-related problems are best qualified and situated to analyze and resolve them. Advocates of team-based organizations believe that the tasks of government are now so complex, the amount of information to be assimilated so overwhelming, and the pace of change so great that decisions can no longer be made effectively by omniscient administrators at the top of the organizational pyramid. Nor can they be made effectively by specialists working in isolation. Ordinary employees are much better educated than in the past, and the use of teams, according to advocates, not only improves decision making and problem solving but also allows a fuller and wiser use of human potential. This occurs as individuals with unique talents and specialized knowledge are charged with working together to improve core work processes. Empowering workers in this way not only keeps everyone focused on their common mission but also increases motivation, morale, and commitment, and leads to a higher level of performance.

Teams and Decision Making

The kinds of teams now in use may be differentiated according to the degree to which they delegate decision-making authority downward within an organization.

Problem-Solving Teams. A problem-solving team is a semipermanent group of 5 to 12 workers within a particular work unit who meet one to two hours each week to discuss their problems and make recommendations regarding needed changes. Problem-solving teams can be established in various functional areas and charged with continuously improving work processes and product or service quality. Experience with this type of team effort suggests that participation in decision making is not sufficient by itself to increase motivation, morale, and commitment. Managers must be willing to work closely with these teams and to implement recommended changes whenever possible. If recommendations are unwarranted or cannot be implemented, managers must be willing to offer team members full and frank explanations.

Special-Purpose Teams. A special-purpose team is a temporary team of 5 to 12 members established for a specific purpose, such as redesigning a work process, introducing a new technology, investigating a work-related problem, or resolving labor-management difficulties. It is often called a cross-functional team when members are drawn from various units of the organization to resolve problems that cross departmental lines.

Self-Directed Teams. A self-directed team is a permanent team of workers who are fully responsible for a particular work function or process. The defining characteristic of this type of team is that workers manage themselves rather than receive direction and control from a work supervisor. The team is delegated an unusually broad scope of decision-making authority and is held accountable for producing positive results. Team members typically schedule their own work, set their own goals, select and train new members, appraise and reward their team's performance, and cross-train so that they can perform each other's tasks. As responsibility and decision-making authority are passed to self-directed teams, fewer middle managers and supervisors are needed. This type of team is based on the idea that those who do the work are the experts and that enormous gains in work performance and product quality can be had by empowering them to take charge of their own work situations.

Self-directed work teams are not widely used in the public sector. Unlike the other types, which can be adopted without changing the basic structure or culture of the organization, self-directed teams require fundamentally different structures and cultures. They aim to achieve a flatter organization in which operational decisions are no longer made by managers and first-line supervisors; those individuals must be willing to relinquish control, delegate authority, and take on new roles as facilitators and coaches. The success of this concept also requires the identification of concrete measures by which the group's performance, as well as each individual's contribution, can be evaluated and rewarded, something that is often difficult in the public sector.

Nonetheless, it is a concept worth investigating. Self-directed road maintenance teams, for example, might be given responsibility for the repair and maintenance of roads in specific geographical areas. The concept tends to work best where there is a distinct work process or geographical area over which a team can exercise meaningful control. Conversely, it works less well where stakes are high and decisions must be made quickly, such as in police, fire, and emergency units; where employees tend to work in isolation, such as accountants and building inspectors; and where employees see very little personal value in assuming additional responsibility, such as clerical workers performing highly routine duties.

Tips for Successful Teamwork Efforts

❑ Do not assume that all workers are eager to accept responsibility or that all managers are willing to delegate authority. Test job applicants for their ability to assume various roles in work teams.

❑ Create teams only where there is a clear problem to solve or a distinct work product, function, or process for which to hold members accountable.

❑ Create problem-solving teams only if managers are fully committed to acting on their recommendations or explaining why they cannot act on them.

❑ Prepare the way for self-directed work teams by first establishing a high degree of trust and team-oriented norms.

❑ Be prepared to invest in a broad range of training programs if a decision is made to move toward a team-based organization.

❑ Be prepared to modify classification, pay, and performance appraisal systems to sustain a flatter, team-based structure.

❑ Replace an adversarial union culture with a consensus-seeking labor-management partnership culture.

Prerequisites for Team Success

Although research has documented the benefits of working in teams, these benefits do not come automatically. First, many employees are initially uncomfortable with assuming more responsibility, and supervisors are generally uncomfortable with relinquishing control. A high degree of trust must be built into the organizational culture if teamwork is to succeed. It then takes time for teams to trust that they will be allowed to make mistakes and for managers to trust that they will not be called on the carpet every time one of their teams makes unwanted headlines.

Second, moving toward a team-based organization requires considerable investment

Exhibit 1-10   Effective and Ineffective Teams

Characteristics of Effective Teams	Characteristics of Ineffective Teams
Clearly defined, mutually set team goals	Unclear/unrealistic goals
Understanding and commitment to team goals	Low commitment
Atmosphere that encourages discussion by all members; free expression of feelings and ideas	Conformity; lack of disagreement
Prompt distribution of minutes of meetings to team members; informed members	Failure to share information
Good communication with each other and with other parts of the organization	Formal or structured communication; cautious or guarded communication
Efficient task-oriented meetings that focus on improvement	Poor meetings
Problem solving rather than blaming	Reliance on criticism
Frequent performance feedback	Lack of individual feedback; performance evaluation based on personal opinion
Cooperation and support of members	Competition among team members
Tolerance with emphasis on resolution	Failure to use team members' talents
Support of management	Low confidence in others
Decisions based on facts, not emotions or personalities	One-person decisions
Pride and spirit	Negative attitudes

Source: Adapted from Patricia A. Harris, *Total Quality Management: Strategies for Local Government* (Washington, D.C.: International City/County Management Association, 1993), 30.

in training. Team members require training in interpersonal, communication, and problem-solving skills; team leaders require training in how to keep meetings on track; and managers require training in coaching and facilitating skills. Third, a team-oriented culture must be sustained by a clear set of norms that state, for example, that scapegoating, or placing individual goals ahead of team goals, is unacceptable. Fourth, information must be shared to a much greater degree than in position-based personnel systems. Full and complete information is needed for those at the bottom of the organizational pyramid to make informed decisions. The characteristics of effective and ineffective teams are summarized in Exhibit 1-10.

The team concept provides administrators with additional options for structuring work. Problem-solving and self-directed work teams are relatively permanent features, whereas the special-purpose teams are temporary and ad hoc in nature. All three involve the delegation of authority downward in the organization, with problem-solving teams requiring the least delegation and self-directed work teams the most. With the recent concern for quality, all three are typically charged with making continuous improvements to products or services and with satisfying the needs of customers or clients.

Although teamwork has been shown to produce greater innovation, risk taking, and productivity, team-based organizations require fundamental shifts in philosophy, attitude, and skills among managers and employees alike. Leadership practices, job descriptions, classification and pay systems, and career advancement policies may also have to be adjusted to support the team concept. Finally, upper management must be very strongly committed to the team concept if the inevitable resistance to change and fear of losing control is to be overcome.

Unions also have to be convinced that the team approach will benefit their members. This generally means that wages should be raised when rank-and-file employees increase their value to the organization through cross-training and by assuming management functions. Overall, traditionally adversarial labor-management relations have to be replaced with a more trusting work culture. Labor-management partnerships and interest-based bargaining are consensual methods of decision making promoted by the federal government through Executive Order 12871.[12]

[1] For more information on strategic planning, see John M. Bryson, *Strategic Planning for Public and Nonprofit Organizations: A Guide to Strengthening and Sustaining Organizational Achievement* (San Francisco: Jossey-Bass Publishers, 1995); Gerald L. Gordon, *Strategic Planning for Local Government* (Washington, D.C.: ICMA, 1993).

[2] Penelope Lemov, "Deficit Deluge," *Governing* 15 (May 2002): 20–24.

[3] Jonathan Tompkins, "Strategic Human Resources Management in Government," *Public Personnel Management* 31 (Spring 2002): 95–109.

[4] For detailed information on workforce planning, see International Personnel Management Association, *Workforce Planning Resource Guide for Public Sector Human Resource Professionals* (Washington, D.C.: IPMA, 2002); and the U.S. Office of Personnel Management, OPM Workforce Planning Web site at http://www1.opm.gov/workforceplanning/index.htm.

[5] Donald E. Klinger and John Nalbandian, *Public Personnel Management: Contexts and Strategies* (Upper Saddle River, N.J.: Prentice-Hall, 1998), 70.

[6] See David Osborne and Ted Gaebler, *Reinventing Government* (Reading, Mass.: Addison-Wesley, 1992).

[7] Sunnyvale, California, was one of the first local governments to adopt performance budgeting.

[8] National Commission on the State and Local Public Service, *Hard Truths/Tough Choices: An Agenda for State and Local Reform* (Albany, N.Y.: Nelson A. Rockefeller Institute of Government, 1993).

[9] Siegrun F. Fox, "Professional Norms and Actual Practices in Local Personnel Administration. A Status Report," *Review of Public Personnel Administration* 13, 2 (Spring 1993):5–28.

[10] Jon L. Pierce, John W. Newstrom, Randall B. Dunham, and Alison E. Barber, *Alternative Work Schedules* (Boston: Allyn and Bacon, 1989).

[11] Peter Mears, *Organization Teams* (Delray Beach, Fla.: St. Lucre Press, 1994), 3.

[12] The National Performance Review, a project of the Clinton administration, provides information on ways to overcome an adversarial union culture and to implement teamwork. The NPR Web site has been archived at the University of North Texas and can be accessed at http://govinfo.library.unt.edu/npr/.

CHAPTER 2

Recruiting for a High-Performance Workforce

STEPHANIE L. WITT AND W. DAVID PATTON

The quality of any work organization depends on its people, and the best way to ensure excellence is to hire highly capable employees. The first step in hiring is to recruit well-qualified applicants, and the next step is to find the one person in the applicant pool who is the best match for the job. Careful selection procedures can help managers avoid personnel problems by weeding out applicants who are not capable or motivated. Yet the need for thoroughness in selection procedures must be balanced with the need for speed in finding the most desirable candidate because the most qualified candidate tends to be courted by several employers.

Standard procedures have been developed to select the best candidates for new or existing jobs. Federal and state laws, court rulings, local civil service ordinances, and collective bargaining agreements provide the legal protocol for many personnel decisions, including the hiring process. The most important principle to follow throughout the hiring process is that all recruitment information, tests, and selection decisions must be based on the specific requirements of the job to be done.

The recruitment process ends with the signing of the employment documentation and employee orientation. The purpose of both is to prevent misunderstandings between the employer and the employee about job-related expectations. Applicants not selected should be promptly notified about the decision to hire another applicant and thanked for applying.

A favorable public image can lighten the chore of filling vacant positions. Careful and ongoing public relations efforts by the city or county can convey the impression in the community that the government is a good place to work. However, word of mouth also is an important tool to attract talented job applicants, and being a model employer is as important as image management.

Recruitment

Guiding Principles

- All recruitment information, tests, and selection decisions must be based on the specific requirements of the job to be done.

Equal Employment Opportunity and Affirmative Action

fyi

Local governments with 15 or more employees fall under Title VII of the 1964 Civil Rights Act, as amended in 1972, and Title I of the Americans with Disabilities Act (1990). All public employers are also included in the Age Discrimination in Employment Act (1967). Combined, these federal laws prohibit discrimination in all employment-related decisions, including recruiting, on the basis of race, color, religion, gender, national origin, physical disability, or age if the person is at least 40 years old. Public employers are also required under the Equal Employment Opportunity Act of 1972 to maintain records relevant to the determination of whether unlawful employment practices have been committed. (See Chapter 5 for more on Equal Employment Opportunity compliance.)

Entities with which the federal government contracts work also must comply with affirmative action requirements. Contracts between federal agencies and local governments are rare, but the Equal Employment Opportunity Commission (EEOC) issued a "Policy Statement on Affirmative Action Programs for State and Local Agencies" in 1976, encouraging state and local jurisdictions to adopt affirmative action programs voluntarily. The encouragement was repeated two years later when the EEOC issued the "Uniform Guidelines on Employee Selection Procedures."*

* 41 CFR 60-3; 60-3.13B; 60-3.17. The Equal Employment Opportunity Commission was created by the 1964 Civil Rights Act.

- Communication with all applicants should be open and fair.

Challenges

- Attracting highly qualified candidates.
- Complying with equal employment opportunity (EEO), affirmative action, and Americans with Disabilities Act (ADA) requirements.

Recruitment is the process of finding the best people to fill vacancies in new or existing jobs. Candidates can be recruited internally from among eligible employees, or externally. The nature of the job determines the extent of the search. An adequate recruitment effort is expensive: costs include money spent on advertising and candidates' travel expenses, and staff time spent reviewing applicant files and interviewing and evaluating candidates. Usually, the more professional the job, the higher the cost of recruiting and the longer it takes to fill the open position.

Who Does What?

In the absence of a personnel director or personnel department, the chief executive of the jurisdiction or the head of the department with the job opening will probably handle recruitment. The person doing the recruitment should consult and work with the direct supervisor of the available position since the latter individual is one of the best sources for information about the knowledge, skills, and abilities (KSAs) needed to fill the vacancy. However, the supervisor's understanding of the opening should be based on a carefully researched job analysis.

The chief administrative officer may wish to establish a search committee including, if possible, the direct supervisor of the open position. The team can collaborate in writing the job description, reviewing applications, and interviewing the finalists.

Support staff is needed to handle the clerical aspects of the recruitment process. A set of recruitment files that include application documents has to be compiled and put in a secure place to ensure confidentiality and the integrity of the files. It is also appropriate to develop a recruitment information system so that applicants know where they stand in the selection process, and one person should be made responsible for communication with the candidates.

Regardless of who is in charge of the recruitment process, the EEO/affirmative action officer should be included in planning for the recruitment effort. If the city or county does not have such an officer, the legal counsel of the jurisdiction should review the process for compliance with legal requirements. (Also see Chapter 5.)

The Job Announcement

The job announcement should include the essential job functions, qualifications for the job, location of the job, and pay range.[1] The best tool with which to begin the recruitment process is a recently completed job analysis, since that describes the nature of the work, lists the essential job functions, states minimum education and experience required, indicates the physical demands of the job, and places the incumbent in the chain of command. (See Chapter 1, page 10, for more on job analysis.) From this analysis comes the job description, which is included in the announcement of the open position. The job description needs to be carefully thought through before its announcement because changes made to the job description during the selection phase may violate EEO principles. (Again, see Chapter 1, page 11, for more on the job description.)

It is important to ask for only those qualifications—KSAs, education, training, and experience—necessary for the successful performance of the job. For example, the employer should require a high school diploma only when it can be demonstrated that the duties of the job require such an education.[2] Basing the recruitment effort on the job analysis—that is, linking the selection criteria to the specific job tasks—avoids potential EEO/affirmative action problems later on.

The pay range for the new position should be based on several criteria, including the salary paid to the previous occupant, the qualifications needed for the job, and the relevant external labor market—local, regional, or national. (See Chapter 1 for more on determining the proper pay level.)

The job announcement is posted to inform current employees if the local government is doing an internal recruitment. Many local governments also place job announcements on their Web sites.

A job announcement from the city of Boise, Idaho, is shown in Exhibit 2-1. Sample announcements can also be viewed at the Local Government Job Net site (www.govtjob. net) maintained by the Local Government Institute <www.lgi.org>). This and other Web sites listing local government job openings are described in Chapter 9.

Internal vs. External Recruiting

Early in the recruitment process, the hiring authority must decide whether to hire someone from inside or outside the organization. There are advantages and disadvantages to either strategy. Some positions are better suited to internal as opposed to external searches.

Internal Recruiting. Recruiting from the current workforce is appropriate for positions for which existing employees are likely to have the necessary skills. The job announcement can be placed in an employee newsletter, posted on bulletin boards, and, if appropriate, distributed to the collective bargaining unit. Employees can then nominate themselves for the opening. Internal recruiting needs to comply with EEO principles, existing civil service procedures, collective bargaining agreements, and other personnel rules under which the jurisdiction may be operating.

An advantage of internal recruitment is its lower demand on resources. It is less expensive and takes less time than an external search. A second advantage is that the candidates' strengths and weaknesses are known to the agency. Finally, internal recruitment may enhance employee morale by providing opportunities for advancement.

Exhibit 2-1   Sample Job Announcement

PLANS EXAMINER II
City of Boise

Opening Date: April 13, 1998   **Closing Date: May 4, 1998 or Until Filled**

OVERALL RESPONSIBILITIES: Reviews and checks construction and hillside excavation plans, engineering calculations and specifications to ensure compliance with pertinent codes and ordinances; establishes routing procedures to nine (9) other agencies.

ESSENTIAL FUNCTIONS OF THE JOB: Examines building plans for compliance with building, mechanical, zoning, hillside, flood plain, and life safety codes and ordinances; assures plans are in compliance with accessibility requirements for the disabled; verifies that engineering calculations and specifications are accurate and correct; reviews plans and engineering for excavation and grading of commercial site work; establishes compliance criteria prior to issuance of permits; determines construction value for basing permit fees; provides technical assistance to inspectors, architects, engineers and builders regarding code interpretation and plan clarification; acts as liaison between City, County, State and Federal agencies, and builders and developers; establishes routing procedures to nine (9) other agencies; provides technical support and work direction to office personnel; performs site investigations.

REQUIRES: Thorough knowledge of structural engineering principles and design of wood frame and non-combustible construction; of Uniform Building Code; of City, County, and State building regulations, zoning and related ordinances; good knowledge of National Fire Protection Association Standards and UL directories; of construction materials and techniques.

Ability to accurately read and interpret multi-level multi-family residential and commercial building plans, engineering reports, calculations and specifications; to interpret excavation plans; to determine value of construction; to communicate effectively orally and in writing; to deal effectively with architects, developers, contractors, inspectors, co-workers and supervisors; to work effectively under time constraints and deadlines.

QUALIFICATIONS OF SUPERIOR CANDIDATES: I.C.B.O. Plans Examiner certification; minimum of two (2) years previous work experience reviewing commercial plans as a Plans Examiner.

SALARY RANGE: $31,272 - $46,908 per year. (Individuals may be hired anywhere within this range depending upon qualifications.)

BENEFITS: Membership in the Public Employee Retirement System of Idaho; group health, life and dental insurance for employee and family; flexible spending account; long-term disability plan; ten (10) paid holidays annually; sick leave accrual at one (1) day per month; vacation leave accrual at one (1) day per month; deferred compensation plan; employee assistance program; employees credit union; employee wellness program.

HOW TO APPLY: Applications may be obtained at Boise City Human Resources, 601 W. Idaho St., P.O. Box 500, Boise, ID 83701.

FILING DEADLINE: Applications will be accepted by Boise City Human Resources until 5:00 p.m. on Monday, May 4, 1998 or until opening is filled.

SELECTION PROCEDURE: Boise City Human Resources will notify all applicants of the status of the recruitment process within 3 weeks of the application deadline. The initial screening of applications will normally occur within 2 weeks of the closing deadline. All applications will be assessed. War and disabled war veterans residing in the State of Idaho who provide required documentation, will receive credit in accordance with Idaho State Law. The top rated group of applicants will proceed further in the hiring process. A referral list of qualified applicants will be established for consideration in filling future openings which may occur within six (6) months following the list's development.

EMPLOYMENT ELIGIBILITY VERIFICATION

As required under the Immigration Reform and Control Act, any person wishing to work for Boise City, regardless of the nature of the job or the number of hours or months employed, will be required to show proof of identity and work eligibility.

AN EQUAL OPPORTUNITY/AFFIRMATIVE ACTION EMPLOYER M/F/D/V

Internal recruiting has some possible disadvantages, however. In some jurisdictions, the employee with the most seniority has the first claim to an open position, even if he or she is only minimally qualified. Another drawback may be the ripple effect created when several people in the organization change jobs. Factions in the workforce may be aggravated when the internal promotion strengthens one faction. Employees left out of the promotion cycle may respond by reducing their work effort and causing dissent. To avoid negative repercussions, employers are advised to adhere to open and fair selection procedures and to keep all applicants informed about the selection process.[3]

The advantages of both internal and external recruiting can be realized when local governments judiciously employ both strategies in their hiring decisions. If the recruitment policy is not rigid, managers can consider the needs of the organization for each position and decide whether to hire from the existing pool of employees or to look for new resources outside the organization. A policy statement outlining the criteria to use in deciding whether to recruit internally or externally should be established. Many local governments have policies describing recruitment procedures that begin with internal recruitment and proceed to external sources if no internal candidate is found.

External Recruiting. If the local government is going to recruit from outside the organization, the administrator first determines the proper pool of candidates on the basis of the type of job to be filled. For example, it is not necessary to recruit nationally for a secretary-receptionist position, and an advertisement in the local newspaper will probably generate an adequate number of applicants. Other positions, however, such as engineer or information services director, will require a regional or nationwide search. The jurisdiction should allow for the increased cost and time associated with a national search. Generally, the

greater the responsibilities, the longer the time needed to fill the position. Costs include advertising the position, long-distance phone calls to check references, and travel expenses if candidates are invited for in-person interviews.

There are many resources available to assist with external recruiting. Technical assistance in conducting the search is available through professional organizations, some of which are listed at the end of this chapter and in Chapter 9. On-line services bring employers and job seekers together. Employment services may also be available through state employment agencies.

Recruitment firms will assist in finding professional employees. In exchange for a fee, the human resource management consultant locates professionals meeting the job description. Care should be taken, however, in using this option. The recruiter should have worked with public sector agencies before and should understand the jurisdiction's commitment to affirmative action and any other priorities. The cost of a recruiter also needs to be carefully investigated, as it is likely to be high, often up to a third of the open position's salary.

On the other hand, the cost of a recruiter may be justified by the fact that most public organizations underestimate the indirect costs incurred when staff completely handles a search. There is some evidence also that external recruiters can complete a search more quickly than an internal committee.[4]

Advertising the Job Opening

Where to Place the Advertisement. The decision about where and how to advertise should be based on the nature and size of the likely applicant pool. Placing an advertisement in a local or regional newspaper or in the local unemployment office can fill many entry-level positions. Other, more specialized positions must be advertised in national publications. Most professions have their own journals, newsletters, and on-line services. (See the resource list at the end of this chapter and in Chapter 9.) Innovative methods include sending direct mail to professional associations and schools, contacting employers that have recently laid off large numbers of employees, and using outplacement firms.[5] (Outplacement firms help organizations find jobs for displaced employees and can be an excellent resource for finding potential employees who have recently lost their jobs and are seeking work.) If the city or county is attempting to attract more minority applicants, it should consider placing advertisements in neighborhood weeklies that are based in ethnically diverse areas or contacting placement offices at colleges and universities with large minority student populations.

As schools, libraries, and homes become connected to the Web, many people routinely look for work on-line. Posting jobs on a Web site allows the employer to use creative techniques in marketing its job openings. Newspaper ads, which are more expensive than announcements on one's home page, can be used as teasers to encourage job seekers to look at the full description on-line. For examples of local government job postings on-line, see Eugene, Oregon's site at www.ci.eugene.or.us/JOBS/.

The Content of the Advertisement. The advertisement should attract applicants with the right qualifications. It should be specific enough to attract interest, but not so specific (e.g., with regard to compensation level if compensation is open) that it obligates the jurisdiction to contractual arrangements prematurely.

The advertisement should avoid any mention of gender, race, religion, age, ethnic origin, and physical capabilities unless those characteristics are considered bona fide occupational qualifications—in other words, requisites to the successful performance of the job. For example, it is illegal to advertise for "male lifeguards" for your city swimming pool or for a "female receptionist." If testing of any kind is involved, the advertisement should notify potential

The Job Ad

An effective ad should include the following components:

- A job title
- Minimum acceptable qualifications with respect to education or experience
- Essential job functions
- Typical duties and responsibilities
- Skills, certifications, or licenses required
- Forms and documents needed to apply for the job, as well as phone number or location where application forms can be obtained
- Notice of whether successful applicants will have to undergo drug testing and pass a medical exam
- The nature of skills tests or other examinations and the approximate time and place for taking them
- Address of where to send the documents
- The deadline for application
- The time when those who meet minimum qualifications can expect notification about exams
- A statement confirming the jurisdiction's status as an equal opportunity employer
- Whom to contact in case applicants wish to exercise their rights under the Americans with Disabilities Act and request reasonable accommodation during the application process.

applicants of specific selection procedures to be used (e.g., pen and paper testing, physical agility testing, etc.) so that applicants who wish to ask for reasonable accommodation under the ADA will be able to do so in a timely manner.[6]

Advertisements placed in periodicals outside of your geographical area may contain general information about your jurisdiction, including size, amenities, and other character-

Tips for Successful Recruiting ✓

❑ Include the supervisor of the position in the hiring team.

❑ Use an up-to-date job analysis to determine the job requirements.

❑ Ensure that all advertising, application, testing, and selection procedures comply with equal employment opportunity and affirmative action regulations as well as Americans with Disabilities Act requirements.

❑ Check the personnel manual and collective bargaining contracts for recruiting regulations.

❑ Tailor the scope of your search to the requirements of the position.

❑ Develop a recruitment information system so that applicants know where they stand in the selection process, and assign responsibility for communication with them.

Red Flags ⚑

⚑ Avoid any mention of gender, race, religion, age, ethnic origin, marital status, and physical capabilities in job ads unless those characteristics are considered bona fide occupational qualifications and essential for the job.

⚑ Be prepared to make reasonable accommodations for applicants who may request them under the ADA.

istics that you think might attract interested applicants.

Selection

Guiding Principles

• All selection methods must be valid and reliable tests of the KSAs that candidates need to perform on the job being filled.

• The selection process should be open to anyone who feels qualified to apply.

Challenges

• Ensuring that all selection criteria are job related.

• Ensuring that all selection criteria are applied consistently to all applicants.

• Balancing speed against thoroughness in selecting new employees.

The first objective of the selection process is to find the individual who can perform most successfully in a specific position. To do this, the employer must understand the duties and responsibilities of the job and then test qualified candidates on the specific requirements of the job and the KSAs needed. Courts have determined that for selection criteria to be valid, they have to be job related as documented by the job analysis. Factors unrelated to the job, such as political affiliation or friendship, are not valid selection criteria. Employees hired on the basis of extraneous factors may not be capable of doing the jobs they are hired to do; more important, invalid selection procedures can lead to claims of illegal discrimination.

In fact, the second objective of the selection process is to provide a fair opportunity for all applicants to be hired. The selection process should be open to anyone who feels qualified to apply, and each test administered should provide each applicant who reaches that testing level with the same opportunity to demonstrate his or her abilities.

Who Does What

In most organizations a number of people are involved in the selection process. A clerical employee may receive and review applications for completeness. The agency or department with the job opening may screen applications on the basis of minimum qualifications and prepare a list of qualified or eligible candidates. The department head, the chief administrator, or a committee then can test the candidates and interview the most promising ones.

Even though in most cases only one manager will have direct responsibility for the future employee, there are advantages to having more than one person involved in making a hiring decision. A variety of perspectives allows for several people to provide information about the job and input about each candidate's ability to perform in it. Several people on a hiring panel can discuss the advantages and disadvantages of each candidate and make a decision based on a consensus of needs instead of the job requirements as interpreted by one person. Finally, with the potential for claims of discrimination, it is a good idea to have several people involved in the selection process to help keep the questioning job related and to provide documentation against false claims.

Minimum Qualifications

Minimum qualifications describe the essential KSAs an employee needs to actually perform the job. Applicants who do not meet the minimum qualifications need not be considered.

Usually, minimum qualifications include knowledge of the principles related to the work to be performed, experience doing similar work, and specific job skills needed to perform the job duties. Each qualification must be a valid indicator of performance. Quite often, employers specify qualifications that are not clearly job related. For example, many employers use a college degree as a minimum qualification for jobs without stopping to consider whether earning that degree is directly related to the performance of a specific job. It may be that the knowledge needed could be obtained through experience or a combination of education and experience.

Minimum qualifications are often established by law or public policy. Child labor laws apply to all government employment. Professional certifications are required or preferred for certain jobs in local governments—teaching, nursing, lifeguarding. In some cases, city attorneys, clerks, engineers, finance officers,

and even human resource managers are required or requested to have professional certification. In some communities, residency requirements are allowed as one of the minimum qualifications for a local government job.

If women and minorities are underrepresented in certain jobs and ranks, the affirmative action officer, chief executive, or other top staff member should keep a separate record of all applicants by gender and ethnicity, specifying the reasons why they were or were not retained for further consideration. (See Chapter 5 for more information on record keeping.)

Selection Methods

Most organizations use several selection tools in sequence, such as application forms, performance tests, interviews, and reference checks. Each of these selection instruments must be designed to measure an applicant's abilities as they relate to actual job requirements, and should not disqualify candidates because of factors not related to the job. However, candidates who at any step do not meet the qualifications identified in the job description can be disqualified and removed from further consideration.

Since not all jobs are the same, selection methods differ. The least costly selection method is the application form, which can be administered to many applicants and used to find those candidates who meet the minimum requirements of the job. Because of the time commitment, the most expensive approaches are performance tests administered at assessment centers or skill demonstration tests. Such tests should therefore be administered toward the end of the process, when a final choice is being made among a very small number of highly qualified candidates.

Actually, every step of the selection process, from the application form to the final interview, is a test and should be viewed as such by those making the hiring decision. Each testing component should specify minimum levels for the KSAs being evaluated and can also include a list of preferred or desired qualifications. Each component must also assign points for minimum and desired qualifications. Cutoff points can be designated to help in grouping candidates for further consideration, for example,

Minimal	70–79%
(candidate satisfies minimal qualifications)	
Good	80–89%
(candidate exceeds minimal qualifications by at least 10%)	
Excellent	90–100%
(candidate exceeds minimal qualifications by at least 20%)	

In addition, each test in the hiring process must be valid and reliable. To be valid, tests must measure factors related to specific requirements of the job; to be reliable, tests must be applied consistently. The manager should also be certain to treat all applicants and eventual candidates in the same way. At every step of the hiring process, the manager should constantly ask whether the question is job related and whether he or she is being consistent with all candidates.

Application Forms and Resumes. Application forms or resumes are used to screen out applicants who do not meet the minimum qualifications and to gather information for personnel records. In addition to an applicant's personal employment information such as name, address, Social Security number, and telephone number, these selection devices can provide information on the applicant's basic qualifications, such as level of education, employment experience, and job skills. An example of an application form from Boise, Idaho, is shown in Exhibit 2-2.

The information requested on applications must be related directly to the job being filled. Questions that directly or indirectly lead to

information about age, race, color, sex, religion, national origin, or physical disability or to personal information not related to required employment information or potential job performance should not be included. For example, many application forms include questions about age and marital status, but this information is usually irrelevant to the eventual performance of the job and could be used to make illegal hiring decisions. If such information is needed for determining benefits, it should be collected only after a hiring decision has been made.

Managers should exercise caution when reviewing application forms because there is evidence that nearly half of all applicants exaggerate their qualifications on application forms and resumes.[7] Factual information (e.g., places of employment, degrees earned, certifications, etc.) can be verified. Managers should ask for supporting documentation (e.g., education transcripts, certificates, degrees awarded) and contact former employers to confirm prior work experience.

Most organizations use a single application form for all applicants applying for any job within the organization. In this case, there may be serious questions of job relatedness, and the information may not be sufficient to determine minimum qualifications for the specific job to be filled. A supplemental application form may be required for some jobs, asking for information specific to the job in question.

An example of a criminal history and driving record form, also from Boise, is shown in Exhibit 2-3 (but see page 140 for a discussion of the legality of asking about arrest records).

Eligibility Lists. Following a review of application forms, many organizations establish an eligibility list, or a list of those who meet the minimum qualifications and are considered the most promising candidates for further evaluation. The most common number of candidates passed on to management for consideration is three although the trend is toward including as

Exhibit 2-2   Sample Job Application Form

APPLICATION FOR EMPLOYMENT

The City of Boise is an Equal Opportunity/Affirmative Action Employer. It is our policy to recruit, hire and promote qualified and qualifiable persons without regard to race, religion, national origin, age or disability.

Give special attention to experience relative to the job in which you are applying. Be specific and thorough. Include all relevant temporary, part-time or volunteer work.

To: **City of Boise Human Resources**
601 W. Idaho St.
P.O. Box 500
Boise, ID 83701-0500

Phone: **(208) 384-3850**
Fax: **(208) 384-3868**
Web: **www.cityofboise.org**

Position Applied For: _____

Name: _____
Last _____ First _____ Middle

Present Address: _____
Street _____ City _____ State _____ Zip

Home Phone: _____   Work Phone: _____

Message Contact: _____
Name _____ Address _____ Phone

1. Are you willing to work: ☐ Full-Time   ☐ Part-Time   ☐ Temporary
2. Acceptable Salary: $ _____ per _____
3. If you are applying for a clerical position, you will be considered for openings in all departments unless you specify a particular department.
4. If considered for a position with the Police Department, are you willing to submit to a polygraph (lie detector)?
   ☐ yes   ☐ no
5. When can you report for work? _____
6. Are you currently employed by the City of Boise?   ☐ Yes   ☐ No
7. Have you previously been employed by us?   ☐ Yes   ☐ No   If yes, when _____
8. Have you previously been employed under another name?   ☐ Yes   ☐ No   If yes, what name? _____
9. As required under the Immigration Reform and Control Act, any person working for the City of Boise, regardless of the nature of the job or the number of hours or months employed, will be required to show proof of identity and work eligibility.

   Do you legally have the right to work in the U.S.?   ☐ Yes   ☐ No

EDUCATION

Do you have a high school diploma or equivalent? (GED)   ☐ Yes   ☐ No

Circle the highest grade completed – not including college.
1 2 3 4 5 6 7 8 9 10 11 12

Special Training or Education Beyond High School

Name of School/ Location	Courses	Credit Hours Completed	Type of Degree/ Date Received

EMPLOYMENT HISTORY

In the spaces below, list the specific tasks and responsibilities included in your work history, beginning with your present or last employment. If you have a long history of employment, **be sure to list those jobs which best relate to the position for which you are applying.** Employment verification may be made regarding all of your past experience. Please note if you do not want your present employer contacted. Use additional pages as necessary. **A resume will not be accepted in lieu of completing this portion of the application.**

Starting Date:	Ending Date:	Starting Salary:	Ending Salary:	Hours per Week:

Your Title: _____   May we contact your present employer?   ☐ Yes   ☐ No

Present or Last Employer - Name/Address & Phone: _____   Supervisor - Name & Title: _____

Reason for Leaving: _____

Duties (be specific): _____

Starting Date:	Ending Date:	Starting Salary:	Ending Salary:	Hours per Week:

Previous Employer - Name/Address & Phone: _____   Supervisor - Name & Title: _____   Your Title: _____

Reason for Leaving: _____

Duties (be specific): _____

AFFIRMATIVE ACTION DATA REQUEST

To assist the City of Boise in its commitment to Equal Employment Opportunity, applicants are asked to voluntarily provide the following information. This questionnaire will be separated from the application and will not be used in any employment decisions.

Date: _____   Position applied for: _____
Name: _____   Age: _____

Sex: □ Female □ Male   Disabled: □ Yes □ No

Race: □ African American   □ Hispanic   □ Asian American/Pacific Islander
□ American Indian/Alaskan Native   □ Caucasian

How were you informed of this opening?

□ I am currently employed by the City of Boise   □ Walk-In   □ Private Placement Service
□ Newspaper/Magazine Ad   □ College Placement Office   □ Job Interest Card
□ Department of Employment   □ Internet Website   □ Other _____

WAR ERA VETERAN'S PREFERENCE STATEMENT

Idaho law provides veteran's preference for residents of Idaho who:

have been in active service in the armed forces of the United States during a recognized war period or other recognized conflict as defined by law; or,

are disabled veterans who served on active duty in the armed forces at any time; or,

are widowers of such individuals, who have not remarried; or, are a qualifying spouse of an eligible disabled veteran who is unable to perform the work in the position for which the spouse seeks to apply the preference.

If you are claiming eligibility for veteran's preference, please complete a Veteran's Preference Form and submit it with your application along with any required documentation. A copy of the Veteran's Preference Form may be obtained from the City of Boise Human Resources or by visiting our website at *www.cityofboise.org* .

Starting Date:	Ending Date:	Starting Salary:	Ending Salary:	Hours per Week:
Previous Employer - Name/Address & Phone:			Supervisor - Name & Title:	Your Title:
Reason for Leaving:				
Duties (be specific):				

Starting Date:	Ending Date:	Starting Salary:	Ending Salary:	Hours per Week:
Previous Employer - Name/Address & Phone:			Supervisor - Name & Title:	Your Title:
Reason for Leaving:				
Duties (be specific):				

Starting Date:	Ending Date:	Starting Salary:	Ending Salary:	Hours per Week:
Previous Employer - Name/Address & Phone:			Supervisor - Name & Title:	Your Title:
Reason for Leaving:				
Duties (be specific):				

Exhibit 2-2 Sample Job Application Form (continued)

CITY OF BOISE
Applicant Information

Introduction:

Thank you for your interest in employment with the City of Boise. The following information is provided to assist you in completing the application. Our goal is to find the best qualified applicant for the job.

If you have any questions, please call Human Resources at (208) 384-3850.

The City of Boise will provide reasonable accommodation to applicants applying for employment. If you wish such accommodation, please call Human Resources (208) 384-3850 or (208) 384-3760 (TDD & Voice).

Tips for Completing Your Application:

Review the qualifications listed in the job announcement. If you believe that you meet these qualifications, we invite you to complete the appropriate application material.

The job announcement identifies job duties as well as the knowledge and abilities needed to perform them. It is important that you describe your experience in detail in order to identify the knowledge and abilities that make you a good candidate for the job. *Some positions may require a resume or cover letter to be included with the application. For these specific instances, a notation on the job description will be made.* ***However, a resume will NOT be accepted in lieu of the City application.***

The information you provide will be used to determine your level of qualifications for the current recruitment opening(s). When completing application papers, be as thorough and complete as possible. Do not overstate or claim experience that you do not have. The following information may be helpful:

★ Read the entire job announcement. Consider the responsibilities of the position you're applying for and their relationship to your training and experience (paid or unpaid).

★ Organize your responses in draft form, then prepare your final response.

★ When identifying duties you performed for each employer, include your most pertinent experience.

★ Include your most complex or important accomplishments.

★ If you do not include important experience and abilities, Human Resources cannot properly assess your qualifications.

★ You must give specific, detailed accounts of your related education, training and experience. Once your application is submitted, no additional information will be accepted.

★ Make sure your statements clearly describe your experience and accomplishments. Avoid describing your experience with general words such as: coordinate, responsible, facilitate, etc. Avoid non-specific statements about experience such as: "I have done this for 10 years."

★ When describing education and training, identify specific course content, and special projects completed.

★ Avoid using words, phrases and acronyms that are common only to your profession or previous employer.

★ Be as clear, concise and legible as possible.

★ If you do not have enough space to identify your job duties, additional sheets may be attached.

It's a good idea to keep a copy of the application and job announcement to prepare for any test or interview that may be required. Copies will not be provided for you.

(OVER)

List any experiences and/or skills that you feel would especially qualify you for this position.

Typing	Licenses /Certificates	Seminars/Training	Association/ Membership	Computer Software/Equipment
WPM _____ **Ten-Key by Touch:** ☐ Yes ☐ No				

EMPLOYMENT REFERENCES
(Include individuals who are qualified to evaluate your capabilities.)

Name:	Address:	City:	State:	Phone:

SIGNATURE OF APPLICANT

I certify that all information given on this application is true, correct, and complete to the best of my knowledge. I also certify that I have accounted for all of my work, experience, and training on this application, and that I have not knowingly withheld any fact or circumstance which would, if disclosed, affect my application unfavorably.

The City of Boise is hereby authorized to make any investigation of my employment, educational or background history through investigative agencies or bureaus of its choice. I release all relevant parties from all liability of any damages resulting from furnishing such information.

If employed by the City of Boise, I agree to abide by its rules and regulations. I understand that discovery of misrepresentation or omission of facts herein will make me ineligible for employment or be cause for immediate dismissal. I agree to furnish additional information as may be required to complete my employment file. I understand that operating conditions may require me to temporarily and/or regularly work shifts other than the one for which I am applying and I agree to such scheduling change as directed by my supervisor.

I have read and reviewed the description of the job for which I am applying. I understand that I must be capable of performing the essential functions of the job effectively and safely, with or without reasonable accommodation.

I also understand that my employment may be subject to the successful completion of an employment physical examination, and that my continued employment may be conditioned upon satisfactorily continuing to meet job-related physical and mental requirements. If requested, I agree to submit to a job-related physical examination performed by a qualified medical person of the City of Boise's choice. Such exam shall be paid for by the City of Boise. I also agree that all information concerning said physical examination can be supplied to the City of Boise, or an authorized agent of this municipality, upon their request.

I further understand that the City of Boise is committed to providing a safe, productive, and efficient work environment and to employing a work force free from the use of illegal drugs, either on or off the job. The City of Boise has established a pre-employment drug and alcohol testing policy. Pre-employment testing of applicants: As a condition of hiring, applicants will be required to submit to a pre-employment drug and alcohol test conducted by the City of Boise's authorized representative. Applicants will provide a urine sample for drug testing. Breath alcohol testing will be performed by an evidential breath testing device. The test results will be maintained in a confidential file, and only released to the City of Boise, its representatives, or as otherwise authorized or required by law. The applicant releases the City of Boise and its representatives from all liabilities relating to the drug testing carried out under this policy, including, without limitation, the release of the test results. Any applicant who fails to report for a test, refuses to take a test, fails to provide a specimen, tampers with a test specimen or who is identified with verified positive test results will be denied employment at that time. Applicants identified with verified positive test results may reapply after one (1) year from the date of the initial test with proof of successful completion of a rehabilitation program through a state-licensed facility.

I understand that this is an application for employment and that no employment contract, either express or implied, is being offered. I also understand that if employed, such employment is for an indefinite period and can be terminated at will by either party, with or without notice, at any time, for any or no reason, and is subject to change in wages, conditions, benefits, and operating policies.

Date: _____   Signature of Applicant: _____

Exhibit 2-3   Sample Criminal History and Driving Record Form

CRIMINAL HISTORY/DRIVING RECORD CHECK

All acceptable applicants for the position for which you have applied must successfully pass a criminal history and driving record check. In order to make the proper identification, the following information is necessary; Human Resources will not be responsible for omission of information needed to obtain an accurate record check. A conviction may or may not be grounds for disqualification. Each case will be considered individually.

Position applying for: _____

_____
Last Name   First Name   Middle Name

_____
Alias Names (Include Maiden/prior Married Names   Birth date   Sex   Social Security Number

Please list the name of any city or town in which you have lived during the last five (5) years:

_____   _____   _____
City, State   City, State   City, State

_____   _____   _____
City, State   City, State   City, State

****

In the space below, please list **ANY** misdemeanor and felony offenses, including D.U.I., for which you have been convicted or received a withheld judgment **within your lifetime**. Some juvenile offenses for which an individual is charged as an adult (tobacco, alcohol and drug charges) and traffic citations or moving violations such as inattentive driving <u>may</u> also fall into this category; it is the applicant's responsibility to verify the accuracy of the information contained within their record.

Approximate
  Date   City/State   Offense or Violation

****

Please list the approximate date and place of all traffic citations and moving violations received within the last **FIVE** (5) years including any driving related misdemeanor and felony offenses such as D.U.I., D.W.P., etc. Do not list parking tickets.

Approximate
  Date   City/State   Citation

****

I authorize Boise City to receive any and all information concerning myself related to my criminal records, and <u>I understand that any of the above requested information not listed which appears on the security check will automatically disqualify me on the basis of falsification of the application.</u>

_____   _____
Applicant's Signature   Date

many as five or ten. Other ideas for certifying eligible candidates are to use a percentage of those who meet minimum qualifications, or to establish categorical groupings such as satisfactory, good, and excellent and to test everyone in the "excellent" category.

It is the policy of many public organizations to give extra consideration in the selection process to veterans and especially to veterans with disabilities. This is often done by assigning them extra points in a ranking system.

Written Tests. Standardized methods of measuring knowledge or ability in specific job areas fell into disfavor with the courts and public employers in the 1960s and 1970s because many general tests at that time (such as intelligence and mechanical comprehension tests) were not clearly tied to performance in a specific job and had an adverse impact on minorities. However, more recently, tests have been carefully reconstructed to measure indicators related to job performance.

Standardized tests for specific jobs are available from various firms and organizations. The International Public Management Association for Human Resources has tests avail-

able for common public sector jobs (see Chapter 9). Multiple-choice tests are easy to score, require little interpretation, and can be given to large numbers of applicants with little cost to the organization.

Performance Tests. Performance tests assess proficiency in or aptitude for executing essential job functions. These tests are given to applicants to measure their ability or skill at performing some specific aspects of a job or their ability to be trained to do the work. The tests often simulate a major facet of the job and are therefore considered highly valid. However, they are also expensive to administer. For instance, when firefighters are tested for the job of engineer, they have to be individually observed demonstrating their ability to drive the engine, mentally calculate the engine pressure, pump water from a fire hydrant, and draft water from an open water source, all within a specified time period.

Physical tests are often given to candidates who will be required to perform physical tasks in their jobs. These tests must accurately reflect the common physical requirements of the job and cannot eliminate candidates for inability to perform in extreme cases.[8] The ADA requires that written and physical tests allow for "reasonable accommodation" for applicants requesting it, and it prohibits employers from discriminating against employees who cannot perform tasks of a marginal, infrequent, or nonessential nature (see Chapter 5).

Interviews. Besides the application form, interviewing is probably the most common selection device used by employers. By itself the interview may also be the least valid and reliable method of selecting future employees.[9] Managers can use the interview to determine a candidate's ability to communicate verbally and to ask probing questions about performance and behavior in circumstances similar to potential job situations. Because of the personal interaction in an interview, managers can explore interests or

Validity and Reliability

Validity

Validity refers to the adequacy of the test instrument—whether it accurately measures those attributes of a job that it is intended to measure. To be valid, a test must be job related. Three types of validity apply to testing: content validity, criterion validity, and construct validity.

To have **content validity,** the test has to be directly related to the knowledge, skills, and abilities (KSAs) needed to perform the duties and responsibilities of a job, and must cover the whole domain of the job and not exclude essential KSAs. A recent job analysis should capture the job content.

To have **criterion validity,** a test has to measure a specific criterion of the job, such as the ability to make quick decisions or to assume a leadership role in an unstructured situation. A test has criterion validity if its results have a strong relationship to required job behaviors and future performance. Examiners infer from the candidates' performance on the test how well they will perform in a similar situation on the job.

Construct validity applies to psychological tests for which theoretical constructs, such as the IQ test measuring intelligence, have been developed. Other test instruments can assess aptitudes or personality traits that research has identified as predictors for high or low performance in certain positions. Psychological pro-file tests have been developed for stressful jobs such as police officer or fire-fighter, in which little room for human error can be tolerated. However, because these tests are grounded in psychological theory, they need to be administered by qualified psychologists.

The U.S. Supreme Court has ruled that selection criteria not directly related to job performance are not valid and are therefore prohibited (see *Griggs v. Duke Power Company* and *Wards Cove v. Atonio*).* The federal "Uniform Guidelines on Employee Selection Procedures" provide generally accepted rules for selection procedures and standards for validation of selection tests.

Two approaches to validate tests are concurrent validation and predictive validation. **Concurrent validation** uses a sample of current employees who take the proposed selection test while evaluators simultaneously collect information on their job performance. The test is considered valid when the range of low to high performance parallels the range of low to high test scores. In **predictive validation,** the test results of job applicants are compared against their actual performance after being hired and on the job for a period of time. Regression analysis is the proper statistical procedure for both types of validation approaches. If the jurisdiction does not have the expertise in statistics or the necessary software, the resources of a nearby university can perhaps be used.

Reliability

Reliability refers to the consistent use and unambiguous nature of the test instrument. Tests are supposed to be applied consistently over time and across a variety of applicants. Reliability is also ensured when the test instrument is unambiguous and elicits consistent responses from test takers. In other words, a reliable testing method should consistently obtain similar scores from applicants with similar KSAs.

* *Griggs v. Duke Power Company,* 28 L. Ed. 2d (1971); *Wards Cove Packing v. Atonio,* 104 L. Ed. 2d (1989).

fyi

Common Interviewing Errors

The following errors are easy to make in an interview:

- **Similarity error:** one candidate may appear similar to the interviewer and therefore be favored.

- **Comparison error:** one candidate may stand above the rest of the applicants by comparison and be favored even though he or she still does not meet the requirements of the job.

- **First-impression error:** one candidate may become a favorite of those interviewing because of some information on the application form or other communication, and may gain an advantage before any interviewing actually takes place. Research on interviewing finds that managers make up their minds about a candidate being interviewed in an average of four minutes.

- **Halo-and-horns effect:** one candidate may qualify in one aspect of a job, which influences the remainder of the interview, or the interviewer may overreact to one unfavorable response. Unfortunately for the job candidate, one bad impression tends to influence those conducting the interview more than the positive responses.

accent, friendliness, posture, and enthusiasm, as well as the clothing worn by candidates. Research indicates that nonverbal behavior in an interview situation tends to have a greater influence on a hiring decision than verbal responses.

Finally, administrators may not be well trained in conducting interviews properly and may have poor listening and communication skills. Much of the important information in an interview may never be heard or may be misinterpreted as a result of error and bias.

Interviews can be conducted by more than one person to gain the advantages of multiple perspectives and to protect the interviewers from any false claims from disgruntled candidates. Although agreement between interviewers on the facts and overall evaluations of candidates is fairly good, inter-rater reliability or consistency on subjective characteristics such as candidate leadership or honesty is often low. To assure consistency in how the interview is conducted among candidates, it is common to have an established list of questions that are asked of each candidate, but it is also common to see the line of questioning diverge from the plan.

The most common errors interviewers make are not knowing the specific duties and responsibilities of the job to be performed, not planning questions (related to job duties) in advance of the interview, and straying into areas during the interview that are either not job related or unnecessary (and a waste of time). These errors can be avoided by following the tips on page 49 before beginning the interview process.

Questions listed in the sidebar on page 50 are usually prohibited because they lead to information that could be used to illegally discriminate against protected classes of applicants. Other questions provide information that is simply irrelevant to a candidate's future performance on the job. In rare cases there is a real and important job requirement, referred to as a bona fide occupational qualification, that

concerns in greater detail than can be revealed in written tests or application forms. However, this characteristic of the interview also opens the door to questions that are not job related and could lead to information that could be used to make discriminatory or unfair decisions.

The validity of interviews becomes questionable when the interview strays into areas not related to the job. Personal interaction and human nature can combine in the interview to produce bias. Factors that can inappropriately influence the outcome of an interview include nonverbal behaviors such as body language, may require interview questions related to otherwise illegal information. In most public sector job interviews, however, questions that call for illegal or unnecessary information are to be carefully avoided. If necessary for personnel records or employment benefits, some questions can be asked after the hiring decision has been made.

The best questions are those that provide the interview panel with information about the candidate's KSAs and attitudes necessary to perform successfully in the job. Questions that ask whether a candidate has a given skill or could perform a task rely on the candidate's own assessment of his or her abilities. More thoughtful questions would ask what the candidates would do in a hypothetical situation (related to the job to be performed) or, better yet, what they have actually done in other jobs similar to the one they would fill. Behavioral and situational questions have been found to be both valid and reliable and good predictors of future performance.

These kinds of questions are especially useful for assessing a candidate's temperament. Violence in the workplace has become a common concern, and one thing managers can do to avert problems in this area is to carefully screen job applicants for violent tendencies. Résumés do not reveal proclivity to disruptive behavior, former employees may not report incidents for fear of defamation suits, and direct questions can expose the hiring authority to a lawsuit for violation of privacy. An alternative is to use role playing to find out how the applicant handles stress and anger in typical job situations.

Scenarios can be set up in which the candidate must handle a disgruntled client who is giving the public employee a hard time, respond to a citizen who doesn't understand a departmental decision, or answer an employee who is insulting. The candidate is asked to think through each scenario and describes his or her response. The objective of this "test" is to give the interviewer an idea of the candidate's ability to get along with difficult people and to deal with frustrating situations and challenges to authority.[10]

If your local government is an at-will employer, it is very important to instruct interviewers not to promise job security in the course of an interview. (Neither should job security be promised at any stage of the recruitment process; see the sections in Chapter 5 on employment at will and on oral and implied contracts.)

Assessment Centers. An assessment center is not a place but a process. It is a series of individual and group exercises used to appraise the abilities of candidates applying for managerial

---

Tips for Successful Interviews

- Before beginning the interview process, conduct a careful job analysis of the position to determine the duties, responsibilities, and required knowledge, skills, and abilities.

- Assemble a panel of individuals with a strong interest in the selection outcome and train them in proper interviewing techniques and ways to avoid common interviewing errors.

- Decide on the objectives you wish to accomplish during the interview. These should include information items that are not accessible through other selection methods.

- Plan past-behavior and hypothetical-situation questions in advance of the interview to direct the meeting into areas important to understanding how each candidate will perform in the job.

- Use a standardized rating scale to evaluate each candidate on the same questions and then discuss these evaluations with the panel of interviewers after all the interviews have been held.

Illegal Questions

It is illegal to ask the following questions on an application form or in an employment interview.

Race, creed, national origin

What is your race? What organizations do you belong to?

What country does your family come from?

Where are you a citizen?

What is your previous foreign address?

What is your birthplace?

What is the name of a relative to be notified in case of emergency?

What is your native language?

Legal alternatives: Are you legally able to work in the United States? Who would you like to be notified in the event of an emergency? What languages do you speak or write fluently (assuming foreign language skills are an essential job function)?

Sex, marital status

Are you male or female?

What is your maiden name?

Have you changed your name?

What is your sexual orientation?

Are you married?

Are you pregnant?

How many children do you have?

Do you have child care?

Do you plan on having any more children?

Legal alternative: Do you have relevant work experience while using another name?

Age

What is your age?

When were you born?

Information about age can be required, however, to ascertain whether the applicant meets minimal age requirement for the job.

Disability

Do you have any disabilities?

Have you had certain diseases?

Legal alternative: Is there any reason you would not be able to perform the responsibilities and tasks of this position?

Height and weight

What is your height?

What is your weight?

Legal alternative: Can you perform the essential job functions?

Religion

What is your religion?

What religious holidays do you celebrate?

In what groups are you a member?

Legal alternative: Can you meet the work schedule for this job?

Military service

Have you been dishonorably discharged from the military?

Legal alternative: What was your occupation while in military service? Did you receive training related to this job?

Criminal record

Have you been arrested?

Have you been convicted of any crime?

Legal alternative: Have you been convicted of a crime related to the duties and responsibilities of this position?

Source: Paul Balbresky, "An Employment-Related Lawsuit May Put Your Local Government at Risk," *Public Management* 73 (November 1993): 13–15. See also James A. Buford, Jr., *Personnel Management and Human Resources in Local Government* (Auburn, Ala.: Auburn University Press, 1991), 170–171.

The Cone Method

A popular technique for conducting employment interviews is known as the "cone method." The interviewers first determine their objectives for the interview and then examine each selected topic by using broad questions, followed by more specific questions related to that topic. For example, if one of the objectives for the interview is to determine the amount of supervisory experience a candidate has had, the questions on this topic might move from the general to the specific as follows:

Opening question	Describe your experience supervising employees.
More specific questions	What were your responsibilities as a supervisor?
	What problems did you experience as a supervisor?
Probing questions	How did you handle that problem?
	Did you seek advice in responding to the problem?
More specific questions	How did you improve the performance of your employees?
	What were the duties of the employees you supervised?

Source: Thomas L. Moffatt, *Selection Interviewing for Managers* (New York: Harper and Row, 1979), 81–101.

and other complex jobs.[11] Assessment centers may include tests measuring executive skills, such as leadership, management style, and intelligence. The set-up may also involve taking performance tests, writing memos, handling a problem employee, using listening skills, preparing and delivering a speech, and dealing with sexual harassment problems. Group exercises or games can shed light on the candidates' abilities in areas such as delegation, team building, and conflict management. In simulations, a rather elaborate series of job-related situations is presented to a group of candidates, who behave in roles assigned by the assessors. The simulation allows for multiple responses and has pre-planned, progressive steps for the candidates to act upon as the simulation unfolds.

Assessment centers commonly use an in-basket exercise. Each candidate is given an in-basket full of letters, memos, and telephone messages and is asked to deal with these items by first determining their importance and then deciding about how to act on the information. Another test is the leaderless group problem. A small group of candidates is brought together and asked to solve a management problem. The solution is not as important as the process, and the candidates are observed and scored on their leadership traits and ability to work in groups.

The assessment centers usually include interviews in which the candidates are asked about their behavior on some of the tests and their experience handling work situations similar to those they can expect to encounter on the job.

Typically, a group of candidates for the same position is tested simultaneously in an assessment center. A larger number of candidates enables assessors to compare the highest-rated candidates against each other after they have passed a series of preliminary tests.

Red Flags

The following can ruin your selection process:

- Unclear job requirements
- Invalid or unreliable tests
- Untrained interviewers
- No reference check

Assessment centers usually use a team of trained evaluators who conduct the tests and then discuss the results as a group. These assessors may include representatives from the departments or areas in which the candidate is to be employed, and they provide a wide range of perspectives for deciding who is the most acceptable candidate.

The most important advantage of assessment centers is that the tests can be designed to focus on very specific aspects of the job and are therefore highly content valid. Assessment centers can also reliably test a number of candidates using very similar testing procedures.

The biggest problem with assessment centers is their cost. Their procedures can run from one to five days and can occupy the time of several assessors and candidates. Because of the cost, assessment centers are usually made available only to candidates applying for upper-level management or highly technical positions.

Assessment centers also carry the risk of bias related to measurement standards. The accepted characteristics of good managers or leaders are sometimes biased against women, who often display different management traits from men. Successful managers may display these male-oriented management traits, but female-oriented traits may be equally valid predictors of good leaders and managers.

For example, in an in-basket exercise, some evaluators would give high marks to participants who act independently and decisively. Others might favor a deliberative and consultative approach to decision making. The *right* answer should be justified by specific requirements of the job.

Background Investigations (Reference Checks). As with any other selection method, the objectives of conducting background or reference checks should be decided on before the procedure is begun. The simplest objec-

tive is to verify information obtained from candidates on the application forms and in interviews. Another valuable use of reference checks is to determine past performance. One of the best indicators of future performance is how the employee performed in similar situations in the past. It is a must to develop a set of questions before beginning any reference interviews to ensure that the questions are job related.

It is a good idea to inform the candidate that you will be asking former employers and others who are familiar with the candidate's work for confidential personnel information. This can be accomplished with a notification and checkoff on the application form or a separate signed release.

The list of references can come from the candidate and from the candidate's list of former employers and instructors. Additional references not volunteered by the candidate can be obtained by asking the listed references for others who are familiar with the candidate's work history.

Reference checks are frequently conducted by telephone to save time and to hear spontaneous responses from those interviewed. Background checks by mail are slow, and the responses can be carefully crafted and uninformative. On the other hand, these responses can be more thoughtful than spontaneous answers, and the sources will include clues to the real performance history of the candidate. Reference checks can also be conducted in person, but this is typically done only for high-ranking, security-sensitive positions.

Reference checks are useful for weeding out candidates who have given false information in the selection process and for uncovering behavioral problems in the past. Employers are obligated to find any problems related to the candidate's ability to perform the job before hiring that individual, especially in the event of harm or injury to someone else. If the

Red Flag

⚑ To avoid violating privacy rights of job applicants, you must have their written consent before contacting high schools or colleges for transcripts, previous employers for references, or credit-reporting firms for credit reports.

hired employee causes harm when a pattern of behavior in past employment indicated the danger, the employer can be sued for negligent hiring. (Similarly, former employers can be held liable for negligent referral if they hold back information that could have prevented a person from causing harm to others in a future job situation. However, liability suits from former employees also threaten those employers who give poor references to prospective employers. Because of this possibility, many organizations do not allow their managers to give any more information than the job description and the former employee's dates of employment.)

For jobs requiring good financial management skills, the employer may want to review the finalists' credit history. However, the employer must have written permission to do so. If an applicant is denied employment because of information in the credit report, the Fair Credit Reporting Act requires the employer to inform the applicant of this in case the credit report is inaccurate.

The legality of inquiring into a finalist's criminal record varies among the states. Many states have no statutes while some prohibit asking about arrest records. Questions about convictions, however, are lawful, but even then the refusal to hire a person because of a conviction has to be for job-related reasons. When a position involves the use of a government car, the driving record should be checked by contacting the state agency that issues driver's licenses.

Hiring

Guiding Principle

- A probationary period and careful orientation can help ensure strong performance in the future.

Even after the final selection is made, the process is not finished. First of all, the selected candidate may have to pass additional tests. Paperwork has to be completed, and the employee has to be oriented to the organization and the specific job responsibilities. Then, it is wise to use a probationary period to find out whether the new employee can perform on the job.

The Conditional Job Offer

Because of cost and privacy concerns, certain steps in the selection process are taken only after the preliminary job offer has been made and accepted. The job offer should be conditional on the new employee passing the final screening phases. These include verification of employment eligibility, a drug test, and medical screening.

Employment Eligibility. To verify the employee's right to work in the United States, the employee and employer have to complete CIS Form I-9. To prove identity and work eligibility, the employee has two options:

- Submit an original document that establishes both identity and work eligibility (a U.S. passport, an alien registration card with a photo, a certificate of U.S. citizenship, a naturalization certificate, an unexpired foreign passport with employment authorization attached).

- Submit an original document that establishes identity (driver's license, state-issued I.D. card, U.S. military card or draft record) *plus* an original document that establishes employment eligibility (Social Security card, U.S. birth certificate with official seal).

Employers are advised to keep photocopies of the documents that were examined and to retain Form I-9 as long as the employees work for them. Information about compliance with immigration and naturalization rules about hiring foreign workers immigrating for purposes of employment can be found at www.dol.gov/asp/programs/guide/pewbi.htm.

Drug Testing. From a legal standpoint it is less problematic to subject conditional hires to drug testing than to subject employees who are already on the payroll. Therefore, many jurisdictions routinely screen new recruits for the use of illegal drugs. However, the job announcement should list the drug test as a condition for employment so that applicants are forewarned, and testing procedures should be carefully controlled.

Public employers are by definition the government, which is held to a higher standard than private sector employers in respecting employee privacy. The Constitution limits the government from illegal searches and other privacy infringements (see Chapter 5). The courts have attempted to balance this right to privacy with the public interest in safety and have usually allowed drug testing for applicants and current employees who are involved in dangerous occupations (firefighters, public works employees), for jobs in which harm may come to others (drivers), or for jobs in which drug laws are enforced (police).

Drug testing is expensive, and evidence shows that most job candidates, whether drug users or not, say they are less likely to apply for jobs where drug testing is practiced. However, there are some good reasons to aim for a drug-free workplace. Research shows that drug and alcohol abuse is directly related to employee absenteeism and accidents on the job.[12] There may also be employer liability concerns when an employee who is under the influence of a drug causes an accident.

Medical Examination. After the conditional job offer and before the new hire starts work,

employers can require a full medical exam. Questions can be asked and tests can be conducted to ascertain whether the individual has the physical and mental capabilities needed to perform the job and does not pose a threat to himself or herself, to co-workers, or to customers. However, all new employees in the same job class have to be subjected to the same medical exam. Under the ADA, the conditional job offer can be withdrawn after the medical exam if the employer demonstrates all of the following:

- The conditional hire could not perform an essential job function.
- No reasonable accommodation was possible, or the accommodation requested would mean an undue hardship for the employer.
- The withdrawal of the offer was solely for job-related reasons.

The conditional job offer can also be withdrawn if the employer can show that the new hire would pose a threat to himself or herself or to others.

The Probationary Period

Obviously, the most valid predictor of future performance is actual performance on the job. Most public organizations have a probationary period of three months to a year. The length of the probationary period is determined by the amount of time it takes to learn the responsibilities of the job and to accumulate a record that can be evaluated. The probationary period is an opportunity for managers to carefully evaluate the performance of the new employee. During probation, the worker is subject to termination at will and has fewer employment rights than permanent employees.

Many local governments do not consider the probationary period as part of the employee selection process. Instead, it is used as a learning period for new employees, during which they are trained, observed, counseled, and

Employment Contracts

Individual employment contracts are agreements between the local government and key employees, such as the city and county manager or department heads. These contracts are legally binding on the local government and the employee for the term stipulated, and great care should therefore be taken in drafting the documents.

The contracts describe job responsibilities, reporting arrangements, the terms of employment, and separation provisions. These contracts are useful to attract executive-level personnel because they specify salary, benefits, and incentives and can include protections against arbitrary firings. This latter point makes them especially useful for managers in politically sensitive positions, such as city and county managers, because their employment can otherwise be terminated for reasons completely unrelated to work performance. Individual employment contracts are not offered to rank-and-file employees because case law protects them against arbitrary dismissal unless the employer clearly identifies the work relationship as "at-will employment." (See the beginning of Chapter 5 and Rosenbloom's discussion on pages 147–148 of procedural due process.)

Completing the Hiring Process

The following documents should be created or filed to complete the hiring process:

- Letter offering the job to finalist
- Letter from finalist accepting offer
- INS Form I-9
- IRS Form W-4
- Forms to sign up for employee benefits
- Letters to applicants not selected.

evaluated while actually performing the work they were hired to do.

Whatever the purpose of the probationary period, managers are responsible for properly training probationary employees and evaluating their performance. These evaluations should be regular and frequent and should provide the employee with an assessment of performance and guidance on how to improve. At the end of the probationary period, a final evaluation should be scheduled with the employee to determine whether that individual has the potential to perform successfully in the job. If proper training and regular guidance have been conducted, the outcome of the final evaluation should come as no surprise to the employee.

The Orientation

Employee orientation training sessions introduce recent hires to the requirements of the new jobs and to the general operation of the organization. Formal orientation can prevent misunderstandings and guard against informal orientation that may be inconsistent and misleading. Orientation training can also speed up the socialization process by introducing the new employees to co-workers, supervisors, and those who can help answer questions and make the newcomers become comfortable in the new work environment.

All employees should be carefully prepared to perform their work assignments and familiarized with the setting in which they will be working. Employees should understand the culture of the organization, including its history, the important people involved in the community, the structure of the local government, and the way in which each department is integrated into the overall mission of the city or county. New recruits should be briefed on organization rules and regulations, introduced to those who will either affect the work product or receive the work of the employee, and trained so that they fully understand the demands of the work expected of them. A separate orientation can be scheduled with supervisors, who can explain the work product needed and the supervisory arrangements. An orientation session should also be scheduled to explain employee benefits and the method of paying the employee's salary.

A small investment in time and orientation training materials can provide substantial benefits in employee productivity much sooner than if new employees are left alone to figure out their responsibilities. An employee orientation checklist (see sidebar on page 56) can help supervisors ensure that all the topics needed for new employees are covered.

Many things cannot be taught in a formal employee orientation training session. The best source of information is often co-workers, who can explain facts and situations in the context of the organization's way of doing things. Mentoring or arranging for the opportunity to meet with several co-workers informally, such as in a lunch setting or after work, can help new employees feel comfortable asking questions and can provide them with an opportunity to learn many of the values, professional and ethical norms, and attitudes of important people within the organization.

Employee Orientation Checklist

The following orientation segments can be conducted by the chief executive, department head, or supervisor, as appropriate.

General orientation to the organization

Organization mission and goals
Organization history
Services provided
Organization structure
Who's who in the organization
Culture, values, ethical principles

Specific orientation to the organization's policies and procedures

Employee handbook
Work hours
Vacation and leave rules and procedures
Provision of pay and description of benefits
Discipline system
System for complaints and suggestions

Specific orientation to the department

Departmental goals
Relationship to other units and departments
Operational procedures
Work flow
Facilities
Schedule
Introduction to co-workers

Specific orientation to the job

Goals and performance standards
Job duties, responsibilities, and performance
   expectations
Workstation
Computer system and capabilities
Tools and equipment
Supervisory arrangements
Where to go: whom to ask for help
On-the-job and other job-training plans and
   schedule
Performance appraisal schedule and content
Promotion criteria
Salary increase schedule and criteria
Training plans

Source: Gary Dressler, *Personnel Management* (Reston, Va.: Reston Publishing Company, 1984), 237–239.

Recruitment Advertising Outlets

American Foreign Language Newspapers Associates, 8530 Wilshire Boulevard, Suite 404, Beverly Hills, CA 90211. Phone: 310/652-5444; fax 310/652-8080.

American Planning Association, 1776 Massachusetts Avenue, NW, Washington, DC 20036. Phone: 202/872-0611; Web site: www.planning. org

ASPA Recruiter Online, Web site: http://aspanet. jobcontrolcenter.com/

Electrical Construction and Maintenance, 1221 Avenue of the Americas, PO Box 900, New York, NY 10020.

International Association of Chiefs of Police, 515 North Washington Street, Alexandria, VA 22314-2357. Phone: 703/836-6767, 800/THE IACP; fax: 703/836-4543; Web site: http://theiacp.org

International Association of Fire Chiefs, 4025 Fair Ridge Drive, Fairfax, VA 22033-2868. Phone: 703/273-0911; fax: 703/273-9363; Web site: http://iafc.org

International Code Council, 5203 Leesburg Pike, Suite 600, Falls Church, VA 22041. Phone: 703/931-4533; fax: 703/379-1546; Web site: www.iccsafe.org

Career Resource and Recruitment Center, www.careerbuilder.com/

ICMA Job Center, ICMA, 777 North Capitol Street, NE, Suite 500, Washington, DC 20002-4201. Phone: 202/962-3650; Web site: http://jobs.icma.org

Jobs Available, PO Box 1040; Modesto, CA 95353. Phone: 209/571-2120; fax: 209/576-1249.

Library Journal, 360 Park Ave South, New York, NY 10010. Phone: 646/746-6819; fax: 646/746-6734. Web site: http://library journal. reviewsnews.com

Nation's Cities Weekly, 1301 Pennsylvania Avenue, NW, Suite 550, Washington, DC, 20004, Phone: 202/626-3000; fax: 202/626-3043; Web site: www.nlc.org/nlc_org/site/newsroom/nations_cities_weekly/index/cfm

PORAC Law Enforcement News, 2495 Natomas Park Drive, Suite 555, Sacramento, CA 95833. Phone: 800/655-6397; Web site: http://porac. org/employment.html

Public Works Online Edition, www.pwmag.com

URISA Marketplace, Urban and Regional Information Systems Association, 1460 Renaissance Drive, Suite 305, Park Ridge, IL 60068. Phone: 847/824-6300; fax: 847/824-6363; Web site: www.urisa.org/jobsmktpl.htm.

[1] W. David Patton, Stephanie L. Witt, Nicholas P. Lovrich, and Patricia J. Fredericksen, *Human Resource Management: The Public Service Perspective* (Boston: Houghton Mifflin Company, 2000), 210.

[2] Paul Balbresky, "An Employment Related Lawsuit May Put Your Local Government at Risk," *Public Management* 73 (November 1993): 13–15.

[3] Patton et al., 211.

[4] Catherine Rush and Lizbeth Barclay, "Executive Search: Recruiting a Recruiter," *Public Management* 77 (July 1995): 20–22.

[5] Patton et al., 212.

[6] Balbresky, "An Employment Related Lawsuit," 14.

[7] Thomas E. Becker and Alan L. Colquit, "Potential Versus Actual Faking of a Biodata Form: An Analysis Along Several Dimensions of Item Type," *Personnel Psychology* 45 (1992): 389–408.

[8] For information on pre-employment testing for public safety personnel, see Glenn R. Jones, "Police and Fire Physical Fitness," *IQ Report* 36, no. 1 (Washington, D.C.: ICMA, 2004).

[9] Richard A. Posthuma, Frederick P. Morgeson, and Michael A. Campion, "Beyond Employment Interview Validity: A Comprehensive Narrative Review of Recent Research and Trends over Time," *Personnel Psychology* 55 (Spring 2002), 1:79; and Gregory S. Jelf, "A Narrative Review of Post-1989 Employment Interview Research," *Journal of Business and Psychology* 14 (Fall 1999), 25.

[10] Michael Barrier, "When Laws Collide: Legally Screening Out Potentially Violent Employees," *Nation's Business* 83 (February 1995): 23.

[11] Maurine Moody, "Ready Aim Hire," *Directo* 52 (1999), 53.

[12] Edward F. Etzel, Christopher D. Lantz, and Catherine A. Yura, "Alcohol and Drug Use, and Sources of Stress: A Survey of University Faculty, Staff, and Administrators," *Employee Assistance Quarterly* 11 (1995): 51–58.

CHAPTER 3

Maintaining a High-Performance Workforce

ARTHUR H. MCCURDY AND NICHOLAS P. LOVRICH

This chapter discusses the predominant approaches to maintaining a high-performance workforce, including evaluating performance, setting goals, linking performance to compensation, linking performance to employee advancement and development, building teams and workgroups, and managing special circumstances that can affect performance. These various approaches are interrelated with other personnel policies, such as compensation (Chapter 1), employee benefits (Chapter 6), setting expectations (Chapter 7), and disciplinary procedures (Chapter 8).

An assessment of the approaches to managing a high-performance workforce must take into consideration the labor relations environment and other laws, rules, and regulations governing the jurisdiction. These factors establish the broad parameters for what the city or county can and cannot do in its personnel practices. The environments within which local governments exist vary considerably, but it is often possible to find similar jurisdictions and compare personnel policies.

A note of caution is due about adopting private sector practices. In one frequently cited discussion and review of the public administration literature, the authors observe that "a century of dialogue concludes that the public and private sectors are different."[1] Because they are indeed quite different, any private sector practices that would be adopted must first be scrutinized in the light of the unique legal and political contexts within which the public sector operates.

Evaluating Employee Performance

Guiding Principles

- The organization's mission should determine important performance goals.
- Evaluation techniques must fit performance goals.

The authors gratefully acknowledge the assistance of Carol Greene, the director of the Association of Washington Cities Local Government Personnel Institute, in reviewing the first-edition version of this chapter from a practitioner's viewpoint and providing many useful insights. We also wish to acknowledge the support and assistance of numerous members of the Section on Personnel Administration and Labor Relations of the American Society for Public Administration for providing sources of information and research as well as serving as a sounding board for our observations on personnel issues. Steve Hays, Rick Kearney, Brent Steel, and Meredith Newman all deserve special recognition in this regard.

- Performance evaluation techniques must be valid and reliable.
- Cooperation between management and rank-and-file employees is as important as the technique selected.
- Performance evaluations should report both strengths and weaknesses.

Challenge

- Determining whether to develop in-house expertise or to contract out for the service.

One of the primary means of maintaining a high-performance workforce is through the evaluation of employee performance. The aim of the individual performance evaluation is to ensure personal accountability to the goals of the organization. Thus, it is very important both to select a performance evaluation technique that supports achievement of the organization's goals and to connect the expectations for employee performance to the mission of the organization.

Evaluations may be directed toward either individual or team performance. Their multiple applications fit broadly into one of two categories, depending largely on the outcomes desired from the performance appraisal system. First, there are summative evaluations, which are designed to assess an employee's overall strengths. These are developed primarily to review performance for a specified period in the immediate past, and to recognize employee accomplishments or successes and distribute performance-based pay increases or bonuses. Second, there are formative evaluations, which are designed to diagnose an employee's weaknesses. These are developed primarily to improve performance for some specified future period. These evaluations set goals or objectives and identify employee training and development needs in order to broaden the organization's knowledge base or prepare individuals for promotions. When these two types of performance appraisal purposes are confused and combined, the

process can be very stressful for the evaluated employee, and it may tempt him or her to hide weaknesses and avoid needed training, actions detrimental to organizational performance in the long run.[2]

It is important to ensure that all employees understand the purposes of the performance appraisal system. Beyond associating the performance evaluation with the mission of the agency and the various applications mentioned above, the organization might also use its evaluation system to enhance employee motivation; enhance communication between managers and employees; and conduct personnel system research for evaluating (or defending) personnel selection, promotion, demotion, and termination decisions. To the extent that performance evaluation is linked to the accomplishment of the mission of the organization or its principal subdivisions and that employees are expected to do challenging and meaningful work in which they can take pride, high performance in the task will likely persist and even improve over time.

Protecting the Performance Appraisal System from External and Internal Challenges

When an organization develops a performance evaluation system, several issues can cause severe problems and therefore require careful attention.

Validity and Reliability. Performance evaluation systems must meet the same standards for validity and reliability as do selection procedures for hiring (see Chapter 2 sidebar "Validity and Reliability" on page 47). Validity for performance evaluation refers to the relevance of the performance evaluation system design; that is, does the system provide accurate job-related measures of the employees' work? Additionally, validity is concerned with measuring job-related behaviors that do not discriminate or adversely affect protected

Tips for Developing Valid and Reliable Performance Appraisal Instruments

☐ Use a job analysis to develop the appraisal instrument.

☐ Develop a behavior-oriented or results-based instrument rather than a personal-trait-oriented instrument.

☐ Give evaluators specific written instructions on how to use the performance appraisal instrument.

classes of employees. Again, it is important to employ job analysis techniques to identify job-related criteria used to design the performance evaluation system.

As is true for selection techniques, reliability refers to the level of consistency with which the evaluation techniques are applied. Discriminatory impacts must be avoided. Thus, training is necessary to ensure that the evaluation system is understood and applied similarly by the different actors involved in the process—principally managers, supervisors, and employees.

Court Challenges.[3] Legal challenges to performance evaluation systems are not uncommon (for example, employees have charged that personal traits were used for rating criteria, that rating standards were subjective, that the employer failed to inform them of rating standards, that rating standards were not job-related, that standards had a disparate impact on particular groups of employees, that raters were improperly trained). Amendments made in 1972 to the Civil Rights Act of 1964 require public sector employers to validate any personnel evaluation technique that affects an employee's chances for promotion. Consequently, performance evaluation systems that are used to determine employee promotions must not discriminate against protected employees as defined in Title VII of the act (see Chapter 5). Court decisions issued prior and

subsequent to the issuance of the "Uniform Guidelines on Employee Selection Procedures" in 1978[4] show that performance evaluation systems that were developed with the characteristics described in the sidebar on page 74 are best able to withstand judicial scrutiny.

Clear, Consistent Top-Level Support. If managers and employees are to take an evaluation system seriously, top-level management and the political leadership must give the system clear, consistent support. The failure to present the evaluation system as a priority management issue will lead to lax implementation, and the organization will not attain the full benefit that such a system is designed to produce. Lack of management support can also lead to morale problems. The seriousness of top management's support should be reinforced in the following ways.

Policies and Procedures to Ensure Appropriate Implementation of the System. The evaluation system must feature sufficient documentation to provide clear guidance for implementation. The documentation should include policies that reinforce the goals and objectives of the system. For example, it is increasingly recognized that managers and supervisors should have a performance standard and be evaluated for the timely completion of their subordinates' evaluations.

Employee Participation in Selecting and Designing Procedures. Involving employees in the selection and design of an appraisal system can have a very positive impact. Employees may be selected for participation by the employer unilaterally or from nominations made by managers, supervisors, and employees—even those wishing to nominate themselves. Committees of employees may be empowered to select an appraisal system, or they may be advisory in nature. Additionally, participation can be encouraged by allowing employees sufficient on-the-job time to participate in the evaluation process, including release time for those who are involved in the development, assessment, and redesign of evaluation systems.

Training of Managers, Supervisors, and Employees.[5] Managers, supervisors, and employees must be provided with sufficient training to understand and complete performance evaluations. Specifically, they need adequate training on the following:

- Subjectivity and bias. Even the most objective performance evaluation systems call upon raters to make tough decisions. Unavoidably, subjective rater judgments can be influenced by biases irrelevant to actual performance. Supervisors must be made aware of the subjective elements of their ratings and receive training on avoiding biases in their assessments. Failure to be open about this subjectivity and potential for bias can lead to morale problems and undermine the acceptance of the system.

- Cross-rater comparisons. The subjective elements of most appraisal systems necessarily mean that one supervisor may interpret and implement an assessment system differently from another. In addition, the performance objectives of employees are often quite different and so might not be directly comparable.

- Periodic updating of evaluation processes. Most evaluation systems contain elements that are time-bound; for example, key individuals or the technologies being used may change. Consequently, the evaluation system should be reviewed periodically to keep it up-to-date.

The importance of continuous training cannot be overemphasized. It is absolutely necessary to develop and maintain a shared understanding and consistent administration of the evaluation system.

Unions and Employee Associations. Rights granted to union- or association-represented employees differ across jurisdictions, so it is important to obtain legal advice with respect to those rights when appraising employee per-

formance. However, regardless of the specific rights of bargaining agents, it is important to involve the union or employee association in developing the appraisal system. Failure to do so will likely lead to troublesome resistance by the union or association, to employee grievances, and to subsequent negotiation problems. Should the union or employee association and the organization not reach agreement, the employer should explore options with the assistance of labor relations or legal advisors. These options may include, but should not be limited to, exempting employees subject to the labor agreement from coverage under the evaluation system.

Choosing an Evaluation Method

The choice of an evaluation method depends on the organization's purposes for evaluating performance. In all likelihood, the organization wishes to pursue several objectives simultaneously. In addition, the organization could have different evaluation purposes for different categories of employees. Consequently, one of the initial decisions that must be made is whether the development of a single evaluation system is appropriate for all employees. If a single system is not appropriate, the organization should consider the development of several parallel systems—systems that match the purposes for each agency and/or group of employees.

There are two methods commonly employed for evaluating job-related performance, both of which use job analysis techniques. It should be noted that elements of these two methods can be mixed to create a hybrid method. The first uses the job descriptions (see Chapter 1) for singular positions or groups of similar positions. Job descriptions are written by supervisors (and perhaps involve the employee) and are analyzed and refined by personnel job analysts. The information they yield—for example, the tasks, responsibilities, level of supervision—provide the foundation for developing the performance appraisal instrument. Whoever creates the instrument, whether it be the chief administrator or a human resources consultant, then questions the job experts (i.e., the employees who perform the jobs and/or their supervisors) to identify desired work-related behaviors. These behaviors become the performance standards necessary for the employee to meet to successfully complete the tasks for the position or class of positions. Scales ranging from exceeding to not meeting expectations are specified for each behavior.

A second method uses either job analysts and/or job experts who gather information about specific tasks (often called "critical incidents") that employees perform and the behaviors that are thought to contribute to the successful or unsuccessful completion of those tasks. Once these tasks and behaviors are identified, the personnel staff and/or job experts write a performance standard scale for the critical incidents representing the range of behaviors against which the employees will be evaluated.

Techniques of Performance Appraisal

The techniques described here are categorized by their primary focus: comparison of employees against an "average" employee, comparison of employees against each other, evaluation by someone other than the supervisor, participatory techniques, upward and 360-degree techniques, and pass-fail techniques. Most of these techniques may be implemented with substantial employee participation.

Techniques That Compare Employees against an "Average" Employee

Narrative Essays. The rater writes substantial comments about the employee's job-related behaviors (see Exhibit 3-1 for an example). This technique is sometimes combined with employee-ranking techniques described in the next section, "Techniques That Compare Employees against Each Other" (but see Red Flags on page 76).

Exhibit 3-1   Example of Appraisal Technique with Narrative

Employee Name: _____   Rating Period: _____

Rating Criteria

1. Delegating work to subordinates

2. Meeting deadlines

3. Keeping current with applicable regulations

Narrative Description of Performance

1.

2.

3.

Overall Rating of Employee (circle the most appropriate):

Outstanding	Exceeds Expectations	Meets Expectations	Needs Improvement	Not Acceptable

Rating instructions: Write a paragraph to describe how the employee performed in each of the rating criteria. Include examples of the employee's work in the description. Then select the performance rating that best describes the employee's overall performance.

Exhibit 3-2   Example of Appraisal Technique with Objective (Pre-Established) Standards

Employee Name: _____   Rating Period: _____

Primary Duties or Responsibilities	Performance Standards	Rating	Comments
1. Assesses if clients meet requirements for benefit eligibility	A. Contacts clients by phone once per month to reapprove benefit receipt	Outstanding Exceeds standard Meets standard Needs improvement Not acceptable	
	B. Meets client in client's home once per quarter to review client needs for types of benefits	Outstanding Exceeds standard Meets standard Needs improvement Not acceptable	

Rating instructions: Mark the performance level that best describes the performance of the employee for each primary responsibility and note the reason(s) for the choice in the comments column.
Note: The evaluator must also have definitions for each of the rating levels.

Narrative essays provide substantially more information as to why particular ratings were given than do simple numerical rating systems, but they have several disadvantages:

- They are time-consuming.

- They require substantial training of raters.

- They create a bias in favor of employees blessed with supervisors who have strong writing skills.

- They are subject to rating inflation over time as raters try to find new superlatives to describe their more able employees.

- It is extremely difficult to make comparisons between ratings since different raters describe their employees differently.

- Raters tend to focus mostly on either the positive or the negative aspects of an employee's performance.

Objective (Pre-Established) Standards. This technique uses pre-established standards for such indicators as quality of work, quantity of work, timeliness, etc., and for related indicators, such as the number or percentage of total claims processed in a month by an employee. (An example of this format is provided in Exhibit 3-2).

This method focuses on uniform, quantifiable measures and is relatively easy to design and implement. However, it ignores qualitative elements of work that might contribute to performance and is not well suited to positions for which quantitative measures are difficult to develop.

Exhibit 3-3   Example of Forced-Choice Appraisal Technique

Employee Name: _____   Rating Period: _____

Item

1   MOST   LEAST
     A   Does not anticipate problems   A
     B   Grasps explanations quickly   B
     C   Rarely wastes time on the job   C
     D   Easy to talk to   D

2   MOST   LEAST
     A   Leader in group activities at work   A
     B   Wastes time on unimportant things   B
     C   Cool and calm under stress   C
     D   Hard worker and good example to others   D

3   MOST   LEAST
     A   Polite with clients   A
     B   Avoids taking on new responsibilities   B
     C   Takes advantage of training programs   C
     D   Able to delegate responsibilities   D

Rating instructions: In each item the rater circles the letter of the phrase that is *most* like the subject being evaluated *and* the letter of the phrase that is *least* like the subject being evaluated.
Note on scoring: If one of the positive (favorable) items is checked as most characteristic, the employee receives credit; similarly, one of the negative items marked as least descriptive also merits a positive credit.

Forced-Choice Rating. This technique identifies positive behaviors that are related to successful job performance. Supervisors choose from among multiple behaviors those that best describe the employee's performance (see Exhibit 3-3). There is no apparent right or best answer known to the rater. In larger jurisdictions the personnel office uses a weighted scale to score the rater's choices. Smaller communities can contract with an outside human resources consultant (see Chapter 9 for resources).

This technique reduces rater bias since the rater does not know the weighting scheme for scoring the ratings. Supervisors tend to dislike the technique, however, because they do not know how they are rating each employee. Moreover, the technique grants the personnel office or human resources consultant ultimate

control since the job evaluation is used to develop the rating instrument. It also requires the maintenance of confidentiality regarding the weighting methodology. However, this claim to confidentiality may result in suspicion and distrust of the methodology on the part of those displeased by outcomes of the process.

The Weighted Checklist. This technique is similar to the forced-choice rating technique but features some noteworthy differences (see Exhibit 3-4). The first step in developing the weighted checklist involves obtaining a "laundry list" of statements from supervisors describing effective and ineffective behaviors that contribute to or detract from successful job performance. The second step is for a smaller group of experienced "judges" to rank the statements in order of importance. Those state-

Exhibit 3-4   Example of Weighted Checklist Appraisal Technique

Employee Name: _____   Rating Period: _____

Item	*Weighting*
❐ Employees enjoy working with him or her.	(+)
❐ Takes a long-range viewpoint.	(+)
❐ Expects too much of subordinates.	(−)
❐ Schedules his or her work well.	(+)
❐ Wastes much time preparing for meetings.	(−)
❐ Works well with managers from other agencies.	(+)
❐ Knows where important questions can be directed.	(+)
❐ Is unable to delegate responsibilities.	(−)
❐ Makes all efforts to involve subordinates in work decisions.	(+)
❐ Can be expected to maintain work schedules and deadlines.	(+)

Rating instructions: Check all items that apply to the employee's work behavior.

---

ments that most of the judges agree on and rank similarly are included in the rating checklist given to the supervisor, to whom the weighting values of the statements remain unknown.

This technique has the same advantages and disadvantages as the forced-choice rating.

The Critical Incident Assessment. This technique lists job-related behaviors or agreed-upon objectives. The rater records examples of critical incidents (samples of work) and assesses the employee's performance—good and bad—against the list (see Exhibit 3-5).

This technique focuses the supervisor's attention on high-priority behaviors and goals. The supervisor is trusted to record truly representative critical incidents of the employee's work, while employees feel trusted to do a good job using their own discretion on lower-priority goals. However, to the extent that critical incident examples are not representative, the technique is subject to rater bias. This system is relatively more time-consuming than others since supervisors need to write up and maintain notes of employee work examples.

Behaviorally Anchored Rating Scales (BARS). This technique, like the weighted checklist, begins with supervisors providing descriptions of effective and ineffective behaviors that contribute to or detract from successful job performance. Personnel specialists use job analysis techniques to ensure that these behaviors are job related. A group of experienced judges then evaluates and ranks the statements on a performance scale ranging from excellent to poor. Those descriptions that most of the judges agree on, and rank similarly, are included in the BARS instrument (see Exhibit 3-6). Supervisors then compare the employee's performance against the descriptive statements and choose the statements that most closely describe the *typical behaviors* of the employee. The chosen statements for each behavior correspond to points on the BARS rating scale.

This technique reduces rater bias and has withstood the scrutiny of the courts. However, it requires substantial effort, time, and cost to develop. It also requires either considerable personnel office expertise to implement or a contract with a human resources consulting firm.

Exhibit 3-5 Example of Critical Incident Assessment Appraisal Technique

Employee Name: _____ Position: _____

Rating Period: _____ to _____

Objectives	Representative examples of performance (successful and unsuccessful)
1. Train field workers well	1. 2. 3. 4.
2. Improve quality of services to walk-in clients	1. 2. 3. 4.
3. Achieve better cost control over long-distance telephone use	1. 2. 3. 4.

Rating instructions: Note both successful (good) and unsuccessful (poor) examples of the employee's work efforts to meet the objectives as they occur throughout the rating period.

Techniques That Compare Employees Against Each Other

Paired Employee Comparisons. This technique requires the rater to rank each employee against other employees for a number of work behaviors (see Exhibit 3-7). A summary score is tallied for each employee to determine the employee's rank in comparison with other employees the rater supervises.

This technique reduces rater bias by eliminating the ability to rate employees similarly on all behaviors, and it is relatively easy to develop and implement. However, it makes it difficult for supervisors to rank more than a handful of employees. Employees and supervisors alike tend to dislike these comparisons.

Forced Distribution of Employees. This technique requires the supervisor to place employees in a percentage distribution breakdown of performance, such as the top 20 percent, lowest 20 percent, etc. Employees are ranked in distributions for several categories of merit that are considered important for the organization (see Exhibit 3-8).

Forced distribution has the same pros and cons as paired employee comparisons. Moreover, employees prefer to work in settings where all pull their weight—no stars and no slackers.

Techniques That Use Evaluators Other Than the Supervisor. The techniques described in this section could use any of the rating formats for

Exhibit 3-6   Example of Behaviorally Anchored Rating Scale (BARS) Item

Willingness and ability of employee to meet deadlines:

	5	Could be expected to meet deadlines, no matter how unusual the circumstances, by increasing efforts until the work is done.
Could be expected to meet deadlines comfortably by delegating the less important duties to others		
	4	Could be expected always to meet deadlines on time by delegating most of the work to others
Could be expected to meet deadlines within a reasonable length of time		
	3	Could be expected to offer to work at home after failing to get work out on the deadline day once in a while
Could be expected to fail to meet deadlines on a regular basis, but be ready to devote personal time to catching up		
	2	Could be expected to be behind schedule all the time, but appear to work hard to catch up
Could be expected to be behind schedule and display little effort to catch up		
	1	Could be expected to ignore deadlines and get work in on time only infrequently

Rating instructions: Select the statement that best reflects the work behavior of the employee.
Note: This is an example of one of the possible items that could be used on a BARS rating instrument. In addition to selecting the statement that best identifies the employee's typical behavior, the rater could also be asked to write examples of the employee's work to support the selection made.

which examples have already been provided. The wording of the questions may need to be modified, however, to reflect the change in who completes the evaluation.

Self-Ratings. The self-rating technique is based on the employee's participation in establishing objectives, and then rating his or her own performance in working toward those objectives.

Self-rating establishes clearer patterns of communication of expectations between supervisor and employees and often generates greater employee commitment. Its disadvantages are that it can be subject to bias and rating inflation (self-ratings tend to be higher than supervisory ratings), and it requires substantial supervisor and employee time and effort to complete.

Exhibit 3-7　Example of Paired Employee Comparisons Appraisal Technique

Supervisor Name: _____

Department/Unit: _____

Rating Period: _____

Employees Supervised:　　　　Employee A
　　　　　　　　　　　　　　Employee B
　　　　　　　　　　　　　　Employee C
　　　　　　　　　　　　　　Employee D
　　　　　　　　　　　　　　Employee E

Comparisons of Employee Pairs

1.	Employee A	Employee B
2.	Employee A	Employee C
3.	Employee A	Employee D
4.	Employee A	Employee E
5.	Employee B	Employee C
6.	Employee B	Employee D
7.	Employee B	Employee E
8.	Employee C	Employee D
9.	Employee C	Employee E
10.	Employee D	Employee E

Rating instructions: Circle the employee whose overall performance is better between each pair of employees. *Note on scoring:* Add the number of times each employee is circled and then rank the employees in descending order by the total number of times each is chosen.

Exhibit 3-8　Example of Forced Distribution of Employees' Ratings Appraisal Technique

Supervisor Name: _____　　　Rating Period: _____

Department/Unit: _____

Highest 10%	Next 20%	Middle 40%	Next 20%	Lowest 10%
	_____	_____	_____	_____
		_____	_____	
		_____		
_____	_____	_____		

Rating instructions: Place the names of your 10 employees in the appropriate categories according to their overall performance.

Peer Ratings. The underlying concept is that co-workers are in the best position to know how well or how poorly a fellow employee does his or her job.

Anonymous ratings by co-workers tend to be more accurate than either self-ratings or supervisory ratings, and they can encourage more of a group commitment to work. However, there are several disadvantages to peer ratings:

- Anonymity is difficult to maintain in smaller groups.

- Accuracy is less reliable if the co-workers do not work closely with the evaluated employee or do not perform similar kinds of work.

- Peer ratings are not well liked by employees.

- Differences in co-worker ratings can cause conflict.
- Co-workers can easily conspire—consciously or subconsciously—to inflate each other's ratings or to scapegoat unpopular employees.

Field Review. This technique uses the services of a neutral outsider to perform the evaluation. The outsider should be unquestionably knowledgeable about the work.

Field review is well suited to situations in which interpersonal relationships between supervisors and employees are poor, or in which the organization detects biased supervisory reviews. However, neither employees nor supervisors like the use of outside raters, nor is there any guarantee that field reviews will be free of the same kinds of bias that are found in supervisory evaluations. Also, field reviews may incur additional costs and disrupt work.

Participatory Techniques. In participatory reviews, the employee is drawn into the process of setting performance objectives. Management by objectives (MBO) and work planning and review (WPR) are examples of participatory techniques. Goal setting establishes standards against which the employee is evaluated, so the focus of evaluation is on outcomes or results. Exhibit 3-9 provides an example of the MBO-type format. WPR is less comprehensive than the MBO technique and stresses periodic supervisor-employee reviews of work plans and employee progress in meeting plans, mid-course plan revisions, and the identification of employee training needs.

Participatory techniques improve communication, clarify work expectations, and increase the employee's commitment to goal attainment. They can also have the following disadvantages:

- When results become the focus of the evaluation, the organization must guard against overzealous individual competitiveness, a "results by any means" mental-

ity, and, where quantity or timeliness is the objective, a potential drop in work quality.
- Participatory techniques require a time commitment by supervisors and employees to discuss and set goals, review progress, and complete the appraisal.
- Evaluative decisions must be made even though factors beyond the control of the employee can influence attainment of results.
- Participatory techniques tend to be less successful for positions that are not executive, managerial, or professional.

Upward and 360-Degree Feedback Techniques. These techniques use evaluators other than the supervisor to rate employee performance, and they could use any of the rating formats for which examples were provided in the sections on techniques that compare employees against an average employee or against each other. The wording of the questions may have to be modified, however, to reflect the change in who completes the evaluation.

Upward Feedback. The solicitation of supervisor ratings by subordinates technique represents an effort to underscore the importance of feedback in an organization.

The anonymity of raters produces more accurate evaluations, but it makes reconciling differences in ratings by individual employees difficult. However, anonymity tends to be difficult to maintain. Moreover, a potential exists among employees for conspiring to inflate or deflate ratings to make their boss look good or bad, depending on their personal feelings.

360-Degree Feedback. The 360-degree technique, also known as multisource performance evaluation, obtains evaluations from multiple sources—supervisors, managers, peers, and co-workers, as well as people outside the organization such as agency clients. All sources are people with whom the employee works or interacts. This technique uses observable work

---

Exhibit 3-9   Example of MBO Goal-Setting Approach (a Participatory Technique)

Employee Name: _____   Rating Period: _____

In the coming six months, the following objectives will be pursued and success will be determined by these associated results.

Objectives	*Results Sought*
1. Train field workers well	Preparation of five staff members to assume supervisory duties at field offices in rural areas
2. Improve quality of services to walk-in clients	Conduct search for and locate the most willing/able employee to take on receptionist duties as required
3. Achieve better cost control over long-distance telephone use	Hold a staff meeting to discuss the problem of telephone charges and appoint a committee to formulate a plan to achieve a 15 percent reduction in charges

Agreed to on: _____
                          (Date)

Agreed to by: _____
                          (Evaluatee)

                       _____
                          (Evaluator)

---

behaviors that are considered important for the successful accomplishment of the work; these are behaviors that personnel specialists usually validate as being performance based. The employee's behaviors are ranked against a scale by those asked to complete the evaluation. The resultant product is a report to the employee based on the various responses obtained on the evaluation instrument. Commonly, the evaluations are submitted anonymously.

Self-rating may also be used in conjunction with this technique. Whether or not self-rating is used formally, the accuracy of the employee's self-perception of performance is increased by the feedback of the participants from within and outside the employee's work unit. It should be noted, though, that when the gap between self and other ratings is relatively wide, the employee concerned requires greater attention with respect to training and development.[6] Through 360-degree feedback, employees are made aware of how essential they are to the organization and how they stand with their peers and customers. Most employees consider this kind of evaluation fair, which makes it more effective. However, the 360-degree feedback is time-consuming and administratively burdensome.

Anonymity tends to be difficult to maintain, especially in small workgroups or where the number of outside contacts of the employee is limited. Moreover, reconciling differences in ratings from the various sources can be problematic, and report writing can be difficult. Finally, in jobs where the employee has to enforce the law (e.g., police officer or building code inspector), citizens cited for violations may give poor ratings to employees who actually do an excellent job.

Pass-Fail Techniques. In recognition that most evaluation approaches are time-consuming and supervisors as well as employees tend to dislike the process, designers of evaluation systems have been seeking methods that keep it simple and require less time and effort to complete. A recent innovation has been the pass-fail evaluation in which there are only two performance categories—one either passes (meets or exceeds expectations) or fails (does not meet expectations). In a now classic article on performance appraisal, John Nalbandian noted that supervisors believe they know how their employees perform based on an informal assessment and that formal reviews are duplications of an assessment already made.[7] Also, because many evaluators tend to rate in the middle of the scale and few employees fail in performance, the performance appraisal system is often considered meaningless by employees and supervisors.[8] Another noted problem with most evaluation systems is a failure to complete evaluations on a timely basis, especially when there is no performance standard for completion in manager and supervisor performance plans. Since the vast majority of employee evaluations are favorable, the pass-fail method eliminates a substantial amount of the paperwork and should improve the rate of timely completion.

Pass-fail evaluation simplifies the process by adopting the informal evaluations of supervisors and limiting the choice in performance categories to two. Pass-fail evaluation focuses attention on employees who are not performing to expectations. Supervisors and employees

who are performing to expectations are freed from the time-consuming formal process. Supervisors can devote more time and effort to poor performers, with the goal of improving their performance.

It is important to note that formal documentation is necessary for those employees judged not to meet expectations. The pass-fail technique may be used in conjunction with any of the previously discussed techniques for the required documentation. While the fundamental advantage in the pass-fail technique is the reliance on informal assessments of employees and diminished time commitment, there are disadvantages.

- The pass-fail focus may be perceived as more negative since written documentation is produced only for those who "fail" in the evaluation. To avoid this pitfall, the organization needs to ensure that the evaluation and disciplinary processes are separate so the evaluation process can concentrate on development of the employee.

- Pass-fail may place more pressure on both formal and informal methods of employee recognition. Employees need positive reinforcement of their on-the-job performance. Eliminating the formal evaluation and their participation in the process requires supervisors and managers to provide positive feedback regarding performance by other means.

- The absence of formal evaluations on "passing" performance may not provide documentation to support compensation, promotion, or other human resource decisions.

- Pass-fail does not eliminate the need for training of employees, supervisors, and managers or the need for consistent standards against which employee performance is judged, both informally and formally.

Exhibit 3-10   Example of a Trait-Based Appraisal

Employee Name: _____   Agency: _____   Review Period: _____

	Outstanding	Good	Satisfactory	Fair	Unsatisfactory
1. Job knowledge	❑	❑	❑	❑	❑
2. Interpersonal relationships	❑	❑	❑	❑	❑
3. Quantity of work	❑	❑	❑	❑	❑
4. Quality of work	❑	❑	❑	❑	❑
5. Dependability	❑	❑	❑	❑	❑
6. Initiative	❑	❑	❑	❑	❑
7. Supervisory skills (if applicable)	❑	❑	❑	❑	❑

Supervisor: _____   Date: _____

Comments:

Evaluation Techniques to Avoid. Appraisal techniques that use personal traits (such as neatness, honesty, dependability, or initiative) in the abstract, without relating them to a particular task, seldom, if ever, withstand court scrutiny, and should therefore not be used. (See Exhibit 3-10 for an example of a trait-based system that uses a graphic rating scale format.)

Implementing the Program

To reinforce the organization's commitment to its mission, managers and supervisors should be subject to the same kind of evaluation as employees. To ensure their compliance and commitment to the evaluation system, top management should include in their evaluations specific performance objectives that support the implementation and maintenance of the evaluation system under which the supervisors and managers are being rated.

Training. Proper training of employees, supervisors, and managers in the use of the performance evaluation system is essential to ensure that the system is applied consistently by different raters and to reduce the potential for rater error and bias, factors that can reduce the perceived fairness of the system. Supervisors need to understand how the evaluation solidifies power relationships and how to manage those relationships sensitively. Training should cover how to write performance objectives.

It will be necessary for training purposes to prepare manuals and worksheets that explain the performance appraisal system and provide solutions for commonly encountered problems. A pilot agency can be used to test out a new system, and supportive materials can be developed if necessary after the pilot test is debriefed. A new performance appraisal system can also be phased in by implementing the system for a pilot group of employees, such as the top-echelon management group. This technique has the advantage of familiarizing (training) top management with the system before they administer it to their subordinates, and it helps support a perception of fairness since the system is applied to all employees— even top management.

Elements of a Good Appraisal

- Objectives are established at the beginning of the appraisal period (pre-established).
- Specific competencies or skills to be measured are listed with examples of successful behaviors.
- A rating scale that fits the organization's culture and objectives is used.
- Space is included for employee self-appraisal.
- Space is included for supervisor's appraisal.
- Space is included for specific comments from the supervisor about the employee's performance.
- Suggestions for employee development are made.

Source: Adapted from Carla Joinson, "Making Sure Employees Measure Up," *HR Magazine* 46, no. 3 (March 2001).

Timing. Appraisals may be made either on an individual employee's employment anniversary or on an established time schedule for all employees. Each has advantages and disadvantages. In a nutshell, a universal evaluation date may align performance reviews with the budget cycle and organization goals and objectives. Universal evaluation dates also mean that the supervisor is evaluating all employees under the same environmental conditions. However, a universal evaluation date may cause a time crunch for supervisors who must review all employees simultaneously. Anniversary date evaluations avoid the time crunch problem, but very likely mean that the supervisor is producing evaluations for employees under different circumstances. For example, one employee may be evaluated when the supervisor is under very tight deadlines for completing other tasks while another employee may be appraised when the supervisor is not under such pressures.

Periodic Employee-Supervisor Performance Status Reviews. Periodic reviews between the supervisor and employee on the employee's progress toward the accomplishment of performance objectives are important to communication efforts. Periodic reviews allow the supervisor and employee to exchange ideas on options for continued progress, and also allow for discussion and negotiation of any changes that may need to be made in the established performance objectives. The length of time between periodic reviews may vary depending on the type of work involved, but as a general rule they should be conducted quarterly. Three months usually allows enough time between reviews for the employee to demonstrate additional accomplishment of performance objectives and is not overly burdensome for supervisors.

Criticism in performance reviews must be handled very carefully.[9] When supervisors use reviews as a vehicle for criticism, they risk intensifying the conflicts that may be at the root of the negatives that emerge from the evaluation. Criticism is rarely a motivator; even well-placed and modulated criticism is very often seen as a personal attack on the employee.[10] If the supervisor adds sarcasm or contempt, the employee may feel humiliated, defensive, and angry, and these feelings lead to evasion of responsibility, passive resistance, and other noncompliant behaviors. The first sidebar on page 75 offers some tips for keeping performance reviews positive.

Employee Response and Appeals. Employees must be provided with the results of their evaluations and the evaluator's report. They have a right to inspect and review their performance evaluation records. They should also be informed that they have a right to respond and rebut negative entries.

Employees may also have a right to ask for arbitration or grieve their evaluation. Because of the due process rights of public employees and the potential for using performance evaluations in disciplinary proceedings, some form

Tips on Communicating Performance Appraisals

- Do not delay providing feedback to employees about performance.
- Balance criticism with praise and appreciation for the positive.
- Focus on the results of a person's performance. Avoid any criticism that focuses on character or a person's innate deficiencies.
- Be specific, focusing on incidents or problems.
- Offer solutions.
- Be empathetic. As an appraiser, put yourself in the place of the person being evaluated.
- Operate on the assumption that even an objective and dispassionate appraisal may be interpreted as a deprecation causing embarrassment and hurt feelings.

Source: Daniel Goleman, *Emotional Intelligence* (New York: Bantam Books, 1994), Chapter 10.

Tips for Evaluating Employee Performance

- Take the time to thoroughly determine why the organization desires to implement a performance appraisal system, and then identify the appraisal techniques that most closely fit these purposes.
- Identify goals that are associated with the agency's mission. This process moves from the top down, with each level of the organization selecting goals that assist the next level up to achieve its goals.
- Begin communication about the evaluation system early and continue through the development process.
- Develop a comprehensive training plan for managers and supervisors as well as for all employees.
- Ensure that the performance appraisal instrument elicits a balanced account of the employee's performance.
- Review appraisal results with employees, identifying both strengths and weaknesses.
- Reinforce management's commitment to the evaluation system by including accurate and timely completion of employees' evaluations in the managers' and supervisors' appraisal criteria.

of appeal of adverse actions needs to be established. However, if the employer makes a procedural mistake in the performance appraisal, an employee is not entitled to any relief unless the employee would otherwise have been retained, promoted, or rewarded.[11] (See Chapter 5 for further discussion of employee rights in this context.)

Performance Evaluation and Termination.

Summative performance evaluations are useful for terminating individuals who do not perform up to standards. However, it must be remembered that one of the primary purposes of performance evaluation is to provide feedback to employees so that they may improve their performance if it is deficient. Consequently, the initial thrust of performance evaluation should be rehabilitation of the substandard employee and only secondarily support for decisions to terminate the employee.

In other words, performance evaluation should be used to support termination of those employees who, after being given the opportunity through sufficient counseling and direction by the organization, nonetheless fail to improve their substandard performance.

When employees are terminated for performance-related reasons, a written record of the organization's efforts to correct performance deficiencies is invaluable. Certainly, there may be occasions when an employee does something so egregious that immediate termination is warranted. In most cases, however, deficient performance is a longer-term problem. Performance evaluations, properly done, document the employee's job behavior deficiencies, record the organization's efforts to correct them, and establish that the employee was given sufficient time to make the corrections. Such documentation is often critical for withstanding adverse-action appeals, grievances, or court challenges to termination decisions.

Improving Performance through Goal Setting

Guiding Principles
- Goals should be specific, clear, realistic statements of potential attainment.
- Goals should be set jointly with the employee.
- Goals may be changed when circumstances change.

Challenges
- Developing and maintaining communication between employees and management.
- Establishing and maintaining periodic progress checks.
- Providing appropriate opportunities for employee development.
- Creating realistic expectations regarding pay adjustments and job advancement.

A distinction must be made between goals and performance standards; the terms are often used interchangeably but may define different things. *Performance standards* are the general expectations established by the employer for performance and are identified by terms such as "exceeds expectations," "meets expectations," etc. *Goals* may be understood as target levels toward which the employee is to work. They should stretch the employee's capabilities— that is, be high enough to challenge the employee to perform at an increased capacity—but not be so high that they are impossible to attain. The employee may not fully attain the goals that have been set in the performance contract (see below), but may very well meet or exceed the standards established for measuring satisfactory performance.

Red Flags

- Federal law requires public sector employers to validate any personnel technique that affects an employee's chances for promotion. Consequently, if performance evaluations are used in determining employee promotions, the appraisal system must not discriminate against protected employees (as defined under Title VII).
- Evaluation techniques that make use of personal traits, such as dependability or initiative, should be avoided.
- Too little employee and supervisory involvement in the process of selecting and designing the procedures or too few resources for supporting a performance evaluation system (money and time for training, time for supervision and monitoring) can cause failure.
- Using the performance evaluation system as an alternate disciplinary process will undermine its purposes and erode employee support for it.
- An appraisal system cannot violate provisions of a negotiated labor agreement.

All employees have strengths and weaknesses that are reflected in how they approach their work. Performance evaluation provides the opportunity to work with employees to identify the types of knowledge, skills, and abilities (KSAs) that could be developed either to improve performance in their current work, to enable them to perform work that may be assigned in the future, or to prepare them for promotions. These can be referred to as the employee's development needs.

Performance evaluation systems can thus use goal setting for three distinct purposes: to improve performance deficiencies, to develop employees' capabilities to increase productivity, and to challenge employees to perform at higher levels.

Requirements for Effective Goal Setting

Communication and Employee Participation. The identification of development needs for the employee to improve performance deficiencies can create stress because such needs are unavoidably personal. It must be remembered that the supervisor is in a position of power over the subordinate employee, which leaves the employee feeling vulnerable. Consequently, supervisors and managers need to be trained in how to build and maintain positive communication with employees. If the local government does not have in-house expertise to develop such comprehensive training, it should contract for services.

Employees will be more committed to attaining goals if they participate in establishing the standards that will be used in appraising their performance. Meaningful participation is multifaceted and includes meaningful input in developing performance standards and the rating form, self-evaluation, and two-way communication.[12] Employee participation facilitates communication between the employee and the supervisor, promoting a clearer understanding between the two of precisely what is expected. In turn, the enhanced communication allows an exchange of ideas on how to approach goals most effectively and can also enlighten the supervisor about the employee's interests and career plans.

A performance evaluation system that includes goal setting can create an expectation that the employee should receive increased compensation for acquiring higher KSA levels. The organization must be open and very clear about its intentions with respect to this issue. Employees must know whether they will receive development pay, and if they do not, they must understand what the long-term value of increasing their KSAs is to themselves and the organization. (See next section, Linking Performance to Compensation.)

Progress Checks. It is necessary to establish a pattern—and an expectation on the part of supervisors and employees—of periodic checks on the employee's progress in pursuing and completing development assignments or training. This will require a concerted effort by supervisors, reinforced by management, to allot the time necessary for follow-up meetings with the employee.

Employee Development Opportunities. Once development needs are identified by the supervisor and employee, the organization must make a commitment to provide the employee with the opportunities required to fulfill them. Depending on the course of action identified, these opportunities may include on-the-job training, workshops, continuing education, or other related avenues. It is important to recognize that the identification of development needs creates an expectation on the part of the employee to have development opportunities provided. Failure to provide them will likely result in morale problems and a general loss of trust in management and the evaluation system.

Elements of a Goal-Setting System

Performance Contracts. Goal setting that establishes challenging or "stretch" performance levels fosters higher levels of productivity. The commitment the employee makes to achieve the goals is a "performance contract." Performance contracts identify targets toward which the employee strives to achieve—targets that are higher than "satisfactory" performance levels—but are not the standards against which the employee will be evaluated. Stretch goals are meant to challenge the capabilities of the employee, not to establish ever-higher levels for performance evaluation.

The stretch goals need to have two characteristics. First, they must be specific goals written in concrete terms. For example, "I will process the payroll in five hours," *not* "I will process the payroll as fast as I can." Second, they must be high enough to challenge the capabilities of the employee to perform at an

Tips for Improving Performance Through Goal Setting

❑ Provide comprehensive training on goal setting for managers and supervisors.

❑ Fund employee development and make sure that managers release employees for development opportunities.

❑ Clearly communicate the local government's policies regarding pay adjustments and job advancement.

increased capacity, but not so high that they are beyond the realistic reach of the employee. For instance, if it is known that an employee can process the payroll in seven hours, establishing a stretch goal of six hours may be realistic whereas a goal of three hours is not. If goals are not realizable by the employee, they will not improve the employee's motivation or productivity, and in fact may act as a demotivator.

The Individual Development Plan. An individual development plan provides a means of confronting any deficiencies of the employee in a constructive way, especially if the employee is involved in the planning. The focus should be on providing the employee with opportunities to expand his or her KSAs not only to meet current performance standards, but also to prepare for future advancement. The supervisor

Red Flags

❧ Ignoring the distinction between "performance contract" goals (stretch goals) and performance standards will increase supervisor-employee conflict as employees press for lower goal levels and weaken support for the evaluation system.

❧ Any appearance of favoritism should be avoided because the development of trust is essential in goal setting.

and employee should work together to determine the specific KSAs the employee could develop and identify the means to do so.

Employee Assistance Programs. Another means of redressing performance deficiencies is to refer employees to an employee assistance program (EAP) (if the organization has one) or to a certified counselor under contract with the jurisdiction. While this is usually a delicate matter psychologically and legally, discussion with the employee as well as the referral must be made in the context of performance deficiencies in the employee's work; any focus on personality, such as perceived addiction problems, should be avoided. (See Chapters 5 and 6 for additional pertinent information.)

Linking Performance to Compensation: Merit, Skill-Based, and Competency-Based Pay

Guiding Principle

• Linking performance evaluation to compensation decisions positively affects employee performance.

If performance evaluation is linked to the organization's reward structure, especially compensation, it becomes a powerful means of motivating employees to maintain or improve their performance levels. This linkage is one of the attributes of successful performance evaluation systems. When performance and pay are linked, pay is based not on job classification but on the individual employee's success. This approach is especially appropriate in competitive labor markets where retention is a problem and employers wish to establish the understanding that employees will "grow with the company" and should stay the course.

Research indicates, however, that rewards must be more than minimal for the benefits of an assessment-based pay system to work well.[13] Consequently, development of merit, skill-based, or competency-based pay systems requires a long-term commitment to fund the pay structure adequately. Failure to do so will weaken the link between performance evaluation and pay. Similarly, when employees are evenly skilled or possess different but equally valuable skills or competencies, the link between performance and pay expectations is weakened if limits are placed on the proportion of employees that can be rated within each level of performance.

As with other aspects of performance evaluation, job analysis again plays an important role no matter which assessment-based compensation system the organization is using. (See Chapter 1 for more information about job analysis.) And again, managers, supervisors, and employees must be trained on the nature and purposes of the system to understand how such elements as performance standards, skill sets, or competencies are determined. Managers and supervisors must also be thoroughly trained to explain the system to their employees and to describe its relationship to the organization's mission. Training should emphasize the principle that employees are to be treated equitably.

Finally, because of the due process rights of public employees and the potential for pay increases to be denied as a result of adverse performance evaluations, some form of appeal to adverse actions needs to be established. (See Chapter 5 for further discussion.)

Pay that is linked to an individual's performance is categorized as either merit or development pay. Merit and development pay are not mutually exclusive; elements of both may be used in a pay system.

A consideration with respect to merit or development pay is whether the annual compensation increment will be added to the employee's base pay, which would permanently increase the employee's compensation level. An alternative to a base pay increase is a one-time bonus. The advantage of one-time payments for the organization is that they hold down increases in compensation budgets.

However, Carnevale notes that the effectiveness of merit pay is predicated on acceptable levels of base pay.[14] If base pay levels in conjunction with one-time bonuses are not perceived as adequate, then the disadvantage is that employees may feel the system does not reward them enough for adding value to the organization. As a consequence, employees may not be sufficiently motivated to increase their skill or competency levels permanently. One way to resolve this issue is to provide a combination of a base pay increase and a one-time bonus payment.

Pay for Performance (Merit Pay)

Merit (or bonus) pay is designed to reward employees according to their level of performance. Higher levels of performance are eligible for larger salary adjustments; unsatisfactory levels of performance may receive smaller or no pay adjustments. This concept of merit pay is distinctly different from how merit pay is conceived of in many public jurisdictions. In the public sector, merit pay is often associated with automatic pay increments—typically called "steps" on a pay plan—usually granted on an employee's hiring date anniversary. In pay for performance, the merit concept is not based on longevity or tenure in position, but on the employee's level of performance.

True merit pay programs require that the organization develop clear standards of performance for evaluating employees. This is important so that employees may be treated equitably; that is, employees who are rated the same with respect to work standards should be rewarded similarly. Clear standards are also needed to ensure that the organization rewards the right behaviors—that is, those activities that contribute to the success of the organization.

As has already been noted, performance standards must be developed on the basis of job analysis to measure the individual employee's work accomplishments. Such measurements are typically expressed in terms such as "outstanding," "exceeds expectations," "meets expectations," or "does not meet expectations." For purposes of compensation, a distinction may be made between performance standards against which the employee is measured and performance goals for the position that the employee hopes to attain or is asked to work toward. In other words, the employee may be rewarded for performance above a "meets expectations" ranking even when performance goals are not met.

Equity is an important consideration in pay-for-performance systems. Similar jobs should have similar performance objectives because inequities will create the perception of favoritism among employees. Clear guidelines and training of supervisors and managers are essential to ensure that such consistency is maintained.

Tying performance measures to compensation tends to cause employees to focus their work only on those areas for which they will be rewarded. Neglect of noncompensated areas of work may mean that some important work will not be performed, or at least not performed with enthusiasm. Additionally, employees may not pursue potential areas of innovation because there is no clear perception that such work will be compensated. Since these outcomes could be detrimental to the organization, it is important to establish a clear understanding of expectations at the outset.

Skill-Based and Competency-Based Pay (Development Pay)

Skill-based and competency-based pay systems are similar, and both differ from merit-based pay systems in that they focus on the attributes of the employee rather than on a review of performance. The employer decides what skills or competencies promote the organization's goals and identifies the skills or competencies to be compensated. Increases to base pay can become an alternative to promo-

Tips for Linking Performance and Compensation

❑ Establish a funding source for performance-based pay and a long-term commitment to continue funding.

❑ Develop comprehensive training for managers and supervisors in linking performance to compensation, or contract for services if personnel staff are not available to do so.

tion—for example, in a skill-based compensation system, instead of being promoted to "heavy equipment operator," a truck driver who achieves certification to operate heavy equipment might simply be given an increase in base pay in recognition of his or her attainment of a higher skill level.

The difference between skills and competencies is that skills are associated typically with manual functions, such as truck driving, whereas competencies are more broadly applicable. Competencies may include such things as education or certification required (e.g., an M.P.A. degree or a C.P.A. certification) and capacity for building teamwork. Consequently, competency-based pay systems are viewed as

Red Flags

⚑ Abandonment of a performance-based pay program will almost certainly alienate employees and depress performance.

⚑ An evaluation and compensation system cannot violate any provisions of a labor agreement.

⚑ Inequities will create the perception of favoritism.

⚑ Using performance evaluations to determine pay can raise due process issues.

being applicable to all types of work within the organization, including management positions.

The skills or competencies for which an employee is compensated do not have to be limited to those necessary for performance in the employee's current job. The focus is not on the minimum qualifications necessary to perform a job. Instead, employees are rewarded for developing skills or competencies that can enhance their ability to perform in their current jobs, that can boost their eligibility for potential future jobs, or that will provide them with a broader understanding of other functions of the organization. It should be noted that skill and competency-based pay arrangements may tend to increase compensation budgets as they mature. However, the underlying benefit of rewarding employee development is that if employees have a wider range of skills or competencies generally, they are more valuable to the organization as a fungible asset that can be moved to wherever the skill or competency is needed, enabling the organization to adjust to demands from its environment.

Linking Performance to Advancement or Desirable Assignments

Guiding Principles

- Selection criteria for advancement must be job related.
- Classification and pay grades must be flexible enough to support the link between job performance and advancement or desirable assignments.

Challenge

- Ensuring that advancement procedures are clear and fair.

Advancement opportunities are a scarce commodity: there are fewer opportunities than there are people who want them. The employer must decide whether advancement will be awarded strictly on the basis of merit—that is, to the best qualified—or whether other considerations, including affirmative action (either voluntary or court ordered), promotion of diversity, or seniority, should play a role. Merit system rules may also be a constraining factor.

Any selection criteria for advancement must be job related for two reasons. First, if such criteria discriminate against employees in a protected class under Title VII of the Civil Rights Act, the employer must be able to prove such discrimination to be the result of a compelling business necessity and that no less discriminatory alternative practice is available. (See the section on court challenges earlier in this chapter.)

Second, not basing advancement decisions on job-related behaviors can lead to the perception that favoritism is the determining factor in compensation. To avoid creating such a perception, it is also a good idea to have several parties with a stake in the agency's work share in the decisions on advancement.

Past performance is not an infallible indicator of future performance—either in the same position or in a promotional slot.[15] For example, a top performer as an individual contributor (nonsupervisor) simply may not have the required KSAs (such as people skills) to be a successful supervisor or manager. Even if the employee has demonstrated possession of the required KSAs, he or she may simply not like the social and interpersonal consequences of being a supervisor.

Elements of an Effective Advancement System

Base the System on Job Analysis. To ensure that employee advancement is based on job-related behaviors, job analysis should be used to identify essential job-related KSAs and use them as the basis for developing career tracks or ladders.

Establish Career Tracks. Various positions within the organization that have common or related KSAs can be identified to develop career tracks—natural progressions from position to position that employees may choose to follow, either in the same job or in related jobs. Career tracks show employees that a currently held job—and previously held jobs—can prepare them for higher-level positions of the same or a related type.

Negotiate with Unions/Employee Associations. The organization's labor relations and/or legal advisors should be consulted with respect to the necessity or desirability of negotiating with the unions/employee associations over the selection of employees for promotion, desirable work assignments, and developmental opportunities. If the unions/employee associations are unwilling to subject represented employees to the same rules for advancement that apply to nonrepresented employees, different procedures for employees covered by labor agreements may be necessary.

Develop Clear, Consistent, and Fair Procedures. Employee advancement and development procedures must be perceived by employees as fair so that no one feels unfairly excluded from opportunities. Part of ensuring that procedures are clear and fair is to apply them carefully and consistently. Also important are clear and consistent communication and training for employees, supervisors, and managers.

Do Succession Planning. Succession planning helps the organization identify and develop a pool of workers who are eligible to fill vacancies as they occur. Through this process, the organization helps ensure that there is a ready supply of employees who have the requisite KSAs for successfully achieving the organization's mission. Succession planning may thus entail identifying and maintaining records of the KSAs of individual employees. It may also be used to identify career paths that provide the essential KSAs for employees.

Provide Opportunities for Development. Development opportunities may be provided either within or outside of the employee's career track. Using job analysis techniques, the organization can identify a range of KSAs that are considered strategic—that is, those that organization needs to accomplish its mission. Once the strategic KSAs are identified, the positions requiring them also may be identified. For example, if managing contracts and contractors is a critical part of the organization mission, then essential KSAs associated with contracting need to be developed in employees.

Developmental assignments outside the employee's normal career path necessarily mean that employees (and the organization) are taking a risk to learn new KSAs. However, both the employee and the organization can gain in the process: employees acquire new KSAs, and the organization gains by having employees who have a broad understanding of multiple facets of the organization and additional KSAs that it considers to be strategically important.

Constraints on Linking Performance to Advancement

Union/Employee Association Contractual Provisions. Many labor agreements contain provisions governing promotion, lateral assignments, temporary assignments, training opportunities, and other areas that may affect employee advancement decisions. It should be noted that court reviews have found bona fide seniority systems established by such provisions to be valid under most circumstances. The organization's labor relations and/or legal advisors should be consulted when the jurisdiction is developing its career track and promotional policies.

Civil Service Rules and Procedures. If the jurisdiction has a civil service system, it must comply with civil service rules and procedures. These rules and procedures may have to be amended to accommodate such objectives as

Broadbanding

Broadbanding is an alternative to traditional job classification and pay-grading programs that combines multiple grade levels into a smaller number of job and pay bands. Using the broadbanding approach requires a substantial investment in development, training, and communication with managers, supervisors, and employees alike. The advantage of broadbanding is that the organization has greater latitude in assigning work to employees. Their responsibilities may be expanded or substantially changed without the necessity of reclassifying their jobs. Consequently, the organization spends much less effort on activities that are not directly related to the organization's mission, such as attempting to get employees upgraded.

Even with the increased latitude for assignment of work possible with broadbanding, it is important that the selection of employees for development opportunities be made within the guidelines established by the courts and the "Uniform Guidelines for Employee Selection."

Broadbanding vs. Traditional Classification and Grade Level Example

Classification	Grade	Banding Title	Band Level
Department Director	18	Senior Executive	9
Deputy Director	17	Executive	8
Assistant Director	16	Executive	8
Division Administrator 2	15	Senior Administrator	7
Lawyer 2	14	Senior Advisor	7
Division Administrator 1	14	Senior Administrator	7
Bureau Chief 2	13	Administrator	6
Lawyer 1	12	Advisor	6
Bureau Chief 1	12	Administrator	6
Supervisor 2	11	Supervisor	5
Supervisor 1	10	Supervisor	5
Lead Worker	9	Senior Professional	4
Professional 3	9	Senior Professional	4
Professional 2	8	Professional	3
Specialist 3	8	Senior Specialist	3
Professional 1	7	Professional	3
Technician 4	7	Senior Technician	3
Specialist 2	6	Senior Specialist	3
Technician 3	6	Senior Technician	3
Specialist 1	5	Specialist	2
Administrative Assistant 4	5	Senior Administrative Support	2
Technician 2	5	Technician	2
Administrative Assistant 3	4	Senior Administrative Support	2
Technician 1	4	Technician	2
Clerical Worker 4	4	Senior Administrative Support	2
Administrative Assistant 2	3	Administrative Support	1
Clerical Worker 3	3	Administrative Support	1
Administrative Assistant 1	2	Administrative Support	1
Clerical Worker 2	2	Administrative Support	1
Clerical Worker 1	1	Administrative Support	1

Note: Banding reduces both the number of grade (pay) levels and the number of job titles. Pay ranges for banding are wider than grade levels to accommodate the multiple grade levels that have been incorporated by the band. Banding also accommodates high-level individual contributor positions, such as lawyers, at band levels equivalent to positions that have supervisory responsibilities.

Tips for Employee Advancement

- ❏ Establish career tracks.
- ❏ Establish clear, consistent, fair procedures.
- ❏ Involve several parties with a stake in the agency's work in decisions on advancement.
- ❏ Do succession planning.
- ❏ Provide opportunities for employee development.

job classification reform for more flexible employee assignment (broadbanding) or diversity promotion.

Equal Employment Opportunity and Affirmative Action. Although the law is continuing to evolve with respect to affirmative action, making it less of a consideration than in the past, the equal opportunity requirements are likely to remain strongly in force. If the organization is subject to a consent decree or court order regarding employee advancement,

Red Flags

- ◗ An employee's past success may not predict future performance in a higher position.
- ◗ Public employers that partially rely on performance evaluations to make career track or developmental assignment decisions affecting the chances for promotion of a protected class of employees must be able to show either that the evaluation system does not discriminate against protected employees or that its discriminatory results reflect a compelling business necessity and that no less discriminatory alternative is available.
- ◗ Techniques developed for employee advancement cannot violate provisions of a labor agreement.

procedures must be carefully scrutinized and enforced to ensure such compliance. Even organizations that are not subject to a consent decree or court order should avoid the possibility of future court involvement by ensuring that advancement procedures do not discriminate and are properly enforced.

Other Motivators

Guiding Principles

- Pay is not the only motivator for high performance.
- Employee motivation is significantly influenced by the quality of supervisory skills.

Challenges

- Determining which motivators are most effective in your organization.
- Adapting the reward system to a team-based environment.

Unquestionably, pay is a powerful motivator of employee behavior. However, it has long been recognized that other factors also affect the level of employee motivation to a major extent. Different things motivate different people, so it is a challenge for the organization to determine what is important to their employees. And it is essential that the rewards, whatever they are, motivate the behaviors that the organization most needs. Job-related criteria must be used to identify the desired behaviors and distribute the rewards. Reward structures should be monitored to ensure that inappropriate and counterproductive behaviors are not being encouraged.

The skills with which a supervisor is able to coach employees, coax their best efforts, resolve conflicts among them, mediate between his or her workgroup and outsiders, and otherwise maintain a productive work environment are vital to the effective motivation of employees in a workgroup. Additionally, supervisors should understand how to adjust their style to obtain the best results from each employee. Consequently, the development of people skills in supervisors and managers is important to the success of any motivational system.

Finally, the legal rights of represented employees vary across jurisdictions, so it is important for an organization to consult with its labor relations and/or legal advisors and to involve the union/employee association when designing a reward system.

Rewarding Teams and Workgroups

Historically, organizations have rewarded individuals for their solitary accomplishments. More recently, however, considerable attention has been focused on the organizational contributions made by groups of employees. Consequently, employers now must determine to what extent group contributions should be motivated and rewarded. This issue is particularly important when employees are expected to participate in group problem solving to improve services to their customers (internal and external). If employee empowerment is a significant part of a jurisdiction's activities, some attention to group awards is advisable.

Development of trust among managers, supervisors, and employees is also essential. While there is a natural tendency for people to like some people more than others, perceptions of favoritism must be avoided so that trust is not eroded. Employees must have the confidence that rewards will be distributed equitably and on the basis of contribution to a common effort rather than on the basis of favoritism.

As is true for individual rewards, the organization must make sure that the behaviors being encouraged are central to its mission. The more clearly behaviors are central to the mission, the more effective will be the offer of rewards for group accomplishment. The performance evaluation techniques discussed previously can be designed to include team-oriented standards for evaluation. Team-oriented standards can then be tied to a team reward structure.

Unions/employee associations historically have been suspicious of employer proposals for group reward systems, and this will most likely present a substantial obstacle to implementation for represented employees. Failure to allow the unions/employee associations to participate in the development of a group reward system will likely lead to their resistance and to grievance as well as negotiation problems.

Monetary Rewards Other Than Salary Adjustments

Monetary rewards may take several forms other than salary adjustments or bonuses. In addition to those discussed below, monetary rewards may be granted in the form of employee benefits such as child care, flexible work hours, or paid parking. (See Chapter 6 for further discussion.)

Training Opportunities. The local government can pay for training opportunities of the employee's choice, including workshops and classes offered through accredited schools. These opportunities should be related, however, to the needs of the organization.

Development Opportunities. Providing opportunities for acquiring new KSAs through more challenging assignments may improve the employee's chance of being promoted. Development assignments may include some additional compensation to reward the employee for the risk in taking on the new assignment.

Bonuses. One-time payments for job-related behaviors, successful accomplishments, innovative ideas, and so on do not add to the employee's base pay. While bonuses can range in size, they must be large enough to be viewed as meaningful.

Extra Time Off. Depending on the amount of paid time off currently offered by the organiza-

> ## Tips for Motivating Employees ✓
>
> ❑ Provide training to supervisors regarding the impact of their supervisory style on employee motivation.
>
> ❑ Use job analysis to ensure that rewarded behaviors help the organization accomplish its mission.
>
> ❑ Informally solicit ideas from employees about monetary and nonmonetary rewards they consider valuable.
>
> ❑ Select an array of monetary and nonmonetary rewards for potential distribution and develop clear guidelines for making awards.

tion, many employees may consider extra time off desirable. This is a particularly important area to explore for jurisdictions seeking to become more family friendly.

Gifts. Gifts can range from inexpensive to expensive. They can be prespecified (such as computer equipment) and may include monetary gift certificates at stores or restaurants.

Nonmonetary Rewards

The importance of specific monetary rewards should be assessed since they may not be meaningful to all employees. Since the importance of any specific type of reward will vary among employees, administrators should attempt to determine the kinds of nonmonetary rewards that are considered desirable. (See Chapter 6 for additional pertinent information and possible alternative rewards, such as preferred parking spaces.)

Flexible Work Arrangements. Allowing employees to arrange their workdays or hours to meet family or other obligations may entail job sharing or telecommuting.

Participation. The opportunity to provide their talent and input on special projects or in

routine decision making (including budgets) can be a motivator for some employees.

Special Projects. Assignment to special projects of interest can provide opportunities for employees to develop or use special talents and can motivate employees.

Awards/Recognition. Awards such as certificates of achievement should be accompanied by public recognition from the supervisor and by special publicity, such as being featured in an employee newsletter, in news releases to the local media, and so on.

Managing Organizational Change

Guiding Principle

- Performance objectives for employees must change as the organization's mission changes.

Challenge

- Helping supervisors and employees adapt to new procedures and work structures.

Managing organizational change is an important function of chief administrators. It means assisting employees to adapt to new procedures and work structures.

It is important for the organization to keep employees informed about changes that it is planning, or that are in process. Communication requires a commitment of time and money to provide information to employees on a continuous basis. If employees understand what the organization is doing and why, they are less likely to lose motivation and more likely to maintain trust in the organization.

Performance Evaluation in the Midst of Change

Organizational changes may alter the mission of the organization and consequently require the organization to review whether its current performance evaluation system supports the accomplishment of its new mission. Even without a major change in mission, it is worthwhile to evaluate a performance evaluation system periodically to ensure that it encourages productive behaviors. It is highly useful to have a diverse group conduct the review and formulate recommendations for improvements; this group can be composed of employees, supervisors, and managers from different agencies. The union/employee association must also be involved.

Similarly, the performance objectives established for each employee should not be considered cast in concrete. Previously identified performance objectives may no longer contribute to the accomplishment of the organization's newly defined mission. Managers and supervisors must thus be willing to amend the performance objectives of their employees, and employees must be encouraged to renegotiate performance objectives that are no longer priorities for the organization or may not be attainable as initially constructed. For example, if a performance standard is set to improve outreach activities, budget reductions may have an impact on full attainment of the standard, and the supervisor and employee should discuss revision. As noted earlier, periodic reviews by the employee and supervisor of performance objectives and the employee's progress are advisable.

When Objectives Change. When performance objectives are abandoned or replaced, the supervisor and employee should be given sufficient time to change the performance appraisal instrument and work behaviors. If adequate time cannot be provided, either some interim level of accomplishment should be agreed upon or the new objectives should not be included during the performance rating period in question. The employee can still be assigned to work on the new task, but it must be recognized that the employee will naturally focus on those work assignments for which he or she will be evaluated.

Tips for Managing Organizational Change

❑ Develop and stick to a communication plan regarding any organizational change.

❑ Make sure that clear guidelines are in place and that training is provided for managers and supervisors regarding changes to performance objectives.

❑ Establish a periodic review schedule to ensure that the performance evaluation system continues to support the organization's mission and organizational objectives.

When the Supervisor Changes. Procedures for evaluating employees whose supervisor has changed should be fair to both the employee and the new supervisor. The supervisor must have sufficient time to observe and work with the employee. The employee must have sufficient time to work on the performance objectives during the new supervisor's tenure. In addition to fairness, the organization must consider two other issues that will affect how it deals with changes in supervisors: first, the date the organization has established for completing performance ratings—that is, timing for ratings; and second, whether the organization prefers to have new supervisors establish new performance objectives with their employees. (See the first section of this chapter for more on the timing of evaluations.)

If the performance rating period is not a universal, established period for all employees, the new supervisor could work with the employee to establish performance objectives for a new rating period. However, two considerations should be addressed if this approach is taken. First, the new supervisor must have enough time to understand the mission and tasks of the work unit for which he or she is responsible before attempting to negotiate with employees on performance objectives. Consequently, there will likely be a period during which employees receive too little guidance on what work they will be held responsible for accomplishing. Second, if a new rating period is established, the date on which the employee is rated shifts—perhaps from the employee's anniversary date to a new rating cycle date—and thereby complicates record keeping. And if the performance evaluation is tied to pay, some provision needs to be made for granting pay adjustments under this circumstance.

One way to deal with these issues is to have the vacating supervisor complete a "close out" performance evaluation for the portion of the rating period during which the employee worked under his or her supervision. The new supervisor can then evaluate the employee for the remainder of the rating period using the performance objectives the employee established with the previous supervisor—subject to any changes that the new supervisor may have negotiated with the employee. Ideally, both the vacating and incoming supervisors will have sufficient time to observe the employee, and the employee will have sufficient time to achieve some progress on the performance objectives for each supervisor. If the new supervisor does not have enough time to observe and evaluate, the vacating supervisor may be required to complete the evaluation in consultation with the new supervisor. Alternatively, both supervisors may jointly complete the performance evaluation. This approach does not necessitate changing the evaluation period, so it is suitable in systems that use either a universal rating date or the employment anniversary date. However, there may be circumstances in which it may not be desirable or possible to have the vacating supervisor participate in the evaluation.

Downsizing the Workforce

Guiding Principles
- Downsizing decisions should be based on job-related criteria.
- Performance evaluations should be only one of many considerations in making layoff decisions.

- Appropriate documentation must be maintained for all employees, including those who are terminated for poor performance.

Challenges
- Retaining employees whose positions and competencies are central to the organization's mission.
- Making certain that employees will be evaluated, and layoff decisions made, fairly and consistently.
- Maintaining morale among employees.

Downsizing decisions should *not* be seen as an opportunity to get rid of employees who are viewed as troublesome or undesirable for one reason or another. Rather, the focus of a downsizing program should be on retaining employees whose positions and competencies are central to agency survival and service function accomplishment. Failure to base downsizing decisions on performance criteria and centrality to mission will likely lead to legal challenges and a lesser likelihood of the organization prevailing in those challenges.

It is just as important to keep employees informed about what the organization is planning in downsizing situations as it is in other, more desirable agency expansion situations. Although downsizing inevitably affects employee morale and productivity, employees who understand what the organization is doing and why are less likely to lose motivation and trust in the organization than are employees who are kept in the dark.

Determining Whom to Lay Off. Performance evaluation is only one tool to use when layoff decisions must be made. Moreover, it should be one of the last criteria to consider since there are many other decisions that must precede the identification of specific employees for termination.

One of the first decisions the organization must make is what functions or responsibilities need to be downsized. It must then decide how many positions must be laid off, and at what levels within the organization, to meet downsizing targets. Another decision to be made is whether to provide for bumping or transfer rights for affected employees. Such rights may enable the organization to retain employees who have attained higher levels of competencies, skills, and abilities, as well as higher performance evaluation results. However, they can also be disruptive. They add an element of uncertainty for the organization and employees. Additionally, transfer rights require a great deal of administrative effort both to document and to implement. Other decisions may include issues such as what assistance, if any, to provide employees who will be laid off and how much notice the employees should be given.

Only after all the planning decisions have been made should performance evaluations be used to compare employees for making the specific decisions about whom to lay off. Again, however, the performance evaluations should not be the sole decision criterion since other work-related attributes of the employee might be important. For example, an employee with a higher attainment of important competencies, skills, or abilities may be the appropriate choice for retention even if his or her recent evaluations have not been as good as those of other employees. A related concern is whether other employees are available to perform the work of the ones being laid off. Additionally, equal employment opportunity, workplace diversity, and consent decrees or court orders may be issues for consideration when determining the specific employees to be laid off (see below).

Cross-Rater Comparability. One of the challenges in a downsizing environment is making certain that employees will be evaluated, and layoff decisions made, on the basis of the same criteria. Inequities create the perception of favoritism among employees. Consequently, it is important that downsizing criteria and decisions are consistent among jobs and employees, whether or not the employees have the same supervisor. Clear guidelines and consistent themes in the training of supervisors and managers are therefore essential to maximize the likelihood that equity is maintained.

Union/Employee Association Agreement Provisions. If employees subject to the evaluation system are covered by a labor agreement, it is essential that downsizing and termination procedures comply with relevant provisions of that agreement. Seniority rights tend to be included in union contracts and thus are typically protected in the case of a reduction in force. As with other issues, the organization's labor relations and/or legal advisors should be consulted when policy is being created in this area.

The union/employee association may not be willing to become involved in planning a layoff. However, informing the union/employee association about downsizing plans and offering it the opportunity to contribute ideas will reduce the likelihood of grievances, unfair labor practice charges, or even court challenges. The union/association may have specific rights under its labor agreement or the law governing labor relations. Furthermore, it

---

Tips for Downsizing the Workforce

- ❑ Develop a communication plan for dealing with downsizing.
- ❑ Provide guidelines and training to managers and supervisors on the criteria for selecting employees for layoff.
- ❑ Establish a position or committee to coordinate layoff decisions made by the various units affected by the downsizing to ensure that the agency's mission is not compromised, to ensure consistency in making layoff decisions, to lessen bumping or transfer problems, etc.

may have alternative ideas of how to meet the goals of the downsizing, or it may be willing to amend procedures in its labor agreement in possibly helpful ways.

Additionally, employees have specific rights—often called *Weingarten* rights (see Chapter 8)—to representation for actions that they reasonably expect will lead to discipline. Consequently, the organization should involve the union/employee association early on for cases in which it may terminate an employee for cause.

Civil Service Rules/Regulations/Procedures. If the jurisdiction has a civil service system, it must comply with the rules and procedures of that system. These rules may limit the options available to the organization with respect to downsizing. They may also give employees bumping and transfer rights that must be taken into account.

Consent Decrees and Court Orders. If the organization is subject to a consent decree or court order regarding employee advancement, it should seek legal advice to ensure that downsizing decisions do not violate that decree or order. Procedures must be carefully scrutinized and enforced to ensure compliance. Those organizations that are not subject to a consent decree or court order should also ensure that their downsizing procedures do not unfairly discriminate. Recent decisions in the adjudication of affirmative action indicate that the granting of preference to protected groups in layoff situations in adherence to affirmative action goals generally is not permitted, and may be viewed as reverse discrimination.

Appeal to Adverse Action. Because of the due process rights of public employees and the perception that termination is the workplace equivalent of capital punishment, some form of appeal to adverse actions needs to be established. In some cases, the appeal procedure will be specified in a labor agreement or in civil

service rules, but employees who are not covered by such agreements or rules should also be afforded some appeal process. (See Chapter 5 for further discussion.)

---

[1] Marc Holzer and Kathe Callahan, *Government at Work: Best Practices and Model Programs* (Thousand Oaks, Calif.: Sage Publications, Inc., 1998), 6.

[2] Janet L. Barnes-Farrell and Angela M. Lynch, "Performance Appraisal and Feedback Programs," in *The Human Resources Program—Evaluation Handbook*, Jack E. Edwards, John C. Scott, and Nambury S. Raju, eds. (Thousand Oaks, Calif.: Sage Publications, 2003), 155–176. Herbert H. Meyer, Emanuel Kay, and John R. P. French, "Split Roles in Performance Appraisal," *Harvard Business Review* (January–February 1965): 123–129.

[3] This section is based on Donald E. Klingner and John Nalbandian, *Public Personnel Management: Contexts and Strategies*, 5th ed. (Upper Saddle River, N.J.: Prentice-Hall, Inc., 1998), 262–268, 317–326; and Jonathan Tompkins, *Human Resource Management in Government: Hitting the Ground Running* (New York: HarperCollins College Publishers, 1995), 249–252.

[4] *Albemarle Paper Company v. Moody* (1975), 422 U.S. 405; *Rowe v. General Motors Corporation* (1972), 457 F. 2d 248; *Wade v. Mississippi Cooperative Extension Service* (1974), 372 F. Sup. 126; *Watson v. Fort Worth Bank and Trust* (1988), 487 U.S. 977; *Zell v. U.S.* (1979), 472 F. Sup. 356.

[5] ICMA produces materials for supervisory skills training, such as the training manual *Employee Performance Appraisal and Management*, published in 1997, and the group course entitled Effective Supervisory Skill Building.

[6] Francis J. Yammarino and Leanne E. Atwater, "Implications of Self-Other Rating Agreement for Human Resources Management," *Organizational Dynamics* (Spring 1997).

[7] John Nalbandian, "Performance Appraisal: If Only People Were Not Involved," in *Classics of Public Personnel Policy*, 2nd ed., Frank J. Thompson, ed. (Belmont, Calif.: Wadsworth Publishing Co., 1991. (Article reprinted from *Public Administration Review*, May–June, 1981).

[8] Dennis Daley, "The Trials and Tribulations of Performance Appraisal: Problems and Prospects on Entering the Twenty-First Century," in *Public Personnel Administration: Problems and Prospects*, 4th ed., Steven W. Hays and Richard C. Kearney, eds. (Upper Saddle River, N.J.: Prentice Hall, Inc., 2003), 154–166.

[9] See Robert A. Baron, "Countering the Effects of Destructive Criticism: The Relative Efficacy of Four Interventions," *Journal of Applied Psychology* 75, no. 3 (1990): 234–245.

[10] Daniel Goleman, *Emotional Intelligence* (New York: Bantam Books, 1994), Chapter 10.

[11] See W. H. Holley Jr. and H. S. Feld, "Performance Appraisal and the Law," 7 *Labor Law Journal* 523 (July 1975).

[12] Gary E. Roberts, "Employee Performance Appraisal System Participation: A Technique that Works," *Public Personnel Management* 32, no. 1 (Spring 2003), 89–97.

[13] James L. Perry, "Compensation, Merit Pay, and Motivation," in *Public Personnel Administration: Problems and Prospects*, 4th ed., Steven W. Hays and Richard C. Kearney, eds. (Upper Saddle River, N.J.: Prentice Hall, Inc., 2003), 143–153.

[14] David G. Carnevale, *Trustworthy Government: Leadership and Management Strategies for Building Trust and High Performance* (San Francisco, Calif.: Jossey-Bass, 1995), 111–115.

[15] On the question of predicting future performance through test validation, see Janet L. Barnes-Farrell and Angela M. Lynch, "Performance Appraisal and Feedback Programs," in *The Human Resources Program—Evaluation Handbook*, Jack E. Edwards, John C. Scott, and Nambury S. Raju, eds. (Thousand Oaks, Calif.: Sage Publications, 2003), 155–176; Jay M. Shafritz, Norma M. Riccucci, David H. Rosenbloom, and Albert C. Hyde, *Personnel Management in Government: Politics and Process*, 5th ed. (New York: Marcel Dekker, Inc., 2001) 246–251; Donald E. Klingner and John Nalbandian, *Public Personnel Management: Contexts and Strategies*, 5th ed. (Englewood Cliffs, N.J.: Prentice-Hall, Inc., 1993), 193.

CHAPTER 4

Labor-Management Relations and Collective Bargaining

RICHARD C. KEARNEY AND BARRY M. FELDMAN

In stark contrast to unions in the private sector, whose membership has declined precipitously to around 8.5 percent of the nonagricultural workforce, public employee unions remain robust. Labor organizations represent about 38 percent of federal employees, 35 percent of state employees, and an impressive 47 percent of local government workers. The unionization percentage is highest at the municipal level, particularly for teachers, police officers, and firefighters.

A union environment presents special challenges to local government managers. Following brief historical and legal overviews of public sector unionization and collective bargaining, this chapter will note the major labor organizations and examine the current policy environment. This chapter sets out the fundamental elements of the collective bargaining process and concludes with contemporary challenges in local government labor-management relations. Throughout, special attention is given to emerging and best practices.

Historical and Legal Framework

Guiding Principle

• Collective bargaining for local government employees is not federally mandated.

From their early roots in handicraft technologies such as shoemaking and carpentry, through the widespread organization of industrial workers during the 1930s and 1940s, to the recent decline in membership and political clout, labor unions have been controversial components of human resource management in the private sector. Their best days were in the years immediately following passage of the 1935 National Labor Relations Act (NLRA) (also known as the Wagner Act). But broad changes in national and regional economic factors, increasingly unfavorable legal and political environments, and intense management opposition conspired to cut union membership from one-third of the private labor force in the mid-1950s to its low point of 8.5 percent today.

Unions in government have had a quite different experience. Although they had an early presence in federal defense facilities and the postal service, unions did not enjoy significant growth in federal employment until the 1960s. Similarly, police officers, firefighters, teachers, and state workers began organizing during the late nineteenth and early twentieth centuries, but organizational prosperity awaited important changes in their legal environment in the 1960s and 1970s.

Why do public workers join unions? For the same reasons as their counterparts in industry and nonprofit organizations: they are dissatisfied with one or more aspects of their jobs and consequently seek improvement through collective action. They may be discontent with pay, health care benefits, job security, hazardous working conditions, unfair or arbitrary management actions, or any number of annoyances. Their right to organize and join unions is constitutionally protected through the First Amendment to the U.S. Constitution by a string of federal court decisions (e.g., *McLaughlin v. Tilendis,* 1967; *Atkins v. Charlotte,* 1969). Unlike private and nonprofit sector employees, however, public employees do not enjoy the right to be recognized and engage in collective bargaining with their employer unless that right is granted by the employing jurisdiction.

Exhibit 4-1   Major Federal Laws Affecting Public Sector Labor Relations

Social Security Act of 1935
Fair Labor Standards Act (1938) (as amended)
Civil Rights Act of 1964
Urban Mass Transportation Act (1964)
Age Discrimination in Employment Act (1967)
Occupational Safety and Health Act (1970)
Equal Employment Opportunity Act of 1972
Employee Retirement Income Security
    Act (1974)
Americans with Disabilities Act (1990)
Civil Rights Act of 1991
Family and Medical Leave Act (1993)

The NLRA, as amended by the Landrum-Griffin and Taft-Hartley acts, grants the right to unionize and bargain collectively to virtually all nonsupervisory employees in the private and nonprofit sectors. Regulation of *public* employee labor relations, however, is the responsibility of the respective government jurisdictions. Federal employee collective bargaining rights are embodied in the Civil Service Reform Act of 1978 and various agency-specific legislation. Collective bargaining for state and local workers is governed primarily by state law. However, many federal laws apply to the workplace no matter where it is situated (see Exhibit 4-1).

Thus, a key difference between private and public sector labor relations and collective bargaining is that no national law sets bargaining and other rights for state and local employees and their unions. The result is a patchwork of state statutes, attorney general opinions, gubernatorial executive orders, court decisions, and local ordinances. Sunbelt states are generally unsympathetic to organized labor in any venue. North Carolina, South Carolina, and Virginia explicitly prohibit state agencies and local governments from recognizing unions and negotiating with them. Unhappy state and local workers in these three states may organize and join a union, but their collective voice will not be heard through collective bargaining. Other states permit some categories of public employees to bargain collectively but not others. For instance, teachers may bargain in Tennessee, but, with some exceptions, municipal and county employees may not. Idaho and Oklahoma grant bargaining rights to teachers and firefighters. Twenty-seven states, mostly across the northern tier of the country, give negotiating rights to virtually *all* categories of state and local employees. (See Exhibit 4-2 for bargaining status for major local government functions across the United States.)

State bargaining laws cover expansive territory. They generally do the following:

Exhibit 4-2   Local Government Collective Bargaining

(X = collective bargaining; Y = *meet and confer*)

State	Police	Firefighters	K–12 Teachers	Other
Alabama	–	Y	–	Y
Alaska	X	X	X	X
California	Y[1]	Y[1]	X	Y[1]
Connecticut	X	X	X	X
Delaware	X	X	X	X[1]
Florida	X	X	X	X[1]
Georgia	–	X	–	–
Hawaii	X	X	X	X
Idaho	–	X	X	–
Illinois	X	X	X	X
Indiana	–	–	X	–
Iowa	X	X	X	X
Kansas	Y[1]	Y[1]	X	Y[1]
Kentucky	X	X	–	–
Maine	X	X	X	X
Maryland	–	–	X	X[2]
Massachusetts	X	X	X	X
Michigan	X	X	X	X
Minnesota	X	X	X	X
Missouri	–	Y	–	Y
Montana	X	X	X	X
Nebraska	X	X	Y	X
Nevada	X	X	X	X
New Hampshire	X	X	X	X
New Jersey	X	X	X	X
New Mexico	X	X	X	X
New York	X	X	X	X
North Dakota	Y[2]	Y[2]	X	X[2]
Ohio	X	X	X	X
Oklahoma	X	X	X	X
Oregon	X	X	X	X[1]
Pennsylvania	X	X	X	X
Rhode Island	X	X	X	X
South Dakota	X	X	X	X
Tennessee	–	–	X	–
Texas	X[1]	X[1]	–	–
Utah	–	–	X	–
Vermont	X	X	X	X
Washington	X	X	X	X
West Virginia	Y[2]	Y[2]	Y[2]	Y[2]
Wisconsin	X	X	X	X
Wyoming	–	X	–	–

Source: Compiled from various sources; see Kearney, 2001: 61–62.

[1]Local option permitted.

[2]*Meet and confer* established by attorney general opinion.

- Establish employee and employer rights
- Create or identify an existing agency to administer labor relations, often called the public employee relations board (PERB)
- Determine which employees will be included in a bargaining unit and how a union will be recognized
- Identify which personnel policies are appropriate for bargaining
- Establish procedures for resolving negotiating impasses
- Specify how the union will be treated as exclusive representative of the bargaining unit (union security provisions).

Employee Organizations in State and Local Government

A distinction can be made between employee associations and unions. *Associations* exist primarily to provide professional benefits and services to their members. Most, including the State Employees Association of North Carolina and the Texas Public Employees Association, are also engaged in lobbying activities to win favorable treatment for their members by the legislative and executive branches of government. Over time, some associations, such as the National Education Association (NEA), have experienced a metamorphosis into unions that use collective bargaining as the chief means for winning improved wages, benefits, and working conditions from government employers.

Some unions, such as the American Federation of State, County, and Municipal Employees; the NEA; the International Association of Fire Fighters; and the Fraternal Order of Police, concentrate their efforts on organizing and representing public sector employees. Others, such as the Service Employees International Union, American Nurses Association, and the International Brotherhood of Teamsters, are

general purpose organizations that operate across public, private, and nonprofit sectors. (See Exhibit 4-3 for membership figures for the largest organizations of public employees.)

Collective Bargaining Process

Guiding Principles

- Preparation is the key to effective bargaining.
- Bargaining in good faith is critical to successful negotiation.
- Adversarial bargaining is being supplanted by interest-based bargaining.

Collective bargaining is a continuous process in which representatives of government employers (management) meet with employee representatives (the union) to jointly establish the terms and conditions of employment for members of a bargaining unit. Decision-making authority is shared by the parties, who sign a legal and binding contract. In *meet and confer*, union and management representatives meet to discuss terms and conditions of employment, but only management has final decision-making authority. In practice, *meet and confer* has developed into collective bargaining in many jurisdictions. The principal elements of the collective bargaining process are outlined below. The principal steps of collective bargaining are displayed in Exhibit 4-4.

Determining the Bargaining Unit

Which group of employees will a union represent? This group may be initially identified by the employees themselves, by a union seeking to represent them, by the state administrative agency, by management, or by a court. Criteria for determining the bargaining unit vary, but usually take into account a "community of interest" among members, the history and prior extent of collective bargaining in the jurisdiction, and efficiency of agency operations, among other considerations. Most jurisdictions, but not all, follow the NLRA in excluding bona fide supervisors and confidential employees from the bargaining unit. However, some states and localities combine supervisors and subordinates in the same unit, whereas others permit separate bargaining units for supervisors. The general trend is towards consolidating bargaining units into large groups of represented workers, but to segregate bona fide supervisors from other employees.

Deciding the Bargaining Unit Representative

Which union will represent the members in the unit? An employer may voluntarily recognize a union as official representative of the bargaining unit upon a showing of majority support by its members. In some cases a representation election must be held in which members are given a choice between two or more unions along with an option of voting "no union." Voting is usually by secret ballot, and a runoff election is held if none of the

---

Exhibit 4-3   Membership of Largest State and Local Employee Organizations

Organization	Membership	
National Education Association	2,700,000	(2002)
American Federation of State, County, and Municipal Employees	1,400,000	(2003)
American Federation of Teachers	1,000,000	(2003)
Service Employees International Union	1,500,000*	(2003)
Fraternal Order of Police	300,000	(2002)
International Association of Fire Fighters	250,000	(2003)

Source: Organization Web sites.
*Total of public, private, and nonprofit sectors.

Exhibit 4-4   The Collective Bargaining Process

The Duty to Bargain in Good Faith: Basic Principles

- Time limits for commencement of negotiations. Parties must furnish notice of the intent to modify or terminate an existing agreement, usually within at least 60 days.

- Obligation to provide information. The public employer is required to provide relevant information on any matter within the mandatory scope of bargaining that the employee organization requests.

- Prohibitions against bypassing the bargaining representatives. In an effort to avoid the end run, some jurisdictions prohibit communications between the union representatives and any other official not a designated management bargaining representative.

- Requirement that the employer make no unilateral changes in existing wages, hours, and working conditions while negotiations are under way. Unilateral implementation usually is permitted for nonmandatory bargaining subjects.

- Prohibition against work stoppages during negotiations.

- Formal procedures to resolve impasses.

- Duty to reduce the bargaining agreement to writing and to execute it.

- Prohibition against bad faith bargaining, which exists when one or both of the parties simply go through the motions without any real intention of reaching agreement. Indications of bad faith bargaining include dilatory tactics, failure to offer proposals or counterproposals, or refusal to make concessions on any issue.

choices receives majority support. The winning union is certified as bargaining representative by the public employee relations board or other labor relations agency. This arrangement grants the union the right of exclusive representation of the unit for a minimum period of time. During this time, management must not deal with any other union or group of employees purporting to represent all or a portion of the unit. The union may be decertified if it loses majority support of unit members.

Negotiating the Contract

Union and management representatives negotiate the terms of a contract. The union team typically includes the local union president, his or her aides, and, increasingly, a labor lawyer and a representative from the national union. Members of the local government management team may include the city or county manager or an assistant manager, the human resource management director, relevant department heads, the city or county attorney,

mayor's representative, or others. Elected officials rarely sit on the management bargaining team. Both teams designate a chief negotiator to serve as team leader and spokesperson.

The general public may also participate in negotiations in some jurisdictions, as determined by state law or local ordinance. Sunshine laws may permit media access, freedom of information concerning documents and data, public hearings or negotiations, and even a public representative at the bargaining table. Under Florida's sunshine law all negotiations must be held in public. Sunshine bargaining is optional in Iowa, Massachusetts, Nevada, and New Jersey.

Preparation is the key to effective bargaining. Both teams should familiarize themselves with the provisions of the previous contract and their experience with its implementation. Wage and benefit data need to be analyzed, particularly data from other local bargaining units and neighboring jurisdictions. National, state, and local legal developments should also be examined, including relevant court cases.

Both parties must identify their bargaining goals and proposals, amass supporting data, and anticipate the other side's reactions, objectives, and proposals. Finally, dates, times, and places for the negotiations must be agreed to.

Bargaining laws require both parties to negotiate in good faith over all issues properly within the scope of bargaining. Such *bargaining in good faith* is critical to negotiating a successful contract—see the basic principles of good-faith bargaining on page 98.

Collective bargaining is a political process with high stakes. Future wages, benefits, working conditions, and the overall quality of work life are in play. The union leader's reputation and survival are on the line. The mayor and council's reelection chances may be hinging on the public's reaction to the outcomes of the negotiations. The union wants "more," and management seeks to hold the line or perhaps wring concessions out of the union. A single strategic error or miscalculation can be very costly. Meanwhile, the media, voters, and other stakeholders are watching. Under these stressful conditions, astute negotiators will attempt to draw lessons from others' experience.

Conventionally, collective bargaining has been adversarial, with each side predetermining "positions" and trying to force the other side to make concessions by applying negotiating skills, clever tactics, and political power. Personal attacks and implied and overt threats may be employed. This traditional "us versus them" approach is about power and winning at the expense of the other party. It tends to leave behind a reservoir of distrust, ill will, and hurt feelings, along with a gloating winner and a resentful loser.

As labor-management relations change, so does the philosophy of collective bargaining. Today, a growing number of local jurisdictions are experimenting with *interest-based bargaining,* also known as "Getting to Yes," "mutual gains," and "win-win bargaining." As popularized by Roger Fisher and William Ury in *Getting to Yes: Negotiating Agreement Without Giving*

Tips for Maintaining Good Labor-Management Relations

- ❏ Know the legal environment and the provisions of contracts.
- ❏ Prepare carefully for collective bargaining. Gather all relevant wage and benefit data, identify bargaining goals, and anticipate the union's objectives and reactions.
- ❏ Communicate early and often with elected officials about the bargaining process.
- ❏ Negotiate in good faith.
- ❏ Practice patience.
- ❏ Move toward a collaborative approach to bargaining.
- ❏ Look for the underlying causes of grievances.
- ❏ Involve employees in problem solving and decision making.

In, it begins with assumptions very different from traditional bargaining. The parties identify their major issues and interests instead of taking hard, unyielding positions. Thus, "people are separated from the problem."[1] They develop options for themselves and the other side to consider, basing these alternatives on objective criteria and the perceived interests of the other. If it works out as intended, win-win bargaining results in a contract acceptable to both the union and management and does no harm to the long-term relationship between the parties. One permutation of interest-based bargaining is gainsharing, in which dollar savings are shared.

Interest-based bargaining has been declared a success in numerous local government arenas, from public schools to sanitation. But it is not appropriate as a "gateway" change that is intended to propel other fundamental changes in the organization. Rather, a certain level of trust and good faith is required, or must first be built, and formal training in win-win techniques is needed. The most positive

Elected Officials and the Bargaining Process

fyi

The relationship between the legislative body and the local government manager can, at times, be tension-filled. Small tears can periodically appear in the complex web of trust and support that binds legislators and executive together, especially in reformed local governments. The collective bargaining process can cause those small tears to become large fissures if the local government manager is not thoughtful when dealing with the elected officials during the collective bargaining process. While there are no perfect techniques to avoid the pitfalls, there are strategies local government managers can employ prior to and during collective bargaining to maintain and perhaps enhance their relationships with local elected officials.

- **Meet early in the process**—Seventy-five to 90 days before the start of collective bargaining, meet with the legislative body. The local government manager's primary purpose is to listen to the elected officials' opinions and positions regarding wages, benefits, and other topics that are collectively bargained. The manager needs to determine if there is a consensus regarding wages and benefits, and if the legislative body is unified or divided on collective bargaining issues.

- **Offer good analysis quickly**—Within seven days of the first meeting, meet again. (1) Present an analysis of costs of the various issues raised in the first meeting. (2) Give the legislative body feedback as to the practicality of the issues. (3) Identify unrealistic positions that would be nonstarters at the table. This second meeting should help both the legislative body and the local government manager begin to sharpen their positions on the various issues.

- **Meet again**—At this third meeting, held within a week of the second, the local government manager should outline positions to be taken on the issues raised at the two earlier meetings. While the positions may be further refined, the outline represents the local government's bargaining agenda. It is critical that the legislative body sign off on the agenda and affirm its agreement on the issues and positions to be negotiated on the municipality's behalf by the local government manager.

- **Share the union's issues and positions**— Early in the collective bargaining process both sides exchange positions on issues. Even though the initial list (agenda) of positions will be modified through the collective bargaining process, the elected officials should see the union's opening proposal. Sharing the opening positions may give a sense as to how far apart the parties are and how difficult the process may be.

- **Meet again, and again, and again**—For many local governments the collective bargaining team includes senior managers, but not elected officials. While this model has advantages, one of its biggest disadvantages is that elected officials are often the last to know. Don't let that happen. Meet often and regularly with the elected officials to keep them informed.

- **If in doubt, wait**—The manager's ability to verbally agree to settle an issue at the collective bargaining table is a function of the support given by members of the legislative body to settle issues without first checking with them. Local government managers who are not sure how strong their support is or how divided their legislative body is over collective bargaining issues need to practice patience. When in doubt about settling an issue, check with the legislative body first.

Gainsharing

Gainsharing programs have received far more support in the private sector than the public sector, although there have been several high-profile municipalities that have made gainsharing a part of their new labor-management relations.

Gainsharing is the sharing with municipal employees of any dollar savings generated by initiatives or improvements in work procedures. Gainsharing has also been used to retain jobs that might have been cut due to budget problems. It is a way to make municipal costs of providing a public service comparable with private costs and to avoid the contracting out of a service.

The notion of gainsharing has far more support with municipal union leaders than with public officials. Public officials, for the most part, view any savings generated by workplace reforms as belonging to the taxpayers and not the employees. This belief, coupled with the difficulty of accurately measuring dollar savings, has made gainsharing a program viewed with caution by some public officials.

Not withstanding the problems, gainsharing can be an element in creating a different relationship between labor and management. The following are some examples:

- The city of New Rochelle, New York, and the American Federation of State, County, and Municipal Employees (AFSCME) Council 66 and Local 663 developed a gainsharing program where productivity gains were used to help fund wage increases. The sanitation department, through a program of attrition, reduced its crew size from four employees to three employees per truck. The savings from this gain was used to fund wage increases.

- In what has become one of the more notable experiments in gainsharing, the city of Indianapolis, Indiana, and AFSCME Council 62 implemented gainsharing programs in the public works department. The success of the gainsharing programs was the major topic in former Indianapolis mayor Neil Goldsmith's book, *21st Century City.*

- The Monona Grove, Wisconsin, school district and AFSCME Council 40 developed a gainsharing program for their food service costs, where savings were split between the school district and employees.

Source: Examples of gainsharing programs were obtained from the American Federation of State, County, and Municipal Employees (AFSCME) Web site at www.afscme.org.

results achieved by interest-based bargaining tend to occur when both parties go through joint training prior to negotiations and use a facilitator during collective bargaining. For example, the Iowa Association of School Boards and their various unions created a partnership called "Partners for Collaboration" to train school board negotiators in interest-based bargaining and to use professionally trained facilitators during interest-based negotiations. More than 500 negotiation team members representing 88 school districts participated in the program. Another example of a program designed to improve bargaining relationships is found in Frederick County, Maryland, and is described in the sidebar on page 102.

In jurisdictions where management, the union, or both are committed to traditional tactics and not genuinely willing to embrace—or at least entertain—the principles of interest-based bargaining, it is destined to fail. It must also be understood that there are places and times in which traditional, adversarial bargaining is called for because of the nature of the

Relationship-by-Objectives (RBO) *fyi*

The Emergency Services Division of Frederick County, Maryland, has more than 3,000 career full-time and volunteer firefighters available to respond to fires and other emergencies anywhere in the county. In April 2001, labor, volunteer leaders, and management officials participated in a Relationship-by-Objectives (RBO) program conducted by the Department of Labor's Federal Mediation and Conciliation Service (FMCS). FMCS described the RBO program's goal as simply to change how the participants interacted with each other. The RBO program was significant because of the number of participants, which included elected officials.

In a follow-up effort in spring 2002, FMCS brought the parties together again to develop a code of conduct for all firefighters, to develop a problem-solving process to be used when differences or problems arise, and to work through chain-of-command problems that may occur at a fire scene.

Source: Information on the RBO program was obtained from the Federal Mediation and Conciliation Service Web site at www.fmcs.gov/internet.

dispute, the comfort zone of the parties, an ugly history of labor-management relations, intense constituent pressures on the union team, or political problems for management.[2]

Resolving Bargaining Impasses

Guiding Principles

- Contingency planning and good communication can shorten work stoppages.
- Arbitration focuses on equity, the public interest, acceptability to the parties, comparability with similar jurisdictions, and the ability of the jurisdiction to pay.
- The availability of arbitration lessens pressure for a voluntary settlement.

Negotiation impasses are common. There are several proven means of settling them, including the strike, mediation, fact finding, and arbitration.

The Strike

The NLRA permits strikes as a legitimate means for settling private and nonprofit sector differences when they cannot be resolved at the negotiating table. As recently as the late 1970s, strikes were common. Since then the strike rate has declined significantly due to structural changes in the economy, global competition, a growing willingness of employers to hire permanent replacements for striking workers, and other reasons.

In government, federal employee work stoppages are categorically prohibited in the United States. Thirty-five states also outlaw public employee strikes, and the vast majority of labor contracts contain no-strike clauses to preclude work stoppages during the life of the contract. An illegal strike is typically met with an injunction and imposition of fines or other penalties on the union and the strikers themselves.

But some states permit certain local government employees to strike legally. Beginning with Vermont in 1967, ten states have enacted laws granting a limited right to strike. Additionally, courts in another five states have upheld the right of some categories of public employees to strike. In virtually all instances, strikes are forbidden for essential employees (e.g., police, firefighters, correctional employees, hospital workers). Most permissive legislation requires the union to comply with specific provisions before executing a strike, including mediation, fact finding, arbitration, and prior notice.

The record on strike legislation is mixed. A prohibition against work stoppages discourages them, but it does not prevent them. Also compulsory use of arbitration in contract disputes does diminish the incidence of strikes. Permissive strike policies are associated with high strike frequency in some states (e.g., Penn-

Best Practices for Reinventing Labor-Management Relations

The new municipal workplace has incorporated elements of a different philosophy of labor-management relations. The elements of this new philosophy include the following:

- Giving employees enhanced training, knowledge, and information about their jobs and the municipal organization
- Encouraging and training managers and supervisors to be coaches and mentors
- Viewing employees as positive contributors to the municipal team—thus municipal workplace policies are designed to be supportive, not restrictive
- Using measurement tools such as benchmarking, citizen surveys, and outcome measures to improve public services
- Encouraging municipal managers, supervisors, and employees to prevent building barriers and to collaborate when providing public services
- Incorporating technology to enhance employee skills and knowledge; new technology coupled with greater flexibility in work rules leads to productivity gains, which can mean maintaining and enhancing public services
- Teaching front-line municipal workers problem-solving skills to quickly respond to citizens' concerns
- Offering compensation based on skill building, knowledge acquired, and seniority rather than relying on rigid classification plans that fail to recognize employee achievements
- Finding common goals for labor and management to achieve
- Supporting ongoing innovation through efforts like labor-management committees.

sylvania) but low rates in others (e.g., Vermont). Strike incidence actually declined in several states after they decided to authorize work stoppages (e.g., Ohio and Illinois).

Generally, management today does a much more thorough and effective job of contingency planning for work stoppages than it did in the past. Strikes—legal or not—are anticipated and arrangements are made to continue the delivery of basic and essential services by management employees and others. When public management executes its strike contingency plan effectively and also garners public support for the correctness of the management point of view on the dispute, the duration of the strike can be shortened significantly.

Fortunately, the preponderance of impasses is resolved through means other than a work stoppage. The most common techniques for resolving disputes over contracts are mediation, fact finding, and arbitration.

Mediation

Once an impasse is declared by either party or the labor relations agency, the next step is usually to call in a mediator. A mediator is a non-biased third party whose purpose is to help the other two parties attain a voluntary settlement. Mediators may be dispatched by the Federal Mediation and Conciliation Service, the state labor relations agency, or other sources. Successful mediators meet individually and jointly with the parties, help them to understand the other's interests, facilitate a climate conducive to settlement, and steer them to the terms of a final contract. The mediator cannot impose a solution, but he or she may suggest possibilities for resolving the impasse.

Fact Finding

If mediation fails, fact finding begins. It may also be used as a first step. A fact-finding panel, usually composed of three members, is obtained from the same sources tapped for mediators. In some jurisdictions, a mediator's role may be transformed into fact finder. Procedurally more formal than mediation, fact finding consists of a quasi-judicial process with evidence, a written transcript, and, in most cases, written, nonbinding recommendations for settlement. Fact finding is something of a misnomer because all labor disagreements start with at least two sets of "facts." The principal task of the fact finders is to derive from the evidence the most objective facts and bring them to the attention of the parties and the various stakeholders. Like mediation, fact finding cannot impose terms on the parties.

Arbitration

Arbitration resembles fact finding in that it involves each party formally presenting supportive evidence to one or more neutrals. Unlike fact finding, however, arbitration is final and binding on the parties. Its purpose is to produce a fair settlement that protects the parties and the public interest and to avoid work stoppages. Arbitration may be mandated by law or by the administrative agency when negotiations fail, or the union and management may agree voluntarily to use the technique to resolve a negotiation impasse.

The parties may select an arbitrator from a list provided by the American Arbitration Association, the state PERB, or other sources, or arbitrators may be designated by the PERB or a court. When a three-person (tripartite) panel is used, a truly neutral arbitrator typically works with other "neutrals" who are known to favor one side or the other. Thus, tripartite arbitration is, in this sense, a continuation of collective bargaining.

The decision-making criteria arbitrators consider usually include equity, the public interest, acceptability to the parties, comparative data from similar or nearby jurisdictions, and, increasingly, the ability of the jurisdiction to pay.

There are two types of arbitration: conventional and final offer. Conventional arbitration maximizes the neutral person's authority, permitting him or her to favor the interests of one side or the other or to split the difference. Final offer arbitration requires each party to submit its "last best offer" to the arbitrator, who is bound to accept the terms of one or the other as presented. "Final offer by package" means the arbitrator must accept the best offer in its entirety, even if multiple issues are involved. "Final offer by issue" permits separate decisions on each item in dispute.

Arbitration peacefully and effectively resolves interest impasses without the strike and accompanying service disruptions. However, it is controversial for three major reasons. First, it delegates important decision-making authority to an individual or panel of individuals who cannot be held accountable by the voters or elected officials. Arbitrators' decisions can significantly impact the jurisdiction's budget and even precipitate a subsequent tax or fee hike, but such decisions are subject only to limited review by courts and elected officials. For this reason, arbitration has been ruled unconstitutional by courts in five states: Colorado, Maryland, Nebraska, South Dakota, and Utah.

A second criticism of arbitration comes from management, which, in most local governments, is convinced that the arbitration outcomes favor the unions—a conclusion supported implicitly by unions' general enthusiasm for the process. Empirical evidence indicates that arbitration decisions do not significantly favor one party or the other. Nonetheless, the mere *availability* of arbitration does appear to boost salary and benefits. Finally, it is argued that arbitration "chills" collective bargaining by holding open the possibility that one or both parties may obtain more from the arbitrator than from a negotiated agreement. Thus, the availability of arbitration tends to lessen the pressure for a voluntary settlement.

Administering the Contract

Guiding Principles

- Successful contract administration is the responsibility of the union and management.
- Grievances may be symptomatic of an underlying workplace problem.
- The new workplace gives employees more opportunities to participate in problem solving and decision making.

Negotiating contracts and resolving disputes over them capture the labor relations spotlight, but the day-to-day problems of living with the contract define—and test—the labor-management relationship. Conflicts over issues unresolved at the bargaining table often continue after the contract is formally signed. Vague language or legalese, confusing clauses, hurt personal feelings, and other problems must be worked out through side meetings or the grievance process.

The contract serves as the law of the workplace. It has legal standing superior to that of a commercial contract. The provisions of the contract address, often in exquisite detail, obvious issues like union and management rights, wages, hours of work, benefits, union security, antidiscrimination and affirmative action, residency requirements, layoffs, reductions-in-force, union political activities, and employee discipline and dismissal. Hundreds of other, less obvious issues may be covered as well, including wash-up time, laundry expenses, and teacher lunchroom duty.

Administrative oversight for implementing the terms of the contract during its specified life is the responsibility of the PERB, another administrative agency, or, occasionally, the courts. At the end of the day, however, successful contract administration is the responsibility of the union and management.

Grievances

There are a variety of vehicles for addressing conflicts arising from contract interpretation.

As a rule, work stoppages over a disagreement concerning an existing contract are impermissible. A party can file an unfair labor practice charge with the appropriate administrative or judicial body, or register an informal complaint. Civil service procedures may be applied or management may simply take unilateral action. Litigation may be filed. But usually, allegations of a violation of contract language or other disputes under the contract are resolved through formal grievance procedures.

Exhibit 4-5 illustrates a typical grievance procedure. The most common grievances are over disciplinary actions, absenteeism, health and safety issues, vacation assignments, work assignments, promotions, overtime, reductions-in-force, and allegations of discrimination. Note that when the parties cannot settle a grievance voluntarily, grievance arbitration serves as the final step. As is the case with interest disputes, a neutral arbitrator hears the evidence presented by the parties and renders a final and binding judgment. Among the factors considered by the grievance arbitrator are past practice, the prior bargaining record of the parties, and previous arbitration awards.

Grievances may be symptomatic of an underlying workplace problem, such as difficult or insensitive supervisors, a hostile or unsafe working environment, introduction of new technology, or personality conflicts between a union steward and supervisor. Sometimes grievances result from intentional violations of contract language. For example, during a flood or other natural disaster, management may be forced to take preemptive action regardless of contract language.

Unions should be expected to investigate all allegations of contract violations made against management by a member of the bargaining unit, and to proceed with most of them. Grievance representation is a key responsibility of the union and one through which it demonstrates its value to members. Management should also take seriously its responsibility to defend itself and, when appropriate, take up its own grievances against the union.

Tensions between the union and management resulting from formal grievances may escalate and be difficult and frustrating to handle. Grievance procedures demand valuable management time and energy. An excessive number of grievances, even trivial ones, can seriously disrupt the workplace. But, as in a marriage, some disagreements are to be expected, and, when properly and maturely handled, can even strengthen the relationship.

There are other techniques for encouraging and organizing constructive dialogue between unions and management that take place outside the bargaining and grievance processes. Several examples of such employee participation approaches follow.

Exhibit 4-5   A Typical Grievance Procedure

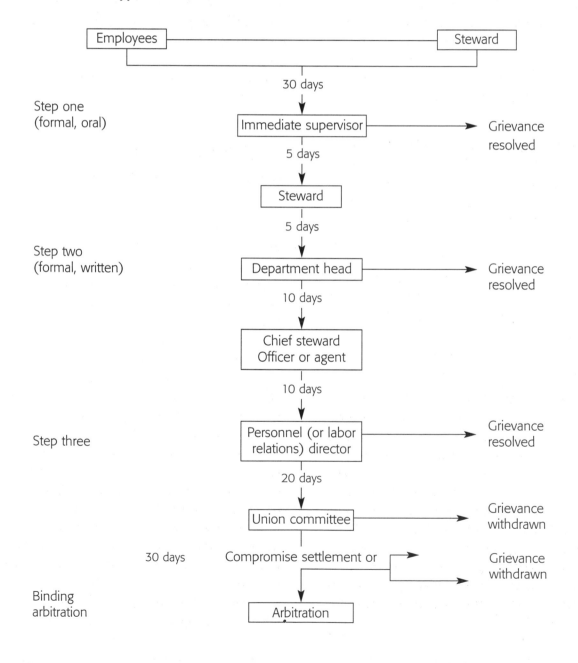

Employee Participation Initiatives

Municipal officials and union leaders are employing different methods to enter into a more constructive dialogue with each other. The new workplace of reinventing and improving government gives employees opportunities to participate in problem solving and decision making as never before.

Quality of Work Life (QWL) Programs.
QWL programs have been used for more than two decades to improve employee workplaces and working conditions, leading to better quality of public services and enhanced productivity. QWL programs are guided by a steering committee of labor and management employees who discuss and implement changes involving service delivery and empowering employees.

Total Quality Management (TQM) Programs.
TQM, as first developed by W. Edwards Deming, focuses on how a service or program is delivered, and emphasizes the quality of the product. Management and union work cooperatively to meet the expectations of citizens and empower first-line employees to be problem solvers to improve the delivery of public services. TQM programs are not as popular today as they were in the early 1990s, but similar initiatives based on involving employees in continuous improvement of work processes continue under other names.

Self-Directed Work Teams.
Self-directed work teams are self-managed groups responsible for the tasks needed to provide public services. Self-directed work teams were originally used in manufacturing facilities starting in the late 1960s and 1970s and gained support in local government in the late 1980s and 1990s. Although self-directed work teams have been implemented, a number of problems have plagued their widespread acceptance. Chief among the problems is redefining the relationship between the former supervisor and the work team.

Labor-Management Committees.
Labor-management committees comprise the most far-reaching efforts to change current labor-management relations. Called by a variety of names, the labor-management committee's common element includes the creation of a partnership committed to improving the relationship. Underscoring the new relationship is the idea that employees are the foundation of the organization, and the organization will be no stronger than the relationship that exists between labor and management. On the national level, the International Association of Fire Chiefs and the International Association of Fire Fighters encourage local fire chiefs and local union leaders to participate in labor-management committees aimed at improving relations.

Challenges in Local Government Labor-Management Relations

Some of the challenges confronting labor-management relations in local government are long-standing, including how to overcome a historically poisonous labor-management environment, finding and using alternatives to adversarial processes, and coping with persistent taxing and spending constraints. Other challenges are of more recent vintage, such as the movement to reinvent government.

Taxing and spending limitations have always plagued local governments. At the bottom of the fiscal food chain, municipalities, counties, towns, and townships are highly dependent on their respective state governments and, to a much lesser extent, on the federal government. Tax-resistant citizens aggressively attack tax and fee increases. Thus, local governments are at the mercy of economic forces they cannot meaningfully influence. For unions and management, this means that reductions-in-force must be considered from time to time and that pay hikes and benefit contributions are constrained. Collective bargaining is much more difficult when the size of the financial pie is shrinking.

Positive union-management relations are critical to successful reinvention efforts. The development of new techniques for delivering services, adoption of labor-saving technology, contracting out for services and jobs, and implementation of human resource management innovations, such as broadbanding position classification and performance-based pay, are among the many reinventing-government reforms that call for solicitation and encouragement of union participation and cooperation. Union resistance has doomed many a reinventing-government initiative.

The old saying, "necessity is the mother of invention," is particularly fitting given the approach local governments have taken to deal with cutbacks in federal and state aid, perceptions of inefficiency, the lack of public support for higher taxes, and citizens' growing demands for increased public service. Local government leaders realize that maintaining the status quo will not make government work better and cost less. What is needed, in part, to initiate reforms is to change the relationship between management and unions.

Although changing employee relationships built over decades will not be accomplished by quick fixes, there are a growing number of

Red Flags

The following missteps can get a local government manager in serious trouble:

- Failing to prepare properly for collective bargaining
- Using delaying tactics or refusing to make concessions
- Leaving elected officials "in the dark" about labor negotiations
- Neglecting training for collaborative bargaining
- Ignoring grievances.

local governments seeking ways to create an environment that empowers workers to solve problems and improve the delivery of public services. Changing the relationship requires elected officials, local government managers, and their employees to end the contentious relations and find ways to work together.

---

[1] Roger Fisher, William Ury, and Bruce Patton, *Getting to Yes,* 2nd ed. (New York: Penquin Books, 1991).

[2] Richard C. Kearney, with David G. Carnevale, *Labor Relations in the Public Sector* (New York: Marcel Dekker, 2001), 132–136.

CHAPTER 5

Employee Rights: Avoiding Legal Liability

JOHN A. DiNOME, SAUNDRA M. YAKLIN, AND DAVID H. ROSENBLOOM

An important responsibility of public managers is to balance the citizens' right to receive efficient, effective, equitable, and responsive service from government with the public employees' right to be treated with equity and dignity. The U.S. Constitution, state constitutions, codified law, and common-law practices set the legal framework for the rights and responsibilities in the public employer-employee relationship.

Other chapters in this book address many of these rights and responsibilities in the context of specific personnel procedures. This chapter summarizes the major federal laws and court rulings affecting personnel matters. It also describes important documents used to communicate employment-related rights and duties, provides practical tips, and offers sample language. Employers may not be able to completely avoid lawsuits filed by unhappy job applicants or employees, but they can at least protect themselves and the jurisdiction from liability claims by not violating the rights of job seekers and employees.

Employee Contracts and the Personnel Policy Manual

Employment at Will

The doctrine of employment at will provides that an employer may discharge an employee for any reason not prohibited by law, or for no reason at all. However, when an employee has an employment contract or there is a statutory restriction, an employer does not have this freedom.

Most public employees are covered by civil service statutes or collective bargaining agreements and are, therefore, not employees at will. Rather, the requirements of the statute or collective bargaining agreement must be met before the employee may be terminated. However, some municipal employees are at-will

---

Editor's Note: Most of this chapter was written by John A. DiNome and Saundra M. Yaklin, with assistance from Caroline A. O'Connell. Alexander E. Gallin, Samuel Veytsman, Sara S. Kennedy, and Jarrod J. Malone assisted with updating the chapter for the 2nd edition. The last section, which addresses constitutional rights, was written by David H. Rosenbloom. The sections on oaths and whistle-blower protection were contributed by Charles R. Wise.

employees. For example, in many states, city managers, chiefs of police, and department heads are at-will employees.

Employers should be aware that their written or oral statements, including employee policy manuals, may create an employment contract with their at-will employees or create additional rights for employees protected by civil service statutes and collective bargaining agreements.

Oral and Implied Contracts

In many states, oral statements made by an employer—for example, "you will be employed as long as you do your job"—may create an oral employment contract and rebut the presumption of employment at will. Most states require objective evidence of intent between the parties to create an oral contract and to dispel the at-will employment rule. Examples of objective evidence include statements and documents that indicate an intent to create an employment contract. Ultimately, the employee may have the burden to prove that the employment relationship is not at will.

Many state courts have found that an implied contract also exists where an employee supplies "additional consideration" to the employer. Sufficient additional consideration is found when an employee gives an employer a substantial benefit or undergoes a substantial hardship. For example, courts commonly find that an employment contract has been created when an employee relocates to take a job that he or she believes has been offered. If the court deems this to be adequate consideration, the employee is not at will and must be employed for a reasonable amount of time.

Personnel Policy Manual

Guiding Principles

- The personnel policy manual should include an employment contract disclaimer.
- The personnel policy manual should use clear, concise language.

- The personnel policy manual should be kept up to date, and changes should be well publicized.

Many employers, particularly nonunionized ones, publish personnel policy manuals for their workforce. As a general rule, employers should use these manuals as a means of communicating with their employees, setting forth standards for workplace performance and conduct, and describing employee benefits. The manual should be written in clear, concise language and it should be kept up to date. Changes made to the manual should be publicized. An easy-to-use and straightforward personnel policies manual comes from the City of Rancho Cordova, California, and is available on ICMA's Web site at http://bookstore.icma. org/freedocs/43081.

However, employers must also carefully design their personnel manuals to avoid making unintended contractual guarantees to their employees. This and other legal issues surrounding personnel policy manuals are discussed in the paragraphs below.

Personnel Policies as Contracts

In many jurisdictions, statements and policies contained in an employee handbook can create contractual obligations. For example, if an employee handbook states that an employee will be fired only for just cause, an employee terminated without cause may have a breach of contract claim. There are a few states, such as Pennsylvania, that have held that handbooks are generally not employment contracts. An employer should check state law to see whether and how its personnel handbook may give rise to contractual liability.

Disclaimers and Acknowledgment Forms

Disclaimer. Employee handbooks should contain a disclaimer stating clearly that the handbook is not a contract and is subject to change; otherwise, an employer may be contractually bound by any statements contained in the handbook. Disclaimers must also be conspicuous; for example, a disclaimer that appears in the middle of a paragraph on page 25 may be insufficient. Therefore, an employer must carefully draft a disclaimer and place it within the first few pages of the handbook. Such a disclaimer might read:

> Your employment relationship with [*employer*] is considered "at will." This means that your employment with [*employer*] has no defined or definite duration. Either you or [*employer*] may terminate the employment relationship with or without cause, with or without notice, for any reason that is not prohibited by law. This handbook is not a contract and is subject to change without notice.

Acknowledgment Form. Employee handbooks should also include an acknowledgment form to document that the employee has received the handbook and understands its contents. Further, by signing the form, employees acknowledge that their employment is at will and that the handbook creates no contractual obligations between them and the employer. The acknowledgment might be worded as follows:

> I have this day received a copy of [*employer*] employee handbook. I understand that the handbook contains management guidelines only and that the [*employer*] may, from time to time and at its discretion, change, modify, or delete rules, policies, or benefits contained in the handbook.
>
> I understand that neither the handbook nor any other communication by a management representative, whether oral or written, is in any way intended to and does not create a contract of employment. I understand that my employment relationship with [*employer*] is, as described in this handbook, an employment-at-will relationship. As such, my employment with

[*employer*] is voluntarily entered into, and I am free to resign at any time. Similarly, [*employer*] may terminate the employment relationship whenever it believes it is appropriate, with or without cause, with or without notice.

Political Patronage

A public employer may not make decisions regarding lower-level public employees on the basis of political affiliation.[1] This includes hiring decisions, promotions, transfers, discharges, and other job actions. "Lower-level" public employees include all nonconfidential and non-policy-making employees. Further, an employer may not recommend that an employee support a particular political candidate. It is important to include this information in the employee handbook.

Equal Employment Opportunity and Harassment Policies

All employee handbooks should contain a statement of policy on equal employment opportunity (EEO), for example:

> The [*employer*] strictly follows a policy of nondiscrimination in all employment policies and practices. Our employment policies and practices treat everyone equally. We hire and develop the best people available on the basis of job-related qualifications. No distinctions are made in rates of pay or employment opportunities, including recruiting, hiring, training, benefits, promotions, transfers, or treatment on the job, on the basis of color, religious belief, sex, age, race, national origin, disability, handicap, or other prohibited criteria as these terms are used under applicable law.

In some jurisdictions, discrimination on the basis of sexual orientation is prohibited and the employer's policy must also include "sexual orientation" in the list of prohibited criteria. It is also very important that an employee handbook set forth the jurisdiction's policy on sexual and other types of prohibited harassment (see Exhibit 5-1). An established policy may discourage employees from committing any illegal activity. And, in the event that there is a claim of harassment, a policy can provide the basis for defense. (See section, Sexual Harassment, on page 126, and section, Other Types of Prohibited Harassment, on page 129.)

First Amendment Rights of Public Employees

Public employees enjoy certain First Amendment protections against speech restrictions in the workplace. There are, however, certain limitations upon those free speech rights. The Supreme Court has established that only speech that involves "a matter of public concern" and does not interfere with the effective functioning of the workplace is protected under the First Amendment.

Exhibit 5-1   Sample Harassment Policy

All employees have a duty to report sexual and other types of prohibited harassment whether they feel they are a victim of harassment or they believe they have observed harassment.

It is the policy of the [*employer*] to maintain a working environment for employees free from sexual harassment and harassment because of an employee's color, religious belief, sex, age, race, national origin, disability, handicap, [*sexual orientation*], or other prohibited criteria. This type of harassment in any form or manner is expressly prohibited. All reported or suspected occurrences of harassment will be promptly and thoroughly investigated. If harassment in violation of this policy has occurred, this municipality will take appropriate corrective action, including discipline or discharge of the offending employee.

Sexual Harassment Defined

Sexual harassment includes unwelcome sexual advances, requests for sexual favors, or other verbal or physical conduct of a sexual nature when

- Submission to the conduct is an explicit or implicit condition of employment.
- Submission to or rejection of the conduct is used as the basis for an employment decision.
- The conduct has the purpose or effect of unreasonably interfering with an individual's work performance or creating an intimidating, hostile work environment.
- Slurs, jokes, or derogatory comments are based on an individual's gender. This includes verbal comments as well as written comments in e-mails, posters, memoranda, or other documents.

Reporting Harassment

Any incident of prohibited harassment from a co-worker or others who deal with the [*employer*] should be reported immediately to the supervisor or to the Personnel Office. Complaints of harassment from a supervisor should be reported immediately by the employee to the department head or to the Personnel Office. [*List title and telephone number of individual to receive report*].

To the extent practicable, all complaints of harassment will remain confidential. It may be necessary, however, to disclose the nature or the origin of the complaint in order to investigate it properly or to take corrective action. The [*employer*] will take all necessary steps to ensure that a person who makes a good faith complaint, or any witness who comes forward in an investigation, will not be retaliated against in any way.

Corrective Action

If the municipality concludes that harassment prohibited by this policy has occurred, it will take immediate steps to ensure that the harassment is stopped and does not recur. This may include suspension or termination of the individual(s) responsible for the harassment.

As a result of the First Amendment protection given to public employees, a government employer may impose restrictions on speech in the workplace only if it can demonstrate that the restriction is vital to the efficient operation of the workplace. An employer may require professional conduct by its employees and may prohibit profanity in the workplace. A public employer may not, however, restrict its employees from possessing particular types of magazines (for example) at work because the mere possession of these magazines does not compromise workplace efficiency.[2] Public employers should consider these First Amendment issues before including rules that restrict employee speech and expression in the employee handbook. (See the last section of this chapter for more on public employees' constitutional rights.)

Leave of Absence and the Family and Medical Leave Act

Employers should clearly outline in the employee handbook their policy on leaves of absence. Further, the handbook should describe how the Family and Medical Leave Act (FMLA) is implemented. It should explain that although the FMLA allows certain employees to take up to 12 weeks off for reasons defined by the act, if an employer has its own leave-of-absence policy, an employee is not entitled to both the leave of absence and the FMLA time. An employer may also include in the handbook a statement that employees are required to use their sick and vacation time as part of their 12-week FMLA time. (See sections on the FMLA on pages 124 and 129–133.)

Workplace Violence

As discussed below, government employers have a duty to maintain a safe work environment and, therefore, should also state a policy prohibiting workplace violence in their employee handbook. (See section on workplace violence beginning on page 137 and Exhibit 5-2.)

Other Policies

These are just a few of the policies that should be included in an employer's policy manual. In particular, many states have laws regarding employee pay and break requirements. Employers are encouraged to consult their

---

Exhibit 5-2   Sample Policy on Workplace Violence

It is [employer]'s policy to promote a safe environment for its employees. [Employer] is committed to working with its employees to maintain a work environment free of violence, threats of violence, harassment, intimidation, and other disruptive behavior. While this kind of conduct is not pervasive at our facilities, no workplace is immune. Every workplace is affected by disruptive behavior at one time or another.

Violence, threats, harassment, intimidation, and other disruptive behavior in our workplace will not be tolerated; that is, all reports of incidents will be taken seriously and will be dealt with appropriately. Unacceptable behavior can include oral or written statements, gestures, or expressions that communicate a direct or indirect threat of physical harm. Individuals who commit such acts will be removed from the premises and will be subject to disciplinary action (up to and including termination), criminal penalties, or both.

We need your cooperation to implement this policy effectively and maintain a safe working environment. Do not ignore violent, threatening, harassing, intimidating, or other disruptive behavior. If you observe or experience such behavior by anyone on [employer]'s premises, whether he or she is an employee of [employer] or not, report it immediately to [title and telephone number of individual to receive report]. Individuals who receive such reports should seek advice from [title of person primarily responsible for investigating workplace violence] regarding investigating the incident and initiating appropriate action.

counsel regarding state, local, and other legal requirements that affect policy manuals.

Personnel Records

Guiding Principle

• Every employee should have a complete, up-to-date personnel file.

Employers should maintain a complete and up-to-date personnel file for each employee. This is simply a good management practice, but it is also required in case of an adverse personnel decision. Employers are tempted to create a paper trail only for poorly performing employees. However, in case of a lawsuit, judges want to see evidence of how the problem employee's performance differed from that of co-workers, and therefore, for the purpose of comparison, proper records need to be kept for all employees.

Record Retention

Most employment laws require employers to maintain records. The chart in Exhibit 5-3 on pages 116 and 117 lists the records that must be kept and the time period for retention. To prevent tampering and to maintain their confidentiality, personnel files must be kept in a secure place. Government employers should contact their legal counsel to find out about state and local record-keeping requirements.

Confidentiality of Personnel Files

Personnel files of public employees may or may not enjoy protection, depending on the state and political culture in which the public employees operate. Some states such as New

Confidential Records

• Medical and mental health histories and personal records on client or patient treatment in medical facilities
• Information on human immunodeficiency virus (HIV) or acquired immune deficiency syndrome (AIDS) conditions
• Adoption records, child protection services files
• Correctional files
• Credit or loan histories, tax returns
• Information that, if disclosed, would result in economic or personal hardship to the subject party
• Information of a personal nature reported in confidence to an agency and not relevant to the ordinary work of such agency
• Lists of names and addresses (including public employees) that could be used for commercial or fund-raising purposes
• Employment records or personal references of applicants for employment
• Test results (employment and educational)

Personal information may not be regarded as confidential information when identifying details are deleted or when the person to whom the record pertains consents in writing to the disclosure.

Source: Theodore Pedeliski.

York exempt from disclosure the personnel files of police, firefighters, and paramedics to ensure that these employees are not the object of opportunistic civil suits.[3] Other states exempt material from the personnel files of public employees and teachers, as well as applicant files for public positions.[4]

Personnel files may be open to disclosure under a state's open records statutes, or disclosure may turn on a balancing of the employee's privacy interests against the public's "right to know," and where the balance is equal, the

Contents of Personnel File
(also see Exhibit 5-3)

Job description (see Chapter 1)

Application form and related documents, such as test results (see Chapter 2)

Letters with conditional job offer and final job offer, including pay rate (see Chapter 2)

CIS Form I-9 and copies of documents presented to affirm identity and work eligibility (see Chapter 2)

Requests for reasonable accommodation

Internal Revenue Service Form W-4

Employee benefits forms (see Chapter 6)

Form acknowledging receipt of employee handbook (see this chapter)

Regularly scheduled performance appraisals (see Chapter 3)

Participation in training and educational programs

Promotions, special recognitions, and awards

Written reprimands and other disciplinary decisions (see Chapter 7)

This list is based on a similar list published in Fred S. Steingold, *The Employer's Legal Handbook* (Berkeley, Calif.: Nolo Press, 1996), Chapter 2, page 3.

Tips for Success in Maintaining Personnel Records

☐ Adhere to federal, state, and local law in retaining personnel records.

☐ Maintain a complete personnel file for each employee, and keep the files in a secure place.

☐ Abide by state and local laws in allowing employees access to their personnel files.

☐ Keep medical files separate from regular personnel files, and restrict access to them to a need-to-know basis.

judgment is tilted in favor of disclosure. Schoolteachers are particularly vulnerable to disclosure of their personnel records in this context as there is a public interest in the revelation of any behaviors that would be harmful to children or of any lack of fitness to teach. Some states preserve confidentiality of records for the period of the administrative hearings and permit disclosure only once proceedings are complete.

The Americans with Disabilities Act (ADA) requires that information from physical or medical exams be kept in separate, locked files and that access to them be restricted. According to the ADA, an employee's need for reasonable accommodation can be disclosed to supervisors or the need for special attention in case of an emergency evacuation can be shared with security staff.

Right to Inspect Records (State Law)

Many states have laws that require employers to let employees access their own personnel records at least once a year. Again, an employer should contact its legal counsel regarding state and local laws. Some states may have on-line information on record keeping and open records.

Discrimination

Guiding Principles

- All employees and all candidates for employment must be treated fairly.
- The local government's legal counsel, the state equal employment agency, and the Equal Employment Opportunity Commission (EEOC) can provide guidance in case of EEO and affirmative action questions.
- EEO principles should be applied to all aspects of human resource management, including planning future jobs; determining pay; advertising job openings; and hiring, developing, promoting, and disciplining employees.

Exhibit 5-3   Records That Must Be Kept

Statute	Records to be kept	Time period
Title VII of the Civil Rights Act of 1964 (Title VII); Americans with Disabilities Act (ADA)	All personnel or employment records, including application forms; job advertisements; documentation concerning hiring, firing, promotion, demotion, transfer, or layoff decisions; payroll records; job descriptions; employment handbooks; documentation referencing training programs, employee evaluations, and requests for reasonable accommodation	For one year from when the record was made or the personnel action was taken
	Records relating to bias or discrimination, including but not limited to appraisals, job description, payroll, and other records relating to charging party and all similarly situated employees	Until the Equal Employment Opportunity Commission charge and suits are resolved
	EEO-1 Forms (for employers with 100 or more employees)	A copy of most recently filed report must be available
Fair Labor Standards Act (FLSA) (including the Equal Pay Act of 1963)	Payroll records with the following information: employee's full name, address including zip code, date of birth, sex, and occupation; the time of day and day of the week on which the employee's workweek begins; the regular hourly rate of pay for any workweek in which overtime compensation is due and an explanation for the basis of the pay rate as well as a notation of any payment excluded from the employee's regular rate, the hours worked each workday and the total hours worked each workweek; the total daily or weekly straight time earnings; the total premium pay for overtime hours; the total additions to or deductions from wages paid each pay period; and the date of payment and pay period covered by payment	For three years
	Collective and individual employment contracts	
	Records of sales or business	
	For administrating executive or professional employees, documents regarding the basis on which wages are paid	
	Employees' time sheets or time cards	
	Wage rate tables used to calculate wages, salaries, or overtime	
	Records of deductions or additions to the individual's pay (and any records used to determine the deductions or additions)	
	Order, shipping, and billing records, including customer orders and invoices, shipping records, and delivery records that the employer makes or retains in the normal course of business	

Statute	Records to be kept	Time period
	Certificates of age for employees who are minors	
Age Discrimination in Employment Act of 1967 (ADEA)	Payroll records with each individual employee's name, address, date of birth, occupation, rate of pay, and compensation weekly computation	For three years
	Employee benefit plans	For one year after the termination of plan
	All employment and personnel records that relate to promotion, demotion, layoff, job applications, résumés, recall or discharge; job orders submitted to either a labor organization or employment agency for the recruitment of personnel; test papers of employer-administered aptitude test and physical examination test results; and advertisements	For one year
	Application forms for positions known to be of a temporary nature	For 90 days
Family and Medical Leave Act of 1993 (FMLA)	Same records as FLSA	For three years
	In addition, employers must maintain all documentation related to FMLA leave, including but not limited to dates and hours of FMLA leave taken, employee handbook provisions outlining employer policies and referencing leave benefits, copies of employee's notices of leave to employer, and records of disputes with employees over FMLA benefits	For three years
State Occupational Safety and Health Administration (OSHA) laws	Employers may be required to maintain medical records and exposure information on each employee. Check your state's OSHA law for exact requirements.	Varies for each state
Immigration Reform and Control Act	U.S. Citizenship and Immigration Services (CIS) Form I-9 and Employment Eligibility Verification Form	For three years from hiring or one year after employee's termination
Employee Retirement Income Security Act (ERISA)	Records regarding employee's health and/or welfare benefit plan, including but not limited to • Benefit plans • Summary plan descriptions • Employee notices	For six years
Department of Labor requirements	Records reflecting the benefits that are, or may become, due to any employee, and the name and address of each such employee	As long as any possibility exists that they might be relevant to a determination of benefits entitlement

Many laws regulate discrimination by local government employers. To help public administrators spot problems before they spiral into lawsuits, this section identifies and briefly explains the major discrimination laws and describes how the EEOC enforces many of them. When municipal employers suspect a problem, they should contact legal counsel. The EEOC provides useful information online, accessible through its home page at http://www.eeoc.gov.

Major Discrimination Laws

The chart in Exhibit 5-4 on pages 120 and 121 gives a condensed summary of some of the major laws governing discrimination by employers.

Title VII of the Civil Rights Act of 1964 (42 U.S.C. § 2000e, *et seq.*).

Employers (but not individual supervisors or managers) may be sued under Title VII if they (1) are engaged in an industry affecting commerce, and (2) have 15 or more employees for each working day in 20 or more calendar weeks in the current or preceding calendar year. In 1972, Title VII was amended to include state and local governments, agencies, and political subdivisions.[5] Title VII protects both employees and applicants.

What It Prohibits. This statute, including its amendments, prohibits discrimination in employment on the basis of race, color, religion, sex (including pregnancy), and national origin. It also prohibits sexual harassment and harassment based on the other categories protected by Title VII, which is explained in detail in the next section of this chapter (see page 126). Title VII's nondiscrimination provision applies to all aspects of the employment relationship, including recruitment, hiring, compensation, promotion, discipline, and discharge.

Employees may bring discrimination suits under Title VII for several reasons:

- *Disparate treatment.* Often employees sue because they feel they have been treated differently from other employees who are not in their protected class.
- *Disparate impact.* Employees may sue because they believe that a test or employment policy unfairly excludes their protected class.
- *Harassment or hostile work environment.* Employees may sue because they feel that they have been harassed because of their protected class or that their work environment is abusive toward their protected class.
- *Reasonable accommodation.* Employees may sue because they feel that their religious needs are not being accommodated.

How It Is Enforced. Employees who feel that they have been discriminated against must file a charge with either their local EEOC office or a local or state discrimination agency that the EEOC has certified. (See page 124 for an explanation of what happens when an EEOC charge is filed.) Employers who have violated the employment provisions of Title VII may be required to hire or reinstate their employees with or without back pay. In 1991, Congress enacted the Civil Rights Act of 1991 (42 U.S.C. § 1981a), which provides that employers who violate Title VII may also be required to pay up to $300,000 in compensatory damages, such as damages for pain and suffering, and punitive damages. Political subdivisions cannot be required to pay punitive damages but can be required to pay compensatory damages.

Civil Rights Act of 1871 (42 U.S.C. § 1983).

This act covers local governments and individual public officials who are acting in their official capacities.[6] Government officials may be immune from liability if they are carrying out an official legislative or judicial function, such as enacting an ordinance. However, in most employment situations, public managers are immune from liability only if "their conduct does not violate clearly established statutory or constitutional rights of which a reasonable person would have known."[7] The jurisdiction itself is not immune from suits by its employees.[8]

What It Prohibits. Section 1983 prohibits "state actors" from depriving a person of rights, privileges, and immunities secured by the Constitution or laws of the United States. Claims under Section 1983 in the public employment context usually involve alleged violations of the equal protection, free speech, and due process clauses of the Constitution. In the discrimination context, employees generally claim that they have not been treated equally or have been discriminated against on the basis of race, color, sex, religion, national origin, age, disability, or some other distinction.

How It Is Enforced. Employees often bring Section 1983 suits instead of Title VII suits because they do not have to follow any of the administrative procedures required to bring suit under Title VII. They may file directly with either a federal or state court. The relief available to employees under Section 1983 is now similar to the relief available under Title VII. Employers may be ordered to reinstate or hire an employee; they may also be required to pay back wages, emotional damages, and attorneys' fees. While local officials may be required to pay punitive damages,[9] the jurisdiction itself cannot be required to pay punitive damages.[10] However, unlike Title VII, compensatory and punitive damages are not capped at $300,000.

Civil Rights Act of 1866 (42 U.S.C. § 1981).

This act covers local government employers who have an employment contract with an employee. Section 1981 provides that "all persons . . . shall have the same right to make and enforce contracts . . . as . . . white citizens." The Civil Rights Act of 1991 defines "make and enforce contracts" in Section 1981 to include the "making, performance, modification, and termination of contracts, and the enjoyment of all benefits, privileges, terms, and conditions of the contractual relationship." There is no minimum number of employees. Both local government entities and officials may be sued under this act, either directly or indirectly through Section 1983 described above.[11]

What It Prohibits. Courts have found that Section 1981 prohibits discrimination based on race, color, and ethnic characteristics.

How It Is Enforced. Employees often bring Section 1981 suits instead of Title VII suits because they do not have to follow any of the administrative procedures required to bring suit under Title VII. They may file directly with either a federal or state court. The relief available to employees under Section 1981 is now similar to the relief available under Title VII. Employers may be ordered to reinstate or hire an employee; they may also be required to pay back wages, emotional damages, and attorneys' fees. While local officials may be required to pay punitive damages,[12] the jurisdiction itself cannot be required to pay punitive damages.[13] Like suits under Section 1983 above, there is no cap on compensatory and punitive damages.

Title I of the Americans with Disabilities Act of 1990 (42 U.S.C. § 12101, *et seq.*).

Employers generally (but not individual supervisors or managers) are covered if they (1) engage in an industry affecting commerce, and (2) have 15 or more employees for each working day in 20 or more calendar weeks in the current or preceding calendar year (42 U.S.C. §§ 2000e(a), 12111[5]). Most local governmental employers are covered by this act.[14]

What It Prohibits. Title I of the ADA prohibits employment discrimination against a qualified individual with a disability because of the disability. A person with a "disability" is an individual who (1) has a physical or mental impairment that substantially limits one or more major life activities, (2) has a record of such an impairment, or (3) is regarded as

Exhibit 5-4   Laws Regarding Discrimination

Discrimination law	Who is covered?	What is prohibited?
Title VII of the Civil Rights Act of 1964 (42 U.S.C. § 2000e *et seq.*)	Employers (1) engaged in an industry affecting commerce with (2) 15 or more employees for each working day in 20 or more calendar weeks in the current or preceding calendar year. In 1972, Title VII was amended to include state and local governments, agencies, and political subdivisions.	Discrimination against employees with respect to their "compensation, terms, conditions or privileges of employment, because of [their] race, color, religion, sex or national origin" (42 U.S.C. § 2000e-2).
Civil Rights Act of 1871 (42 U.S.C. § 1983)	Persons acting "under the color of state law." Local governments are generally covered by this act as well. (There is no minimum number of employees.)	Deprivation of employees' constitutional and legal rights, privileges, and immunities because of their race, color, religion, sex, or national origin.
Civil Rights Act of 1866 (42 U.S.C. § 1981).	Local government employers who have an employment contract with an employee. (There is no minimum number of employees.)	Discrimination against employees in the "making, performance, modification, and termination of contracts, and the enjoyment of all benefits, privileges, terms, and conditions of the contractual relationship" because of their race, color, or ethnicity (42 U.S.C. § 1981b).
Title I of the Americans with Disabilities Act of 1990 (42 U.S.C. § 12101 *et seq.*)	Local government employers who are (1) engaged in an industry affecting commerce with (2) 15 or more employees for each working day in 20 or more calendar weeks in the current or preceding calendar year (42 U.S.C. § 12111[5]).	Discrimination against qualified individuals with a disability with respect to job application procedures, compensation, terms, conditions, and privileges of employment because of their disability.
Section 504 of The Rehabilitation Act of 1973 (29 U.S.C. § 794 *et seq.*)	Any department, agency, or instrumentality of a state or local government that receives or distributes federal financial assistance.	Discrimination against an otherwise qualified individual with a disability because of the disability.

Discrimination law	Who is covered?	What is prohibited?
Age Discrimination in Employment Act of 1967 (29 U.S.C. § 621 _et seq._)	Employers (1) engaged in an industry affecting commerce with (2) 20 or more employees for each working day in 20 or more calendar weeks in the current or preceding calendar year (29 U.S.C. § 630). Since 1991, local government employees generally have been protected by this act; however, law enforcement officers and firefighters are partially exempt.	Discriminating against employees "with respect to [their] compensation, terms, conditions, or privileges of employment" because of age.
The Equal Pay Act of 1963 (29 U.S.C. § 206)	Most public employees.	Prohibits employers from paying their employees different wages on the basis of gender.
Family and Medical Leave Act of 1993 (29 U.S.C. § 2601 _et seq._)	State and local governments are covered by this act regardless of the number of employees (29 C.F.R. 825.108). An employee is covered if the employee (1) has worked for 12 months for the employer, (2) has worked at least 1,250 hours during the previous 12 months, and (3) works at a work site where the public agency employs 50 or more employees within 75 miles (29 U.S.C. § 2611[2]).	Under the FMLA, employees are entitled to leave time. It is unlawful for employers to (1) interfere with an employee's right to request or take leave or (2) discriminate against an employee for opposing actions that are illegal under this act (29 U.S.C. § 2815).
Uniform Services Employment and Reemployment Rights Act of 1994 (38 U.S.C. § 43) (USERRA)	All employers in the public and private sectors.	Prohibits discrimination against veterans and grants reemployment rights to those serving in the military.

having such an impairment. The ADA covers job application procedures; testing; hiring; advancement; discharge; compensation; job training; and other terms, conditions, and privileges of employment.

To enable "otherwise qualified" individuals with disabilities to perform the essential functions of the job, employers must also make "reasonable accommodations" for those individuals unless doing so would impose an "undue hardship" on the organization. Under the ADA, "undue hardship" requires a showing of significant difficulty or expense by the employer. Employers who are trying to accommodate an employee's disability can call the Job Accommodation Network at 800/526-7234 for reasonable suggestions.

How It Is Enforced. The ADA is enforced by the EEOC under the same administrative scheme as Title VII discussed above. The Title VII remedies are available to employees who sue under the ADA. In reasonable accommodation cases, however, an employer is not liable for emotional pain and suffering or punitive damages if it can show that it consulted with the employee and made a good-faith effort to provide reasonable accommodation.

Sections 504 and 503 of the Rehabilitation Act of 1973 (29 U.S.C. § 794 *et seq.*). Any department, agency, or instrumentality of a local government that receives or distributes federal financial assistance is covered by Section 504 of the Rehabilitation Act (29 U.S.C. § 794). Section 503 (29 U.S.C. § 793) applies to local government employers who enter into a contract in excess of $10,000 with the federal government to provide nonpersonal services such as construction.[15]

What It Prohibits. Section 504 prohibits recipients of federal funding from discriminating on the basis of non-job-related disabilities and requires employers to make reasonable accommodation for their employees. The requirements and cases under this law are very similar to those under the ADA. Section 503 also requires government contractors to take affirmative action to employ and advance qualified persons with disabilities.

How It Is Enforced. The Civil Rights Division of the Department of Justice coordinates enforcement of Section 504. Section 503 is enforced by the Department of Labor's Office of Federal Contract Compliance Programs.

Age Discrimination in Employment Act of 1967 (29 U.S.C. § 621, *et seq.*). According to the Age Discrimination in Employment Act (ADEA), employers are generally covered if they (1) are engaged in an industry affecting commerce, and (2) have 20 or more employees for each working day in 20 or more calendar weeks in the current or preceding calendar year (29 U.S.C. § 630). In 1991, Congress extended the ADEA to cover local and state government employers. More recently, in 2000, the U. S. Supreme Court held that Congress overstepped its authority and found that the ADEA did not validly abrogate the states' Eleventh Amendment immunity from suit. Therefore, the ADEA does not apply to state governmental employers.[16] Local governmental employers are still generally covered by the ADEA, however, with only a few governmental employers who are considered "arms of the state" exempt from the ADEA.[17] Individual governmental employers should contact their local counsel to determine whether they are covered by the ADEA and other federal discrimination laws. As a practical matter, even if a governmental employer is exempt from the ADEA, it will still be subject to a similar state law.

Police officers and firefighters are partially exempt from the requirements of the ADEA. Although this exemption expired on December 31, 1993,[18] Congress restored it on September 30, 1996. Under the restored exemption, a governmental employer does not violate the ADEA when discharging its firefighters or police officers on the basis of age if the following three criteria are met:

- The employer has complied with EEOC regulations allowing police officers and firefighters to take mental and physical fitness tests. As of the printing of this book, however, these regulations have yet to be enacted and, therefore, under the statute, do not currently apply.

- The employee has either (1) attained the age of retirement under a state or local law in effect on March 3, 1983; or (2) attained the age of retirement specified in a state or local law enacted after September 30, 1996, that provides for retirement at age 55 or after.

- The retirement is taken "pursuant to a bona fide . . . retirement plan that is not a subterfuge to evade the purposes of [the ADEA]."

What It Prohibits. The ADEA protects individuals aged 40 and over from discrimination based on age. Like Title VII, the ADEA's protection extends to hiring, discharge, promotions, compensation, benefits, and all other conditions or privileges of employment.

Under the 1990 amendments to the ADEA, known as the Older Workers' Benefit and Protection Act (26 U.S.C. § 626), employees cannot waive their ADEA claims unless employers strictly comply with the following requirements:

- The employee must receive something of value in addition to his or her normal salary and benefits.

- The release must be in plain English and specifically mention the ADEA.

- The employee must be notified in writing of his or her right to consult an attorney.

- The employee must be given at least 21 days to consider the offer.

- The agreement must provide the employee with the right to revoke the agreement for up to seven days after signing the agree-

ment. Employers should not pay any release amount until after the seven-day waiting period.

- When a severance agreement or release is made in connection with an exit incentive plan offered to a group of employees, the employer must meet more imposing requirements. The employer must provide written notice of (a) the plan's eligibility factors, (b) the groups of employees eligible for the plan, (c) the job titles and ages of employees eligible for the program, (d) the ages of all employees in those same job classifications or organizational units who are not eligible, and (e) any time limits for accepting. After providing this notice, the employer must give the employees 45 days to consider the offer (as opposed to 21 days for individual employees).

How It Is Enforced. The ADEA is enforced by the EEOC but under a slightly different administrative scheme than Title VII. Employees must file with the EEOC, but may then file suit directly with a court within 60 days. Employers may be ordered to reinstate or hire employees; they may also be required to pay back and front wages and attorneys' fees. Although punitive damages are not available, employers may have to pay double damages if a violation was "willful."

The Equal Pay Act of 1963 (29 U.S.C. § 206). The Equal Pay Act stipulates no minimum number of employees and applies to most public employees.[19] Local government employees are exempt if they (1) are not subject to civil service laws, and (2) hold an elected office or are appointed by an elected official to be a member of the official's personal staff or to make policy.[20]

What It Prohibits. The Equal Pay Act prohibits employers from paying their employees different wages on the basis of gender. "Wages" refers to any form of compensation, including benefits and retirement plans.

How It Is Enforced. The EEOC is in charge of enforcing the Equal Pay Act, and employees may file with the EEOC. Employees may also file suit directly with a court as long as they bring their claims within two years. Employees may recover back pay, double damages, and attorneys' fees.

The Family and Medical Leave Act of 1993 (29 U.S.C. § 2601 *et seq.*). Both state and local governments are covered by this act.[21]

What It Prohibits. Under the Family and Medical Leave Act (FMLA), employees are entitled to leave time. It is unlawful for employers to (1) interfere with an employee's right to request or take leave, or (2) discriminate against an employee for opposing actions that are illegal under this act (29 U.S.C. §2815).

How It Is Enforced. The FMLA is enforced by the Wage and Hour Division of the Department of Labor. Employees may file complaints with the department and may also sue in either state or federal court. Employees may be reinstated or promoted and receive back pay, attorneys' fees, and double damages.

Uniform Services Employment and Reemployment Rights Act of 1994 (38 U.S.C. § 4311) (USERRA)

What It Prohibits. USERRA is intended to minimize the disadvantages to an individual that occur when that person needs to be absent from his or her civilian employment to serve in this country's uniformed services. USERRA defines the cumulative length of time that an individual may be absent from work for uniformed services duty and retain reemployment rights.

USERRA covers employees who serve in or have served in the uniformed services. The law seeks to ensure that those who serve their country can retain their civilian employment and benefits, and can seek employment free from discrimination because of their service. The discrimination provisions of USERRA address problems regarding initial employment, reemployment, retention in employment, promotion, or any other benefit of employment. USERRA provides enhanced protection for disabled veterans, requiring employers to make reasonable efforts to accommodate the disability.

How It Is Enforced. USERRA is administered by the U.S. Department of Labor, through the Veterans' Employment and Training Service (VETS). VETS provides assistance to those persons experiencing problems with their civilian employment that are related to their military service and provides information about the act to employers.

State and Local Discrimination Acts. Most states and many local governments have laws prohibiting discrimination that are very similar to the federal acts outlined above. In addition, some state and local governments have laws prohibiting discrimination on the basis of sexual orientation. These jurisdictions usually have a special agency that enforces these rights and coordinates efforts with the EEOC. Public managers should contact legal counsel to find out about their state and local laws.

Retaliation Claims. Most discrimination laws also contain provisions prohibiting employers from retaliating against employees who complain about discrimination or bring actions to enforce their rights.

EEOC Charges

Who Files. Individual employees may file a charge of discrimination with the EEOC under Title VII, the ADA, the ADEA, or the Equal Pay Act. In some cases, associations such as unions may also file discrimination charges against an employer. Additionally, the EEOC may file its own charges against an employer.

The Charge and Notice. Generally, a charge contains the name of the employee, the name of the employer, and a statement of the facts constituting the alleged discrimination. The EEOC usually accepts employee statements that are vague and allows employees to amend their charges if the new charges are related to or grow out of the original charge. Once a charge is filed, the EEOC sends a copy to the employer.

Timing. Charges must generally be filed with the EEOC within 180 days after the alleged discrimination occurred. In some cases, the deadline is "tolled" or stopped. For example, if an employer maintains a policy that is discriminatory or that repeatedly subjects an employee to the same type of harassment, the violation is continuous and an employee may file within 180 days of the last violation. Employees may also file after 180 days if they did not know that an employer action, such as termination, was taken for discriminatory reasons. If an employee files in a state that has an authorized state discrimination agency, the employee has 300 days from when the discrimination occurred to file with the EEOC. The EEOC has various arrangements with state agencies, many of which allow an employee to file with both agencies by simply filing with one. However, only one agency will investigate at a time.

Document Requests and the Employer Position Statement. The EEOC generally sends employers a list of the documents it seeks. Employers should also file a letter with the assigned EEOC investigator stating their position on the charge (known as a position statement). If an employer does not provide the requested documents, the EEOC has the authority to issue subpoenas that will be enforced by the federal courts provided the charge is valid, the description of the relevant documents is clear, and the subpoena is issued for a legitimate purpose.[22]

Fact-Finding Conferences. The EEOC may require a fact-finding conference, at which the investigator questions both the employee and an employer representative. The conference, usually held at the EEOC field office, is used to define the issues, resolve issues that can be resolved, and determine whether settlement may be possible.

Interviews and On-Site Investigations. The EEOC also has the power to interview witnesses and conduct on-site investigations of an employer's premises and documents. The employer has the right to have an attorney present during interviews of management employees only. The employer also has the right to have a company representative accompany an investigator who comes on site.

EEOC Determinations/Right to Sue. Employees may withdraw their charge only if the EEOC consents to the withdrawal. However, should the EEOC determine that a charge was not filed in time or that, based on the evidence before it, it cannot conclude that discrimination occurred, it must dismiss the charge. The EEOC may also dismiss the charge if the employee is uncooperative, cannot be found, or refuses a settlement offer made by the employer that provides full relief for the discrimination.

After the EEOC concludes its investigation, it issues a letter of determination to the employee and employer. The letter states whether, based on the information obtained in the investigation, the EEOC has concluded that discrimination occurred. The letter also informs the employee that he or she has 90 days to sue in federal court. The EEOC is supposed to issue its determination within 120 days after the charge is filed, but this requirement is not mandatory and is seldom observed. If an investigation is ongoing, an employee may request, in writing, a right-to-sue letter at any time after 180 days from the date the charge is filed. Employees have the right to sue regardless of the EEOC's finding.

Dispute Resolution Duties. If the EEOC finds reasonable cause to believe that discrimination has occurred, it must make an attempt

Tips for Avoiding Discrimination Suits

❑ Review hiring practices to ensure that the jurisdiction is reaching out to a diverse applicant pool.

❑ Ensure that employees have the opportunity to discuss and seek redress of grievances before going to an outside agency (such as the EEOC).

❑ Conduct workplace training on racial sensitivity and sexual harassment.

for 30 days to have the parties reach a conciliation agreement. Employees are not required to sign a conciliation agreement, however, and may bring an individual suit after receiving the right-to-sue letter.[23]

On July 17, 1995, the EEOC issued an alternative dispute resolution policy indicating that it intended to begin using alternative dispute resolution procedures such as mediation. The commission has now instituted mediation programs in all of its district offices. The EEOC mediation program encourages parties to resolve their disputes voluntarily through the use of a neutral mediator and is not binding unless the parties reach a settlement agreement.

Suits. Both the EEOC and individuals have the power to bring suit or intervene in a suit in a federal court on discrimination charges. Employers may be required to hire or reinstate their employees with or without back pay. Under the Civil Rights Act of 1991 (42 U.S.C. § 1981a), governmental employers may also be required to pay up to $300,000 in compensatory damages for pain and suffering. In reasonable accommodation cases under the ADA, compensatory damages are not awarded if the employer shows that it has consulted with the disabled person who asked for an accommodation and made a good-faith effort to provide a reasonable accommodation. See pages 118–124

for discussion on the relief available under each law enforced by the EEOC.

Sexual Harassment

Guiding Principles

• Courts allow public employers significant leeway in regulating employees' conduct because these employers have a significant interest in providing government services effectively.

• Employees who feel that their concerns have been addressed may be less likely to sue.

• Employers must conduct sexual harassment investigations fairly and discreetly to avoid suits by wrongly accused employees.

Challenges

• Drawing a line between acceptable office romance and unacceptable sexual harassment.

• Stopping clumsy or boorish behavior before it becomes sexual harassment.

• Protecting the privacy rights of the alleged victim and the alleged perpetrator while gathering evidence concerning the charges.

Title VII of the Civil Rights Act of 1964 (42 U.S.C. § 2000e *et seq.*), and many state and local laws prohibit both sexual discrimination and sexual harassment. This section is designed to help local government employers identify and deal with sexual harassment.

The Law

Title VII explicitly prohibits sexual discrimination. Sexual discrimination occurs when an employer treats an employee, male or female, differently because of the employee's gender. Examples of sexual discrimination include paying a woman a lower salary than a man who performs the same job and has the same experience, refusing to promote women, or providing lower benefits for male employees.

Courts have broadened Title VII by finding that sexual harassment is a form of sex discrimination. Sexual harassment involves unwelcome

Exhibit 5-5　What Is Sexual Harassment?

Sexual discrimination = different or unfair treatment of an employee because of his or her sex

Examples:　limits on an employee's job opportunities or different levels of pay, bonuses, or benefits

Sexual harassment = unwelcome sexual advances, requests for sexual favors, or other contact that is sexual

There are two types of sexual harassment:

* Quid pro quo—when submission to or rejection of sexual harassment is used for employment decisions

  Examples:　demotion, discipline, or discharge for refusing to have sex

* Hostile work environment—sexual harassment that unreasonably interferes with an employee's work or creates an intimidating, hostile, or offensive workplace

  Examples:　sexual comments, jokes, repeated sexual advances, pornographic displays

---

sexual advances, requests for sexual favors, or other contacts of a sexual nature. The illustration in Exhibit 5-5 demonstrates the different types of behavior that are prohibited. Courts have ruled that Title VII covers sexual harassment claims not only between persons of the opposite sex but also between people of the same sex, whether heterosexual or homosexual.

There are two types of sexual harassment: quid pro quo and hostile work environment. Quid pro quo harassment is usually easy to spot. It involves sex in exchange for hiring, promotion, job security, or other employment benefits or detriments.

Hostile work environment harassment is more subtle. It involves sexual advances, requests for sexual favors, or other verbal

or sexual conduct that interferes with an employee's work or creates an intimidating, hostile, or offensive workplace.

Under two Supreme Court cases decided in 1998,[24] employers are strictly liable for either type of sexual harassment (quid pro quo or hostile environment) committed by their supervisors if the employee suffers a tangible job detriment. If the employee has not suffered a tangible job detriment, an employer may be able to defend itself successfully against a sexual harassment claim if it can show that (1) it exercised reasonable care to prevent and correct promptly any sexually harassing behavior, and (2) the plaintiff employee unreasonably failed to take preventive opportunities provided by the employer.[25] To avoid liability, it is essential that employers take all necessary steps to prevent sexual harassment (see below). Further, if an employee does claim sexual harassment, employers must promptly investigate and take action as appropriate.

Many states and local jurisdictions also have laws that prohibit sexual harassment. Public administrators should ask their legal counsel about the laws in their state. Often employees sue under a state or local law in order to receive large monetary awards because many state discrimination laws do not have the cap on punitive damages contained in Title VII. Employees may also sue under a state or local law in order to sue the individual accused of harassment because individual employees are not liable under Title VII.

Red Flags

* Employees today are suing for discrimination and receiving multimillion-dollar awards.
* Employees who are wrongly disciplined for harassment may sue for discrimination or defamation.

Solutions and Approaches

To minimize liability for sexual harassment, employers must take steps before harassment occurs, investigate employee complaints of harassment, and take appropriate measures to correct the problem. Prompt investigation and disciplinary action aids in the defense of a lawsuit involving a hostile work environment claim. In addition, employees who feel that their concerns have been addressed may be less likely to sue. Employers must conduct their investigations fairly and discreetly to avoid suits by a wrongly accused employee.

To protect themselves against potential sexual harassment claims, employers may want to adopt a policy prohibiting relationships between supervisors and subordinates. There are some concerns about an employee's right of privacy and freedom of association, and some state statutes prohibit employers from regulating off-hours activities, which protects all legal recreational activities. In general, however, courts allow public employers significant leeway in regulating an employee's conduct because these employers have a significant interest in providing government services effectively, and employers may adopt a clear policy prohibiting romance while in the workplace.[26]

Several steps can be taken before harassment occurs.

Carefully Recruit Employees.
Employees should be asked in their interviews why they left their prior jobs. They should also be asked if they have ever been accused of sexual harassment or of violating an employment discrimination law. Employers should check potential employees' references.

Adopt a Written Policy against Sexual Harassment.
This policy should give examples of sexual harassment. It should then clearly state that the employer does not tolerate sexual harassment and will discipline offenders up to and including discharge. The policy should require employees to report harassment imme-diately and should also set forth a clear procedure for doing so. (See Exhibit 5-1 for a sample harassment policy).

Set Up a Procedure for Addressing Sexual Harassment.
The employer should designate the person or persons to whom employees should bring their harassment concerns. There should also be an alternate person for employees to contact in case the person doing the harassing is precisely the person to whom the employee has been instructed to report such behavior. Large employers often provide a phone number where employees may complain and get advice anonymously.

Train Managers, Supervisory Employees, and Human Resource Employees.
An employer should conduct a sexual harassment awareness seminar for its supervisory employees, in which the supervisors are given problems and examples and asked to identify sexual harassment. Courts have dismissed some sexual harassment claims partly because the employer had a good prevention program.

Train All Employees.
All employees should be taught how to recognize sexual harassment. They should be told that sexual harassment will not be tolerated. They should also be told what to do if sexual harassment occurs. Every employee should be given a copy of the sexual harassment policy and required to sign a form acknowledging its receipt.

Unfortunately, employers and employees can also be falsely accused of sexual harassment. A worker threatened with an adverse personnel decision—demotion or firing—may try to deflect the action by claiming sexual harassment. Managers can take a few steps to avoid the appearance of wrongdoing:

- Keep the door open when meeting with a problem employee.
- If confidentiality and a closed door are required, a staff member (e.g., a secretary) should be present at the meeting and should take notes.

Tips for Avoiding Sexual Harassment Problems

❒ Make sure that all employees, both management and rank and file, understand that sexual harassment is sex discrimination and prohibited under Title VII of the Civil Rights Act.

❒ Develop a sexual harassment policy, including steps that alleged victims should take to deal with the problem.

❒ Post the sexual harassment policy on bulletin boards devoted to personnel issues.

❒ Train all employees to recognize and avoid the two types of sexual harassment—quid pro quo and hostile work environment.

For information on dealing with sexual harassment charges, see Chapter 8.

Other Types of Prohibited Harassment

Courts have found that employees can also bring suits for harassment based on other types of prohibited criteria, including race, color, national origin, religion, age, and disability. Therefore, employers must broaden their sexual harassment policies to prohibit other types of illegal harassment, and the discussion above regarding preventing, investigating, and promptly correcting sexual harassment applies with equal force to these other types of harassment. (See Exhibit 5-1 for a sample harassment policy.)

Family and Medical Leave Act

Guiding Principles

• Employers should notify the employee that requested leave qualifies as FMLA leave and to designate it as such.

• Employers may require that the employee produce a medical certification for a serious health condition.

The FMLA requires employers to provide employees in certain circumstances with 12 weeks of unpaid leave with benefits. Employers must pay special attention to the notice requirements under the FMLA.

Which Employers, Employees, and Reasons for Leaves Are Covered?

The FMLA generally covers state and local government employers regardless of the number of employees. (See endnote 21.) However, an individual employee is only covered if he or she (1) has worked for the employer for 12 months, (2) has at least 1,250 hours of service within the previous 12 months, and (3) works at a work site where the public agency employs 50 or more employees within 75 miles of that work site.

To be eligible for FMLA leave, employees must need the leave

• To care for a newborn, newly adopted child, or new foster child

• To care for a spouse, child, or parent who has a serious health condition

• Because a serious health condition makes the employee unable to perform the functions of his or her position. A "serious health condition" is defined as an "illness, injury, impairment, or physical or mental condition that involves: (a) inpatient care in a hospital, hospice, or residential medical care facility; or (b) continuing treatment by a health care provider" (29 U.S.C. § 2611 [11]). Employers may require that the employee produce a medical certification of the serious health condition. The Department of Labor has published a form to be used for medical certification (see Exhibit 5-6a).

Exhibit 5-6a   Department of Labor Form for Certification of Health Care Provider

Certification of Health Care Provider
(Family and Medical Leave Act of 1993)

1.   Employee's Name: _____

2.   Patient's Name (if different from employee): _____

3.   The attached sheet describes what is meant by a **"serious health condition"** under the Family and Medical Leave Act. Does the patient's condition[1] qualify under any of the categories described? If so, please check the applicable category.

   (1)_____   (2)_____   (3)_____   (4)_____   (5)_____   (6)_____, or   None of the above_____

4.   Describe the **medical facts** which support your certification, including a brief statement as to how the medical facts meet the criteria of one of these categories: _____

5.a.   State the approximate **date** the condition commenced, and the probable **duration** of the condition (and also the probable duration of the patient's present **incapacity**[2] if different): _____

   b.   Will it be necessary for the employee to take work only **intermittently or to work on a less than full schedule** as a result of the condition (including for treatment described in Item 6 below)? _____

If yes, give the probable duration: _____

   c.   If the condition is a **chronic condition** (condition #4) or **pregnancy**, state whether the patient is presently incapacitated[2] and the likely duration and frequency of **episodes of incapacity**:[2] _____

6.a.   If additional **treatments** will be required for the condition, provide an estimate of the probable number of such treatments: _____

If the patient will be absent from work or other daily activities because of **treatment** on an **intermittent** or **part-time** basis, also provide an estimate of the probable number of and interval between such treatments, actual or estimated dates of treatment if known, and period required for recovery if any: _____

   b.   If any of these treatments will be provided by **another provider of health services** (e.g., physical therapist), please state the nature of the treatments: _____

   c.   **If a regimen of continuing treatment** by the patient is required under your supervision, provide a general description of such regimen (e.g., prescription drugs, physical therapy requiring special equipment): _____

7.a.   If medical leave is required for the employee's **absence from work** because of the **employee's own condition** (including absences due to pregnancy or a chronic condition), is the employee **unable to perform** work of any kind? _____

   b.   If able to perform some work, is the employee **unable to perform any one or more of the essential functions of the employee's job** (the employee or the employer should supply you with information about the essential job functions)? _____ If yes, please list the essential functions the employee is unable to perform: _____

   c.   If neither a. nor b. applies, is it necessary for the employee to be **absent from work for treatment?** _____

8.a.   If leave is required to **care for a family member** of the employee with a serious health condition, **does the patient require assistance** for basic medical or personal needs or safety, or for transportation? _____

   b.   If no, would the employee's presence to provide **psychological comfort** be beneficial to the patient or assist in the patient's recovery? _____

   c.   If the patient will need care only **intermittently** or on a part-time basis, please indicate the probable **duration** of this need: _____

_____   _____
(Signature of Health Care Provider)   (Type of Practice)

_____   _____
(Address)   (Telephone number)

To be completed by the employee needing family leave to care for a family member:
State the care you will provide and an estimate of the period during which care will be provided, including a schedule if leave is to be taken intermittently or if it will be necessary for you to work less than a full schedule:

_____   _____
(Employee Signature)   (Date)

A "**Serious Health Condition**" means an illness, injury, impairment, or physical or mental condition that involves one of the following:

1.   Hospital Care

Inpatient care (i.e., an overnight stay) in a hospital, hospice, or residential medical care facility, including any period of incapacity[2] or subsequent treatment in connection with or consequent to such inpatient care.

2.   Absence Plus Treatment

(a) A period of incapacity[2] of **more than three consecutive calendar days** (including any subsequent treatment or period of incapacity[2] relating to the same condition), that also involves:

(1) **Treatment[3] two or more times** by a health care provider, by a nurse or physician's assistant under direct supervision of a health care provider, or by a provider of health care services (e.g., physical therapist) under orders of, or on referral by, a health care provider; *or*

(2) **Treatment** by a health care provider on **at least one occasion** which results in a **regimen of continuing treatment[4]** under the supervision of the health care provider.

3.   Pregnancy

Any period of incapacity due to **pregnancy,** or for **prenatal care.**

4.   Chronic Conditions Requiring Treatments

A **chronic condition** which:

(1) Requires **periodic visits** for treatment by a health care provider, or by a nurse or physician's assistant under direct supervision of a health care provider;

(2) Continues over an **extended period of time** (including recurring episodes of a single underlying condition); and

(3) May cause **episodic** rather than a continuing period of incapacity[2] (e.g., asthma, diabetes, epilepsy, etc.).

5.   Permanent/Long-term Conditions Requiring Supervision

A period of **incapacity[2]** which is **permanent or long-term** due to a condition for which treatment may not be effective. The employee or family member must be **under the continuing supervision of, but need not be receiving active treatment by, a health care provider.** Examples include Alzheimer's, a severe stroke, or the terminal stages of a disease.

6.   Multiple Treatments (Non-Chronic Conditions)

Any period of absence to receive **multiple treatments** (including any period of recovery therefrom) by a health care provider or by a provider of health care services under orders of, or on referral by, a health care provider, either for **restorative surgery** after an accident or other injury, **or for a condition that would likely result in a period of incapacity[2] of more than three consecutive calendar days in the absence of medical intervention or treatment,** such as cancer (chemotherapy, radiation, etc.), severe arthritis (physical therapy), kidney disease (dialysis).

---

[1] Here and elsewhere on this form, the information sought relates only to the condition for which the employee is taking FMLA leave.

[2] "Incapacity," for purposes of FMLA, is defined to mean inability to work, attend school or perform other regular daily activities due to the serious health condition, treatment therefor, or recovery therefrom.

[3] Treatment includes examinations to determine if a serious health condition exists and evaluations of the condition. Treatment does not include routine physical examinations, eye examinations, or dental examinations.

[4] A regimen of continuing treatment includes, for example, a course of prescription medication (e.g., an antibiotic) or therapy requiring special equipment to resolve or alleviate the health condition. A regimen of treatment does not include the taking of over-the-counter medications such as aspirin, antihistamines, or salves; or best-rest, drinking fluids, exercise, and other similar activities that can be initiated without a visit to a health care provider.

Checklist of Basic Employer Requirements

- Employers must provide eligible employees with up to 12 weeks of unpaid leave during a 12-month period.

- Employers must provide the notices described below.

- Employers must continue to provide health benefits that the employee would normally be entitled to during the leave.

- Unless the employee is a "key employee"—one who is paid on a salary basis and is among the highest-paid 10 percent of employees within 75 miles of the work site—the employer must return the employee either to his or her previous position or to "an equivalent position" that has equivalent pay, benefits, and other terms of employment. Key employees may be denied a position if "denial is necessary to prevent substantial and grievous economic injury to the operations of the employer" (29 U.S.C. § 2614b) (see Exhibit 5-6b).

Designation of FMLA Leave

Employees must give 30 days prior notice when leave is foreseeable. When leave is not foreseeable, employees must generally notify the employer within two business days or as soon as practicable. Employees do not have to say they want FMLA leave. They must merely state that they need the leave to take care of a new child or a family member with a serious health condition or because they have a serious health condition themselves.

Under the federal Department of Labor regulations, it is the employer's duty to designate the leave as FMLA qualifying. The employer may generally do so only after it has notified the employee that the absence will be FMLA leave and must generally notify an employee that the absence is FMLA leave within two days after the employer discovers that the leave qualifies as FMLA leave. The Department of Labor regulations put the bur-

den on the employer to designate leave as FMLA qualifying and penalize employers who fail to so designate leave by requiring the employer to grant up to an additional 12 weeks of leave (29 C.F.R. § 825.700(a). For example, under the Department of Labor regulations, if an employee goes out on leave for surgery and receives 12 weeks of leave, but the employer does not tell the employee that the leave is FMLA leave until the 13th week, the employer must grant an additional 12 weeks of leave. In 2002, the United States Supreme Court struck down this regulation and found that the penalty to employers was generally too harsh and granted more leave than required by the FMLA.[27] However, the Supreme Court left open the possibility that employees could be entitled to more than 12 weeks of leave when an employer fails to designate leave as FMLA qualified if the employee proves that his or her FMLA rights were impaired and that he or she suffered prejudice because of the failure. Therefore, to avoid lawsuits, discord, and confusion, it is strongly recommended that employers continue to designate in writing whether an employee's leave qualifies as FMLA leave as soon as possible.

Notices Required

- The employer must post in the workplace an FMLA notice approved by the Department of Labor (see Exhibit 5-6c on page 134).

- The employer must also have an FMLA policy in the employee handbook if it has a handbook. The policy should stipulate any medical certification requirement that the employer intends to enforce.

- When an employee requests leave or an employer designates leave as FMLA leave, the employer must give the employee written notice of the employee's rights and obligations (see Exhibit 5-6d on pages 136 and 137). If the employer does not have a handbook policy, it must also give the

Exhibit 5-6b   FMLA Notices for Key Employees

Notification of "Key Employee" Status

This will serve as notice that you, _____, are considered a "key employee" of the Township. As one of the most highly compensated employees of the Township, it is anticipated that it may cause substantial and grievous economic injury to restore you to your prior position or an equivalent one at the conclusion of your FMLA leave period. If, during the period of your FMLA leave, it becomes apparent that restoration would cause the Township substantial and grievous economic injury, we will notify you at that point and provide you with an opportunity to return to work immediately. If you choose to remain on leave, you may request reinstatement at the conclusion of your leave period, and the Township will restore you to your prior position or an equivalent one if no substantial and grievous economic injury would result. In the event that the Township cannot restore you to employment, you will have incurred no liability for the cost of your health care premiums during the period of leave.

Notification of Anticipated Substantial and Grievous Economic Injury

This will serve as official notice that the Township faces substantial and grievous economic injury if it were to reinstate you at the end of your Family and Medical Leave. Consequently, unless you return to work immediately, it may be necessary to deny you restoration to employment at the conclusion of your leave. If you elect to remain on leave, the Township will nevertheless consider if it is possible to reinstate you, at the conclusion of your leave period. However, if it is determined that to do so would cause substantial and grievous economic injury at that time, restoration to employment will be denied. If you choose to remain on leave and the Township is unable to reinstate you at the conclusion of your leave, you will not be obligated for the cost of the health care coverage which the Township will have maintained on your behalf.

employee a document summarizing the FMLA.

- The employer must notify the employee that the leave has been designated as FMLA leave. The notice can be verbal and must generally occur within two business days after the employer learns of the need for leave. The designation notice must be confirmed in writing by the next payday.

- The employer must notify the employee verbally whenever medical certification is required. The employer must also either (1) notify the employee in writing every time medical certification is required, or (2) provide notice of the medical certification requirements in both the employee handbook and the

employer response notice (see Exhibit 5-6e on page 138).

Workers' Compensation

Guiding Principles

- Every workers' compensation claim should be routinely investigated.
- Injured workers should be encouraged to come back to work as soon as they have recovered.
- Safety training programs prevent injuries.

Workers' compensation is a state program created by statute. Employers should check their particular state laws because workers' compensation laws vary from state to state. Workers' compensation acts are designed to compensate workers for injuries or death arising out of

Exhibit 5-6c   Department of Labor Notification of Rights under FMLA

Your Rights
Under The
Family and Medical Leave Act of 1993

FMLA requires covered employers to provide up to 12 weeks of unpaid, job-protected leave to "eligible" employees for certain family and medical reasons.

Employees are eligible if they have worked for a covered employer for at least one year, and for 1,250 hours over the previous 12 months, and if there are at least 50 employees within 75 miles.

Reasons For Taking Leave:

Unpaid leave must be granted for *any* of the following reasons:

- to care for the employee's child after birth, or placement for adoption or foster care;
- to care for the employee's spouse, son or daughter, or parent, who has a serious health condition; or
- for a serious health condition that makes the employee unable to perform the employee's job.

At the employee's or employer's option, certain kinds of *paid* leave may be substituted for unpaid leave.

Advance Notice and Medical Certification:

The employee may be required to provide advance leave notice and medical certification. Taking of leave may be denied if requirements are not met.

- The employee ordinarily must provide 30 days advance notice when the leave is "foreseeable."
- An employer may require medical certification to support a request for leave because of a serious health condition, and may require second or third opinions (at the employer's expense) and a fitness for duty report to return to work.

Job Benefits and Protection:

- For the duration of FMLA leave, the employer must maintain the employee's health coverage under any "group health plan."

- Upon return from FMLA leave, most employees must be restored to their original or equivalent positions with equivalent pay, benefits, and other employment terms.
- The use of FMLA leave cannot result in the loss of any employment benefit that accrued prior to the start of an employee's leave.

Unlawful Acts By Employers:

FMLA makes it unlawful for any employer to:

- interfere with, restrain, or deny the exercise of any right provided under FMLA;
- discharge or discriminate against any person for opposing any practice made unlawful by FMLA or for involvement in any proceeding under or relating to FMLA.

Enforcement:

- The U.S. Department of Labor is authorized to investigate and resolve complaints of violations.
- An eligible employee may bring a civil action against an employer for violations.

FMLA does not affect any Federal or State law prohibiting discrimination, or supersede any State or local law or collective bargaining agreement which provides greater family or medical leave rights.

For Additional Information:

Contact the nearest office of the Wage and Hour Division, listed in most telephone directories under U.S. Government, Department of Labor.

U.S. Department of Labor
Employment Standards Administration
Wage and Hour Division
Washington, D.C. 20210

WH Publication 1420
June 1993

employment. It is important that all employers educate their employees about their workers' compensation policies and procedures before an employee is injured. When an employee is injured, an employer should (1) evaluate the injury, (2) determine if the injury arose in the course of employment, and (3) investigate the injury.

Antifraud Measures and Investigation of Workers' Compensation Claims

Approximately 20 percent of all filed workers' compensation claims are fraudulent. To discourage fraudulent claims, an employer should routinely investigate all workers' compensation claims filed. Employers should begin by taking a written statement from the injured worker. Some states have particular requirements regarding statements, so employers should check state laws first. An employer may also want to interview and obtain written statements from witnesses to the accident.

The employer should also make use of return-to-work programs, which are designed to motivate employees to return to work promptly, as soon as their injuries are healed. Without this type of program, employees often stay out of work longer than is necessary while still collecting workers' compensation.

Note that return-to-work accommodations (e.g., light duty, etc.) must be temporary in nature and not "guaranteed" positions. In addition, to minimize liability under the ADA, these positions should be limited to workers' compensation cases and not include all classes of off-duty injuries.

Cost Control

An employer can take other steps to lower workers' compensation costs. First, it is important that employers have safety training programs to teach employees how to handle themselves in dangerous situations. Employees who are trained to use equipment safely will be less likely to injure themselves.

Second, an employer can create wellness programs for employees. These programs should be designed to educate employees about healthy lifestyles and should offer screenings for the early detection of high blood pressure, lung disease, and other ailments. Wellness programs generally encourage employees to exercise, maintain a proper diet, and not smoke. If employees are healthy, their chances of being injured are greatly reduced. Some employer health maintenance organizations offer wellness incentives such as reimbursement for health club expenses.

Access to Physicians

In some states an employer has a statutory right to have the injured worker examined by the employer's physician, or may permit the injured employee to choose the examining physician. A few states require that an impartial physician be appointed for the evaluation. Employers should check their state's workers' compensation statute to determine who has the right to choose the physician to examine the injured employee. More often than not, the initial evaluation is the most critical element of a claim for benefits.

Other Disability Statutes

Workers' compensation may not be the only aspect to be investigated when an employee is injured. Some states have created specific funds that offer broad protection for uniformed public sector employees with temporary disabilities. In Pennsylvania, for example, the Heart and Lung Act (53 Pa. Stat. Ann. § 637 [1974]) specifically applies to police officers and firefighters injured during the performance of their job duties and provides full benefits to injured individuals who are temporarily disabled as a result of work-related injury. An employer should check its particular state's law to determine whether a statute other than workers' compensation applies.

Exhibit 5-6d Notice to Be Given at Time of Leave Request

Employee Rights, Obligations, and Responsibilities When Exercising Family and Medical Leave

As an employee requesting Family and Medical Leave, you should already have been provided with a summary of your rights. This notice is to serve as a reminder of your corresponding obligations and what we at the Township expect of you when you exercise Family and Medical Leave. Specifically, the Township expects and requires that you comply with the following requirements:

1.   The leave you have requested for _____ will be counted against your annual leave entitlement. This entitlement allows you to exercise up to twelve (12) weeks of qualifying leave in a 12-month period. This 12-month period is calculated on a rolling basis by counting backwards from the date of your leave. When requesting leave, you must give advance notice; otherwise, leave will be denied until the expiration of the applicable notice period.

2.   The Township requires that when you exercise FMLA leave because of a personal illness or the illness of a family member, the physician must provide us with medical certification of the need for leave, and additional recertifications of the need for leave every thirty (30) days or at the expiration of the period of incapacity as indicated in the prior certification form. The Township will provide medical certification forms for you to submit to the physician. Failure to obtain requested medical certification within fifteen (15) days will revoke an employee's entitlement to continued leave.

3.   An employee may substitute accrued paid leave for unpaid Family and Medical Leave. Unless written authorization is granted from the Township, accrued sick leave may be used only for purposes specified in the sick leave policy. (In accordance with our policy, employees must substitute accrued paid vacation and personal days before unpaid leave is permitted.)

4.   During any period of Family and Medical Leave, the Township will continue to make premium payments to maintain an employee's health care coverage. However, this does not eliminate the requirement of employee copayments for those employees who normally have copayments toward their insurance coverage. As part of your leave information package, you will be provided with information on how to make your copayments while on leave. If any copayment is more than thirty (30) days past due, the Township will terminate your health care coverage for the duration of the leave period after 15 days' notice. Health care coverage will be restored upon return to work.

Reforming Trends

Dramatic legislative reforms instituted by many states in the early to mid-1990s to reduce workers' compensation costs shifted the balance from an extremely employee-oriented slant to one that attempts to address long-neglected employer concerns. The beginning of the new millennium has brought even more economic hardship to struggling employers and workers' compensation programs. In response, states have enacted a flurry of new legislation. Such legislation includes the following:

- Investments in technology and software to enhance efficiency and streamline services by digitizing case files and automatically cross-checking those on disability with those also reported working

- Creation of special antifraud investigation units combined with tougher penalties for workers' compensation fraud

- Various attempts to reduce the massive litigation backlog, including creation of many informal resolution methods outside the traditional hearing process and reduction of attorneys' fees

5. In accordance with our policy, all employees who are absent from work on a leave of absence for personal illness or injury must present a medical certification indicating that he or she is fit for duty and is able to return to employment. No one will be reinstated to work until his or her fitness-for-duty certification has been received.

6. Included in your FMLA information package will be notification if you are considered a "key employee." If you have received "key employee" notification, it means that under appropriate circumstances, you may be denied restoration to employment. If it is determined that restoring a key employee from a leave period would cause substantial and grievous economic injury, the Township will be forced to deny that employee restoration to employment. If the Township becomes concerned that a key employee may have to be denied restoration, it will provide that employee with written notice and an opportunity to return to work. Once notified, that employee may return to work or may remain on leave. An employee who remains on leave will be entitled to a continuation of health care benefits and will be considered for restoration of employment at the conclusion of his or her leave period if to do so will not cause substantial and grievous economic injury at that time.

7. At the conclusion of a Family and Medical Leave period, an employee will be returned to his or her prior job whenever possible. If that is impossible, the employee will be placed in an equivalent position with equal benefits, pay, and other terms and conditions of employment. The Township is not obligated to reinstate any employee whose job position is eliminated while on leave.

8. The Township will be entitled to recoup the costs of providing health care coverage for an employee during the leave period if that employee fails to return to work at the conclusion of his or her Family and Medical Leave period. This obligation does not apply in certain situations where the Township grants an additional leave of absence and the employee subsequently returns to work, or where the employee is unable to return to work for reasons beyond his or her control.

9. Falsification of any leave request, medical certification, or other form or document will be punishable by termination.

10. The Township has always had an open door policy. If you should ever have questions or concerns about your rights or obligations with regard to Family and Medical Leave, management is always willing to assist you.

- Revision of medical fee schedules in an attempt to control costs and improve services.[28]

Workplace Violence

Guiding Principle

- Local government employers should not permit even the slightest threat or indication of violence in the workplace to go unchecked.

Workplace violence is a problem faced by all employers. To deal with it, some states have adopted legislation that protects state employees from workplace violence. For example, in 1996, the governor of New Jersey signed an executive order stating that the state of New Jersey will not tolerate threats of violence by or against its employees.[29] Government employers should contact legal counsel to determine whether their states have enacted workplace violence laws. In addition, although local governmental employers are exempt from the federal Occupational Safety and Health Act, they may be subject to state safety and health laws that deal with violence in the workplace.

Exhibit 5-6e   Notices of Requirement of Medical Certification

Notice of Requirement of Medical Certification for Personal Illness

The Township hereby notifies you that since you have requested leave for the care and treatment of a personal medical condition, the Township will require the attached medical certification form to be filled out by your physician prior to the granting of any leave, unless circumstances make this impracticable. You have fifteen (15) days to provide this certification. In addition, the Township will require that your physician submit continuing medical certifications of the need for leave every thirty (30) days or at the expiration of the period of incapacity as indicated on the prior medical certification form. Failure to submit this certification within fifteen (15) days will revoke your entitlement to continued leave. In accordance with our uniform policy, no employee exercising leave for a medical condition may return to work without certification from his or her physician that the employee is fit to return to work.

Notice of Requirement of Medical Certification for Family Member

The Township hereby notifies you that since you have requested leave to care for the medical condition of a qualifying family member, you must submit the attached medical certification form to be completed by the treating physician. Additional medical certification of the continuing need for leave will be required every thirty (30) days or at the expiration of the period of incapacity as indicated on the prior medical certification form. Leave will not be granted until the appropriate medical certification form is submitted, unless it is impracticable to do so, and the failure to provide subsequent certifications within fifteen (15) days shall revoke your entitlement to continued leave.

Prevention of Workplace Violence

To prevent workplace violence, employers should have a written workplace violence prevention plan. This plan should include a policy that forbids workplace violence, threats, and related actions. The Occupational Safety and Health Administration (OSHA) has recently reissued voluntary guidelines for health care and social service workers that detail how an employer can implement a workplace violence prevention program. There are four elements to such a program:[30]

Management Commitment and Employee Involvement. Management commitment refers to management's support and aid in implementing a workplace violence prevention program. Employee involvement means that employees have the opportunity to express their own commitment to the prevention of workplace violence by providing suggestions and their own evaluations of the program.

Work Site Analysis. An examination of the workplace for any potential workplace hazards may include a review of security procedures and an analysis of any prior incidents of violence.

Hazard Prevention and Control. Once potential hazards are discovered through the work site analysis, the next stage is to develop measures through different work practices to prevent or control these hazards.

Safety and Health Training. Through proper training, employees can learn how to avoid a violent situation and how to protect themselves when faced with one.

Discipline of Violent Employees

Once an employer has identified a violent or potentially violent employee, it must carefully balance the rights of the identified employee against the rights of other employees. Before terminating an employee for violent tendencies, the employer should consider referring the employee to psychological counseling. If the employer decides to terminate an employee, it should make sure that police or other security personnel are available to escort the employee off the premises and to monitor the workplace.

If an employer terminates an employee for being violent, it must be aware of potential ADA and defamation claims. Employees may fall under the ADA if they suffer from a mental impairment that substantially limits them in a major life activity. Although courts generally reject such claims when an employee has exhibited violent behavior, defense of even an unwarranted suit is expensive.

An employee may also have a defamation claim if an employer tells other persons about the employee's violent acts. For example, when an employer gives a negative reference regarding an employee who has been fired for a violent act, that employee may have a cause of action for defamation against the employer. To avoid such a claim, an employer should give only the relevant employment history of the employee, such as his or her dates of employment. On the other hand, some public entities have been sued by subsequent employers of terminated employees because when they called for references, they were given only positive information and were not warned, for example, about the employee's history of violence. This then is another situation in which it would be wise to get input from an employment lawyer.

To deal with the legal ambiguity, at least 34 states have passed job reference immunity laws, which protect employers who provide information about current or previous employees to a new employer. Usually these laws stipulate that the reference must be provided at the request of the employee or the prospective employer, and that the information has to be job related and truthful.[31] Please note, however, that even in states that have job reference immunity laws, a public employer may still be subject to a defamation lawsuit when a former employee alleges that the information provided was not "truthful." Therefore, even where there are immunity statutes, public employers must be careful concerning the type and quantity of information they disclose.

Victims of Workplace Violence

In addition to suits by violent former employees, employers are subject to suits by employees who are victims of workplace violence. Government employers have a duty to maintain a safe work environment for their employees. They may be liable to an employee or third party for the violent acts of their employees under state OSHA statutes, as landowners, and under common-law negligence actions.

An employer may be vicariously liable for actions of its employees if the actions occurred on the job. An employer also has a duty to warn its employees of any foreseeable risks of harm that may be caused by another employee. For example, if an employer is aware that an employee poses a particular risk, it may be required to alert its employees of the potential danger. But, before an employer discloses such information, it must consider that it may be subject to a defamation claim by that employee if it discloses false, medical, or private information.

A victim of workplace violence may also have a cause of action against an employer for the negligent hiring or retention of the violent employee. An employer may be liable in this regard if it knew or had reason to know of dangerous characteristics of an employee. Negligent hiring is found when the employer knew or should have known of the employee's unfitness before the employee was actually hired. The focus of negligent hiring is on whether the employer used reasonable care during the recruitment process. To avoid potential liability, employers should check all references given to them by job applicants.

Tips for Avoiding Workplace Violence

❏ Assess the potential for workplace violence in your organization.

❏ Implement a workplace violence prevention program.

❏ Act with prudence, balancing your duty to protect your employees from harm with your duty not to defame an employee.

Further, employers whose employees regularly deal with customers may consider conducting a criminal background investigation, although criminal background checks may require notice to the employee who is the subject of the investigation, and the employer may be prohibited from requesting certain information, such as arrest records or convictions that are not related to an employee's job. Negligent retention occurs when an employer becomes aware of problems with an employee that indicate the employee's unfitness but fails to take any action. If an employer becomes aware of any unusual conduct of an employee that suggests that the employee is potentially dangerous, it should investigate and evaluate the situation and then choose an appropriate course of action.

For more on avoiding violence in the workplace and handling potentially violent employees, see Chapters 7 and 8.

Healthy Workplace

Guiding Principle

• Many local governments are responsible under state law for protecting employees against hazardous conditions and materials in the workplace.

Smoking

Smoking in the workplace is generally regulated by state law. Most states require that employers have at least a written policy on smoking. Some states require employers to implement a policy designating smoking and nonsmoking areas in the workplace. Government workplaces are often covered by statutes that ban smoking in public buildings (except in designated areas), and some states, such as New York, have nearly banned smoking in the workplace altogether. On the flip side, many states have enacted "smokers' rights" laws, which prevent employers from discriminating against employees who smoke while off-duty or outside the workplace.

Employers who implement "no smoking" policies often include in their policies an allowance for smoking breaks. This break time is usually taken from an employee's lunch period. For example, an employer who generally gives employees 45 minutes for lunch may instead give two 10-minute smoking breaks and reduce the lunch period to 25 minutes. However, before implementing such a policy, employers must check the break requirement for their state to make sure that the lunch break meets state requirements. In New York, for example, employers must give employees a 30-minute lunch break (N.Y. Lab. L. § 162(2)).

Several states have statutes stipulating that government employers may be liable for injuries suffered by their employees from fumes and smoke. For example, in Pennsylvania, the Heart and Lung Act (53 Pa. Stat. Ann § 637[a]) provides that municipal employees engaged as police officers, corrections officers, or firefighters will receive their full salary for temporary disabilities, including diseases of the heart and respiratory failure, caused by such things as fumes and smoke. Therefore, employers who are considering implementing a "no smoking" policy should consider their states' particular laws. Employers whose workforce is unionized must first negotiate with union representatives before implementing a "no smoking" policy.

Sample "No Smoking" Policy   *fyi*

The state of [__] does not permit smoking in places of public accommodation except in designated areas. In accordance with this law, it is the policy of this department that smoking is permitted only in designated areas. Employees who violate this policy will be subject to disciplinary procedures, which may include dismissal.

Infectious Diseases

Bloodborne Pathogens. Policies and procedures to prevent and control infections are key elements in providing a healthy and safe work environment. Because emergency and public safety workers are at risk of exposure to bloodborne pathogens such as HIV and hepatitis B, such procedures may also be required for government employers under state safety and health laws.

The risk of infection with bloodborne pathogens depends on the employee's likelihood of exposure to blood and other possibly infectious materials. The Centers for Disease Control and Prevention (CDC) has recommended hepatitis B vaccinations for occupational groups such as emergency medical technicians, police officers, and firefighters who are frequently exposed to blood.

The CDC has also updated its guidelines for protection of emergency and public safety workers who may be exposed to HIV, hepatitis B, and hepatitis C.[32] The updated guidelines still emphasize exposure prevention as the primary means of reducing bloodborne pathogen infections, but also require that employers have exposure control plans in place for prompt reporting and treatment of exposure to bloodborne pathogens. The new guidelines discuss when pre-exposure hepatitis B vaccinations are required and the effectiveness of post-exposure treatment for hepatitis B and HIV, including HBIG, hepatitis B vaccine, and HIV PEP, all of which are most effective when administered as soon after the exposure as possible.

Tuberculosis. The spread of tuberculosis increased in the 1990s. As a result, the CDC published a model for tuberculosis control programs in 1994, which generally applies to health care facilities,[33] and updated that model in 2003.[34] OSHA has withdrawn its proposed guidelines, but occupations in which the spread of tuberculosis is high have taken their own precautions. For example, almost all states require teachers and other school officials to be tested for tuberculosis upon employment. To the extent that they have not already done so, local governments should implement their own tuberculosis control program to combat the spread of this deadly disease.

Constitutional Rights

Guiding Principle

• Efficiency, economy, discipline, harmony, and other administrative values do not trump employees' constitutional rights.

Public employees have broad constitutional rights in addition to the job protections they may enjoy under civil service laws and regulations. These rights are not abrogated by the need to serve the public with efficiency, economy, discipline, and harmony. Rather, the judiciary assesses these rights by balancing the interests of the employer, the employees, and the public. Understanding the logical structure of public employees' constitutional rights will help managers and supervisors avoid violating them.

Ambiguous Law, High Stakes

Upon hearing of an assassination attempt on President Ronald Reagan, a deputized employee in a constable's office said, "Shoot, if they go for him again, I hope they get him."[35] A public school security guard failed to note

Red Flags

▶ "Insubordination" may turn out to be constitutionally protected speech. Even comments made only to a supervisor or manager may be protected if they deal with matters of public concern.

▶ Never compel or pressure an employee to join any organization, no matter how civic-minded it may be.

▶ Be very careful when taking any personnel action based on partisanship. Because the constitutional law has changed drastically since the mid-1970s, past practices may no longer be constitutional.

▶ Where an employee has a reasonable expectation of privacy, a search of his or her work space, files, desk, and so forth must be reasonable in both inception and scope. No fishing expeditions; the objects of the search should be identified beforehand.

▶ Avoid implicitly classifying employees, whether on the basis of age, gender, ethnicity, creed, or race, in ways that reinforce social stereotypes.

on his application that he had been convicted of a felony.[36] At a dinner break, a nurse told a trainee about problems in a public hospital's cross-training program and, allegedly, in its obstetrics department.[37] A public school teacher wrote a letter to a local newspaper criticizing the school board, opposing greater funding for the schools, and apparently mistakenly suggesting that money earmarked for education previously had been diverted to sports.[38] All four employees were fired. In one way or another, each dismissal was constitutionally defective.

Because public employees have a broad array of constitutional rights,[39] constitutional law is a significant concern of public human resource management. This differentiates the public sector substantially from the private sec-

tor, where the employer's sole *constitutional* responsibility is compliance with the Thirteenth Amendment's proscription of slavery and involuntary servitude. The concept of employment at the will of the employer, which still prevails in much of the private sector, does not fully apply to local governments because of constitutional constraints as well as civil service protection, union rules, and state laws.

Contemporary constitutional law poses significant problems for public managers. Caution is required in adopting private sector models and techniques, so often popular with reformers and the media and, apparently, in the public culture.[40] Constitutional law is "what the courts say it is," which is sometimes opaque or counterintuitive.[41] Key standards may be vague, or subjective, or may require the complicated balancing of a number of factors. Yet the stakes are high. Violating a public employee's constitutional rights can trigger substantial liability damages, both compensatory and punitive.

Public managers need not become constitutional lawyers to do their jobs, but they should understand the logical structure of employees' constitutional rights. Even though Supreme Court justices, circuit courts, and lawyers may disagree over the appropriate outcome of specific cases, knowledge of these structures will prevent many violations and much liability. It will also increase productive thinking about how to integrate employees' constitutional rights with core human resource management values. It is toward this end that this section provides a general guide to the current constitutional law of public personnel management.

The Public Service Model: A Framework for Analyzing Public Employees' Constitutional Rights

The current model for analyzing public employees' constitutional rights crystallized in the mid-1980s. Called the "public service model," it seeks to promote the public interest by balancing three sets of concerns: the interests of the government as employer, the interests of the employees in exercising their constitutional rights, and the public's concern with the way its affairs are run by administrative agencies.[42]

The model's fundamental premise is that "the government's interest in achieving its goals as effectively and efficiently as possible is elevated from a relatively subordinate interest when it acts as a sovereign [dealing with ordinary citizens] to a significant one when it acts as employer."[43] This enables governments to require their employees to sacrifice some constitutional rights as a condition of joining and remaining in the public service. However, to be constitutional, such conditions must on balance serve the public interest. The public interest generally includes open government, accountability, safety, customer service, honesty, and political responsiveness.

In applying this balancing model, the courts may side with either the government or the employee. For instance, the Supreme Court has supported restrictions on the partisan political activities of public employees[44] but has opposed governmental efforts to suppress employees' whistle-blowing.[45] In terms of the public service model, there is no inconsistency in these opinions even though they have disparate impacts on the scope of public employees' First Amendment rights. Context becomes all-important. Restrictions on political activity serve the public interest by reducing the likelihood that partisanship will interfere with office operations and service to the public. Protecting whistle-blowers, on the other hand, promotes the public's interest in learning of governmental mismanagement, waste, fraud, abuse of power, and specific dangers to community health or safety.

The public service model determines the general structure of public employees' First Amendment, Fourth Amendment, procedural and substantive due process, and equal protection rights. Each of these structures, in turn, requires additional balancing of one kind or another.

Red Flags

▶ Common sense and constitutional law don't always mix. When in doubt, consult an attorney who is familiar with public employment law and practices.

▶ Don't confuse administrative convenience and standard managerial values, such as efficiency and economy, with the public interest. The courts respect these concerns but typically subordinate them to individual rights.

The Structure of First Amendment Rights

Restrictions on Partisan Speech and Activity. Restrictions on public employees' partisan speech, electioneering, or campaign management are generally constitutional.[46] However, care should be taken to avoid vagueness in drafting or applying such regulations. It is also important that they not be overly broad—that is, not prohibit more than is necessary to achieve the governmental objectives of efficiency, the appearance of partisan neutrality, and protection of employees from partisan coercion.

General Speech on Matters of Public Concern. Public employees' general speech on matters of public concern enjoys considerable constitutional protection. It is valued by the public service model precisely because it can inform the citizenry about government and public affairs. Remarks on matters of public concern made privately "will rarely, if ever, justify the discharge of a public employee"[47] because they have little potential to harm legitimate governmental objectives. If such remarks are made publicly, however, it is necessary to "arrive at a balance between the interests of the [employee], as a citizen, in commenting upon matters of public concern and the interests of the State, as an employer, in promoting the efficiency of the public services it performs through its employees."[48]

On the basis of such a balancing, the deputized employee's comments regarding the assassination attempt on President Reagan were constitutionally protected because (1) she had a strong interest in making them during a general discussion with a co-worker as a means of underscoring her opposition to Reagan's civil rights policies; and (2) the remarks posed no threat to the constable's mission as her position was purely clerical and involved no law enforcement activity.

Adverse action based on an employee's speech on matters of public concern is more likely to be constitutional when the remarks impair discipline or harmony in the workplace, interfere with close working relationships or normal operations, or cast doubt on the employee's ability to do his or her job. Situational factors, including the time, place, manner, and context of the remarks, must also be taken into account in determining their likely impact. For instance, an offhand statement to a co-worker by a low-level employee may be treated more favorably than a similar one made to a large public crowd by a high-level career executive.

Inaccuracy is potentially a basis for discipline only if the government can show that the employee knew the remarks were incorrect or acted with disregard for their truth or falsity.[49] Consequently, the public employer faces a very heavy—indeed, almost impossible—burden of persuasion when trying to discipline an employee such as the teacher whose newspaper letter allegedly contained damaging falsehoods. Finally, non-work-related expressive activity by public employees, such as publishing novels, cannot constitutionally be treated differently than similar activity by any member of the public unless the government can show a "nexus" to a significant governmental interest as an employer.[50]

The application of these rules and balances is sometimes complicated by dispute over what the employee actually said. In such cases, whoever is acting on behalf of the governmental employer must take "reasonable steps" to ascertain the content of the remarks. This requirement gives public employees some procedural protection against being disciplined for comments they may not have made. However, the current standard for what is reasonable is exceptionally vague: "only procedures outside the range of what a reasonable manager would use may be condemned as unreasonable."[51] To be on the safe side, public managers should at least interview the employee involved and any witnesses to the remarks at issue.

Because they are of no particular interest to the public, employees' publicly made remarks on matters of *private* concern do not enjoy constitutional protection when they impede legitimate governmental interests.[52] For example, a public comment about a co-worker's annoying habits is not of public concern and can be the basis for discipline if it harms the governmental employer's efficiency or public image. In some instances, it can be difficult to determine whether a remark is of private or public concern. Generally, matters of office politics and personalities are considered of private concern only, unless they can be construed as legitimate whistle-blowing.

Although the Supreme Court has not yet dealt with public employees' speech via voice or e-mail, use of these channels should not affect the constitutional analysis with respect to whether the *content* of the remarks is of public or private concern. However, they may present some thorny issues regarding whether their *context* is private or public. Either channel can be used to communicate with one, a few, or many individuals, any of whom may reveal the remarks to the employer. Direct monitoring of voice or e-mail by the public employer is potentially constrained by the Fourth Amendment (see discussion in the section, Fourth Amendment Privacy).

Freedom of Association. Under the public service balancing model, public employees are generally free to join organizations insofar as their membership does not create a conflict of interest with their jobs. Membership in unsavory or even subversive organizations is not per se grounds for dismissal because "those who join an organization but do not share its unlawful purposes and . . . activities, surely pose no threat, either as citizens or as public employees."[53] By contrast, membership can be off-limits to employees when it conflicts with their official responsibilities or appears to invite impropriety.[54] For example, managers are commonly banned from joining unions representing rank-and-file employees.

Public employees also have broad protections against being forced to join organizations. With limited exceptions, partisan patronage is now an unconstitutional basis for public personnel decisions to hire, fire, train, transfer, promote, discipline, or undertake similar actions. In a series of three cases beginning in 1976, the Supreme Court reasoned that, on balance, the contributions patronage makes to the government's interests in loyalty, accountability, and party competition are outweighed by its infringement on public employees' freedom of association and belief.[55]

Nor can public employees be compelled to join labor unions. Nonmembers even have constitutional protections against the assessment of unreasonable "counterpart" or "fair share" fees by the unions representing the bargaining units in which they work. "[T]he constitutional requirements for the Union's collection of agency fees include an adequate explanation of the basis for the fee, a reasonably prompt opportunity to challenge the amount of the fee before an impartial decisionmaker, and an escrow for amounts reasonably in dispute while such challenges are pending."[56]

Religion. The Constitution's dual guarantees that government will neither establish religion nor abridge individuals' religious freedom present complex issues, but limited guidance, for public human resource management. The "establishment clause" is read to mean that government cannot require, encourage, or foster any religious behavior at all. The clause is not satisfied merely by nondenominationalism or nonsectarianism. Under the leading test, to survive a challenge based on the establishment clause, government regulations or practices must meet three criteria: (1) they must have a secular purpose, (2) their principal effect must neither advance nor inhibit religion, and (3) they cannot excessively entangle government in religion.[57] In public employment, these restrictions are bolstered by the specific constitutional provision that "no religious Test shall ever be required as a Qualification to any Office or public Trust under the United States" (Article VI, clause 3).[58] Clearly, the public employer cannot put pressure on employees to engage in religious activity, such as prayer breakfasts, or to discuss their religious beliefs.

The extent to which governments can constitutionally abridge the exercise of religious freedom in the workplace is less certain. When ordinary citizens are involved, religious expression is currently treated like expression generally. If a public space is open for any type of public speech or display, there is a strong presumption that religious speech and displays must be permitted as well. The fact that public property is used by private parties to express or encourage religion does not violate the establishment clause.[59]

However, transferring this general model to public employment presents problems. As noted above, public employees' workplace speech on matters of private concern is not constitutionally protected when it is detrimental to an agency's mission. Does this mean that an employee can be disciplined for private religious expression that causes disharmony? No doubt that proselytizing at work, like partisan speech, can be prohibited, but what about displaying religious symbols, headgear, or jewelry; putting "I Love Jesus" (or the Pope or Louis Farrakhan) on a screen saver; or hanging the picture of a religious leader on one's cubicle wall? The Supreme Court has given little guidance, and there are no definitive answers.[60]

Reasonably accommodating employees' religious practices is generally favored by civil rights law, but exceptions to workplace rules should be made with caution. When a practice is prohibited if motivated by secular concerns but permitted as religious activity, such as deviation from uniform dress or dress codes, accommodation can be in tension with the establishment clause.[61] Again, the parameters are uncertain and reasonableness may be the only guide.

Oaths. Governments sometimes try to limit an employee's freedom of association by having the employee swear an oath of allegiance. So long as the scope of the oath does not exceed a statement of allegiance, it is constitutional. Courts have struck down oaths because of vague language or for requiring employees to give up constitutional rights of speech and belief.[62]

Oaths come in positive and negative form. Positive oaths that are struck down usually are too vague. Far more common are negative, disclaimer-type oaths that require applicants or employees to forswear membership in certain kinds of organizations. Courts have been skeptical of such disclaimer oaths, especially when they have been so specific as to name forbidden organizations.[63]

Whistle-Blower Protection. The Supreme Court has substantially ensured First Amendment protection of public employees who criticize government policy.[64] A whole new set of procedural safeguards is necessary to protect the rights of individuals who uncover waste or wrongdoing within government. In recent decades, courts have increasingly ruled in favor of whistle-blowers, and there are many specific provisions in federal and state law that seek to protect employees who reveal corruption.

But these antiretaliation clauses are limited to protecting employees who report violations of the particular law in which they are found. The Whistle Blower Protection Act of 1989 introduced some important innovations in safeguarding outspoken federal employees

from retribution. This legislation makes it much easier for whistle-blowers to prove their cases; it increases the burden on the government to defend against these claims; it allows whistle-blowers to appeal their own cases; it enhances confidentiality safeguards; and it puts the federal Office of the Special Counsel more surely in the corner of the whistle-blower.

One important difference between whistle-blower protection and free speech protection is that whistle-blower retribution cannot even be one of the factors leading to an adverse action. Courts have ruled that an adverse action cannot be based even partly on reprisal because of the "chilling" effect it would have on other employees.[65] Although this act applies only to federal employees, some state legislators have used it as a model. County and municipal managers should consult legal counsel about laws protecting whistle-blowers at their level of government.[66]

Fourth Amendment Privacy

It is firmly established that "individuals do not lose Fourth Amendment rights" against unreasonable searches or seizures "merely because they work for the government instead of a private employer."[67] Their Fourth Amendment rights are structured as follows:

First, in order to enjoy any protection at all, the employee must have a "reasonable expectation of privacy" under the circumstances. For instance, an employee who has a private office to which only he or she and a janitor have a key will have a reasonable expectation of privacy in it. In a building in which briefcases, handbags, suitcases, and so forth are not screened, employees will have a reasonable expectation of privacy in their contents even if work spaces are open or shared.

Second, any governmental search must be reasonable in both inception and scope.[68] That is, the purpose must be sound and defined in such a way that it limits the search's scope. The ambiguity of this standard invites litigation, but the standard is intended to be flexible.

The governmental interests in efficiency and effectiveness preclude requiring warrants or findings of probable cause for undertaking workplace searches of public employees' desks, files, and other work-related spaces that are not prompted by law enforcement.

Third, searches may be reasonable even when they are not based on a suspicion that any particular employee has violated a workplace rule. They may be used in administrative (noncriminal) drug-testing schemes for personnel in law enforcement, public safety, or other positions where, on balance, the employees have a reduced expectation of privacy and the government and public interests outweigh their privacy interests.[69] However, drug testing for human resource management purposes must be reasonable and avoid entanglement with criminal actions.

As noted earlier, applying these principles to voice and e-mail may raise some difficult questions. Technologically, e-mail is a relatively open communication channel so it may be difficult to demonstrate a reasonable expectation of privacy in its use at work. Voice mail, of course, is more akin to a telephone conversation, in which one does have a reasonable expectation of privacy. But the employer may be able to reduce this expectation by not providing private passwords or by informing employees that voice mail (or even telephone conversations) will be monitored for business reasons (e.g., efficient and appropriate communication with customers). Nevertheless, Fourth Amendment protection may be applied to communications that are clearly private in content, such as between spouses about family matters.

Procedural Due Process

The Fifth and Fourteenth Amendments protect individuals against the deprivation of life, liberty, or property without due process of law. Procedural due process requires fundamental fairness. It is a check on incorrect, arbitrary, capricious, and discriminatory decisions in individual cases. However, it does not involve a specific formula, and it ranges from a mini-

Tips for Constitutional Practice

❏ Think in terms of the "public service model." Remember that the employer's interests may differ from the public's interest.

❏ Each of the constitutional rights discussed in this section has a logical structure. By understanding these structures, you will be able to ask the right questions and better analyze situations. It is especially important to know threshold questions. For instance, was the employee's remark on a matter of public concern? Did the employee have a reasonable expectation of privacy under the circumstances?

❏ When balancing claims according to the public service model or procedural due process, do not overestimate the importance of administrative values and concerns.

❏ Whenever possible, before disciplining an employee, give him or her notice of the reasons and at least an informal opportunity to respond.

mal give and take (notice and opportunity to respond) to elaborate hearings with courtroom-like procedures (oral presentation of evidence and arguments, confrontation and cross-examination of adverse witnesses, right to counsel, disclosure of opposing evidence, impartial decision maker, determination on the record of the proceedings, and written explanation of the decision).

The structure of procedural due process is based on the premise that there is often a tension between the government's interest in using less elaborate procedures for the sake of speed, efficiency, and economy on the one hand, and the individual's desire for maximum procedural protection on the other. Consequently, determining when procedural due process applies and what it mandates requires a balance among the following concerns:

(1) the private interests affected by the government action; (2) the risk that the procedure used will result in error, and the probable value of alternative procedures in reducing the error rate; and (3) the government's interest in using the procedure afforded, including the administrative and financial burdens of alternatives.[70]

In the context of public human resource management, procedural due process is most commonly triggered by civil service statutes that establish an employee's property right or interest in his or her job. Once a regulation establishes an expectation of continuing employment, termination depends on constitutional due process rather than on civil service rules and procedures.[71] Prior to termination, "the tenured public employee is entitled to oral or written notice of the charges against him, an explanation of the employer's evidence, and an opportunity to present his side of the story."[72] Depending on the circumstances, the employee will often be entitled to a more elaborate post-termination hearing as well.

Additional employee interests that may trigger a right to procedural due process include abridgment of liberty and harm to reputation or future employability.[73] When any of these interests are involved, hearings may be required even if the employee has no civil service status or tenure, as in the case of probationary employees.[74] The timing and scope of the hearings will vary with the balancing of the other two factors.

The higher the probability that the procedures in place will yield correct decisions, the less likely that they will require augmentation or elaboration. All else being equal (i.e., rules are valid and applied uniformly), if there is no factual dispute, there is no need for a hearing at all.[75] However, caution is necessary as the courts may be prone to hairsplitting. An employee who is dismissed for "lying" on his or her application is entitled to due process since the false information may have been the result of a mistake rather than an intent to deceive: such was the case of the public school security guard who thought his conviction was for a misdemeanor rather than a felony.[76]

Finally, the Supreme Court has recognized that the government has a strong interest in removing or disciplining unsatisfactory employees without having to go through burdensome or prolonged procedures. Thus, hearings need not be held before tenured employees are suspended, without pay, for disciplinary reasons. Postsuspension hearings, held within a reasonable time, satisfy constitutional due process.[77]

Substantive Due Process

The Fifth and Fourteenth Amendments protect individuals against the deprivation of liberty without due process of law. But they do not define *liberty.* "Substantive due process" is the label applied to judicial decisions that give substance to the term *liberty.* It is a hotly contested area of constitutional law because it allows the courts great discretion in determining what is protected. However, in terms of public human resource management, the Supreme Court has thus far limited the concept of substantive due process to "freedom of personal choice in matters of marriage and family life."[78] Thus, it has held that highly restrictive mandatory maternity leaves for schoolteachers are unconstitutional. Taking any action against an employee or applicant because she had an abortion or a child would also trigger substantive due process protection, as filtered through the public service model.

By contrast, the Court has specifically upheld grooming standards for male police officers (length of hair, beards, moustaches) and residency requirements for urban employees in the face of substantive due process challenges.[79] Substantive due process is inherently open-ended and subjective, but the more fundamental the courts consider a right to be, the more likely it is to enjoy protection in the context of public employment.

Equal Protection

The constitutional guarantee of equal protection under the laws, contained in the Fourteenth Amendment (and applied to the federal government through the Fifth), is currently of great importance to public affirmative action and related efforts to achieve socially diverse workforces. It has an elaborate structure.

The threshold question for the application of equal protection analysis is whether a policy, law, regulation, practice, or other governmental action classifies people in order to treat them differently. If there is such a classification, the courts use a three-tiered approach to determining its constitutionality:

Suspect Classifications. Classifications based on race, ethnicity, and, for state and local governments, alienage (noncitizenship) are called "suspect."[80] This is because, in view of the nation's history, it is reasonable to suspect that they will be used to discriminate, thereby defeating the guarantee of equal protection. Suspect classifications are subject to "strict judicial scrutiny." The burden of persuasion is on the government, and the courts are not deferential to government claims of policy or administrative expertise. Such classifications can be sustained only if they serve a compelling governmental interest and are "narrowly tailored." One possible example of a compelling governmental interest in this context is to remedy past, proven racial discrimination against identifiable individuals.[81] The Supreme Court has never held that diversity in the public service is a compelling governmental interest. However, while discussing affirmative action in higher public education, the Court said: "Effective participation by members of all racial and ethnic groups in the civic life of our Nation is essential if the dream of one Nation, indivisible, is to be realized" and "In order to cultivate a set of leaders with legitimacy in the eyes of the citizenry, it is necessary that the path to leadership be visibly open to talented and qualified individuals of every race and ethnicity."[82]

Narrow tailoring requires that the intrusion of suspect classifications on the principle of equal protection be limited. For instance, in terms of remedial racial quotas for hiring and promotion, it requires (1) an assessment of the efficacy of alternative remedies; (2) a fixed duration, in terms of either time or achievement of the policy objectives; (3) hiring and promotion targets that closely reflect the availability of members of the minority group(s) in the relevant workforce; (4) waiver provisions so that it is never necessary to hire or promote an unqualified individual; (5) limited harmful impact on innocent third parties; and (6) an individualized consideration of each candidate.[83]

In the context of today's affirmative action, it should be noted that all race- or ethnicity-based classifications are suspect even if their purpose is to further equal opportunity or workforce diversity. In this context, the purpose does not have to be discriminatory.

Nonsuspect Classifications. Classifications based on age, residency, income, and similar factors are "nonsuspect," or ordinary. There is no particular reason to believe that these classifications threaten the purposes of the equal protection clause. They are subject to "rational basis" judicial review. Ordinary judicial scrutiny is exercised: the burden of persuasion is generally on the challenger to show that such classifications are not rationally related to the achievement of a legitimate governmental purpose.[84]

In terms of public human resource management, this means that qualifications based on age,[85] residency,[86] education, and perhaps low income for certain positions[87] are not likely to be deemed unconstitutional unless they are wholly irrational or interfere with the exercise of a fundamental constitutional right (see section on gender-based classifications). Use of these classifications can also be regulated by statute, as in the case of age discrimination.

Federal classifications based on alienage are treated as nonsuspect because the national government has broad constitutional authority regarding immigration and naturalization.[88]

Gender-Based Classifications. Gender-based classifications fall in between the suspect and nonsuspect tiers. At an earlier time, such classifications received only rational basis review because their putative purpose was to protect women—from long working hours, unsavory workplaces (such as bars), the corruption of electoral politics (by restrictions on suffrage), and the depravity that might be revealed in criminal trials (by exclusion from jury service).

Since the 1970s, as the society and courts became more sensitive to gender inequalities, male/female classifications have been subject to "intermediate" judicial scrutiny. They must be substantially related to the achievement of important governmental objectives, and they require an "exceedingly persuasive justification."[89]

Practices that promote occupational segregation or pay differentials based on gender are vulnerable to constitutional challenge. As the constitutional law now stands, the status of affirmative action for women differs from that for racial and ethnic minorities. The Supreme Court has not decided whether or when promoting gender diversity in traditionally male (or female) occupations is constitutionally acceptable under intermediate scrutiny.

Sometimes nonsuspect or gender classifications interfere with the exercise of a fundamental constitutional right or liberty. For example, in the late 1960s, the Supreme Court held that one-year durational residency requirements for eligibility for state welfare benefits violated indigents' fundamental constitutional right to travel interstate.[90] In such cases, the classification will be subject to strict scrutiny and will need to serve a compelling governmental interest in a way that is least invasive of the protected constitutional right.

Conclusion

Although this section may raise more specific questions than it answers, it provides public managers with the conceptual tools to identify personnel practices that may violate public employees' constitutional rights. Constitutional law is vague and amorphous in some respects, but also has logical structures. Understanding these structures tells us how to think about human resource management problems and issues in a constitutional context. It will help public managers to build systems and procedures that harmonize governmental interests with constitutional requirements. And that, in turn, will help reduce lawsuits with all their attendant expense, in terms of money, time, anxiety, and animosity.

---

[1] *Rutan v. Republican Party of Illinois,* 497 U.S. 62 (1990).

[2] See *Johnson v. County of Los Angeles Fire Dept.,* 865 F. Supp. 1430 (1994).

[3] See N.Y. Civ. Rts. L. § 50-a.

[4] See, for example, in North Dakota, *Hovet v. Hebron Public School District,* 419 N.W.2nd 189 (N.D., 1988), *City of Grand Forks v. Grand Forks Herald,* 307 N.W.2nd 572 (N.D., 1981), and *Forum Publishing Company v. City of Fargo,* 391 N.W.2nd 169 (N.D., 1986).

[5] The United States Supreme Court has long held that Congress had the power to and did abrogate the states' Eleventh Amendment immunity for the purposes of Title VII. *Fitzpatrick v. Blitzer,* 427 U.S. 445 (1976). Therefore, Title VII covers both state and local governmental employers.

[6] *Monell v. Department of Social Services,* 436 U.S. 658, 663 (1978). Local municipalities are subject to suits under Section 1983, Monell, supra, but state governmental entities are not, *Will v. Michigan Dep't of State Police,* 491 U.S. 58 (1989).

[7] *Harlow v. Fitzgerald,* 457 U.S. 800, 818 (1982).

[8] *Owen v. City of Independence,* 445 U.S. 622 (1980).

[9] *Smith v. Wade,* 461 U.S. 30, 56 (1983).

[10] *City of Newport v. Fact Concerts,* 453 U.S. 247, 263–71 (1981).

[11] The federal courts of appeals differ in their opinion as to whether a plaintiff may sue governmental employers directly under Section 1981 or must also simultaneously bring an action under § 1983. Compare *Federation of African-American Contractors v. City of Oakland,* 96 F.3d 1204 (9th Cir. 1996) with *Dennis v. County of Fairfax,* 55 F.3d 151 (4th Cir. 1995). In practice, plaintiffs often bring employment discrimination claims against local governments under both sections.

[12] *Smith v. Wade,* 461 U.S. 30, 56 (1983).

[13] *City of Newport v. Fact Concerts,* 453 U.S. 247, 263–71 (1981). See, e.g., *Ransom Funches v. City of Dallas,* 1999 U.S. Dist. LEXIS 6269 (N.D. Texas, April 28, 1999).

[14] In 2001, the United States Supreme Court ruled that states are not required to make reasonable accommodations under the ADA for their employees so long as their actions toward disabled individuals have a rational basis. *Board of Trustees of the Univ. of Alabama,* 531 U.S. 356 (2001). However, generally local governmental employers are still subject to the ADA. Some governmental employers may be exempt if they are considered to be an "arm of the state." Governmental employers should consult with their local counsel to determine whether they may be exempt from the ADA, but as a practical matter, most governmental employers are subject to similar state disability acts.

[15] Local governments that contract with the federal government are covered by this act. See, for example, *Board of Gov. of Univ. of North Carolina v. Dept. of Labor,* 917 F.2d 812 (4th Cir. 1990).

[16] *Kimel v. Florida Board of Regents,* 528 U.S. 62 (2000).

[17] See *Narin v. Lower Merion School Dist.* 206 F.3d 323 (3d Cir. 2000) (school district covered by ADEA); *Gavin v. Clarkstown Central School Dist.,* 84 F. Supp. 2d 540 (S.D.N.Y. 2000) (school district covered by ADEA); *Sapienza v. Cook County Office of Public Defender,* 128 F. Supp. 2d (N.D. Ill. 2001) (Illinois counties and public defender's office that was arm of county covered by ADEA). Compare *Adams v. Calvert County Public Schools,* 201 F. Supp. 2d 516 (D. Md. 2002) (county board of education not covered by ADEA where it was arm of state under Maryland law).

[18] Age Discrimination in Employment Amendments of 1996, Pub. L. No. 104-208, Subsec. 2(c) & (d), 110 Stat. 3009-25 (codified at 29 U.S.C. § 623j).

[19] Most courts that have considered the issue find that all governmental employers (state and local) may be sued under the Equal Pay Act. See, e.g., *Varner v. Illinois State Univ.,* 226 F.3d 927 (7th Cir. 2000).

[20] 29 U.S.C. § 203(e).

[21] The United States Supreme Court recently affirmed that state governmental employers are not immune from suits under the FMLA. *Nevada Dept. of Human Resources v. Hibbs,* 123 S. Ct. 1972 (2003). Therefore, both state and local governmental employers are covered by this act.

[22] *EEOC v. Shell Oil Co.,* 466 U.S. 54 (1984); 29 C.F.R. § 1601.16(a)(2).

[23] *Sedlacek v. Hach,* 752 F.2d 333 (8th Cir. 1985).

[24] *Burlington Indus., Inc. v. Ellerth,* No. 97-569 (June 26, 1998) and *Faragher v. City of Boca Raton,* No. 97-282 (June 26, 1998).

[25] *Burlington Indus., Inc. v. Ellerth,* No. 97-569 (June 26, 1998) and *Faragher v. City of Boca Raton,* No. 97-282 (June 26, 1998).

[26] *Kukla v. Village of Antioch,* 647 F. Supp 799 (N.D. Ill. 1986).

[27] *Ragsdale v. Wolverine World Wide, Inc.,* 535 U.S. 81 (2002).

[28] N.Y. State Workers' Compensation Board Press Release June 27, 2003; N.Y. State Insurance Dept. Press Release

9/21/2000; N.Y. State Workers' Compensation Board Press Release, January 24, 2000.

[29] N.J. Admin. Code, Executive Order No. 49 (1996).

[30] "Guidelines for Preventing Workplace Violence for Health Care and Social Service Workers," OSHA 3148 (Revised 2003). These guidelines may be obtained by contacting OSHA or by visiting OSHA's Web site at www.OSHA.gov. OSHA also has other helpful publications and information regarding workplace violence on its Web site.

[31] *Individual Emp. Rts. Manual* (BNA) 515:122 (2003).

[32] The Centers for Disease Control and Prevention, "Updated U.S. Public Health Guidelines for the Management of Occupational Exposures to HBV, HCV and HIV and Recommendations for Postexposure Prophylaxis," 2001. This CDC publication and additional information are available on the CDC's Web site at www.cdc.gov.

[33] The Centers for Disease Control and Prevention, "Guidelines for Preventing the Transmission of Mycobacterium Tuberculosis in Health-Care Facilities," 1994.

[34] The Centers for Disease Control and Prevention, "Guidelines for Environmental Infection Control in Health-Care Facilities," 2003.

[35] *Rankin v. McPherson,* 483 U.S. 378 (1987).

[36] *Cleveland Board of Education v. Loudermill,* 470 U.S. 532 (1985).

[37] *Waters v. Churchill,* 511 U.S. 661 (1994).

[38] *Pickering v. Board of Education,* 391 U.S. 563 (1968).

[39] See David Rosenbloom and Rosemary O'Leary, *Public Administration and Law,* 2d ed. (New York: Marcel Dekker, 1997), chapter 6, for a more detailed discussion. See also David Rosenbloom and James Carroll, "Public Personnel Administration and Law," in *Handbook of Public Personnel Administration,* ed. Jack Rabin et al. (New York: Marcel Dekker, 1994): 71–113.

[40] The federal National Performance Review, headed by Vice President Al Gore, sought to make the federal government operate in a more businesslike fashion. See Al Gore, *From Red Tape to Results: Creating a Government that Works Better and Costs Less* (Washington, D.C.: U.S. Government Printing Office, 1993), and Al Gore, *Businesslike Government: Lessons Learned from American's Best Companies* (Washington, D.C.: U.S. Government Printing Office, 1997).

For a review of some of the constitutional problems involved in such reforms, see David Rosenbloom, "Constitutional Problems for the New Public Management in the United States," in *Current Public Policy Issues: The 1998 Annals,* ed. Khi Thai and Rosalyn Carter (Boca Raton, Fla.: Academics Press, 1998).

[41] Justice Lewis Powell in *Owen v. City of Independence,* 445 U.S. 622, 669 (1980).

[42] See "Developments in the Law—Public Employment," *Harvard Law Review* 97 (1984): 1611–1800 for a comprehensive analysis. Authors not identified.

[43] *Waters v. Churchill,* 511 U.S. 661, 675 (1994).

[44] *U.S. Civil Service Commission v. National Association of Letter Carriers,* 413 U.S. 548 (1973).

[45] *Pickering v. Board of Education,* 563. See *Connick v. Meyers,* 461 U.S. 138 (1983) for the Supreme Court's effort

to distinguish between employee speech of public versus private concern.

[46] *U.S. Civil Service Commission v. National Association of Letter Carriers,* 548.

[47] *Rankin v. McPherson,* 378, 327, note 13.

[48] *Id.* at 384.

[49] *Pickering v. Board of Education,* 563.

[50] *U.S. v. National Treasury Employees Union,* 513 U.S. 454 (1995).

[51] *Waters v. Churchill,* 661, 678.

[52] *Connick v. Meyers,* 138.

[53] *Elfbrandt v. Russell,* 384 U.S. 11, 17 (1966).

[54] See Robert Roberts, *White House Ethics: The History of the Politics of Conflict of Interest Regulation* (New York: Greenwood Press, 1988).

[55] *Elrod v. Burns,* 427 U.S. 347 (1976); *Branti v. Finkel,* 445 U.S. 506 (1980); and *Rutan v. Republican Party of Illinois,* 497 U.S. 62 (1990).

[56] *Chicago Teachers Union v. Hudson,* 475 U.S. 292, 310 (1986).

[57] *Lemon v. Kurtzman,* 403 U.S. 602 (1971).

[58] See also *Torcaso v. Watkins,* 367 U.S. 488 (1961).

[59] *Capitol Square Review and Advisory Board v. Pinette,* 510 U.S. 1307 (1994).

[60] In *Goldman v. Weinberger,* 475 U.S. 503 (1986), the Supreme Court upheld the constitutionality of a U.S. Air Force regulation prohibiting religious headgear (an Orthodox Jew's skullcap). However, the majority opinion made much of the military's need for discipline and sacrifice of individuality for the sake of solidarity.

[61] See *id. Sherbert v. Verner,* 374 U.S. 398 (1963); *Thomas v. Review Board,* 450 U.S. 707 (1981); and *Hobbie v. Unemployment Appeals Commission,* 480 U.S. 136 (1987), which require exceptions for some religious practices or beliefs in unemployment compensation programs. The tension between the establishment and free exercise clauses is well illustrated by *Sherbert.* A Seventh Day Adventist could not constitutionally be deprived of unemployment compensation benefits on the basis that he took himself out of the workforce by refusing to work on his Sabbath, Saturday. But an individual refusing to work on Saturday for secular reasons could be denied the benefits. This outcome gives a special, preferential status to religiously motivated behavior. When a personnel decision is the result of the application of a general criminal law, it will presumably be valid if rationally related to the achievement of legitimate governmental objectives. But there is considerable opposition to the Supreme Court's construction of the First Amendment on this point. It raises the specter that long-standing religious practices, such as male circumcision and ritual wine drinking by minors, can be incidentally criminalized under child abuse or other statutes. See *City of Boerne v. Flores,* 117 S.Ct. 2157 (1997).

[62] *Baggett v. Bullitt,* 377 U.S. 360, 362 [1964]; *Elfbrandt v. Russell,* 11, 19. See also *Cole v. Richardson,* 405 U.S. 676 (1972).

[63] *Cole v. Richardson,* 676.

[64] For example, *Pickering v. Board of Education,* 563.

[65] *Kewly v. HHS,* 153 F.3d 1357 (1998). Under the Whistle Blower Protection Act of 1989, the employee must show by a preponderance of the evidence that the employee's disclosure of whistle-blower information was a contributing factor in the agency's adverse personnel action against the employee. If the disclosure was a contributing factor, then the burden shifts to the agency, and the agency must prove by clear and convincing evidence that it would have taken the same personnel action in the absence of the disclosure.

[66] A good source on whistle-blowing, which includes a state-by-state analysis, is Marcia Miceli and Janet Near, *Blowing the Whistle* (New York: Lexington Books, 1992).

[67] *O'Connor v. Ortega,* 480 U.S. 709, 723 (1987).

[68] *Id.*

[69] *National Treasury Employees Union v. Von Raab,* 489 U.S. 656 (1989).

[70] *Mathews v. Eldridge,* 424 U.S. 319 (1976); *Cleveland Board of Education v. Loudermill,* 470 U.S. 532 (1985).

[71] *Cleveland Board of Education v. Loudermill,* 532.

[72] *Id.* at p. 546.

[73] *Board of Regents v. Roth,* 408 U.S. 564 (1972).

[74] See *Rankin v. McPherson,* 378, 383–384: "Even though McPherson was merely a probationary employee, and even if she could have been discharged for any reason or for no reason at all, she may nonetheless be entitled to reinstatement if she was discharged for exercising her constitutional right to freedom of expression."

[75] *Codd v. Velger,* 429 U.S. 624 (1977).

[76] *Cleveland Board of Education v. Loudermill,* 532.

[77] *Gilbert v. Homar,* No. 96-651 (1997); U.S. Supreme Court.

[78] *Cleveland Board of Education v. LaFleur,* 414 U.S. 632, 639 (1974).

[79] *Kelley v. Johnson,* 425 U.S. 238 (1976); *McCarthy v. Philadelphia Civil Service Commission,* 424 U.S. 645 (1976).

[80] See *Adarand Constructors v. Pena,* 515 U.S. 200 (1995) for a recent Supreme Court explanation.

[81] See *U.S. v. Paradise,* 480 U.S. 149 (1987).

[82] *Grutter v. Bollinger,* No. 02-241 (2003), 19–20.

[83] *Id.* and *Gratz v. Bollinger,* U.S. Supreme Court, No. 02-516 (2003), 26–27.

[84] See *Zobel v. Williams,* 457 U.S. 55 (1982), for a Supreme Court explanation of rational basis review.

[85] *Murgia v. Massachusetts Board of Retirement,* 427 U.S. 307 (1976).

[86] In *McCarthy v. Philadelphia Civil Service Commission,* 645, the Supreme Court gave very short shrift to the challenge to public human resource management residency requirements, despite the rather compelling circumstances of the employee involved.

[87] President Bill Clinton's directive that federal agencies endeavor to hire welfare recipients as part of the overall welfare reform of 1996 is an example.

[88] *Hampton v. Mow Sun Wong,* 426 U.S. 88 (1976).

[89] *U.S. v. Virginia,* 518 U.S. 515 (1996).

[90] *Shapiro v. Thompson,* 394 U.S. 618 (1969).

CHAPTER 6

Employee Benefits: Creating an Environment for Excellence

N. JOSEPH CAYER AND WILL VOLK

As part of the total compensation package, employee benefits play a strong role in the success of local governments in attracting and retaining high-performing employees. Local governments face many challenges in designing and delivering benefits programs as the needs of employees continually change and the employment market constantly adjusts to new realities. They must remain competitive in the labor market, but local governments are also under pressure to reduce expenditures and increase services. As with the other personnel issues addressed in this book, employee benefits require continuous assessment and adjustment.

Structure of Benefit Plans

Guiding Principles

- Benefits help the local government stay competitive in the labor market.
- Benefits must be adapted to the needs of employees.

Challenges

- Offering competitive benefits and meeting the needs of a diverse workforce while staying within budget.
- Managing the administration of benefits.

Local government employers need to inventory what types of benefits they offer and how those benefits fit together to serve the needs of all their employees. Some benefits are mandated by federal or state law; others are optional. The appropriate balance between mandated and optional benefits presents another issue for the employer.

Mandated Benefits

Mandated benefits include social security, unemployment compensation, workers' compensation, as well as family and medical leave. Many of these benefits emerged out of the New Deal programs of the 1930s and are often referred to as social insurance programs. Family and medical leave is the latest to be added to the mandated benefits.

Social Security. Social Security provides employees with retirement income and income security for individuals unable to work because of injury or illness. Survivors of employees who paid into Social Security are also covered. For nearly 60 years, local governments could participate in Social Security on a voluntary basis, but in 1991, legislation required that state and local government employees not covered by a public retirement system be included in Social Security.

A challenge for local governments is how to integrate Social Security and local retirement pension packages, especially as concern over the long-term solvency of Social Security grows. One solution that has been suggested is to develop formulas to incorporate Social Security benefits into retirement pensions, but so far, no formal action has been taken. Local governments can choose to include the Social Security benefits as part of their overall retirement benefit plans, but because the national government keeps changing the base salary for Social Security contributions and benefits, it is difficult to develop a formula. Some jurisdictions include Social Security when explaining their complete benefit portfolio to their employees.

Unemployment Compensation. Unemployment compensation, also part of the Social Security Act of 1935, offers temporary income to individuals who have been laid off or, in certain instances, quit their jobs as long as they actively seek employment. Beneficiaries receive a fixed level of income for some specified number of weeks. Employers and the national government contribute to the fund that supports the program.

Workers' Compensation. Workers' compensation provides part of the wages as well as medical and rehabilitation benefits to employ-

ees who are unable to work because of work-related injuries. The major challenge for local government employers is in controlling abuse by a small number of employees who take advantage of the system. (This problem is addressed more fully in Chapter 5.)

Family and Medical Leave. The Family and Medical Leave Act of 1993 (FMLA) established the newest mandated benefit. All employers with at least 50 employees must provide up to 12 weeks of unpaid leave for the birth or adoption of a child; foster care; care of a sick spouse, child, or parent; or the employee's own serious health condition during any 12-month period. In 2002, California became the first state to adopt a paid family leave plan providing employees up to 55 percent of their pay for six weeks. Among the challenges for local government employers has been reconciling the requirements of FMLA with other requirements, such as those of the Fair Labor Standards Act (FLSA) or accommodations under the Americans with Disabilities Act (ADA) and other federal laws, as these regulations have been interpreted. (For more on the FMLA and ADA, see Chapter 5.)

Optional Benefits

Local government employers offer their employees many benefits not required by law, hoping to attract and retain high-performance employees. Health care plans and retirement pension plans are offered by almost all local government employers; 86 percent of state and local government employees received health care benefits in 1998 and 98 percent participated in retirement plans. Similarly, 67 percent earn vacation leave and 96 percent have sick leave benefits.[1] Educational leave and tuition reimbursement for job-related courses and workshops are common. Many local government employers also offset their employees' child care and elder care expenses.

Because the list of discretionary benefits constantly increases and employees have different needs depending on their family circumstances, many employers have created a system called a cafeteria plan (see page 163). The local government establishes a fixed amount of benefit expenditures per employee and permits the employee to determine how to spend part of the allocation. For example, a local government might allocate some portion of each employee's health benefits to single health coverage, some to long-term disability, and some to life insurance, leaving the remainder to the individual employee to use to upgrade health insurance, purchase dental insurance, purchase additional life insurance, or take as taxable income.[2] In most cases, employees can pay for additional coverage beyond what the employer provides.

Health Care. Health care plans are among the most commonly offered benefits provided by local government employers. The Agency for Healthcare Research and Quality found that in 2000, 99.9 percent of state and local governments offered medical insurance. The U.S. Department of Commerce found in 1994 that 65 percent provided dental coverage, and 89 percent offered mental health coverage.[3]

Contemporary health care plans cover many types of health care needs, but that has not always been the case. Traditional plans included only medication and hospitalization to treat physical illness and maintain physical health. Plans gradually added mental-health care and limited dental coverage. Local governments learned that preventive health measures could help contain the growing costs of health care coverage and thus began to focus on prevention. Prevention measures include regular physical exams, wellness programs, nutrition counseling, encouragement of healthy lifestyles, exercise, and reduction of stress.

Health care plans are among the most costly benefits provided, and health care costs have continually gone up. Estimates of the level of expenditure vary widely, but in 2001

about 14.1 percent of the gross domestic product, representing approximately $1.4 trillion, was spent on health care. Efforts by employers to contain costs show results in the decline of premium payments as a percentage of payroll expenses. In 1980, premiums were $245 billion, or 8.8 percent of the total payroll of $2.8 trillion, while in 2001, premiums amounted to $327 billion, or only 6.7 percent of the total payroll of $4.9 trillion.[4] Local government employers did their part in finding new ways to contain costs.

Traditionally, local government employers offered indemnity plans in which employees were free to choose their medical services and providers. The plans paid for specific services rendered for given maladies, and payments were generally made directly to the service provider, such as the physician or hospital. Some argue that such plans fostered abuse by encouraging the use of possibly unnecessary procedures because they would be covered.

To contain spiraling costs, employers switched to health maintenance organizations (HMOs) and preferred provider organizations (PPOs). Under these plans, the employer contracts with the HMO or PPO to cover employee health care costs. The employee selects a particular group practice (HMO) or a particular physician who is under contract with the PPO. The HMO or PPO agrees to provide services according to some fixed cost. Employees may be required to pay some agreed-upon fee (copayment) depending on the service received. Employers have found that costs continue to increase, but at a slower rate for HMOs and PPOs than for the traditional indemnity plans.

Continually increasing health care costs have prompted local governments to ask employees to share in the cost of premiums. Increased deductibles and copayments also help reduce the overall cost to the employer, while increasing the cost to the employee. Along with such sharing, employers may offer more than one option to employees. ICMA

Health Insurance Coverage under COBRA

fyi

The Consolidated Omnibus Budget Reconciliation Act (COBRA) requires local governments with 20 or more employees to offer continued coverage under the jurisdiction's group health plan to former eligible employees and their dependents. The table below identifies the qualifying events that determine eligibility and length of coverage. It is the employer's responsibility to inform the employee, spouse, and dependents about their COBRA rights when they become eligible for the plan. The former employee becomes responsible for paying both the employer's and employee's share of the premium cost. The employer may charge an additional 2 percent administrative fee.

Qualifying Event	Persons Covered	Length of Coverage
Termination of employment	Employee, spouse, dependents	18 months
Reduction of work hours	Employee, spouse, dependents	18 months
Employee's death	Surviving spouse, dependents	36 months
Employee's divorce or legal separation	Former spouse, dependents	36 months
Former employee's Medicare entitlement	Spouse, dependents	36 months
Change in dependent status	Former dependent	36 months
Employee disability	Employee, spouse, dependents	29 months

Source: Consolidated Omnibus Budget Reconciliation Act of 1985 (P.L. 99-272, April 7, 1986; 42 U.S.C. § 300bb). In 2004, the Department of Labor released final regulations and model forms governing the notice requirements for continuing health care coverage under COBRA. To comply with the regulations, which are generally effective for plan years beginning on or after January 1, 2005, employers will have to modify their COBRA forms and procedures, as well as the COBRA provisions of their health plan's summary plan description.

found in 1994 that approximately one-third of local government employers offered some combination of indemnity, HMO, and PPO plans. Thus, employees can choose which plan they prefer, but they bear more of the expense as the cost of the plan increases. For example, the indemnity plan is most expensive for the employee, whereas the HMO is least expensive.

Other Insurance. Disability insurance constitutes another form of insurance benefit. Most local governments provide short-term disability coverage at no cost to the employee and make long-term disability coverage available at the employee's expense. Group rates allow the employee to purchase the coverage at lower rates than if purchased individually. Many employers also purchase life insurance policies

for their employees, usually in an amount equivalent to a single year of salary with the option for employees to purchase additional coverage at group rates.

Legal insurance is another employee benefit program offered increasingly by local government employers. Although government employees are usually indemnified for actions within their authority and undertaken in good faith, employers may offer coverage for non-work-related legal expenses. Employers generally offer this type of coverage at group rates for purchase at the employees' expense.

Leave. Local governments offer many types of leave to their employees, including holiday, vacation, sick, and family care leave. In most jurisdictions, employees receive national holidays, and some jurisdictions offer special holidays such as Statehood Day. Holiday leave totals 10 to 12 working days a year in most local governments. Paid vacation leave typically amounts to a week or two in the first few years of employment. After five years or so, employees receive gradually increasing vacation time up to some maximum amount, such as four weeks per year.

Virtually all local government employers also offer sick leave, normally based on the amount of time worked. Commonly, employees accrue a day a month or so, which they use as needed. As a rule, they may accrue only a certain amount of sick leave and must use it by a certain date or lose it. In some jurisdictions, unused sick leave may be paid out in cash, particularly if the employee leaves the organization, or may be converted to vacation leave at a 4 to 1 (or other) ratio once the employee's unused sick leave reaches a certain level. Some jurisdictions also allow employees to share their unused sick leave with other employees who need it, either through a pool arrangement or by direct donations.

About 60 percent of local government employers provide maternity leave, and about 40 percent offer paternity leave. Family leave other than that required under the FMLA also may be offered for such things as bereavement or special occasions involving children; however, these provisions are usually very limited. Some jurisdictions offer personal leave amounting to a day or two a year, which the employees may take for any reason as long as they plan it in advance. Many employers have introduced personal leave to curb abuse of sick leave.

Because leave policies have become complex and abuses have led to inequities for employees, many employers have developed comprehensive approaches to leave policy, sometimes called paid time-off (PTO) arrangements. The International Personnel Management Association conducted a survey in 1996 in which it found that 43 percent of its agency members (most of which are local government agencies) have comprehensive leave policies.[5] Comprehensive leave policies establish a set number of leave days, which the employee can use for vacation, sick, or other leave. Typically, the employees accrue leave time according to the length of time they are employed by the jurisdiction. More detail on this approach is provided later in the chapter.

Leave for military service has taken on new importance because of the military actions in Afghanistan and Iraq. National policy requires employers, including local governments, to guarantee employees who take leave for military service full re-employment rights. Employees returning from military service are entitled to their former positions with full seniority or to a job of similar pay, rank, and seniority. Returning employees also must receive any pay increases, promotions, or other benefits they would have received if their employment had not been interrupted. See Chapter 5 for information on the Uniform Services Employment and Reemployment Rights Act of 1994.

Family Care. As noted previously, the FMLA mandates certain leave for family care, but many local government employers also offer other forms of leave. As child care is an issue for young families, some local governments provide child care subsidies, and even more employers offer elder care programs for employees with elderly parents or other family members. These services (especially child care) may be offered on premises, but most plans provide for some subsidy.

Employee Development. Local government employers have long recognized that to keep up with changing circumstances, fiscal constraints, and demands for improved services, they must provide for the continuous development of their employees. This can involve internal or external programs. Training and development opportunities, offered internally, are common in larger jurisdictions. These pro-

Bereavement

fyi

In the United States, bereavement leave is generally quite limited and permitted only for the period of the funeral. For instance, California allows its state employees only the equivalent of 24 work hours of leave (with an additional 16 hours if it is necessary to travel some distance). Many policies are also limited in terms of the qualifying relationship with the deceased and thus exclude aunts, uncles, and close friends. As with family and medical leave, bereavement leave is usually either unpaid or counted against an employee's regular leave time. If an organization allows flextime or compensatory (comp) time, most employees are willing to make up this time. These accommodations are usually minor to the employer, but they may loom large in an employee's perceptions and communicate a true concern by the organization for his or her welfare.

Requests for extended bereavement leaves, defined as leave for medical or family care under the Family and Medical Leave Act of 1993, seem to be growing. Employees taking extended bereavement leave may also claim temporary disability (especially for episodic depression). Medical problems should be verified through affidavits of physicians or clinical psychologists.

Supervisors have a responsibility to handle bereavement in the workplace with tact. When a supervisor finds that someone significant to an employee has died, the supervisor should

- Respond immediately to the news
- Avoid platitudes or statements that may offend the employee, who may not share the supervisor's theology
- Inform the employee's co-workers
- Ease the employee back to work
- Check with the employee periodically (every two weeks)
- Refer the employee to bereavement groups
- Watch for signs of depression or sleep disorders that can affect job performance.*

Most supervisors underestimate the time that an employee needs to return to full performance. The workplace culture expects people to carry a stiff upper lip, but it may take weeks, months, or a year or more before the employee is operating at 100 percent.

* Philip M. Perry, "How to Deal with a Grieving Employee," *Law Practice Management* (April 1996): 44–49. For a series of brochures providing helpful advice for handling grief in the workplace, write to the Hospice Council of Metropolitan Washington, 1377 K Street, N.W., Suite 66, Washington, DC 20005.

Source: Theodore Pedeliski.

grams typically focus on the knowledge and skills that employees need to perform their jobs effectively. Workshops can be used for a variety of learning outcomes, ranging from updating basic computer skills to reviewing changes in law and policy affecting employees' work. In some cases, the training and development also address broader professional and personal development issues.

Smaller jurisdictions can make use of external training and development opportunities. There are many workshops, institutes, and seminars available on topics of relevance to local government employees. Most employers provide funds for such programs, offering tuition reimbursement for job-related classes or degree programs that will enhance the skills and abilities of their employees. Professional

The Family-Friendly Workplace

fyi

Since absenteeism and tardiness can be caused by family obligations, creating a family-friendly workplace can reduce attendance problems. Some employers allow employees to participate in student-teacher conferences during work hours or to take their children to medical appointments. More comprehensive family-friendly personnel policies allow for job sharing, part-time employment, flextime, compressed workweeks, and paid time off for personal and family responsibilities. Public employers with flextime and comp-time programs have found that employees are quite willing to make up time lost in dealing with a family emergency. Another experimental accommodation allows employees with child care or nursing demands to carry out their job functions by working out of their homes or telecommuting.

However, telecommuting raises its own problems.* Under the Fair Labor Standards Act (FLSA), there are currently no regulations that deal with record keeping and monitoring of employees who are covered by overtime provisions and who also telecommute. Employers are well advised to take steps to reduce their legal exposure under the FLSA. The employer should implement a written policy against covered employees working overtime unless they obtain prior express permission from a supervisor.

* Deborah A. Sudbury and Douglas M. Towns, "Traps for the Unwary: Employment Law Implications of Telecommuting," *Employee Relations Law Journal* 23 (Winter 1997): 5–29.

Source: Theodore Pedeliski.

conferences permit employees to maintain currency in their fields and also allow for interaction with peers from across the country. Professional organizations often use their annual conferences to conduct training and development sessions. Employees may attend these conferences and qualify for reimbursement.

Increasingly, local governments are allocating a certain number of dollars to individual employees for training and development purposes. Employees are able to choose which approved programs best suit their needs and use the money accordingly. The resources for training and development programs not only benefit the employees in their personal growth, but also benefit the employers by ensuring that employees keep abreast of new developments. But well-trained and well-educated employees are more marketable, and employers also have to keep pay and other benefits competitive in the labor market.

Employee Assistance/Wellness Programs. Recognizing that performance on the job is affected by the well-being of the employee, many local governments provide services to assist employees in dealing with stress. Traditionally, employee assistance programs (EAPs) were developed to provide counseling for substance abuse problems. Subsequently, the programs grew to cover almost any personal problem that leads to stress and that might affect concentration on the job, from family issues to legal and financial problems. While some local governments offer in-house EAPs, many provide access to professional consultants under contract to the local government. Employers recognize that it is more cost-effective to help and retain a good employee than it is to recruit and train a new one. EAPs also often offer training on strategies for stress management that can help reduce illness, accidents, and absenteeism related to stress.

Wellness programs can help employees stop smoking, lose weight, or get regular exercise. Healthier employees are less likely to use sick leave or develop medical problems that will increase the organization's health care insurance costs. Awards and other forms of recognition are sometimes used as incentives, and some employers allow employees to convert unused sick leave to cash.

Flexible Schedules, Telecommuting. Some local government employees enjoy flexible work hours or the right to telecommute, that is, to work at home and stay in touch with the office via computer and telephone. Flextime helps the employee who has family obligations that make an 8-to-5 schedule difficult or who just likes working other hours. When some employees come in earlier than the traditional schedule and some stay later, the local government may be able to offer the public extended office hours. Telecommuting enables employees to work at home and maintain family obligations and reduces travel to and from work, thus helping to reduce air pollution and traffic congestion. The local government may choose to provide work-related equipment such as computers that employees need to work at home.

Housing and Moving Incentives. Moving expenses are commonly offered to managerial and professional employees who are recruited from other areas. Housing allowances are often provided to top-level managers. However, some local governments also offer housing allowances to attract and retain police department personnel, especially in high-cost areas. Some local governments use housing allowances to encourage police personnel to live in neighborhoods where their presence may help to reduce crime or contribute to redevelopment efforts.

Uniforms. For some employees, uniforms or a uniform/clothing allowance may be provided to offset the cost of required dress standards.

Awards. Award programs represent another type of benefit. Employees receive awards for suggestions that lead to the improved performance of the organization. Typically, local governments pay some percentage—perhaps 10 percent—of the first-year savings arising from the employee's suggestion. Theoretically, award programs help maintain and improve morale.

Retirement Pensions. Like health care, local government pensions represent one of the most costly employee benefits. However, pension costs have been declining as a percentage of total compensation, to 5.8 percent in 2001, down from 9 percent in 1996.[6] While most employers offer a specific retirement investment plan, many also allow the employees to choose from among approved financial consultants who can design an investment option for individual employees.

Retirement benefits were originally developed as *defined benefits plans.* They guaranteed the employee a fixed benefit based on the employee's age and number of years of service. Traditionally, these plans were based on a pay-as-you-go approach, which requires the jurisdiction to raise the money to pay for the benefits as employees retire and start drawing pensions. However, pay-as-you-go led to many problems for local governments because, during election years, local political leaders often found it tempting to promise increased retirement pensions, knowing that someone else would have to come up with the money when the bills came due. Political leaders also often bought labor-union peace with agreements to increase retirement pensions. During the 1960s and 1970s, it was common for local governments to agree to generous pension plans. During the 1980s, however, many of those jurisdictions faced severe financial strain as the costs of the pensions came due at the same time that voters were cutting taxes and, thus, the revenue to pay for the increased costs.

As a result, local governments explored other options, the most important of which is the *defined contribution plan.* In defined contribution plans, the employee's ultimate pension is based on both the amount of money invested for the individual employee and the earnings on that investment. Accounts are set up in the name of each employee and money is contributed to the account. Additionally, the individual employee's share of the earnings on the investment is credited to the account. At retirement, the employee receives a pension based on the amount in that employee's account. In most instances, both the employer and employee contribute money to the account. See Exhibit 6-1 for a comparison of defined benefit and defined contribution plans.

With the defined contribution plans, forward funding (in which money is set aside and invested as obligations are incurred) replaces pay-as-you-go so that the costs to the local government are more predictable. Defined contribution plans have not been universally embraced, largely because public pension funds have a reputation for being poor performers. Traditionally, the investment strategies of fund managers have been very conservative. But more recently, some public investment funds have engaged in speculative ventures or politically motivated investment strategies that were unsound. In some states, pension funds have also been used to balance budgets or reduce taxes. On top of that, the performance of the funds depends on the fluctuations of the financial markets. For all these reasons, employees may be mistrustful of defined contribution plans. However, with good management, such a plan can benefit employees and employers alike.

Most states operate retirement systems, which local governments are required to join or for which they are eligible. Thus, the operation of the fund is handled at the state level, and the local government functions within state requirements. The statewide systems help to alleviate some of the fiscal problems that local governments have encountered with their own funds. For example, after many local government systems in Massachusetts found themselves in serious financial difficulties, a statewide system was created that allows local governments to pool resources so that they can forward fund their pension plans. This means money for pensions is invested during the tenure of the employee, and at the time of the employee's retirement, payments are made from this pooled fund rather than from the current operating budget.

Demographic changes present challenges to retirement systems. The aging of the population and questions about the solvency of the Social Security system create concerns about the ability of retirement systems to meet their obligations and of retirees to receive adequate pensions. The concern is particularly important for those with pay-as-you go systems, but it affects others as well. Longer life spans and early retirement place strains on the funds. How to integrate Social Security income into the retirement pension planning provides another challenge to the local government employer.

Many employers also permit employees to defer some compensation. The federal government, through the Internal Revenue Code (IRC), allows employees to shield up to a maximum of $13,000 in 2004 for employees age 49 or under and $16,000 for those 50 and over. The maximum increases by $1,000 annually through 2006 for those 49 and under and $2,000 for those 50 and over. After 2006, the amount increases $500 per year for everyone. The amount the employee wants to set aside is deducted from pay before taxes are calculated. The deferred compensation can be invested in options chosen by the employee. Taxes are paid at the time the employee starts taking payouts from the investments, typically at retirement.

Delivery of Benefit Plans

Guiding Principle

- Benefits must be considered part of the total compensation package and expressed in terms of their aggregate cash value to the employee and their total expense to the employer.

Most compensation programs are designed from a historical perspective around the typical, and often traditional, worker needs. These programs rarely consider today's more common two-wage carner, single-parent, or

Exhibit 6-1   A Comparison of Defined Benefit and Defined Contribution Plans

	Defined Benefit	**Defined Contribution**
Investment account	Plan level	Individual employee
Employee benefit	Specified in advance	Depends on account value
Employer cost	Depends on various factors	Specified in advance
Investment decision making	Employer	Employee

Objectives

	Defined Benefit	**Defined Contribution**
Funding certainty	Plan liabilities change on the basis of changes in actuarial assumptions (e.g., future salary increases, investment earnings, employee turnover).	Employer liability is fulfilled annually as contributions are made to employee accounts.
Predictable costs	Annual cash expenditure for plan varies from year to year on the basis of actuarial assumptions (see above).	Annual cash expenditures are more predictable as they are based on employee salaries.
Recruitment tool	Benefits are not portable and may not be so appealing to an increasingly mobile workforce.	Benefits are portable and may be more appealing to an increasingly mobile workforce.
Reward long-term employees	Benefits are typically based on final year(s) salary, rewarding long-service employees.	Benefits are based on accumulated contributions and earnings.
Lower administrative expenses	Expenses include actuarial evaluation in addition to record keeping and investment management.	Expenses are generally lower than for a defined benefit plan because no actuarial evaluation is necessary.
Reduce investment risk	Investment risk is assumed by the employer. Adverse experience increases employer funding costs.	Investment risk is assumed by the employee. Adverse experience does not increase employer funding costs.
Unlimited benefit potential	Benefits paid at retirement are predetermined by the plan's benefit formula.	Benefits paid at retirement are not limited by a formula. There is a potential to earn greater benefits through superior investment results.
Ease of understanding	Benefits are based on variables that are difficult to predict (e.g., future earnings and years of service at retirement).	Benefits accumulate each year, and contributions are generally based on a percentage of earnings. Participant statements present benefits accumulated to date.
Access to benefits while employed	Benefits may not be withdrawn under any circumstances during active employment.	Benefits may be withdrawn under certain circumstances provided that Internal Revenue Service guidelines are followed.

Source: Adapted from Kathleen Jenks Harm, "Defined Contribution Retirement Plans," *MIS Report* (October 1996): 2.

single-with-no-dependents employees. Moreover, they rarely address changes in the needs as employees age, lose dependent coverage, or plan for retirement.

To better accommodate these considerations, local government employers have in recent years established plans that blur the line between pay (direct compensation) and benefits (indirect compensation). While traditional pay systems focus almost exclusively on cash compensation and employees often view benefits in noneconomic terms, employers recognize the need to control ever-increasing staff costs by expressing these expenses in terms of their aggregate cash value to the employee and the corresponding bottom-line expense to the employer.

Recognizing, communicating, and permitting a degree of employee control over the form in which the aggregate income is paid is the principle at the heart of the total compensation concept. Full expression of this principle includes permitting the opting out from available plans in exchange for higher cash compensation; or the shifting of income from the paycheck to higher-cost medical or dental plans; or perhaps the purchase of additional time off, consistent with established plan rules as well as with accounting, actuarial, and tax considerations.

Flexible Benefits Plans

A more limited form of a total compensation plan is one that focuses primarily on choice within the benefits arena. Such plans often are referred to as flexible or "cafeteria" benefit plans. The key elements that define a cafeteria plan are that (1) participants are employees, and (2) participants may choose from a "menu" of options consisting of cash and "qualified benefits."

Tradable Plans. In a typical cafeteria arrangement, the value and equivalency of tradable plans, stated in terms of dollar cost, internal tender (flex bucks/flex credits), or

other related concepts, are established. Employees are then provided with the opportunity to "purchase" the level of benefits they wish to have and perhaps receive any value not spent, either in cash as a lump sum or in their paychecks. Normally these plans require some level of basic participation in at least the medical plan.

Currently, most cafeteria plans are limited to the following options:

- Medical/dental, eye care, hearing care, etc.
- Group term-life insurance
- Short-/long-term disability plans
- Group legal services
- Cash or IRC-eligible deferred compensation plans
- Vacation or paid time-off plans.

A sample flexible benefits plan configuration is included as Exhibit 6-2, pages 164–165.

Flexible Spending Plans. These plans, also referred to as "income reduction plans," provide employees with a choice between taxable cash and nontaxable compensation in the form of payment or reimbursement of eligible expenses. The employee funds this plan by voluntarily making nontaxed payments into it. These payments represent a reduction in the employee's taxable income. Participants may use this money to pay medical and dental insurance premiums, and eligible medical and child care expenses. Medical savings accounts are an example, but they have unique rules regarding forfeiture, among other things.

A recent development in these plans is to provide a debit card to access these flexible spending funds. Many out-of-pocket costs are eliminated and the administration associated with processing reimbursements is significantly reduced.

Paid Time-Off Plans. Traditional paid vacation, sick leave, and bereavement leave plans have been in place with most employers for decades. Increasingly, these plans are being replaced by paid time-off (PTO) arrangements. A key reason for this shift is the highly structured nature of the traditional arrangements, which typically incorporate extensive rules and procedures. Sick leave rules in particular require supervisors to make highly subjective judgments, and the actual use of the sick leave benefit varies greatly within the typical employee population. For these reasons, it is virtually impossible to achieve equity and consistency across the workforce in the provision of this particular benefit.

Typical PTO plans replace existing policies on vacation, sick leave, funeral leave, and occasionally holidays, and combine these benefits into a single plan. Usually the total number of days available under PTO plans is less than the sum available under the previous policies. This, however, is a function of the specific provisions in place, jurisdiction time-off philosophy, and employee time-off usage trends.

A key feature of PTO plans is the time-off approval process. Although sick leave ulti-

---

Exhibit 6-2   FlexComp Plan—Dakota County, Minnesota

Overview of Plan Components

Medical Plans

HealthPartners Choice Plan is a two-tiered medical plan that offers access to both the HealthPartners network and physicians not participating in the network.

HealthPartners Exclusive Plan is an HMO medical plan that offers access to the HealthPartners network. Premium cost is 10 percent less than the HealthPartners Choice plan.

HealthPartners Plus Plan is a three-tiered medical plan that offers access to the HealthPartners network, to a specialists network, and to physicians not participating in either network Premium cost is 10 percent greater than the HealthPartners Choice plan.

Dental Plans

Preventive Dental Plan is a preventive dental plan that covers preventive care only. After a $5 office visit copay, 100 percent coverage for preventive services. No coverage for restorative, major services, and orthodontia.

Comprehensive Dental Plan is a comprehensive dental plan with two levels of coverage. The

choice of a dental provider determines the level of coverage received. Orthodontia coverage not included.

Life Insurance Plans

Basic Life Insurance & AD&D provides $30,000 life insurance and $30,000 AD&D coverage at no cost to employee.

Employee Supplemental Life: Employees have a one-time opportunity to purchase $40,000 of life insurance without providing evidence of insurability. With evidence of insurability, employees may apply for supplemental life insurance in $5,000 units up to a maximum of $300,000. Rates are based on the employee's age.

Spouse Supplemental Life: Employees have a one-time opportunity to purchase $10,000 of spouse life insurance without the spouse providing evidence of insurability. With evidence of insurability, employees may apply for spouse supplemental life insurance in $5,000 units up to a maximum of $150,000. Rates are based on the spouse's age.

Child(ren) Supplemental Life Insurance: Employees have a one-time opportunity to purchase $10,000 of child(ren) life coverage without providing evidence of insurability. The unit rate for mately ought to be available only when the employee is sick, this is often not the case. Supervisors become entangled in questions that they are ill equipped to handle and that lend themselves to inconsistent application. Time off under PTO plans, on the other hand, typically is subject only to nonintrusive notice/ request/approval procedures that have been developed consistent with labor contracts or other related policy considerations. A sample PTO policy and plan configuration is provided in Exhibits 6-3a and 6-3b, pages 166–169.

Insured vs. Self-Insured Arrangements

While some significant opportunities can be gained through self-insured arrangements (primarily with medical or dental plans), such an approach should be considered with caution. This is particularly true for smaller jurisdictions, that is, those with fewer than 750 to 1,000 plan participants (not the same as the number of employees). As the term suggests, the jurisdiction serves as the "insurance company" with all the corresponding risks and rewards. Size is significant first with respect to

---

$10,000 of child(ren) life is $2.00 per month regardless of the number of children covered.

Plus Account (Pretax Spending Accounts)
Health Care Expense Account
Dependent Day Care Expense Account
Pretax Premium Payment Accounts
Flex Leave credits not used to pay for benefit premiums may be rolled into the Plus Account.

Short-Term Disability Plans
8-Day Elimination Period Plan
30-Day Elimination Period Plan
75-Day Elimination Period Plan

Long-Term Disability Options
40 percent benefit level
60 percent benefit level

Long-Term Care Plan
A direct-bill, group, long-term care program that is after-tax and completely employee-paid. Coverage is available to employees and retirees, spouses, parents and parents-in-law, grandparents and grandparents-in-law.

Flex Leave Credits
Amount of Flex Leave that can be converted:

Enrollment in Short-Term Disability
8-Day Plan
   5 days/40 hours
30-Day Plan
   3 days/24 hours
75-Day Plan
   2 days/16 hours

Enrollment in Long-Term Disability
40 percent Benefit
   1 day/8 hours
60 percent Benefit
   2 days/16 hours

If employees have used 30 percent of their Flex Leave accrual rate during the previous payroll year and have a Flex Leave balance of 80 hours or more, they are eligible to convert an additional 3 days/24 hours of Flex Leave to cover the cost of their benefit elections.

Wellness Credit
Eligible employees may use their Wellness Credit ($5.00 per month) to apply toward the cost of their benefit elections.

Note: The Dakota County flexible compensation program was begun in 1992. Since then it has been adopted in a number of other jurisdictions. There is little question that this approach represents the direction of benefits programs both private and public. The county received an achievement award for the FlexComp Plan from the National Association of Counties (NACo) in 1998.

Exhibit 6-3a Sample Paid Time-Off Plan—Dakota County, Minnesota

Introduction

It has been a continuing objective of Dakota County to provide equity, consistency, and flexibility in the delivery of benefits alternatives to County staff. Where appropriate, certain benefits have also been designed to incorporate employee tenure so as to recognize and reward loyal service to the County. These considerations are particularly significant in the accrual, utilization, and administration of paid time off.

While traditional paid vacation, sick leave and funeral leave have been in place for many years, those programs are highly structured, with extensive rules being applied to the actual use of the benefit. With sick leave in particular, these rules often inject the employer into employees' personal lives and require supervisors to make highly subjective judgments. Utilization of sick leave also varies greatly within the employee population and it is, therefore, virtually impossible to achieve equity across the workforce in the provision of this particular benefit.

The Flex Leave Plan replaces County policies on vacation, sick leave, and funeral leave and combines these benefits into a single plan. All eligible employees accrue Flex Leave based on tenure. Plan provisions discourage unnecessary utilization by providing cash and savings incentives.

Flex Leave can be utilized for any purpose, subject only to normal, non-intrusive request/approval procedures consistent with policy and labor contracts.

With the adoption of this plan, Dakota County firmly accepts and endorses the principles of equity, consistency, flexibility, and the recognition of tenure in the delivery of this benefit.

Policy

It is the policy of Dakota County to provide employees necessary paid time away from work. This policy is implemented by means of the Flex Leave Plan, which covers all paid leave previously available under the County's vacation, sick leave, and funeral leave policies.

Flex Leave can be utilized for any purpose, subject only to necessary request/approval procedures consistent with policy and labor contracts.

Eligibility

All non-union, full-time and part-time Dakota County employees participate in the Flex Leave Plan. Part-time employees accrue Flex Leave on a pro-rata basis.

Accrual Rates (New hires)

Years of Service	Annual Accrual Rate
0 – 5 years	160 hours/20 days
6 – 10 years	192 hours/24 days
11 – 15 years	240 hours/30 days
16 or more years	304 hours/38 days

Non-union employees hired prior to September 6, 1992, will accrue Flex Leave at the rate established under previous vacation and sick leave policies until such time as the Flex Leave provisions are equal to or greater than the previous combined vacation and sick leave provisions.

Use of Flex Leave

Flex Leave is accrued on a per pay period basis and may be used subsequent to the pay period in which it was earned. Non-emergency use must be requested in advance per departmental policies. Emergency use may require documentation of the emergency. Probationary employees may use no more than 16 hours of Flex Leave during their probationary period. Maximum carry over from one year to the next is 125 days/1,000 hours. Employees who are eligible to participate in the County's post-employment health care savings plan will have the cash equivalency of hours in excess of 1,000 deposited in the Minnesota State Health Care Savings Plan (HCSP) according to the provisions in the post-employment health care savings plan.

Annual Conversion Option

Employees with a minimum Flex Leave balance of 60 hours at the end of the 3rd payroll quarter may convert (subject to maximum deferral regulations as stated in IRC Section 457) up to 20 percent of their Flex Leave balance each year to the County's deferred compensation plan if they have used a minimum of 60 hours of Flex Leave during the first three quarters of the current payroll year. Conversion of Flex Leave to deferred compensation will be effective the following year. Employees may additionally convert up to 100 Flex Leave hours to wages to offset the cost of benefits enrollments, provided they maintain a minimum Flex Leave balance of 40 hours after the conversion has occurred. Employees who have terminated County employment and qualify as Dakota County retirees may convert Flex Leave to deferred compensation, subject to maximum deferral regulations as stated in IRC Section 457, on their final paycheck, prior to receiving their severance payment.

Current Vacation/Sick Leave Balances

Existing vacation and sick leave balances shall be converted to the Flex Leave Plan in the following manner. Unused vacation balances shall be converted to Flex Leave accounts of participating employees. New Flex Leave hours, as accrued, shall be added to the converted vacation balance.

Sick leave hours will be converted to the Extended Sick Leave Bank hours.

Extended Sick Leave Bank

For employees hired before September 6, 1992, total unused sick leave hours shall be frozen at the balance in effect at the time of conversion. This account shall become the Extended Sick Leave Bank and may be used for future illness or disability.

In the event of illness, injury, or disability, the first 16 hours of absence in each plan year must be taken from the Flex Leave account before accessing the Extended Sick Leave Bank. Subsequent absence (due to illness, injury, or disability) within that plan year may be taken from the Extended Sick Leave Bank or the Flex Leave account, at the employee's choice.

Employees receiving Worker's Compensation may use their Extended Sick Leave Bank to return to 100% of their current salary.

Termination Benefits

An employee's Flex Leave balance becomes available upon termination or retirement. The following chart provides the details concerning severance benefits.

If the terminating employee:	Severance payment
Qualifies for the post employment health care savings plan	• Post employment healthcare plan provisions apply • Flex Leave termination conversion option is available.
Does *not* qualify for the post employment healthcare savings plan **and** • Does *not* qualify as a Dakota County retiree and • Participates in Flex Leave, and • Has an Extended Sick Leave Bank	• Flex Leave is paid in full • One-half of sick leave to a maximum of 400 hours is paid.
Does *not* qualify for the post employment healthcare savings plan **and** • Qualifies as a Dakota County retiree and • Participates in Flex Leave, and • Has an Extended Sick Leave Bank	• Flex Leave is paid in full • One-half of extended sick leave hours to a maximum of 400 hours is paid • Unpaid extended sick leave hours will be used to create an account from which medical, dental, and life insurance premiums may be paid until it is exhausted or until the retiree dies, whichever comes first.
Does *not* qualify for the post employment healthcare savings plan **and** • Participates in Flex Leave, and • Does *not* have an Extended Sick Leave Bank	• Flex Leave is paid in full.
Does not qualify for the post employment healthcare savings plan **and** • Does *not* participate in the Flex Leave Plan	• Vacation and sick leave hours are paid per union contract.

Exhibit 6-3b Flex Leave Questions and Answers

Q: *Do the following answers on Flex Leave apply to union employees as well as to non-union employees?*

A: Bargaining units will need to negotiate implementation of the Flex Leave Plan. While implementation dates will vary, it is anticipated that the general provisions of the Flex Leave Plan Description and the following questions and answers may apply to some union employees beginning in 1993.

Q: *Since the accrual rate for Flex Leave is slightly less than the combined vacation and sick leave accrual rate, will I lose days when I enroll in the Flex Leave Plan?*

A: No. Employees will remain at their current accrual rate until the Flex Leave Plan accrual rate catches up with them. For example, employees with 3 years of service are currently accruing 24 days of combined sick and vacation leave per year. When they enroll in the Flex Leave Plan, they will continue to accrue at the rate of 24 Flex Leave days per year until they have completed 10 years of service.

Q: *Will my Extended Sick Leave Bank be stored as hours or dollars?*

A: Extended Sick Leave will be stored as hours. The value of your Extended Sick Leave Bank hours will be determined by your rate of pay at the time those hours are used.

Q: *How will I keep track of the hours I have in the Extended Sick Leave Bank?*

A: An employee's current Extended Sick Leave Bank balance will be stated on each paycheck stub under the heading, "EXTED/SICK BAL".

Q: *What are the requirements to access the Extended Sick Leave Bank?*

A: Each payroll year, after employees have used 16 hours of Flex Leave (for any purpose) they are eligible (if sick) to use hours from the Extended Sick Leave Bank. County policy for using sick leave will continue to apply for accessing the Extended Sick Leave Bank.

Q: *I have enrolled in the Flex Leave Plan with 4 hours of vacation to convert to Flex Leave and 125 hours of sick leave to convert to the Extended Sick Leave Bank. The following day I have an emergency operation and need to use my Extended Sick Leave Bank to cover my time off work. How can I satisfy the requirement of first using 16 hours of Flex Leave before being able to access the Extended Sick Leave Bank?*

A: Employees may carry a negative balance in Flex Leave for the first 60 days after their initial entry into the Flex Leave Plan. After that time, employees may only use the time they have accrued.

Q: *Can an employee who is receiving workers' compensation use the Extended Sick Leave Bank to obtain 100% compensation?*

A: Yes. If an employee has an Extended Sick Leave Bank, it can be utilized to receive 100% wages while off work due to a work-related injury. This is consistent with current County policy.

Q: *Is there a requirement that the Flex Leave balance be exhausted before an employee is eligible to receive short-term disability (STD) or long-term disability (LTD) benefits?*

A: Effective March 1, 1993, employees are not required to exhaust their Flex Leave to be eligible for STD or LTD.

Q: *Is there a requirement that the Extended Sick Leave Bank be exhausted before an employee is eligible to receive STD or LTD benefits?*

A: No. Employees are not required to exhaust their Extended Sick Leave Bank to be eligible for STD or LTD.

Q: *How will planned Flex Leave and unplanned Flex Leave be determined and recorded?*

A: A major Flex Leave Plan objective is to encourage the advance planning of absences from work. The Flex Leave Plan Description requires that "non-emergency (planned) use be requested in advance" and that "emergency (unplanned) use may require documentation." A central focus of the Flex Leave Plan is to provide employees with adequate time off work while assuring efficient departmental coverage through providing adequate advance notice. Employees are expected to provide as much notice as possible when requesting time off work. For Flex Leave to be considered "planned", an employee should give the supervisor advance notice—equal to the amount of requested time off, up to 5 days. Department rules and requirements concerning employees' absence from work will continue to be applied.

Supervisors may deny a specific request for non-emergency Flex Leave to assure necessary departmental workload coverage. It is expected that unplanned absences will vary based on individual needs and departments ability to accommodate employees requests while maintaining efficiency.

Both planned and unplanned flex leave will be recorded on the employee's time sheet, which will remain in the department.

Q: The Flex Leave Plan states that Flex Leave can only be taken in 60-minute increments. If I use 1 hour and 30 minutes to go to the doctor, will I be required to use 2 hours of Flex Leave to cover this time away from work?

A: Within the employer/employee relationship, there is a mutual understanding that an employee will provide a day's work for a day's wages. This relationship provides the foundation upon which the following guidelines will be administered.

Flex Leave will only be recorded in 60-minute increments and will always be rolled up to the next 60-minute increment. In the situation stated above, 2 hours of Flex Leave will be recorded and then with the supervisor's pre-approval, the employee may adjust either the lunch time, arrival time, or quitting time or find another mutually agreeable arrangement to compensate for the remaining 30 minutes.

Q: When will employees be permitted to convert Flex Leave to Deferred Compensation?

A: Eligibility for conversion of Flex Leave to Deferred Compensation includes having been enrolled in the Flex Leave Plan for a full 12 months prior to conversion. Therefore, employees who enroll in the Flex Leave Plan in January will have the first opportunity to convert Flex Leave to Deferred Compensation in December of that year.

Q: Can an employee who retires use the Extended Sick Leave Bank to pay for medical coverage continuation?

A: Yes. Depending on the election made by the employee, the Flex Leave Plan provides some opportunities for favorable tax treatment and medical coverage payments for both retirees and their dependents. These opportunities are not available under the current County vacation and sick leave policies. Since tax laws are complex and constantly changing, employees are encouraged to consult with their tax adviser before making their election concerning the retirement options available to them.

Q: How will prior County employment affect my Flex Leave accrual rate?

A: "Limited" employees who are hired as "non-limited" employees and who have not had a break in service will automatically have the "limited" aggregate years of service credited to them. Individuals who have had prior employment with the County and have been re-employed may be eligible for restoration of those previous years of service per current County policy.

In both instances, this restoration of service applies to the benefit accrual date only. An employee's benefit accrual date is defined as the date which determines the rate at which Flex Leave is accrued.

Q: What is the Flex Leave accrual rate for non-limited part-time employees?

A: Flex Leave will accrue at a pro-rated amount based on the actual hours worked. This is consistent with current County vacation and sick leave policy.

Q: What will happen if I have used most or all of my Flex Leave and then get sick and need to be away from work for 2 weeks?

A: One of the basic concepts in the Flex Leave Plan is to encourage employees to plan ahead whenever possible. Since the possibility always exists that a person may become sick and need time off work, employees are expected to take this into consideration when using their Flex Leave. If an employee does not have Flex Leave hours or Extended Sick Leave Bank hours available and is absent from work, the time off work will be considered unpaid.

financial capacity and secondarily with respect to the number of plan participants over which risk can be spread. The volatility in the benefits market in recent years has made self-insurance somewhat unattractive when compared with rate guarantees available in most commercial insurance markets. This consideration, as well as the continuing consolidation of providers, suggests that only a larger employer or a consortium of smaller organizations might continue to benefit from essentially eliminating the insurance company profit portion from the costs of providing the plan in question.

The key advantages of self-insurance include the potential cost advantage noted above as well as substantial opportunity to design and configure the various elements of the plan. Coverage levels, cost-control provisions, administrative service arrangements, funding mechanisms (e.g., a trust arrangement), and provider options all represent available possibilities for flexibility or varying approaches that would benefit both employer and employee.

Administrative Issues

Plan administration often is overlooked when the establishment, expansion, or redesign of the benefit program is being discussed. This oversight can often result in employee concerns because of unmet needs or in employer surprise when the workload and corresponding costs of the plan are fully understood. Administration represents the significant but often hidden cost that at some level is unavoidable. Even when insurance agents purport to handle all plan activities, there remains a substantial effort necessary to the effective delivery of the employer plans.

Often this effort requires staff time and the availability of data management systems and procedures to ensure the smooth implementation and communication of the plan as well as the capacity to ultimately process

claims. As with other aspects of the benefits program, however, a range of options is available to the jurisdiction.

While some benefits support comes from resources internal to the organization, many administrative tasks can—and some should—be left to outside contractors. Key among those that are best contracted out are claims administration. Although available benefits software has made the task dramatically less difficult, heavy claim loads are anything but routine. Plan interpretation can pose regular difficulty, and the speed with which claims are resolved as well as the perceived fairness and consistency of this process sets the tone for the overall program. Any employer would be well advised to ensure that these tasks are handled in the most effective manner possible, whether internally or through contracted services.

Tips for the Successful Implementation of a Cafeteria Plan

If you are considering the establishment of flexible benefit arrangements, seek assistance from a consultant experienced in designing and establishing these kinds of plans. Initial consultant efforts would determine and evaluate

- ❏ Specific objectives that the organization is seeking to achieve
- ❏ The range of plan options the organization may be prepared to consider
- ❏ The present components of the organization's benefits plan
- ❏ Organization readiness for this concept
- ❏ Plan administration and cost considerations
- ❏ Typical pros and cons of establishing a more flexible compensation or benefits arrangement.

Purchase and Design Considerations

Guiding Principle

• Most small local governments must employ a benefits consultant.

Challenge

• Managing the contracting process and working with the benefits consultant to achieve local government goals.

Use of Consultants

The growing complexity of even the most basic benefit programs suggests that retaining specialists experienced in the planning, design, purchase, and evaluation of the plans is unavoidable. This is particularly true in the smaller jurisdiction that simply cannot afford this level of expertise in-house. Rather, employees can focus on developing the skills needed to work effectively in this arena by learning how to select a qualified consultant and manage the output from this relationship.

The chief executive of the jurisdiction should take ownership of the project and focus on understanding each step in the process, questioning the consultant as necessary, to ensure that all jurisdictional objectives in employing the consultant are being met.

The RFQ/RFP Process

While specific requirements differ, political subdivisions are normally subject to a structured process when they are entering into a contract for group insurance for their employees. This process is generally one of two types:

Request for Quotation. Sometimes referred to as "request for competitive bid," this process involves the development of a bid specification that details the exact service or product being sought and that is advertised or communicated to the relevant industry segment. There is typi-

Red Flags

 Do not assume that once a consultant is hired there is nothing left to do but receive the work product.

 Do not purchase a "black box," the contents of which are known only to the consultant.

cally a threshold cost below which such a process is not required (e.g., $10,000), and the contract normally is awarded to the lowest responsible bidder. This is the most common approach to the purchase of benefit products that are relatively uniform across the market and for which the selection decision will be based almost solely on the price of the product. A typical example of this is the purchase of group term-life insurance.

Request for Proposal. When the jurisdiction is establishing or renewing a plan that is subject to vendor or employer design variations, the request-for-proposal approach is typically used. In contrast to a request for quotation or competitive bids, this process normally focuses on the provision of services (e.g., medical care for employees) in which the mechanisms for providing the service and the level of the service may differ significantly from vendor to vendor.

Tips for a Successful Bidding Process

 Make sure the bid specification is comprehensive.

 Ensure that the product or service being described in the request for competitive bid is, in fact, what the jurisdiction is seeking.

 Follow a strict bid administration process.

Red Flags

When bidding the design and
purchase of a benefits plan, avoid

- ▶ Being inconsistent when communicating
  with potential vendors
- ▶ Revealing one vendor's information to
  another vendor
- ▶ Opening bids before the submission
  deadline.

Applicable statutes, jurisdiction policies, or labor contracts often establish the nature or extent of the changes that can be made to plans as a result of vendor- or employer-generated variations from one plan configuration to the next. The aggregate value of the benefits, as certified by an actuary, often cannot be reduced, but variations in the specific level or type of coverage being provided are commonly permitted.

Insurance Agents

It is common practice in many smaller organizations to purchase benefits program components from local insurance agents. Other jurisdictions have found it to be cost-effective to retain a consultant to manage the purchase process directly with carriers. The actual rates for a given coverage often can be less when this second approach is taken. Although insurance agents suggest that they handle plan administration when the program is purchased from them, the carriers' own administrative staff provides a significant amount of assistance to employers; thus, agents may be duplicating services already in place or adding steps to the process and thereby adding to the cost.

Communicating the Benefits Program

Challenge

- Communicating the full value of the benefits program to employees.

The very nature of most benefit programs obscures their true value to the employee and their true cost to the employer. It is, therefore, in the interest of the jurisdiction to fully communicate the plan(s) so that employees recognize the significance of what is available as well as whatever additional compensation the benefits program represents. This is particularly true when a flexible benefits plan is being contemplated since such a plan requires choices that could have a significant impact on the employee and his or her family. The only way to avoid the waste that comes from either indifference to or misapplication of the benefits dollar is through well-planned, adequately funded, professionally delivered, ongoing communication. Effective written communications include materials that carefully and completely describe the plan in plain language and that are presented to employees in small increments to facilitate understanding.

Individual Benefit Statements

A common method of more fully communicating both the range of benefits available and the value of selected plans is the individual benefits statement. This statement is generally prepared through the application of specialized computer software and is provided to employees on an annual basis. It itemizes in detail the actual dollar value of each element of the benefits program, including items that typically are not fully acknowledged by employees. Among the less understood benefits are employer FICA contributions; workers' compensation and unemployment compensation contributions; pension plan contributions; and the value of paid time off, vacation, sick leave, and holidays.

A number of consultants specialize in preparing the annual individual benefits statement. Their services include communications planning, data gathering, statement design, distribution to employees, and ongoing maintenance.

On-line Benefit Communications

A relatively new method of communicating benefits is providing employees with access to computer programs that can call up their individual records, including balances in savings plans and pension plan information. These programs have interactive capabilities so that employees can develop "what if" scenarios and better visualize how their current choices may translate into short- and long-term results as well as how different choices may affect them in the future. This type of approach is of particular importance when employees are considering the implications of flexible benefit choices or are planning for retirement. These computerized communication programs hold the promise of greatly enhancing the tools available to employers, and of providing employees with a simple and reliable financial planning mechanism that permits them to accept the greater responsibility inherent in the delivery of a modern benefits program. Web-based delivery of employee benefits continues to expand and reflects a trend toward self-service for human resource functions.[7]

Open Enrollment

A key opportunity for communicating available benefit choices is the annual open enrollment process. In most plans, this event provides employees with the opportunity to rethink their choices, enroll in plans that they may have declined previously, or purchase higher levels of coverage.

In preparation for the process, employers should carefully review available communication channels and seize the opportunity to hold group meetings and encourage face-to-face dialogue. The result can often be dramatic, both in the employer's understanding of employee needs and expectations and in the employees' comprehension of the existing choices and the related costs to the employer.

Evaluation of Benefit Programs

Guiding Principle

- Demographic and societal changes make it necessary to constantly reevaluate benefits.

The benefit needs of employees change constantly. This is partly the result of changing demographics, but it is also the result of societal change. These changes challenge the local government employer in many ways.

The changing structure of families creates a need for new approaches to benefits. Dual-career couples have somewhat different needs than the traditional family of the 1940s and 1950s. Some elements of standard benefit packages may actually be redundant when both members of the couple are employed outside the home, requiring employers to allow an employee to opt out of a particular coverage if the spouse has similar coverage. Yet allowing employees to opt out of traditionally required coverage, such as health care, can make contracting for and administering the benefit even more complex.

As noted above, the aging of the workforce also creates challenges. As people now live longer, many employees have responsibilities for elderly relatives. Older employees need different benefits than younger employees do. Older employees usually use health care services more intensively, while younger employees have more need for child care and education benefits.

Increasing numbers of unmarried-couple households have led to pressure for domestic partnership benefits, which are highly controversial for many local governments. The controversy arises because most people associate domestic partnership with homosexual couples, although the reality is that unmarried heterosexual couples far outnumber homosexual couples. Gradually, local governments are moving to provide domestic partnership benefits, and this move brings with it implementation challenges, especially in defining what constitutes a domestic partnership.

Cafeteria-style benefit plans appear to be an answer to the challenges brought about by changing demographics. The cost resulting from the increased complexity of administration for cafeteria benefits is offset by the savings that come from not paying for benefits that are not used by some employees. Such plans are also attractive from the perspective of cost containment. Typically, benefits represent approximately 30 percent of total compensation costs of local governments. The cafeteria plans provide alternative approaches to particular benefits—for instance, giving employees a choice of health care provided using indemnity, HMO, or PPO plans.

Many local governments are experimenting with consortia or cooperative approaches with other governmental jurisdictions. By pooling resources and numbers of employees, local governments can often obtain better bids or negotiate better terms for the provision of some of their benefit programs.

Costs can be reduced by lowering the number of people eligible for coverage. Thus, many jurisdictions are dropping part-time and retired employees from eligibility for health care. Retirement costs may be reduced by raising the retirement age. Two-tiered benefit plans also are being used in which current employees retain the level of benefits in place when they were hired, but new employees receive a lower level of benefits.

Regardless of the approaches they use, local government employers are also increasingly asking their employees to pay part of the cost of their benefit programs. Generally, local governments have been generous in fully funding most benefits and in offering a wider range of benefits than is typical among private sector employers, especially smaller ones. Yet they also seem to be less successful in controlling costs, which might be related to the tendency of government to be somewhat more socially conscious in its policies. In some places, local government employees have developed an entitlement mentality regarding benefits, and this mentality is usually encouraged by the employers themselves.

Employee participation in the design of benefit plans is another way of getting employees to accept responsibility for their benefits. Participation gives employees an understanding of the cost factors involved in alternative plans that can lead to wiser use of benefits. One way to engage employees in the design and evaluation process is to survey them on benefits issues. A few questions from such a survey are shown in Exhibit 6-4, pages 176–177.

Evaluation Questions

The effective design and delivery of any benefits program must be grounded in careful consideration of the answers to the following key questions:

1. What benefit plans currently exist?
2. Why does each plan exist?
3. What specific objective is each plan designed to achieve?
4. To what degree is the plan achieving its objective?
5. What are the needs of the workforce?
6. What are the needs of the jurisdiction?
7. How do present plans relate to these needs?
8. Are costs in line with what the jurisdiction can afford?

9. Is the overall benefits plan competitive?

10. How well do employees understand the benefits program?

11. How easily can employees and beneficiaries receive answers to their questions?

The most important issues concern the needs of employees and the employer. Because of changing demographics, competitive pressures, and budget limitations, the answers to the questions are not static. They evolve, and the benefits program should evolve with them.

Strategies for the Future

In the future, five key strategies can reshape a benefits program.

Help Employees Be Mentally and Physically Fit. Unpaid personal leave programs, beyond FMLA and independent of child care considerations, and EAPs are in this category. These programs have seen increased implementation and spending since the terrorist attacks on September 11, 2001. Wellness programs help employees make healthy lifestyle choices, and discounted memberships to fitness centers can be available for little or no cost. These programs pay dividends that include reduced medical plan premiums, reduced absenteeism, increased productivity, and reduced turnover.

Establish Programs That Help Employees Care for Dependents. In recent years this area has developed more rapidly than any other. Programs such as dependent care spending accounts are in place in many jurisdictions and are very popular. Other benefits, such as well baby care and child care referrals and resources, have also become more common.

Elder care services and resources are among the fastest growing benefits today. A recent study by the American Association of Retired Persons (AARP) found that nearly one-third of the American workforce provides some form of care for an older adult family member or friend. Almost two-thirds of employees under the age of 60 believe they will have elder care responsibilities in the next 10 years.

These employees need help balancing job and family care responsibilities. Most employers already offer some form of job flexibility. However, additional programs such as estate planning, long-term care insurance, access to geriatric counselors and social workers, and educational materials for employees should be strongly considered.

Make Work More Flexible. Technology has made work truly portable, and employees can be instantly accessible from almost anywhere. Employers needing to do more with less continue to find new ways to embrace flexible work arrangements. Web-based access to the workplace can make the virtual office a reality.

With the large number of "baby boomers" nearing retirement, it will become increasingly necessary, for both the employer and the employee, to develop forms of phased retirement. This will provide employers a ready pool of knowledgeable employees for an extended period of time, and will significantly reduce the stress often associated with leaving one's "productive years" behind. Some employers are developing plans that ease employees into retirement over a number of years; some are even looking to the post-retirement population as a recruitment resource.

Provide Mechanisms That Save Time. Time is the twenty-first-century employee's most valuable commodity. Programs that reduce or eliminate the many small, time-demanding tasks of modern life are growing in popularity. They can range from providing employees resource lists for home maintenance or housekeeping services, to providing valet services at reduced costs. Well-conceived benefits programs and, specifically, programs that save time can be very attractive to employees.

Support Employees Through Their Financial Life Cycle. Benefits such as long-term care, legal services, housing assistance, dependent care, group rates on auto and homeowners' insurance, retirement planning, and tuition reimbursement rank high among employees' priorities. However, the importance of these priorities to the individual employee changes over time. For example, a young employee new to an area may be more inter- ested in housing assistance than long-term care, yet long-term care may be a very impor- tant benefit to another employee in the later years of his or her career. Since the passage of the Long Term Care Security Act, signed into law in 2002, and the changes in many state tax codes, long-term care insurance has seen a

---

Exhibit 6-4   Sample Employee Benefits Survey

The following text and questions are excerpted from a sample survey instrument published by Richard E. Johnson in Flexible Benefits: A How-To Guide *(see source note below). The complete survey is several pages long.*

This survey is an effort to learn your opinions about your benefits. _____ must regularly make tough decisions about how to best spend its benefits dollars and (administration/personnel) wants to know your views to help in the process.

It is important that you answer the questions honestly so we get a clear sense of your opinions about the benefits here. So that you feel free to answer openly we do not want you to put your name on the questionnaire. For your further protection, seal your completed questionnaire in the envelope provided and (provide instructions for returning the questionnaire to a specific office).

No one at _____ will ever see a completed questionnaire. Instead, _____ will get a report from _____ summing up how groups of people feel about various issues.

While we can't promise that everyone's ideas can be used in planning changes, (personnel/administration) wants to be as responsive as possible to your opinions and concerns on these important issues.

	(1) Strongly Agree	(2) Agree	(3) Disagree	(4) Strongly Disagree
I know where to get the information I need regarding my benefits.	❑	❑	❑	❑
Employee medical claims are paid quickly and fairly.	❑	❑	❑	❑
I'd rather work at this company than any other company in the area.	❑	❑	❑	❑
Increasing my direct pay is more important to me than improving benefits.	❑	❑	❑	❑
The benefits here are as good as at other companies in the area.	❑	❑	❑	❑
The company's paid time-off policy is fair.	❑	❑	❑	❑
Company-paid disability insurance won't give me enough income if I become disabled for a long period of time.	❑	❑	❑	❑
I don't understand how the paid time-off policy works.	❑	❑	❑	❑

growth rate of 18 percent. As baby boomers age and employers offer this benefit via payroll deduction, this trend should only continue.

More than ever, employees need to be educated on their investment and retirement opportunities. Recent business scandals have created a new awareness that employees must take active, personal responsibility for their future, and employers are expected to provide the necessary planning tools.

Section 529 plans remain popular. Employees can put aside savings for higher education and incur no federal tax on earnings. These plans are open to residents of any state and

---

Before you answer these next items, we would like to tell you about two possible new employee benefits. These plans are available due to some recent laws passed by Congress. The (administration/personnel) is considering them, but first we would like to get your opinions.

Pretax savings plans let you deposit some of your pay in a company-sponsored saving account—but before you pay income tax on it. The idea is to leave it there until retirement (or in case of a few specific emergencies which stop your income). Since retired people may have less tax taken out of their income than when they were working, they gain by having "sheltered" that money from taxes during their working years, *plus* those pretax dollars have been growing through investment. Congress hoped that these plans would encourage people to set aside some of their own money for retirement.

Health care reimbursement funds also let you set aside your money before taxes are deducted, in this case for use in paying health care costs that are not covered by insurance. For example, if you need eyeglasses or a routine physical, your expenses can be paid from the money you have in the fund. Since you never pay income tax on this money, it's "worth more" when you use it to pay for these medical expenses.

While there's a good deal more to these plans, please answer the following items as best you can, based on what you know at this point.

	(1) Strongly Agree	(2) Agree	(3) Disagree	(4) Strongly Disagree
I would consider putting some of my pay into a pretax savings plan.	❏	❏	❏	❏
The pretax savings plan sounds like a good way to save for retirement.	❏	❏	❏	❏
It would be a real advantage to me to be able to "shelter" some of my income from taxes.	❏	❏	❏	❏
I like the idea of taking some personal responsibility for my retirement income.	❏	❏	❏	❏

can be purchased by parents and grandparents. While employers do not directly offer these plans, they can provide information and education to their employees.

Similarly, voluntary programs that offer group rates and payroll deductions for auto/home insurance, legal services, supplemental life insurance, and other services generally cost the employer little, yet the convenience factor to the employee is significant. Group purchasing can also reduce employees' fees for health clubs, movie theaters, and other entertainment.

As the cost of mandated benefits rises, employers may not want to add optional benefits. But voluntary programs can signal to employees that the employer cares about their personal well-being. Maintaining a caring organizational culture while insisting on high-performance standards can foster loyalty and group cohesion. Top performers may be less inclined to leave government service, and public employers may find it easier to promote an environment for excellence.

[1] "BLS Reports on Employee Benefits in State and Local Governments, 1998," www.bls.gov/ncs/ebs/sp/ebb0018pdf, accessed July 26, 2003.

[2] Evelina Moulder, *Local Government Health Benefits: Responses to Costs and Customers*, Special Data Issue no. 2 (2003) (Washington, D.C.: International City/County Management Association, 2003), 4.

[3] Agency for Healthcare Research and Quality, *Statistical Brief no. 17: Employer Sponsored Health Insurance for Full Time Employees and Retirees: 1999–2000.* May 2003, www.meps. ahrq.gov/papers/st17/stat17.htm (August 26, 2003); U.S. Department of Commerce, *Statistical Abstract of the United States, 1994* (Washington, D.C.: Economics and Statistics Administration, Bureau of the Census, 1994), 321.

[4] "National Health Care Expenditures, 2001," Facts from EBRI, www.ebri.org/facts/0203fact.htm (July 26, 2003).

[5] K. D. Smith, "Comprehensive Leave: Pros and Cons," *IPMA News* (July 1996): 20, 22–23.

[6] "Compensation Costs in State and Local Governments, March 1999 to March 2001," FACTS from EBRI, www.ebri.org/facts/0901fact.htm (July 26, 2003).

[7] In the private sector, the Cedar 2002 Human Resources Self Service/Portal Survey, the fifth annual survey conducted by Cedar, an enterprise applications consulting company, shows early adopters of self-service delivery for HR saved as much as 50 percent on transaction costs and proved measurable ROI within three years. See www.thecedargroup.com/USA/whitepapers/hrsss_pressrelease.asp?Id1=3&Id2=11.

CHAPTER 7

Employee Responsibilities: Setting Expectations

Don A. Cozzetto, Theodore B. Pedeliski, and Jonathan Tompkins

The employment relationship can no longer be viewed as a simple wages-for-work bargain. Over time it has evolved into a highly complex web of mutual rights and responsibilities. Employees now enjoy many statutory rights, such as the right to be protected from racial or sexual harassment. In addition, public employees are protected by constitutional rights, such as the right to due process in adverse personnel decisions. Beyond these legal safeguards, workers also expect to be compensated fairly and to be treated with respect.

But with rights come responsibilities. In their role as employers, local governments have a right to expect workers to perform assigned tasks dependably and to behave in ways that promote the attainment of organizational objectives, and workers in turn are responsible for doing so. Ensuring that employee responsibilities are fulfilled is every bit as important as ensuring that their rights are protected. Without the full cooperation and productive efforts of their workers, local governments cannot carry out their mandated purposes effectively and efficiently.

This chapter reviews basic employee responsibilities and emphasizes the importance of communicating workplace expectations to employees as clearly as possible. Attorneys often advise managers that they are more likely to prevail during the appeal of an adverse personnel decision when workplace expectations have been clearly communicated to employees, but the truth is that clarifying and communicating expectations is simply the sensible thing to do. Workers cannot be expected to direct their efforts toward the realization of organizational objectives if they have no clear sense of the mission of their departments, the way their work efforts contribute to mission attainment, or the way their personal and interpersonal behaviors contribute to or detract from organizational effectiveness.

Expectations of Attendance

Guiding Principles

- Employees must understand that regular attendance is a basic expectation.
- Repeated absenteeism must be met with counseling and discipline.

Red Flags

Government managers should not discourage the use of sick leave for bona fide illnesses, but are responsible for ensuring that sick leave is not abused by employees. Managers should keep an eye out for patterns of absenteeism or lateness that merit intervention in order to determine the cause and to counsel the employees affected. Such patterns might include

- Employees who are habitually late or absent following weekends or holidays
- Employees whose absenteeism or lateness seems to be associated with a period of great personal stress
- Employees who leave during the day to conduct personal errands (going to the bank before it closes, completing a business deal, seeing a lawyer or other professional)
- Employees who appear to be taking "elective sick leave" for minor annoyances or borderline health problems
- Working parents who elect to use their sick leave for situations covered under the FMLA (because sick leave is paid and FMLA leave is not).

Regular attendance is expected of most employees. If they are not at the office or in the field attending to their assigned duties, the ability of the agency to fulfill its mission is severely compromised. Excessive absenteeism has traditionally provided just cause to discipline or terminate employees, and judges and arbitrators have repeatedly affirmed this.

Absenteeism may have any of several causes. The employee may have a drinking problem or may abuse drugs. The employee may have physical or mental disabilities that have an intermittent effect on both work function and attendance. The employee may not consider work responsibility or regular atten-

dance an important priority, or may consider them secondary to family responsibilities, personal business, or even recreational events.

Organizations invest a great deal in their employees as they are recruited, trained, and developed. Because most employees soon become highly valuable human resources, the wise supervisor will not be too quick to discipline or discharge. The reasons behind a poor attendance record should be investigated, counseling sessions held, and referrals made to employee assistance programs when warranted. In many instances, the causes of excessive absenteeism can be addressed successfully without having to resort to discipline or discharge. However, the prudent supervisor will document every instance of absenteeism or tardiness in case it becomes necessary to justify a disciplinary action to a judge or arbitrator.

Attendance and Discretionary Leave

Organizations that allow employees to use their leave time for discretionary activities with proper notice have noted an increase in requests for day and short leaves. This technically does not become a problem for the agency until the employees have exhausted their leave time and none is left for necessary and nondiscretionary leaves. As both public and private organizations move toward more flexible work periods, the tensions will increase between employees who seek more flexible work schedules and accommodations to their life circumstances and employers who must maintain an orderly work schedule for all employees. (See Chapter 6 for more on leave policies.)

Attendance and Family and Medical Leave

Since 1993, both private and public employers have been bound by the Family and Medical Leave Act of 1993 (FMLA) (see Chapter 5) to allow eligible employees to take leaves of absence for medical reasons that apply to themselves, their spouses, their children, or their parents. The FMLA also permits employees to obtain intermittent leave in limited increments of time.

The FMLA, as well as the Americans with Disabilities Act (ADA), establishes a new set of expectations for employees, employers, and public personnel supervisors. Agencies are expected to be accommodating to genuine family and health needs. Employers may not terminate an employee for excessive absenteeism during the period in which he or she is exercising a family or medical leave right.[1] However, employees also have obligations to comply with certain expectations:

- **Notice.** The employee must provide the employer with reasonable notice of his or her intention to take FMLA leave (30 days' advance notice for foreseeable leave and as soon as practicable for more immediate needs). The employee must also obtain the consent of the employer to take FMLA leave. (In California and Wisconsin, state laws allow the worker to simply notify the employer.)

- **Substitution of leave.** The employer may require the employee (with notice) to substitute any accrued paid vacation leave, personal leave, or sick leave for any part of the 12-week period of FMLA leave.

- **Certification.** The employer may require the employee to submit certification from a health care provider stating the date on which the medical condition commenced, the probable duration of the condition, and supportive medical diagnoses and facts.

Both employer and employees are expected to be able to work out new work schedules, new productivity goals, compensatory work times, use of substitutes, and revision of vacation schedules.

FMLA intermittent leave provisions create special problems for employers who have devised no-fault or paid time-off absenteeism policies. Under such systems, employees can

> ### Tips for Dealing Successfully with Attendance Problems
>
> Supervisors and managers must
> - ❑ Document all incidents of absenteeism and lateness for each employee
> - ❑ Inform employees about attendance policies, including when the workday begins and ends; make sure employees understand these policies; and impress on employees the requirement to give prior notice of absences and report unavoidable lateness
> - ❑ Inform employees with emerging patterns of absenteeism or lateness to their attendance record to the burdens they create, and to the disciplinary measures that may be applied
> - ❑ Work with employees to modify schedules or make up time that may have been lost.

take a certain number of days off with reasonable prior notice to the employer. Warnings and disciplinary actions are triggered after the number of grace days allowed within a 12-month period is exhausted or if the employee does not provide notice. Progressive sanctions can apply, rising ultimately to suspension and termination. Under the FMLA, an employee who has exceeded the maximum number of grace days cannot be denied intermittent or block leave if he or she has demonstrated eligibility for such leave.[2]

Workplace Conduct

Guiding Principles

- Civility is a two-way street.
- Order and decorum are essential to morale and work productivity.

Employees should be informed that threats, vulgarities, personal insults, and deprecatory statements will not be tolerated.[3] They should also

Red Flags

The following behaviors on the part of supervisors can have a negative effect on employees' conduct:

- Ignoring the complaints or questions of an employee

- Criticizing or chastising an employee in front of other employees

- Not believing an employee's story ("My battery went dead and the tow service didn't come for two hours.")

- Failing to give recognition for work well done

- Failing to go first to the employee who becomes the object of an investigation

- Not expressing sympathy for or interest in an employee's personal burdens

- Not being totally professional in dealing with employees.

be informed that the public workplace is subject to public scrutiny and public expectations.

Employers must remember, however, that civility is a two-way street. Employees develop their own perceptions of proper employer behavior, and they may consider some supervisory behaviors unacceptable (see sidebar above).[4]

Alcohol Abuse

Alcohol abuse presents special problems because the recovering alcoholic may be covered by the ADA.[5] However, regardless of the disabling character of the physical condition, the employee is still held to expectations of proper conduct both in the workplace and off duty. The focus on proper workplace conduct should include work-related behaviors (attendance, punctuality, productivity, and customer service) as well as civility. Criminal conduct off duty may constitute grounds for sanctions for a recovering alcoholic just as it would for some-

one not classified as an alcoholic. It is the conduct that is the issue.[6]

Some local governments have implemented a zero-tolerance policy for employees, especially law enforcement officers, appearing for work while under the influence of alcohol. This policy applies even if the employee's blood alcohol level is lower than the threshold for a driving violation.

Off-duty behaviors raise questions, however, because they may have only a tangential relation to job performance and they involve very private choices. The distinction between workplace and private environment may blur when members of a workplace get together for social events. Excessive drinking and inappropriate conduct by employees in such a context may be the occasion for concern and action by managers.

Suffolk County, New York, bans off-duty public consumption of alcohol by members of the sheriff's department. This treads on some very private ground. Do off-duty social sessions involving department members carry an unintended public message? Would such a ban apply to police having alcohol with their meals in restaurants? Protection of employees' conduct involving alcohol (or tobacco use) is extended in 29 states, which have laws prohibiting employment discrimination on the basis of an employee engaging in "any lawful activity" or "using any lawful product." While these laws do protect social drinkers and smokers in their off-duty behaviors, they also restrict employers in dealing with employees who are unable to perform their jobs when health problems associated with that activity arise.

Drug Abuse

Many local governments follow the lead of the federal government to create a drug-free workplace using a three-pronged approach: detection, rehabilitation, and educational awareness.

Drug testing can be initiated before hiring and can continue after employment commences. The preemployment examination, seen as a basic condition for employment, screens out users of drugs without consideration of the applicant's on-the-job performance. While it does involve an intrusion into the applicant's privacy, applicants have advance notice of the test and can avoid that personal cost by not applying. And in point of fact, the very process of being considered for a position carries with it an expectation of reduced privacy since a prospective employer scrutinizes the applicant's full employment history and all job-related variables.

Postemployment drug (or alcohol tests) can be administered

- As part of a periodic medical examination

- As part of an investigation of an accident involving the employee

- If there is reasonable suspicion, based on certain facts, that the employee is using drugs (as indicated by impairment)

Drug-Free Workplace   *fyi*

Following terms of the Drug-Free Workplace Act of 1988, public organizations are required to

- Publish a policy statement notifying employees that it is unlawful to possess, manufacture, dispense, or use a controlled substance in the workplace

- Specify actions (including the possibility of termination) that will be taken if the policy is violated

- Establish a drug-free awareness program that requires employees to be informed of

  - the dangers of drug abuse in the workplace

  - the person's responsibility in maintaining a drug-free environment

  - the availability of counseling, rehabilitation, and employee assistance programs.

- Randomly if the employee is in a position with a zero tolerance for drug or alcohol impairment.

Interpersonal Relationships: On and Off Duty

Guiding Principles

- Workplace relationships can lead to sexual harassment claims and resentment among co-workers.

- Policies affecting the marital activities of workers may be sustained by the courts if the public employer can advance a legitimate governmental interest.

Challenges

- Developing fair workplace policies that protect consenting adults who date or fraternize against sexual harassment claims without fostering employee resentment, impeding normal co-worker interaction, or violating employees' privacy.

- Deciding whether there is a clear nexus between an employee's off-duty activity and the employee's job performance or the proper functioning of the public agency.

Dating and Romance

The workplace is a popular arena for interpersonal relationships: friendships, domestic partnerships, and romances. In the past decade, public employers have begun to develop policies that deal with dating and fraternization issues.

The development of these policies is a natural extension of the development of guidelines and training programs to deal with sexual harassment. Employers have discovered that when workplace relationships turn sour or involve exploitation, the victimized employee may initiate sexual harassment claims. Workplace romances between employees and superiors, however consensual in character, may

raise the same issues of pressure and exploitation that come up in cases where the advances
are unwelcome. Romantic alliances between
employees in power-differentiated positions
may also engender feelings of resentment
among other co-workers and give rise to cases
of "reverse sexual harassment," in which
employees who may qualify for advancement
or job rewards feel that they were passed over
in favor of the employee who has a special
relationship with the superior.[7]

Cohabitation

Workplace romances can raise the issue of
cohabitation. These situations produce conflicts
between couples who assert privacy rights
emanating from the First, Fourth, Ninth, and
Fourteenth Amendments to the Constitution
and public employers who not only feel that
they can prohibit any behavior that, if brought
to the attention of the public, could result in
unjustified criticism of the department, but
also contend that permitting such relationships between workers would negatively affect
workplace morale. Public employers, especially
law enforcement agencies, also assert expectations of integrity and compliance with all laws,
including "blue laws," by those employees
entrusted with enforcement of the law.

Court decisions of the 1970s affirmed the
power of agencies to put moral litmus tests on
employment, generally accepting at face value
the agency's concern for "moral discipline" and
a proper public image. For many years the
courts also limited fundamental privacy rights
to legal marriage relationships. By 1985, however, a federal court ruling on the discharge of
a police officer for cohabiting with a woman
not his wife adopted a different analysis of the
privacy interests involved. The court found that
a concern for "community morals" was insufficient to allow public employers to discipline
workers for engaging in extramarital sexual
activity, given the fact that the activity did not
have any effect on the ability of the parties to

perform their jobs.[8] The key question that public employers must address in the case of non-
traditional lifestyles pursued by employees is
whether there is a clear nexus between the off-
duty activity and the employee's job performance or the proper functioning of the public
agency.

Since the 1980s public employers have
retreated from penalizing employees who are
cohabiting. This has paralleled the repeal in
several states of statutes that criminalize adul-
tery and fornication. But new issues have
emerged with same-sex relationships. In 1997
the federal Court of Appeals for the Eleventh
Circuit dealt with a public employment issue
that involved homosexual "marriage" and religious liberty.[9] The attorney general for the state
of Georgia withdrew an offer of employment
after discovering that the job candidate had
gone through a religious marriage ceremony
that had joined her and another woman in
marriage. The rejected candidate filed suit,
alleging that the employer had interfered with
her constitutionally protected rights of intimate
association, religious exercise, and expressive
association. The public office justified the withdrawal on grounds that the same-sex marriage
would raise issues in conflict with current
interpretations of Georgia law and would interfere with prosecutorial actions. In addition, the
attorney general stated that he simply could
no longer "trust" the candidate. The circuit
court decided that no fundamental rights were
abridged by the office and gave great weight to
the fact that a prosecutor's office must have full
discretion in hiring those employees in whom
it can place its full confidence.

Nepotism

Concerning themselves less with off-duty
relationships than with on-duty relationships,
a growing number of employers, especially
those in the public sector, have implemented
nepotism rules.[10] These rules follow the general trend toward regulating interactions

between related employees who work together in power-differentiated positions. In other words, one member of a working couple cannot be in a supervisory position over another or affect the terms and conditions of the other's employment.

For instance, if one member of a couple is a supervisor, he or she shall not in any way participate in the evaluation or determination of salary levels or conditions of employment of the other member. The fact that a supervisor's name appears on a document relating to the terms and conditions of the spouse's employment can be regarded as a prima facie conflict of interest.

Nepotism rules also prohibit one member of the same immediate family from working in such proximity to the other that interference in job performance might result. The rules require that when these close relationships occur in the workplace, one of the couple (usually the less senior employee) must be transferred or discharged. These nepotism rules have come at a time when more women are entering the workplace and more workers are marrying people they meet at work.

Couples adversely affected by the nepotism rules have challenged these policies, arguing that the policies violate not only their fundamental and constitutional right to marry,[11] but also the Fourteenth Amendment equal protections clause through the disparate impact these rules have on women in the workplace. In 1995, federal courts ruled on three separate cases that challenged nepotism rules.[12] In one case in which one spouse was a nurse employed by a hospital and the other was a helicopter pilot employed by an air-ambulance

---

Tips for Policies on Personal Relationships in the Workplace

❒ Recognize that the public agency has no legitimate interest in interfering with co-worker relationships other than ensuring that the relationship does not affect employee morale, employee productivity, or agency functions.

❒ Restrict dating between co-workers in power-differentiated relationships.

❒ Maintain an open-door policy to allow employees involved in a supervisor/subordinate or other power-differentiated relationship to discuss their situation with appropriate managers. Supervisors should usually let employees take the first step toward such a discussion unless other employees express concern.

❒ Encourage employees to report to appropriate managers or supervisors any relationships that cause them concern.

❒ Ensure that one of the involved parties does not have decision-making authority over terms and conditions of employment of the other party and does not have a role in the latter's performance appraisal process.

❒ Allow for reasonable attempts to accommodate the interest of the couple and co-workers through modification of work schedules, restructuring of jobs, and arrangement of job transfers.

❒ Give all employees full notice of the policy and make compliance a condition of employment.

❒ Specify what sanctions come into play if violations occur. For instance, if a violation has led to favoritism, bias, preferential treatment, harassment, or disruptive incidents, disciplinary action up to termination may be taken.

Source: Adapted from Dan J. Schaner, Exhibit 1: Model Co-Worker Dating and Fraternization Policy, in "Romance in the Workplace: Should Employers Act as Chaperons?" *Employee Relations Law Journal* 20 (Summer 1994): 66–67.

service under contract with the hospital, the employer went so far as to call for the transfer of the married employee. In each of the three cases, the federal courts affirmed the power of the public entities to restrict the working conditions of married co-workers. The courts decided that, while there is a fundamental right to marry, the test of a policy is whether it creates a direct legal obstacle that would actually forbid employees from marrying.

Policies affecting the marital activities of workers are also covered by the rational-basis test. That is, such policies will be sustained if they can be shown to advance a legitimate governmental interest, such as minimizing workplace conflicts, decreasing the possibility of sexual harassment claims, or ensuring the equitable treatment of all employees.

Relationships between life-sharing workers are to be assessed by the same rules as those between married workers: managers should maintain an open-door policy and make accommodation efforts. (See sidebar on previous page.) The employer's reactions toward peer-level romantic relationships should also be limited to those situations that result in disruption.

Use of Public Property: Computers and the Internet

Guiding Principles

- In the past several years, many employers have adopted a no-tolerance policy for personal use of public properties.
- Agency policies must clearly spell out the boundaries of what personal use of government equipment can be allowed.
- Rules must be enforced equally for all job classes and ranks.

Challenge

- Deterring Internet abuse while allowing exploration and creative use of the Internet to improve government functioning.

In government, both managers and rank-and-file employees uphold a public trust. In some jurisdictions, the political culture may tolerate some use of public properties for personal use. This practice is seen as part of the perquisites of office. But in the past several years, employers have moved toward a no-tolerance policy for the personal use of public properties, a policy that extends to all ranks of employees.

The workplace environment is replete with items that can be used for personal benefit. From phones, photocopiers, and computers to office supplies, the employee is constantly tempted to use these items for personal needs because they offer convenience. Thus, agency policies must clearly spell out the boundaries of what can be allowed in terms of personal use. The agency is also responsible for educating its employees as to the more stringent expectations that are found in the public sector as opposed to private corporations, where personal use of equipment and resources may be allowed as a job perquisite. Isolated incidents of misuse can not only erode a climate of trust and integrity but also become epidemic.

Probably the most acute problem involving the use of public property is the use of agency computers and their online capabilities. The term *personal computer* is often taken literally, even though the equipment is public and its intended use is for government business only. Computers can be used for cruising the Internet not only for work-related information but also for personal applications. Some employees may use their e-mail privileges for communication of the most personal nature or may waste time talking in chat rooms. Abuse rises to a more serious level when employees use these channels of information to access and download pornographic or hate material. The intrusion of such material into the workplace sows the seeds for harassment and discrimination suits. Employees may also post or download material that violates copyright laws. In 1997 Congress passed the No Electronic Theft Act, which makes it a federal crime to distribute or even possess unauthorized copies of copyrighted material even when no profit is involved.[13] Employees should also be warned to be careful in posting information that may provide grounds for defamation suits.

Because the First Amendment prevents government from stifling free speech, government has little control over employees who establish their own Web pages on their home computers. Although these Web pages represent an employee's own expressive activity and do not tie up the employer's equipment, they are certainly not private. Rather, they become accessible to everyone and thus may become an issue for the local government if the Web site reveals conduct that is not in the interest of the agency.

At present, the law is unsettled in terms of restrictions that can be put on public employees' use of the Internet. A decision by a federal district court in Virginia struck down as unconstitutional a Virginia law that prohibited state employees from accessing sexually explicit material on state computers except when agency heads had certified that such material was required for bona fide state projects.[14] The judge found that the law restricted employees' ability to "read, research, and discuss" controversial topics that were a matter of public concern. However, the court did recognize that the state is entitled to guard the productivity of its employees against distraction and has a right as well as a legal duty to avoid the creation of a hostile work environment. The court noted that the statute involved was underinclusive in ignoring the limitless variety of disruptive computer activity (e.g., accessing on-line video games, chat rooms, and shopping sites, and using e-mail for non-work-related topics) and left open the question of valid restrictions on computer or Internet abuse under regulations that are carefully tailored to target disruptive activity rather than content of information.[15]

E-mail should be recognized as an open letter box. Managers as well as employees should be aware that everyone can read every-

one else's mail. Public managers should also recognize that their files are open, especially those in states that have open-records and open-meeting laws. In one state, the attorney general ruled that e-mail discussions and straw votes on a personnel decision were open records.[16] As a result, the press published messages exchanged between members of a state board, splashing colloquial speech, personal characterizations, and confidential remarks across news pages. (For a sample county e-mail policy, see Exhibit 7-1.)

Different approaches have been suggested to deter or sanction Internet abuses. These can include blocking sites (which is expensive and not fully reliable) and monitoring employees. Monitoring can prevent some Internet abuses, but it must be approached thoughtfully. For one thing, it demands a great deal of time from

Tips for Successful On-line Policies

❏ Create a policy that prohibits use of work time or agency equipment or resources to access adult or other information that has no relation to work interests and that may disrupt the workplace.

❏ Distribute written and electronic copies of the policy to all employees and take steps to update it regularly.

❏ Inform employees if the agency plans to monitor net usage. The agency should follow through on its monitoring even if it involves only occasional spot checks.

❏ Consider letting employees surf the Web on their own time if they stay within written guidelines.

❏ Trust employees to use common sense when working with the Internet just as they are trusted in the use of any other agency property or resource.

Source: Ian Logan, "You Are Being Watched," *PC World* 15 (November 1997): 245–253.

Exhibit 7-1   Sample Policy for Employee Use of E-Mail

The county e-mail system is county property and may be used for county business. The system is not to be used for employee personal gain or to support or advocate non-county-related business or purposes. All use of the e-mail system is subject to management access pursuant to the following policy.

1. Incidental and occasional personal use of e-mail is permitted, but such messages will be treated no differently from other messages. Any personal message can be retrieved by the county even though it has been deleted from an individual's in-box. Assume that any e-mail message you are drafting will be made public, and draft it accordingly.

2. No computer system is completely secure. The e-mail system is not intended to transmit sensitive materials such as personnel decisions, legal opinions, or confidential material that may be more appropriately communicated by written memorandum or personal conversation.

3. Employees may not intentionally intercept, eavesdrop, record, read, alter, or receive another person's e-mail message without proper authorization in accordance with this policy.

4. This policy applies to all employees, contractors, part-time employees, volunteers, or other individuals provided with access to the county's e-mail system as necessary for business with the county.

5. Employees' e-mail communications should be routinely and regularly deleted from their in-boxes.

6. Under no circumstances shall any employee use the e-mail system for messages that could reasonably be considered as injurious or offensive to others on the basis of race, sex, age, sexual orientation, religious or political beliefs, national origin, or disability. Inappropriate e-mail messages can give rise to claims of discrimination, harassment, defamation, emotional distress, and copyright infringement.

7. Solicitation of funds, political messages, and harassing e-mail are prohibited.

8. Use of the county e-mail system for personal business, whether profit or nonprofit, is prohibited.

9. The county may access e-mail messages within the county system of all individuals covered by this policy for any purpose not specifically prohibited by law. If practicable, employees will be notified in advance of such access or receive notice within a reasonable time after the access. Employees will be notified of date of access, purpose of access, and identity of person who accessed the information, and information obtained.

10. Employees are informed that their department managers or county commission may disclose to parties within or outside the county the contents of e-mail sent to and between individuals covered by this policy without the permission of the individuals if it serves the interests of the county or the public.

Source: Adapted from the policy of Grand Forks County, North Dakota.

supervisors, and the costs may outweigh the benefits. For another thing, it is regarded as an invasion of workplace privacy and can thus foster resentment and the motivation to move on to another employer. For tips on discouraging Internet abuse, see the sidebar on page 187.

A lawyer for the Electronic Frontier Foundation has diagnosed much of the trepidation about Internet misuse as "fear of the future." A prudent approach may be simply to monitor the functioning of the offices to see if productivity or agency focus are affected in any way. In general, adaptation will eventually lead to better-functioning agencies.[17] Certainly, the on-line capabilities of Web pages and e-mail put an agency into more direct contact with its clients and members of the public.

Confidentiality

Guiding Principle

- Public employees have an ethical obligation to guard the confidentiality of personal information in their keeping.

One of the primary expectations attached to a position involving information management is that confidentiality will be preserved. Public agencies develop and record a wide range of information on individuals and businesses that is essential to the conduct of public business. These records include personal and financial information on clients, convicts, patients, wards, recipients of public payments, contractors, parties under regulation, and public employees. Public agencies have an ethical obligation to keep this information confidential and restricted to those with a bona fide need to know. Thus, the local government must provide employees with policies and procedures based on relevant state and local law regarding confidentiality of and open access to public records.

The increasing reliance on computerized information networks makes it more difficult for managers of public records to keep these records confidential. Employees should be thoroughly briefed on security measures involving passwords, blocked information, read-only access rules, and restricted access to printers. The faxing of information to other parties—even to allied agencies—should be strictly controlled.[18]

Confidentiality of records needs to be especially protected where release of information could reasonably be expected to constitute an "unwarranted invasion of privacy." Although this is a subjective concept, a number of states (e.g., California and New York) have specified what constitutes such an invasion.[19]

Political Activity

Guiding Principle

- Most state laws on political activity focus on deterring abuses of power by managers and supervisors.

Challenge

- Becoming thoroughly familiar with the political activity laws of both the state and the local jurisdiction.

At the federal level, the Hatch Act was for decades a major restraint on federal employees' involvement in political activity.[20] Apart from voting, most forms of political participation were closed to employees. The Hatch Act also covered state and local workers whose agencies' activities were federally funded. In 1993 Congress passed the Hatch Act Reform Amendments, which substantially relaxed the restrictions on political activity and stipulated that employees should be encouraged to exercise fully and freely and without fear of penalty or reprisal their right to participate or refrain from participating in the political process of the nation.[21] Actually, the amendments reflect the rules on the political activities of public employees that have evolved at the state level and have been codified in "little Hatch Acts."

Statutory Prohibitions on Political Activity or Influence in Administration

- Any use of authority to coerce or influence an agency action or decision

- Any requirement or pressure from a superior to an employee to contribute to any political fund

- Any personnel action that includes a condition that an employee give or withhold political contributions

- Any recommendations or job evaluations that are based on political affiliations or political opinions expressed by the employee

- Any provision of lists or names of employees to any political candidate or organization

- Any direct or indirect offer to a government employee of an increase in compensation or salary by any person seeking elected or appointed office.

These state laws (see sidebar above) vary widely but focus on managers and supervisory personnel more than on rank-and-file workers. They particularly focus on deterring abuses of power that involve power-differentiated relationships.

In addition, all state political activity statutes implement what is known as politics-workplace separation. Some states indicate that there should be no solicitation of political funds on public premises[22] or no political activity during working hours, and no political activity by an officer or public employee while in public uniform.[23] However, no simple guidelines can answer all the questions about the proper bounds of political activity by government employees. It is, for instance, unclear whether a public employee can engage in political activity on behalf of a spouse, or

whether the officer of an agency can be a delegate to a party convention or an official or campaign manager for another candidate. Managers must become thoroughly familiar with the political activity laws of their states and their local jurisdictions.

Off-Duty Activities

Guiding Principle

- A government employee should be proscribed from holding a second job only if it directly conflicts with the employee's public duties.

A complex question for managers in the public sector involves whether managers themselves or their employees may hold other offices, private or public, or engage in other employment. This issue covers a wide range of circumstances:

- A public employee seeking to hold a political office, such as a seat on a city council or school board

- A public employee holding a directorship in a corporation, for instance, serving on a bank's board of directors

- A public employee offering his or her talents as a consultant in a particular field of expertise or running a consultation service out of his or her home

- An appointee to a public executive position completing terms of contracts he or she entered into before being appointed

- A public employee substantially augmenting his or her income with honoraria from speaking engagements

- An employee taking a part-time job outside normal work hours

- A public professional donating his or her services to a cause.

These situations are covered by common law and by explicit constitutional and statutory provisions that vary from state to state. In addition, home-rule cities may develop their own rules with regard to the outside income activities of municipal employees.

According to common law, the holding of one office does not, of itself, disqualify an officeholder from simultaneously holding another job or contract, provided that there is no conflict of interest in the functions of the two offices and that one office does not extend its regulatory net over the other.

State constitutions and statutes are more explicit in barring dual activities. The most common restriction aims to preserve a separation of powers by preventing a person who has a position in one branch from holding a position in another branch that can make policy or exercise authority over the first position (one cannot be superior and subordinate at the same time). Thus a police officer, an employee of the executive branch, cannot hold a position in a legislative forum, city council, or state legislature. Some states at one time forbade state employees, including university faculty members, from serving as state legislators. Those statutes are now being relaxed (e.g., in Georgia), generally to allow employees to take leaves of absence from their employment while a legislature is in session.[24]

A basic problem is determining whether a government employee's outside activity gives rise to a conflict of interest or an incompatibility with the employee's primary public duties that warrants its forfeiture. A government employee should be proscribed from holding a secondary job only if that job directly conflicts with the employee's public duties. For instance, a public health inspector should not own a business he or she is required to inspect. Similarly, a police officer may be precluded from working in or operating an establishment that serves alcoholic beverages or from engaging in off-duty process serving, since those activities can involve the officer in civil disputes.[25]

Guidelines Restricting Outside Employment and Activity

Full-time employees are permitted to engage in outside employment subject to the following restrictions:

- Employees will not engage in any employment, with the exception of military service obligations, that will interfere with proper performance of city (county) employment. Employees shall report to work refreshed and ready to work.

- Employees will not accept pay or compensation from anyone for work time while they are on duty with the city (county).

- Employees will not engage in employment that would interfere with a worker's obligation to his or her primary public employer (e.g., being on call to respond to emergencies).

- Employees are prohibited from working for any contractor or company that has a current contract with the city (county) or for an employer that would constitute a conflict of interest with the city (county).

- Employees will not accept or solicit private work while they are on duty or as a result of their employment with the city (county).

Source: Adapted from "Employee Reference Guide," City of Grand Forks, North Dakota, 1998.

Generally, state statutes confer almost plenary powers on the local hiring and appointing authority to define and proscribe those activities that are inconsistent with the duties and responsibilities of the officers and their employees. (See Exhibit 7-2 for a list of issues that might be included in a local government ethics manual.) But once those ethics policies for local government are established, the agency or office will still need to deal with each case on an individual basis. An employee has a particular responsibility to come forward with any information on outside employment or income activity that can be considered collateral employment. The manager of the agency and the employee must review the situation together to determine the permissibility and scope of this outside activity.

The manager must then follow through with an assessment of the employee's performance to determine whether the outside activities have not only raised conflicts of interest

but also negatively affected job performance (as evidenced in increased absenteeism or tardiness, decreased alertness at work, or decreased quality of performance).

Honoraria are another issue of outside activity that must be evaluated by agencies. State and local governments have expressed an interest in limiting appearances and honoraria where such activity would interfere with the government's interests as an employer. That interest includes avoidance of dual compen-

---

Exhibit 7-2   Issues to Be Included in a Professional Code of Conduct or Ethics Manual

Policies

Outside employment and activities

- Limits on off-duty earnings (not off-duty income)

- Permitted off-duty contracts, engagements for teaching and lecturing

- Research, writing, and publication of material that is agency related or that covers agency functioning

- Profits and royalties from such publication; on-duty/off-duty use of time to produce such publications

- Attendance at conferences at agency expense (guided by job relatedness)

- Honoraria for engagements that are agency related and/or are for activity during agency time

- Participation in civic activities (generally encouraged but commitments may be limited in time) and use of comp time to cover such participation

- Limits on political activities

Relationships between employees of different ranks

- Exchange of gifts and gratuities between upper-level and lower-level employees; de

minimus gifts (birthday recognitions, employee farewells, etc.)

- Fraternization between upper-level and lower-level employees

Conflicts of interest

- Employment of relatives

- Contracts with the city

- Use of public equipment, facilities, or personnel for private gain

Conduct

- Zero tolerance for harassment

- Zero tolerance for threatening or violent behavior

Confidentiality of information
Adherence to open-meetings and public-record laws

Procedures

Where to seek advice
How to declare a possible conflict
Where to report improper behavior

Key Ordinances and State Statutes

Source: Partially adapted from Office of the Mayor, *Ethics Manual* (Orlando, Fla.: City of Orlando, 1995).

sation for officers or employees and use of agency time to qualify for the honoraria. Ambiguous situations arise when an agency officer represents the agency or presents agency views. Some agencies require that officers turn over any honoraria to agency accounts. And officers cannot request travel reimbursements from the agency when the costs of travel are borne by those making the invitation. Again, this is one area in which an agency should have a policy in place.

Residency

Guiding Principle

• Managers should communicate any residency requirements to job candidates during their initial interviews.

Local governments have a long history of imposing residency rules on their employees.[26] These rules have taken several forms:

• Jurisdictional residency rules that require employees to live within the jurisdictional boundaries of the government for which they work

• Geographic or distance rules that require employees to live within a certain distance of their workplace

• Durational rules that require job applicants to be residents or become residents within a specified period

• Job-specific rules that apply to some classifications of employees and not to others (e.g., police, firefighters, medical emergency crews, school administrators).[27]

Employees and their unions have challenged these rules, alleging that they are unreasonable and violate the rights of privacy and travel and a "fundamental" right to live wherever individuals may choose.

In dealing with these rules, however, both federal and state courts have generally avoided the issue of whether residency is a fundamental right and instead used a rational-basis test to measure the validity of the rules. They have tended to strike down durational rules that bear no relation to the recruitment of persons with the proper qualifications. They have also struck down efforts to retroactively enforce residency rules after a period of nonenforcement. However, they have upheld rules of continuing residency, distance, and job-specific residency requirements. In short, the courts have taken a balancing approach to residency requirements, deciding in favor of the rules where the city can advance valid governmental objectives and against the rules only when the requirements impose genuine hardships on the workers.

Residency rules across the country present a checkerboard of approaches. In California, the state constitution bars jurisdictional residency rules but allows geographic residency rules. Montana and Kentucky require public employees to be registered to vote in the jurisdictions in which they work, affirming their stake in the community and their accountability to the people they serve. Michigan is one state where unions gained the right of public employees to collectively bargain residency issues. At least eleven states recognize that the residency of employees is distinctly a local issue that should be worked out with local authorities. In Colorado, the state's high court even struck down a state law prohibiting home-rule cities from adopting residency rules, stating that "the residency of employees of a home rule municipality is of local concern."

Since residency requirements are a condition of employment, managers should communicate these requirements to job candidates during their initial interviews. If a candidate is qualified for the position, the local government may provide listings or realtor references to assist the new employee in obtaining suitable and affordable housing within the jurisdiction.

Communicating Expectations and Responsibilities

Guiding Principle

- All employees must be fully informed about what is expected of them in their jobs.
- The communication of rules and requirements through handbooks or manuals must be periodically reinforced with memos, fliers, and verbal reminders.
- Do not let rules dominate the work process. Emphasize shared principles in pursuit of the agency's mission rather than the workplace rules.

As emphasized in the preceding sections, employees have certain responsibilities to their employer. Management has the right to expect employees to attend work regularly, carry out assigned duties in a productive and cooperative fashion, ensure that work performance is not adversely affected by the use of drugs or alcohol, avoid entangling personal relationships that might undermine morale or create conflicts of interest, respect norms of privacy and confidentiality, and refrain from using public property for personal benefit.

But administrators cannot rightly and fairly hold employees accountable if they do not make their expectations known. Managing the workforce to best advantage requires the clear communication of expectations of performance, workplace behaviors, and adherence to agency objectives. These expectations can be communicated through several channels: job interviews and orientation, handbooks, memos, posters on bulletin boards, training in workshops, meetings with supervisors, or on-line.

Personnel Policy Manual

Employers should provide all employees with a handbook or manual that specifies in writing all personnel policies and rules. The handbook establishes a reciprocal set of responsibilities for employer and employee. It tells employees what is expected of them in the workplace and what they can expect from their employer in terms of fair treatment. The range of issues that demand policies in order to prevent or resolve employer-employee conflicts has grown substantially in kind and number. A comprehensive employee handbook should cover all the issues listed in the sidebar on page 195.

Conduct policies and workplace rules do not require the legal specificity used in hearing procedures but must pass a "reasonableness" test. That is, whether the local government is an at-will employer or can, under state law, terminate employees only after finding just cause (see Chapter 5), local policies and workplace rules laid out in a personnel handbook should provide "a reasonable employee" with advance notice of what would be regarded as cause for discipline or termination.

Handbooks will indicate the range of behaviors that provide grounds for disciplinary action or termination. (See Exhibit 7-3 for an example of work rules regarding misconduct that can lead to dismissal or other disciplinary action.) Under the federal model, "just cause for termination" has been interpreted to include any conduct, on or off duty, that impairs the performance or disrupts the functioning of an agency. Certain offenses against the state or the employer, such as theft, résumé fraud, fighting, insubordination, and workplace assault, can be prima facie evidence of just cause. But not all misconduct can provide just cause to suspend or remove an employee. Generally, the misconduct must be substantial. Occasional absenteeism, neglects of duty, rudeness, horseplay, and violations of dress codes or other work rules may not be sufficient to establish just cause.

The policies contained in the employee manual should be repeatedly communicated to employees through various verbal and written channels, such as the orientation meetings for new hires and periodic memos to all staff. Public employers who simply hand the manual to their employees and have them sign affidavits that they have received and read it are remiss in their responsibility to ensure that employees are properly informed about the rules that may be applied to them.

Since the employee manual is vital in communicating the parameters of workplace conduct, it should itself be a model of good communication. The best-written policies are succinct and written in language understand-

---

Contents of a Comprehensive Employee Handbook

- At-will employment disclaimer and acknowledgment form (*see Chapter 5*)
- Employment rights as recognized by the local government or as codified in state law or federal statutes
  - Equal employment opportunity statement (*see Chapter 5*)
  - Rights under such statutes as the Fair Labor Standards Act, Equal Pay Act, Americans with Disabilities Act (ADA), Family and Medical Leave Act (FMLA), Pregnancy Discrimination Act, Age Discrimination in Employment Act, and others.
- Agency or city procedures governing appointments, promotions, and transfers
- Pay policies (raises, bonuses, temporary increases, incentive pay, travel expense reimbursements, overtime), including method of payment, pay schedule, and final payment
- Benefits attached to employment (pension, health insurance, life insurance)
- Procedures for evaluation and review of performance
- Employee records, access, confidentiality/privacy/application of open records laws
- Code of ethics (see Exhibit 7-2 for a list of issues that might be covered in a professional code of conduct or ethics manual)
- Work rules
  - *Attendance*
    Holidays
    Vacations
    Sick leave, notice, documentation
    Personal and family leave

Bereavement leave
Jury/witness duty
Military duty
Donated time/compensatory (comp) time/flexible time
Lunch breaks/rest periods

- *Use of equipment*
  Telephones, computers, e-mail (*see Exhibit 7-1*), software
  Agency vehicles, office supplies

- *Conduct and misconduct*
  Dress codes
  No-smoking policies
  Drug- and alcohol-abuse policies
  Sexual, racial harassment (*see Exhibit 5-1* for an example of a harassment policy)
  Fraternization policies
  Workplace civility
  Misconduct (behaviors that trigger notice, counseling, and possible disciplinary action) (*see Exhibit 7-3*)

- *Corrective and disciplinary procedures*
  Handling of complaints
  Investigations
  Notice
  Discussion, counseling, employee assistance programs (EAPs)
  Mediation and arbitration
  Hearings, appeals

- *Channels of communication*
  Suggestions
  Changing work rules
  Grievance procedures

Exhibit 7-3   Sample Work Rules

[*Employer*] is concerned for the safety and well-being of all of its employees. For this reason, certain rules are necessary to ensure a safe work environment. The following, ranging in degrees of severity, is a partial list of categories of improper conduct that, when engaged in, shall constitute grounds for disciplinary action, up to and including immediate dismissal:

Grounds for immediate dismissal include the following:

- Use of alcohol or drugs while on duty
- Unauthorized possession of a weapon on work premises
- Sleeping while on duty
- Assaulting a co-worker, supervisor, or any other employee
- Punching another employee's time card
- Theft of company property

- Insubordination
- Falsifying records, reports, or information of any nature
- Any other serious misconduct [*employer*] believes warrants immediate dismissal.

The following, ranging in degrees of severity, is a partial list of categories of improper conduct that, when engaged in, shall constitute grounds for progressive discipline*:

- Smoking in areas not designated for smoking
- Engaging in horseplay
- Tardiness or absenteeism
- Leaving work before scheduled quitting time
- Failure to punch time clock
- Creating unsanitary or unsafe working conditions.

* Progressive discipline means, for instance, that a first offense incurs an oral warning; a second offense, a written warning; a third offense, suspension; a fourth offense, dismissal.

able on first reading.[28] Because employees increasingly react to adverse employment decisions with litigation and regard the manual as a definitive contract that limits the employer to the specific "causes of actions" within it, employers must avoid including language that suggests the manual is such a contract. Rather, the manual should include a statement to the effect that the provisions within it are informational and that the city or agency reserves the right to interpret any provision and to change the policies with reasonable notice to employees. The rules should allow employers to exercise discretion in dealing with personnel problems.

Reserving some measure of discretion on conduct issues also allows supervisors to reasonably accommodate an employee's unique situation. The employee manual draws a nar-

row line between expectations of scrupulous adherence to work rules and relaxation of rules in special circumstances. In treading this fine line, the employer should aim at consistency. In fact, inconsistency in this regard opens the door to charges of favoritism or discriminatory and disparate treatment of employees.

Despite the counseling efforts of supervisors, disciplinary action sometimes becomes necessary (see Chapter 8). One of the primary tests of just cause is whether workers have been given adequate notice of what is expected of them and the probable consequences that will follow if those expectations are not met. This is one of the reasons that it is so important for personnel manuals to clearly set forth workplace rules and expectations. However, an employee manual containing long lists of dos and don'ts gives the appearance of an old-style

Red Flags

- Avoid legal jargon in communicating information on procedures or conduct. (The following, for instance, would be considered legal jargon: "Employees filing a claim of discrimination shall refer to Section 3406 of the City Code and move to demonstrate that they are members of a protected class and establish a prima facie case of disparate treatment.")

- Avoid language that creates an enforceable contract, particularly with regard to guarantees of continued employment.

- Avoid conduct rules that precisely lay out prohibited behaviors and do not provide for sensible discretion by supervisors and administrators to deal with related behaviors that negatively affect the organization.

- Avoid draconian rules that do not allow for some flexibility and corrective action (e.g., a rule that holds that an employee who is absent for two consecutive days without giving notice to the department head shall be considered to have abandoned his or her job and is liable for termination).

military personnel manual, reflecting distrust of employees and a desire for maximum conformity. Such expressions of distrust and conformity are inconsistent with the contemporary view that valued human resources should be trusted, treated with respect, and given considerable flexibility in determining how best to carry out their delegated tasks.

Perhaps the best solution to this dilemma is to ensure that employees read and understand the behavioral rules set forth in the employee manual, so that disciplinary actions can be sustained, and thereafter to emphasize the shared principles that will guide pursuit of the agency's mission rather than the workplace rules. This approach is consistent with what has come to be known as principle-centered leadership.

Job Interviews and Orientation

Some policies in the employee manual may need to be communicated to a job candidate in his or her interview. These would include, for instance, provisions that require an employee to live within the city. Most candidates are informed of an agency's equal employment opportunity policy during the initial interviews. And a candidate who may have a spouse or relative already employed at the agency should also be informed of the agency's nepotism policies.

A new employee's job orientation session should thoroughly familiarize the new hire with the company's workplace policies. This orientation should be given on the first day of employment or as soon thereafter as practicable. Both the human resources director and the supervisors under whom the employee will be working should be involved in the orientation; the presence of the supervisors shows a new employee that these managers are ready to answer questions and help him or her to succeed. As each section of the handbook is introduced and explained, the employee should have full opportunity to ask questions. The individual conducting the orientation should not be surprised by the naïveté of new employees, even those with degrees and professional training.

The orientation session should also clearly indicate to the employee how to use reporting and appeals channels. Each department should have a reporting procedure that provides at least two places for an employee to go with a complaint. This procedure should include a bypass channel for the employee's supervisor. An employee should not have to report harassment or abusive behavior to the harasser (see Chapters 5 and 8).

The employer should also provide for feedback on the orientation session, allowing the new employee to evaluate the session and its usefulness in a questionnaire. Typically, this would include such questions as the following:

- Did you think the orientation session was helpful in preparing you for your job?

- What part of the orientation was most useful? Least useful?

- Was any part of the orientation unclear? On what issues?

- Have you reviewed the employee handbook? Do you have any questions about it?

- Have your supervisor and co-workers been helpful in familiarizing you with the job and your department?

- Do you have any questions about employment with the city?

Supervisors

Supervisors also play an important role in communicating expectations to employees. Supervisors represent the authority of their parent organizations and are charged with maintaining a productive and safe work environment. They therefore need to direct and control the conduct of employees through verbal guidance, written comments, rewards, and discipline. (All these supervisory activities come together in the performance evaluation process discussed in Chapter 3.) Supervisors are also the primary conduits of information both to and from employees. In a real sense, supervisors represent the personification of a department's policies; they make the pages of the employee manual come alive.

Many supervisors consider themselves first as specialists in their own field, whether it be engineering, fiscal management, or some field of public service, and second (if at all) as human resource specialists. However, a supervisor must wear two hats. All supervisors should have special training in the whole panoply of policies and work rules in the employee manual. They should also expect continued education in changing policies. Vari-

Tips for Successfully Communicating Expectations to Employees

❏ Communicate all policies affecting the employer-employee relationship through a written employee handbook.

❏ Hold orientation sessions for new employees in which agency policies are described, explained, and discussed.

❏ Train all supervisory personnel in the agency's workplace policies and ask them to convey these policies to subordinates on a day-to-day basis.

❏ Educate employees on new policies and changes in existing policies.

❏ Use a variety of methods of communication to educate employees about personnel policies.

ous newsletters are published to keep human resources personnel up-to-date on developments; supervisors can be provided with subscription copies or be on a circulation list for such materials. A knowledgeable supervisory crew can be an agency's best line of defense against employee discontent or problems.

Unfortunately, in both overt and subtle ways, a supervisor can also create personnel problems damaging to the agency. For instance, a supervisor might discriminate racially in job assignments to placate prejudiced subordinates, or might use banter to reprimand male workers for workplace failings while responding to women's shortcomings in harsh or vulgar terms. In the extreme case, a supervisor might engage in sexual harassment. These possibilities make it all the more important to train supervisors well.

Changing Policies

Any amendments to existing policies must be carefully drafted and communicated to employees, and all contrary language must be eliminated. In the case of changes that have their source in court decisions, the employer should wait until legal counsel has thoroughly analyzed the decisions before communicating them. Administrators should be careful in making any amendments or changes that affect or revoke benefits, such as vacation or sick leave, that an employee may have already accumulated.

Employee Participation in Changing Work Rules

While administrators bear the responsibility for formulating work rules, the input of employees can be crucial for arriving at rules that are realistic and inspire employee compliance.

Employers may set up either formal or informal procedures for employee participation in work rule formulation and amendments. A process involving changes in the rules could provide for

- Appointment or election of employees to serve on policy committees
- Prepublication of changes or amendments to work rules
- Solicitation of comments from employees on changes or amendments
- Meetings for employees during which proposed rules are explained, discussed, and justified.

Involving employees in the formulation of personnel policies is important not only in identifying potential problems but also in communicating expectations. As in the initial job orientation sessions, trainers legitimize work rules by explaining why the rules have been made and demonstrating their reasonableness. For instance, a requirement that city garbage workers wear protective eye gear, shirts, and steel guard shoes may seem onerous and picky, especially when those workers are sweltering for hours in temperatures around the 100 degree mark. However, reference to the injuries or health problems that result from noncompliance with such rules can provide the justification that makes them acceptable.

Discussion of conduct rules should continually emphasize the need to maintain respect for all co-workers in the organization. The objective is to develop a knowledgeable workforce with a sense of professionalism from bottom to top.

Communicating Changes in Rules

Once rule changes are finalized, they must be communicated to all covered employees. Proper notice of rule changes may be made via several channels:

- Loose-leaf additions to each employee's manual
- Publication in the department newsletter (with commentary)
- Posting on employees' e-mail
- Posting in prominent workplace locations (lunchrooms, restrooms)
- Notification included with paychecks.

Conclusion

Managers can limit disciplinary problems by leading with integrity. People in charge must be above reproach. A discovery of modern management theory is that managerial ethics matter to employees—and matter a lot.[29] Ethics matter from the perspective of the manager strengthening his or her self-respect, from the perspective of employees trusting their superiors enough to follow their lead, and from the perspective of a successful agency being able to attract and retain the most competent and dedicated public servants.

An important aspect of setting expectations is to see that messages are consistent and clear. Nothing diminishes the integrity of a manager as much as a set of mixed messages. In changing environments where both managers and rank-and-file employees are challenged to know more, to adapt technologically, to be more accountable, to be innovative, and to do more with less, the messages must be consistent and on target.

[1] Robert M. Howie and Laurence A. Shapiro, "How Long Is Enough? Leaves of Absence as Reasonable Accommodation under ADA," *Employee Relations Law Journal* 29 (Fall 2003): 33–49.

[2] Brian F. Jackson and Howard R. Flaxman, "Intermittent Leave and Reduced Leave Schedule: Traps for the Unwary under the Family and Medical Leave Act," *Employee Relations Law Journal* 20 (Summer 1994): 29–46. See also Richard J. Reibstein, "The FMLA and Absenteeism," *HR Focus* 73 (August 1996): 3; Robert B. Gordon and Christopher L. Ekman, "Attendance Control Issues under the ADA and FMLA," *The Labor Lawyer* 13 (Fall 1997): 393; and Arthur F. Silbergeld and Stacie S. Polashuk, "Chronic Serious Health Impairments and Worker Absences under Federal Employment Law," *The Labor Lawyer* 14 (Summer 1998): 1–22.

[3] Pamela Johnson and Julie Indvik, "Rudeness at Work: Impulse Over Restraint," *Public Personnel Management* 30 (Winter 2001): 457–465.

[4] Kirstin D. Grimsley, "Leaner—and Definitely Meaner: The Growing Problem of Incivility on the Job Is Hurting Profits as Well as Feelings," *Washington Post National Weekly Edition,* 20–27 July 1998, 21.

[5] Paul E. Starkman, "Answering the Tough Questions about Alcoholism and Substance Abuse under the ADA and FMLA," *Employee Relations Law Journal* 25 (Spring 2000): 43–77.

[6] Theresa Johnson Holt, "Alcoholism and Misbehavior: Implications of the ADA," *Labor Law Journal* 47 (November 1996): 729–734.

[7] Dean L. Schaner, "Romance in the Workplace: Should Employers Act as Chaperons?" *Employee Relations Law Journal* 20 (Summer 1994): 47–71.

[8] *Briggs v. North Muskegon Police Department*, 746 F.2d 1475 (6th Cir. 1984), cert. denied, 473 U.S. 909 (1985).

[9] *Shahar v. Bowers*, 114 F.3d 1097 (11th Cir. 1997).

[10] James Podgers, "Marriage Traps in the Workplace: Nepotism Rules Make It Harder for Spouses to Be Colleagues in Public Sector," *ABA Journal* 82 (January 1996): 46–47.

[11] Cases supporting this position include *Ross v. Stouffer Hotel Co.*, 816 P.2nd 302 (Hawaii 1991); and *Hughes v. Lipscher*, 906 F.2nd 961 (3rd Cir. 1990).

[12] *Parks v. City of Warner Robins*, 43 F.3d 609 (11th Cir. 1995); *Waters v. Gaston County*, 57 F.3d 422 (4th Cir. 1995); *Wright v. MetroHealth Medical Center*, 58 F.3d. 1130 (6th Cir. 1995).

[13] The act signed into law by President Clinton on December 16, 1997, does not contain traditional fair-use exemptions such as those allowing photocopying by libraries and academic institutions, or quotation for the purposes of review or criticism.

[14] *Urofsky v. Allen*, 995 F. Supp. 634 (E.D.Va., 1998).

[15] Ibid. at 639–40.

[16] North Dakota Attorney General Open Records and Meetings Opinion, 98-0-05 (3 March 1998). E-mail messages are subject to open records and records retention laws. Straw votes conducted over e-mail raise troubling questions.

[17] Quoted by John Schwartz, "New Cultural Battleground Comes with a Mouse," *Washington Post National Weekly Edition*, 23 February 1998, 22–23.

[18] Kathleen A. Frawley, "Confidentiality in the Computer Age," *RN* 57 (July 1994): 59–60; and Note: "Keeping Secrets in Cyberspace: Establishing 4th Amendment Protection of Internet Communication," *Harvard Law Review* 110 (May 1997): 1591–1608.

[19] For typical inventories of information given statutory protection, see *Cal. (Gov't) Code* § 6254 (West 1997) and *N.Y. (Civ. Rights)* § 50a, *N.Y. (Civ. Serv.) Law* § R79.1, 80.8 (McKinney 1997).

[20] 53 Stat 1147, 1939, 80 Stat 525, 1966, codified in 5 USCA Sec. 7321-23.

[21] P.L. 103-94, 107 Stat 1001, 1993, codified in 5 USCA 7321-25.

[22] See for example McKinney's *Consolidated Laws of New York Annotated*. Civil Service, Subdivision 3: Section 107.

[23] See for example West's *Annotated California Code— Government*, Sections 3206-07.

[24] For an earlier discussion on this issue, see Carlton J. Snow and Elliott M. Abramson, "By the Light of Dual Employment: Standards for Employer Regulation of Moonlighting," *Indiana Law Journal* 55 (1979–1980): 581–614.

[25] See *Long Beach Police Officers Association v. City of Long Beach*, 759 P.2d 504 (Cal. 1988).

[26] Richard A. Posthuma, "A Balanced Approach to Residency Rules for Local Government Employees," *Government Union Review* 13 (September 1992): 46–73.

[27] See, for example, Brian R. Johnson, Greg L. Warchol, Vic W. Bumphus, "Police Residential Requirements: An Exploratory Analysis," *Journal of Collective Negotiation in the Public Sector* 26 (Winter 1997): 43–64.

[28] For a guide to the preparation of a good employee manual, see Jean d'Agenais and John Carruthers, *Creating Effective Manuals* (Cincinnati, Ohio: South West Publishing Co., 1985). Also see Stephen E. Befort, "Employee Handbooks and Legal Effect of Disclaimers," *Industrial Relations Law Journal* (now *Berkeley Journal of Labor and Employment Law*) 13 (1991/92): 326–381, see "Lack of Clarity," 353f.

[29] Bob Lewis, "The Ethical Manager Knows How to Apply the Right Motivational Tools," *InfoWorld* 19 (10 November 1997): 134.

CHAPTER 8

When Things Go Wrong

CHARLES R. WISE, BRIAN CLEMOW, SARANNE P. MURRAY, AND LISA B. BINGHAM

Even in jurisdictions with professional managers, well-trained supervisors, carefully drafted personnel policies, and procedures designed to ensure that the policies are followed, things go wrong. People are human, mistakes are made, and problems arise that require attention. The test of a well-managed human resources operation is not how many personnel problems arise, but how effectively the employer addresses them. Where significant litigation is involved, legal counsel generally will coordinate the response. However, there are many other common personnel problems that government managers can effectively resolve merely by following a sound plan of defense.

This chapter is intended only as a first reference for local government managers who see trouble brewing. It is much more cost-effective in the long run to consult counsel early, when a problem starts to develop, and to get advice about how to anticipate a claim and prepare a defense, than to wait until the sheriff serves the jurisdiction with notice of a lawsuit.

Discipline and Discharge of Employees

Guiding Principles

- The first step in discipline is a reasonably thorough yet timely investigation into the alleged employee misconduct.
- Discipline should start at the lowest appropriate level and work up to more significant penalties.
- Disciplinary action should proceed independent of any criminal prosecution proceedings.

One of the most common personnel problems faced by public and private sector employers alike is dealing with unacceptable performance, conduct, or behavior on the part of individual employees. An appropriate response to such problems is one that focuses on correcting the problem, if possible, but that resorts to discipline and ultimately discharge if the employee fails to achieve a satisfactory level of improvement.[1]

Investigating and Documenting Employee Misconduct

The first step in discipline is a reasonably thorough yet timely investigation into the alleged employee misconduct. When a manager takes disciplinary action prematurely, without having first conducted an investigation, that action is more likely to be overturned by a court or an arbitrator, usually because the manager missed some important facts. Ordinarily, a manager will want to hear what both the employee and witnesses have to say and determine what evidence there is before recommending discipline. If a public manager follows the steps outlined in the sidebar on page 203, it is more likely that the final disciplinary action will be reasonable and withstand scrutiny.

A gray area emerges with behaviors that may reflect dissatisfaction, disloyalty, or dissent but that do not rise to a confrontational level. These acts of noncompliant behavior can invoke the protections of the First Amendment for the expressive employee, especially if the workplace or supervisor/subordinate conflict can be characterized as a "matter of public concern." Whistle-blowers, for example, may certainly disrupt an agency with their principled disobedience, but they are protected if their revelations involve issues of public interest and agency accountability.

Managers tread a fine line in dealing with speech they find disruptive. Each circumstance requires a balancing between the right of the employee to ventilate a perceived grievance and the interests of the public agency. Since 1968, following the landmark Supreme Court case *Pickering v. Board of Education*,[2] the courts have assessed these conflicts between employees and their public employers and determined that the public employer can validly assert the following interests:

- The effect of speech on the conduct and discipline of the other employees
- The effect of speech on harmonious relations among the employee's co-workers

- The effect of speech on the job performance of the employee
- The breach of relationships that require personal loyalty and confidence
- The effect of speech on the function of the agency. A disruptive impact can be broadly interpreted to extend to effects beyond the immediate workplace, such as an undermining of confidence in the agency.

More recently, the U.S. Supreme Court has given greater discretion to public supervisors in dealing with disruptive speech in the workplace. In the 1994 case *Waters v. Churchill*,[3] the Court upheld a hospital supervisor's right to fire an employee who criticized the department and her superior before trainees. Even though the disruptive statements were "surrounded by protected speech," the statements were not immunized from sanction. The Court held that the supervisor, prior to moving to terminate the individual, had conducted an investigation from which she could reasonably conclude that the statements were actually disruptive. (See Chapter 5 for more on First Amendment protections of speech in the workplace.)

Managers have a responsibility to deal with internal dissent and prevent such dissent from escalating into workplace misconduct. The open door is the manager's first line of defense. The second line of defense is early intervention—calling in an employee to discuss his or her problems. A third preventive is keeping on top of small issues. Employees can become irritated about issues that seem of minor importance to others, such as the location of a workstation near a draft or away from windows. In dealing with an employee's complaint, it is important to make inquiries of other employees. A manager may find that more than one employee's comfort quotient is affected.

After the employer has decided on appropriate disciplinary action, it is critically important to document for the employee's personnel file both the action and the results of the investigation that preceded it. Even a verbal

Steps to Take before Recommending Discipline

For any event that may give rise to discipline, the manager should

- Interview each eyewitness
- Collect and safeguard any original documents that may be relevant and make copies for legal counsel
- Collect physical evidence (such as broken equipment or an altered time card) and store it securely, making sure that clear records of the chain of custody (the people who had access to the evidence) are maintained in order to protect against claims later that evidence was tampered with or manufactured
- Examine what discipline has been imposed on other employees who have committed the same or substantially similar acts of misconduct
- Interview the employee (in the presence of a union or other representative if *Weingarten*[1] is applicable, as discussed on page 205) to determine whether there are any mitigating circumstances or considerations specific to the employee that should be taken into account
- Inform the employee of the charges and the evidence, giving him or her an opportunity to respond or explain before discipline is imposed (see section on *Loudermill*[2] on pages 204–205)
- Consult with counsel about the investigation if the charges are likely to be serious and contested
- If the conduct is also subject to a criminal prosecution, collect all court documents before they are sealed as part of a plea bargain arrangement; time may be of the essence in getting access to witness affidavits that are part of the arrest warrant, for example.

[1] *NLRB v. Weingarten, Inc.,* 420 U.S. 251, 43 L. Ed. 2d 171, 95 S.Ct. 959 (1975); see also *Epilepsy Foundation of Northeast Ohio v. NLRB,* 268 F. 2d 1095 (2001).
[2] *Cleveland Board of Education v. Loudermill,* 470 U.S. 532, 84 L. Ed. 2d 494, 105 S. Ct. 1487 (1985).

reprimand can be documented through a memorandum recapping the date and basis for it. These documents can refresh a supervisor's memory if there is ever a need for testimony on the events that gave rise to the discipline. They can also provide evidence of progressive disciplinary action and establish just cause to dismiss when the employee persists in the misconduct or performance problem. Due process concerns and most collective bargaining agreements require that the employee receive a copy of any notice of discipline and of any records placed in his or her permanent file.

Progressive Discipline, Affirmative Discipline, and Just Cause

One of the most widely accepted principles of personnel management is the concept of *pro-gressive discipline*. The theory is that discipline should start at the lowest appropriate level and work up to more significant penalties. Employers should terminate employment only as a last resort, when an employee is unable or unwilling to respond to less drastic disciplinary measures. Progressive disciplinary steps might include

- Informal counseling
- Oral warning or reprimand
- Written warning or reprimand
- Minor (one to five days) suspension
- Major (more than five days) suspension
- Discharge.

Of course, it is not always appropriate to start at the lowest rung of the disciplinary ladder. For a significant offense, many employers start with a written warning or suspension, and it is generally accepted that certain major offenses (such as stealing from the employer, drinking on the job, or assaulting a supervisor) call for immediate dismissal. It may also be appropriate to skip certain steps of progressive discipline for certain offenses. For example, many employers think suspension is an inappropriate response to absenteeism since it effectively compounds the underlying problem.

A sometimes faster alternative method to progressive discipline is *affirmative discipline.* In this approach the problem employee signs a contract (also called an action plan or a plan for improvement) that specifies the steps he or she will take to overcome the problem behavior and details the consequences, including employment termination, in case of noncompliance. This approach puts the pressure on the employee to improve performance and show commitment to stay with the organization. The affirmative discipline approach can also be combined with features of the progressive technique, in that a verbal discussion about the performance problem can take place days or weeks before the contract is signed, and one violation of the contract may lead to a temporary suspension rather than to an immediate dismissal.[4]

The principle underlying an appropriate response to disciplinary problems is often referred to as *just cause.* This phrase is used in the vast majority of collective bargaining agreements to define acceptable disciplinary action, and it has been carried over into nonunion settings as well. To determine whether there is just cause for discipline in a given case, managers should ask themselves the questions shown in the sidebar on this page. These questions are sometimes called the Daugherty standards,[5] after a famous arbitrator who helped popularize them. A wide range of other considerations may also come into play, depending on the specific circumstances involved.

Determining Just Cause— the Daugherty Standards

- Was the employee aware (or should he or she have been aware) of the rule or standard he or she is accused of violating?
- Was the rule or standard reasonable?
- Did the jurisdiction conduct a reasonable investigation into the alleged wrongdoing or misconduct?
- Was the investigation fair?
- Has it been convincingly established that the rule or standard was violated?
- What mitigating or aggravating factors are present in the employee's work history (length of service, prior discipline, etc.)?
- Have comparable situations occurred in the past, and if so, how have the employees involved been treated?

Source: Adolph M. Koven and Susan L. Smith, *Just Cause: The Seven Tests,* 2nd ed. (Edison, N.J.: BNA Books, 1992).

Loudermill, the Right to Appeal, and Other Procedural Issues

Before disciplinary action is taken, the employer should be aware of any procedural requirements that apply. All too frequently, even though an employee is proven guilty of an offense and the disciplinary action that is taken is appropriate, that action is nevertheless overturned because the employer violated applicable procedural protections.

In most cities and counties, disciplinary action is subject to appeal, either through a civil service or personnel appeals board, or through the contractual grievance procedure in a union contract. To be sure that the action will stand up under review, it is important not only that the offense be documented and proven, but also that the punishment fit the crime. In many cases, the range of appropriate discipline for a particular type of offense may be commonly understood. In others, the employer should have established and disseminated a listing of offenses and applicable penalties. In any event, the reviewing body usually has the authority to decide not only the employee's guilt or innocence but also the reasonableness of the punishment.

In the public sector, any discipline of an employee is considered to be a government action since the employer is a governmental entity. Under the U.S. Constitution, any government action that deprives any individual, including an employee, of a property or liberty interest, such as employment, must comply with the principles of due process. One of these principles, the U.S. Supreme Court has ruled, is that an employee charged with an offense must have an opportunity to respond to the charges before he or she is dismissed (*Cleveland Board of Education v. Loudermill*[6]). Even if the employee has a legal or contractual right to a post-termination hearing, he or she must nevertheless have a pre-termination opportunity to hear the accusations and offer an explanation or any response he or she wishes to present. This is called a *"Loudermill* hearing," after the case in which the Court first articulated the requirement.

In all likelihood, other procedural requirements are applicable as well. Most collective bargaining agreements contain such protection for union members, and often there are requirements imposed by public sector collective bargaining laws or rulings by state labor relations agencies. For example, private sector principles such as *Weingarten* rights are often carried over to public sector employees. Under the *Weingarten* doctrine, unionized employees who are required to attend interviews from which they reasonably anticipate that disciplinary action may result are entitled to union representation if they request it.[7] In addition, a federal court of appeals has extended this right to nonunion employees as well. Many munici-

pal ordinances, regulations, and personnel rules also contain procedural protections for employees.

Specific Situations Requiring Special Consideration

Certain types of disciplinary situations call for the application of special consideration. In some cases, this is because specific legal requirements come into play; in other cases, practical concerns require a different approach from normal disciplinary situations.[8]

Sick Leave Abuse and Other Attendance Problems. There are two general types of employee attendance problems with which employers often must deal. One is excessive absenteeism or tardiness; the other is misuse or abuse of sick leave or other similar benefits.

Excessive absenteeism or tardiness is generally dealt with as a matter of progressive discipline, perhaps (as noted above) skipping the suspension step of the procedure. Some employers have defined numerical thresholds for different types of discipline so that employees know that a certain number of days or occurrences of sick leave within a stated period of time will result in a specific disciplinary response. In other situations, employers impose discipline on a case-by-case basis when absenteeism becomes unacceptable by any reasonable standard. Even a single instance of sick leave abuse, however, may result in serious discipline. That is because fraudulent use of paid leave for purposes other than the employee's personal illness is a form of theft from the employer.

The key in these cases is to demonstrate that the employee knew the limitations of the employer's sick leave policies and took sick leave knowing that he or she was not entitled to do so. In any disciplinary action involving attendance problems, however, it is important to establish that the employer's expectations were clearly communicated to the employee and that the employee was unwilling or unable to meet those expectations.

Alcohol and Drugs. In cases where substance abuse is involved, it is essential to draw a distinction between prohibited behavior, such as possession or consumption of alcohol or controlled substances in the workplace, and the employee's status as an alcoholic or drug-dependent person. Under various antidiscrimination statutes, it is risky for employers to discipline or discharge employees simply because of alcoholism or drug addiction. These are often considered to be illnesses that call for treatment, not discipline.[9] However, even an alcoholic or drug addict may be prohibited from possessing alcohol or drugs on the employer's premises, or from consuming or being under the influence of such substances during working hours. Discipline for these offenses should be handled in the same manner as it is in other cases, even if the employee claims to have a substance abuse problem and requests treatment.

In dealing with issues involving substance abuse, a manager must untangle the various laws and regulations that establish the public employer's obligation to its employees who demonstrate substance abuse. This includes the Rehabilitation Act of 1973,[10] the Americans with Disabilities Act[11] (ADA), and state statutes and administrative rules.

Following the federal examples of Sec. 501 of the Rehabilitation Act of 1973 and the Comprehensive Alcohol Abuse and Alcohol Prevention Treatment and Rehabilitation Act of 1970 and its amendments of 1979,[12] states and their subdivisions have set up evaluation and treatment programs as well as accommodations for the disability of alcoholism. The issue becomes one of establishing the parameters of accommodative and rehabilitative efforts intended to make the employee a dependable and fully functioning worker.

If the alcoholism is tied to excessive absenteeism, critical absenteeism (absence from a critical meeting or call of duty), disruptive incidents involving other employees or superiors, or job snafus, the employee's conduct or performance is what lays the grounds for discipline or termination. As long as the employee is not sanctioned "solely by reason" of his or her alcoholism, the employer may proceed.

In cases where alcohol may be the reason for an employee's poor performance, the supervisor may want to confer with the employee, pointing out the performance problems and advising about available counseling services if the performance problems are caused by personal or health issues. If the employee subsequently refuses help and his or her performance continues at an unsatisfactory level, the supervisor is to provide a clear choice between submitting to counseling and cooperating with treatment or accepting the consequences of unsatisfactory performance.[13] It is the employee's responsibility to meet the requirements of his or her diagnosis and treatment programs. Should the employee refuse to cooperate with treatment efforts, the supervisor is justified in invoking the hard option of the choice given the employee.

Alcohol consumption may lead to criminal conduct, the most frequent manifestation of which is driving under the influence (DUI). When the conduct occurs off duty, the issue is whether the incident affects the public agency or the job performance of the employee. A DUI conviction can provide cause for dismissal if it involves criminal behavior, creates bad publicity for the organization, or compromises duties such as law enforcement.[14] Courts have noted that while an alcoholic's disability may have compelled that person to drink, it did not compel that person to drive a motor vehicle or engage in other misconduct. DUI convictions may result in the suspension or loss of driving privileges, and if a driving license is a necessary job qualification, loss of those privileges may provide grounds for at least transfer or demotion of the employee.

Employer representatives should be careful not to accuse an employee of having an alcohol or drug problem unless the evidence is overwhelming. Otherwise, the employee may claim he or she is being discriminated against because of a perceived disability. A better approach is to offer the employee help if he or she admits to a problem, rather than requiring treatment for a problem the supervisor has perceived, but the employee has not admitted.

The ADA explicitly exempts from coverage any employee or job applicant who is currently engaging in the illegal use of drugs, and court decisions have made it clear that the ADA may not be used as a shield for illegal conduct. That is, the ADA's protection does not extend to an employee who enters a rehabilitation program only after being confronted with the fact that his or her employer is aware of illegal use. The Equal Employment Opportunity Commission construes the phrase "currently engaged in illegal use of drugs" as applying to use that may have occurred weeks or even months prior to discharge, and the ADA's protections apply to persons in long-term recovery, not to persons just entering recovery.

However, borderline cases abound. What about an employee who has successfully completed a program, relapses, and then voluntarily checks back into a rehabilitation program? While the courts have held that such a person exercises current use, administrative discretion might appropriately decide that the person should be given a second chance at rehabilitation.[15] Here again, however, a clear employer policy allowing only one opportunity for leave to undergo treatment for substance abuse may well justify refusal of a second chance.

One additional variable in these challenging cases is the coverage of the Family and Medical Leave Act[16] (FMLA). FMLA regulations state that when an employee takes leave for substance abuse treatment, he or she has exercised his or her right to do so under the FMLA, and so the employer may not take action against that individual. However, the door still remains open for taking action against the employee for violating a provision of the employer's substance abuse policy. This conflict has not yet been resolved by the courts.[17]

Threats and Violent Behavior. Threats and violent behavior on the part of an employee may give rise to legal claims by co-workers and others with whom the offending employee comes in contact. Therefore, employers in such situations must respond quickly and decisively. It may even be appropriate to remove the employee from the workplace immediately, preferably suspending him or her with pay until a *Loudermill* hearing is conducted, in order to protect others from harm and the jurisdiction from liability.

As with substance abuse, threatening or violent conduct on the part of an employee may be the result of an illness or another personal problem for which treatment is appropriate before an employer resorts to discipline. Sources of violence include competitive pressures, loss of autonomy, changing workforce demographics, domestic dysfunction, and victimization by nonemployees.[18]

It is important to develop a policy and encourage a climate in which employees can communicate their concerns. There are several ways to do this. For example, an employee assistance program can provide an employee with referrals to counseling and assistance outside the workplace. An employee ombudsman program can provide confidential, in-house facilitation for work-related problems or concerns. An accessible grievance procedure is important for communicating claims of harassment or threats. If these resources are available and an employee fails to use them, the employer's position in any subsequent litigation will be stronger. An employee who declines such assistance generally cannot later claim to have been entitled to treatment rather than discipline. In recent years many public organizations have adopted "zero tolerance" policies.

Identifying Potentially Violent Employees

Although there is no way of knowing for sure whether an employee may become violent, below is a list of factors or warning signals that may help an employer identify potentially dangerous employees.

- Has the employee recently had personal problems outside of work—for example, a death in the family or a divorce?

- Does the employee have a history of violent tendencies either at or outside of work?

- Does the employee have severe mood swings or suffer from depression?

- Does the employee have an alcohol- or drug-abuse problem?

- Is the employee resentful toward authority? Is the employee engaged in running conflict with a supervisor?

- Has the employee's work performance suddenly deteriorated?

- Does the employee keep to himself or herself?

Some of these symptoms (or actions) alone—particularly behavior that harms or threatens persons or property—may be grounds for dismissal depending on the situation. The risk of violence increases when several warning signals are present. An employer who suspects that an employee may be violent should contact its labor counsel, offer supervisory counseling, and consider referring the employee for professional counseling.

Source: Robert L. Levin, "Workplace Violence: Navigating Through the Minefield of Legal Liability," 11 *Labor Lawyer* 171 (1995): 181–182.

bringing a weapon into the workplace, pervasive outbursts of profanity, destruction of property, insults. They create a hostile environment, not unlike that defined by the courts in sexual harassment cases. It is an environment that makes it difficult for employers to do their jobs. The worst cases actually create a clear and present danger to other employees.

Criminal Misconduct. Theft, assault, and other behavior that violates criminal statutes may also be grounds for disciplinary action. However, as discussed below, discipline is only appropriate if the conduct occurs in the workplace or has some demonstrable nexus to the job.

If discipline is appropriate, it is important to keep such action independent of any criminal prosecution that may occur. Many employers make the mistake of suspending an employee pending the outcome of criminal prosecution. The problem with this approach is that many prosecutions do not result in conviction but rather in a decision not to prosecute, or produce some other result that does not clearly establish grounds for discipline. Unless the employer has developed and pursued its own case against the employee, it may be left with no grounds on which to base a disciplinary decision. While a city or county may be in a better position than most other employers to obtain the cooperation of law enforcement agencies, it is wise not to assume that criminal prosecution will provide a shortcut that will avoid the customary disciplinary process. If an employer does turn over evidence of criminal wrongdoing to the police or a prosecutor, it is advisable to retain copies of any documents provided for use in disciplinary proceedings.

Off-Duty Conduct. In many respects, government employees have greater rights than their private sector counterparts to conduct their personal life as they wish. In most situations, what a public employee does on his or her own time is not the concern of the public employer. For example, gone are the days

In assessing the conduct of employees, a manager must keep in mind the distinction between an employee's acceptable speech and unacceptable disruptive conduct. Some behaviors speak for themselves: assaults, threats, when a public school teacher could be terminated for cohabitating with another person out of wedlock. However, discipline for off-duty conduct is justified if it affects the employee's ability to do his or her job or is directly detrimental to the government employer. For example, a police officer may be fired for selling drugs, a teacher may be fired for sexually assaulting a minor, and a social worker may be fired for welfare fraud. As in many other situations, the circumstances of the individual case are crucial in making a determination as to whether discipline is appropriate. (For more on off-duty conduct, see Chapter 7.)

Correcting Problems with Supervisors and Managers. In many respects, dealing with disciplinary or other personnel problems involving supervisors and managers brings into play the same considerations that apply when dealing with problems involving any other employee. However, there are important differences resulting from two significant distinctions between supervisors and managers, on the one hand, and the rank-and-file employees who work under their direction, on the other hand. First, public employees who have been hired for, or promoted into, positions of significant responsibility are expected to meet a higher standard of performance and conduct than can be expected from their subordinates. Second, actions of managerial-level employees are often attributed to the municipal employer per se and therefore may expose the jurisdiction to greater potential liability than if a lower-level employee had engaged in the same conduct.

The first of these two distinctions becomes important when dealing with disciplinary offenses such as absenteeism or tardiness. For an entry-level employee, this is the classic situation that calls for progressive discipline. However, if a department head cannot get to work on time or fails to let the office know when he or she will not be in, it may be that only one warning is needed before a determination is

justified that the individual is simply not suited to his or her position. In general, problems with supervisors or managers tend to be dealt with through annual performance reviews rather than through disciplinary procedures. This is particularly true when the issue involves performance on the job rather than some specific misconduct.

Another reason why the steps of discipline may be somewhat attenuated in the case of a higher-level employee is that in dealings with both subordinates and members of the general public, actions and statements of management employees may constitute, both practically and legally, actions of the jurisdiction itself. A good example of this principle is found in court decisions in sexual harassment cases in which the employer may be held strictly liable for the conduct of supervisory and managerial employees, even if the employer has no knowledge that such conduct is occurring. In dealings with third parties, members of management may be perceived to have (and may actually have) ultimate authority to make final decisions on behalf of the government entity. Under circumstances such as these, a public employer cannot tolerate repeated errors in judgment or recurring misconduct. In certain circumstances even a nonsupervisory employee who has some authority over co-workers can create liability for the organization.[19]

Supervisory or managerial employees of municipalities and counties may also have different procedural protections from those that apply to their subordinates. In many states, supervisors do not have the right to unionize and therefore lack the substantive and procedural protections that are often included in collective bargaining agreements. On the other hand, state statutes or municipal ordinances sometimes provide special protection for certain managers and department heads. In certain states, police chiefs, fire marshals, and other selected officials have protections against arbitrary dismissal on political or other grounds. When dealing with discipline or dis-

Red Flags

- A pending criminal prosecution does not make disciplinary action unnecessary. Pursue disciplinary procedures also.
- Adverse actions of management employees may constitute actions by the jurisdiction itself and result in liability for the jurisdiction.

charge of such high-level employees, employers should check for special statutory or other protections that may apply.

Handling an Employee Termination. Many employers who have good grounds for dismissing an employee nevertheless get themselves in trouble because of the way in which the termination process itself is handled. This tends to happen more in private industry than in the public sector, where more procedural protections (such as *Loudermill* hearings) tend to apply. Nevertheless, it is a good idea for employers to take a few simple precautions to avoid trouble.

First, the employee should always be told the real reason for his or her termination. Some employers are reluctant to come out and say that they believe the employee has been engaged in misconduct or to openly address inadequate performance. However, if a discharge is disguised as a job elimination or other no-fault termination, the employer will have some explaining to do if, for example, the employee files a discrimination claim. The investigating agency is likely to assume that if the employer misstated the real reason for the dismissal at the time of the termination, there must have been something to hide. Even if the real reason for the discharge is not particularly well documented, it is better to face that problem head-on than to fabricate another reason for the dismissal that cannot be defended at all.

Another mistake that sometimes occurs in the termination process is not allowing for negotiation of terms that will avoid a contested case. Sometimes, simply allowing an employee the option of resigning is enough to avoid a fight. In other cases, it makes good business sense to negotiate a "separation package" that will allow the employer to implement a high-risk termination decision quietly. When terminating a long-serving employee who is in one or more protected classifications, a few months worth of pay and benefits will be much less expensive than a lawsuit, regardless of the outcome. This is particularly true when the employer has not adequately documented the problems with the individual's performance or other reasons for the discharge.

If the employer and employee decide to use a separation agreement—and it is wise to do so if the jurisdiction is to expend a substantial amount of public funds on severance pay or other benefits—it makes sense to seek legal advice in preparing the document. An important element of any such agreement is a waiver by the employee of any claims against the employer; however, there are various legal requirements that apply if such a waiver is to be valid for certain types of claims, such as age discrimination. It is becoming more common for employees who have signed a waiver of claims to later change their minds and sue their former employers, so it makes sense to have a capable lawyer review the document to ensure that it is valid and enforceable.

Another mistake to avoid is treating the discharged employee "like a criminal." Even a discharge that is completely defensible on the merits can become problematic if the employee is confronted at his or her workstation and hustled out the door as if he or she were a security risk. If such a risk in fact exists, it should be handled in more subtle ways. An employee who feels that he or she has been abused in the process of termination may sue on that basis, even if the reason for the dismissal is not contested.

Finally, it is very important to manage post-termination contacts effectively. Managers should channel all inquiries from third parties to a particular individual, perhaps themselves or a human resources professional, and should give out no information other than "name, rank, and serial number" unless required by applicable law or agreed upon with the employee. Many discharged employees have sued not over their dismissal, but over allegedly defamatory or otherwise improper statements made to prospective employers or other third parties.

On the other hand, it is important not to affirmatively mislead prospective employers since this can also lead to liability claims. Some

---

Tips for Successfully Managing Disciplinary Action

☐ Determine whether in-house or outside counsel should be involved, especially if circumstances indicate that termination might be appropriate and that the employee might seek to contest the termination in an administrative, arbitral, or judicial forum.

☐ Quietly conduct a complete investigation but get facts quickly.

☐ Discreetly obtain corroborating statements from other employees as well as those directly involved.

☐ Review the employee's personnel records during the investigation to determine whether he or she has been involved in other incidents.

☐ Do not assume that the supervisor's accusations are true. Test the veracity of supervisors' statements as well as the statements of lower-level and nonsupervisory employees.

☐ Always allow an employee suspected of wrongdoing to provide an explanation of events, and then interview or reinterview witnesses to determine if the employee's explanation appears valid.

☐ Do not threaten an employee with prosecution, loss of job, or other consequences for wrongdoing. Nonetheless, an employee may be told that there could be job-related consequences for not cooperating in an investigation.

☐ Do not touch employees being questioned or make threatening gestures.

☐ Do not restrain employees from leaving the room where the questioning is taking place. Never lock the room, or stand in front of or block the exit.

☐ Refrain from asking employees about private matters unrelated to the investigation of misconduct.

☐ Obtain a written consent, waiver, or release from employees before conducting polygraph exams, and use a competent experienced examiner when such examinations are permitted by law.

☐ Obtain a signed admission, if possible, from the employee suspected of wrongdoing or misconduct.

☐ Advise the employee that he or she is not being *accused* of misconduct, but rather, that the investigation has provided sufficient information to believe that he or she has engaged in misconduct.

☐ Never state to anyone that an employee has engaged in wrongdoing unless you are required by law or collective bargaining agreement to prove or establish that misconduct has occurred.

☐ If asked, advise the employee's co-workers that you are not at liberty to disclose the reasons for the employee's discipline or separation from employment.

☐ Do not file or institute criminal or civil charges or complaints against an employee without probable cause to believe that the employee is guilty or liable.

Source: Adapted from Ronald Green and Richard J. Reibstein, *Employer's Guide to Workplace Torts: Negligent Hiring, Fraud, Defamation, and Other Emerging Areas of Employer Liability* (Edison, N.J.: BNA Books, 1992), 105–106.

Red Flags

There are several ways a manager can get into trouble when dismissing an employee:

- Failing to tell the dismissed employee the real reason for the termination.

- Generating controversy and perhaps even a lawsuit by dismissing the employee outright rather than negotiating a quiet resignation.

- Treating the dismissed employee like a criminal and embarrassing him or her before co-workers.

- Making defamatory statements about the dismissed employee to co-workers, future prospective employers, or other third parties.

- Misleading prospective employers by providing only favorable information about the dismissed employee. It is better to limit the information given to name, rank, and period in which the individual was employed by the jurisdiction.

- Handling an adverse personnel decision in a way that raises discrimination claims.

public entities have been sued by subsequent employers of terminated employees because when those employers called for references, they were given only positive information and not warned, for example, about the employee's history of violence. Even adopting a policy of providing references only when they are positive may not avoid problems, because an employee may be able to prove a pattern of practice that demonstrates no reference is the equivalent of a negative reference. This is another situation in which it would be wise to get input from an employment lawyer.

To deal with the legal ambiguity, 30 states have passed job reference immunity laws, which protect employers who provide information about current or previous employees

to a new employer. Usually these laws stipulate that the reference must be provided at the request of the employee or the prospective employer, and that the information has to be job related and truthful.[20] (See Chapter 5 for more on this subject.)

Investigating and Responding to Complaints by Employees

Guiding Principles

- A jurisdiction should take all discrimination and harassment claims seriously.
- If the employer can prove just cause to dismiss the offending employee, it will have a defense to most claims arising out of the dismissal.

Challenge

- Avoiding mistakes that can lead to claims against legitimate personnel action.

Until the last third of the twentieth century, almost all personnel problems arose in the context of the employer initiating disciplinary or other action against a problem employee. More recently, however, a growing percentage of personnel problems are the result of complaints initiated by employees or applicants for employment claiming mistreatment by their potential employers, their co-workers, or even third parties. A dizzying array of new laws and judicial decisions creating new rights for both public and private employees has been promulgated in the last few decades. Employee claims have become so common that there is even a specialized type of insurance coverage (Employment Practices Liability Insurance, or EPLI) to deal with them. Examples include claims of discrimination, sexual harassment, wrongful termination, whistle-blower violations, First and Fourth Amendment violations, and related constitutional claims. Employers should be aware, however, that these insurance policies can require that the employer turn over the defense to the carrier and its counsel.

Discrimination Claims

Many employees are members of one or more protected groups. Either they are women, or they belong to some racial or ethnic minority group, or they are in a protected age class, or they qualify for some other statutory protection against discrimination such as disability or religion. Therefore, whenever some adverse action is taken against an employee or applicant for employment, chances are good that he or she will have some basis on which to claim employment discrimination. Managers should be familiar with state and federal antidiscrimination legislation and the classifications that are protected in their jurisdictions. (For a quick review of antidiscrimination laws, see Exhibit 5-4 in Chapter 5.)[21]

Whenever an employee or a job applicant makes a discrimination claim, the jurisdiction should take it seriously. It is easy for an employer to assume that the complaining employee or applicant is simply using his or her age, race, sex, or other protected characteristic as an excuse for complaining about a valid personnel action. However, there are at least two good reasons not to brush aside any discrimination claim.

First, even if the action in question (e.g., a decision on hiring, firing, transfer, or promotion) was entirely justified, there may be circumstantial evidence that suggests otherwise. If a 30-year-old is hired for a position and the other five applicants are over 50, or if a woman is denied promotion to a level at which all the incumbents are men, the employer will have some explaining to do, even if the decision had nothing to do with age or sex. Since the motivation for an employment-related decision is not easy for either side to prove, there is a tendency to look at other circumstances to see what they suggest.

In most jurisdictions, an employer does not actually have to prove the absence of a discriminatory motive. However, if the employee can prove one or more factors that raise an infer-ence of discrimination, the employer may be required to prove a legitimate nondiscriminatory reason for its action. Therefore, it would be a mistake for an employer to take too lightly a discrimination claim under circumstances in which it cannot easily explain its actions by objective—and demonstrably job-related—factors. For example, an employer may not impose a college degree requirement for a particular job unless it can demonstrate that a college degree is necessary for performance. Since higher-education requirements tend to adversely affect minority employees and applicants, maintenance of such standards may be discriminatory unless they can be objectively justified. (See also Chapter 2 on the validity of testing procedures and Chapter 3 on the validity of performance appraisal techniques.)

The second reason for taking discrimination claims seriously is that they may in fact be justified. In a typical municipality or county, employment-related decisions are made by many different people, not all of whom are trained in human resource issues and some of whom may harbor discriminatory feelings. Such individuals may treat certain employees differently from others. Further, even if a personnel action is taken for reasons that are entirely neutral on their face, if there is disparate impact on a protected classification (such as a college-degree requirement), a discrimination claim may be successful even if there was no discriminatory intent.

Taking a complaint seriously involves, at a minimum, conducting a thorough and objective investigation and providing a response to the complainant, preferably with as much supporting documentation as is appropriate under the circumstances. If the investigation produces evidence that suggests some justification for the complaint, it may also be necessary to follow up with prompt remedial action. This in turn involves compensation for any adverse impact the complainant may have suffered and correction of the underlying problem so that it does not recur.

A thorough investigation usually involves interviewing the complainant, those involved in making the decision that brought about the complaint, and other witnesses, who may or may not be employees of the jurisdiction. Simply asking the key decision maker to explain his or her action does not constitute a thorough investigation. Ideally, the person who is in charge of the investigation should be someone who is removed from the events and the people who are the subject of the complaint, and that person's opinion as to the appropriate resolution should be given great weight.

Whether or not the results of the investigation suggest that some remedial action is appropriate, it is important to respond to the complainant and provide as much information as possible about the investigation and its results. In many cases, the complainant is not necessarily expecting a reversal of the decision that occasioned the complaint; he or she only wants someone to review the situation and ensure that there were no irregularities. Of course, some complainants will never be satisfied with the results of an internal investigation. However, the process will almost always produce valuable information that will be useful to the employer if and when the employee or applicant pursues the claim in an administrative or judicial forum.

Sexual and Other Harassment

Sexual harassment is a form of sex discrimination. Sexual harassment is unwelcome attention or harassment, even if not specifically sexual in nature, that is directed only at one sex and that directly affects conditions of employment; interferes with job performance; or creates an intimidating, hostile, or offensive working environment[22] (see Chapter 5). The Supreme Court has also ruled that same sex harassment is illegal.[23]

The same principles that apply to discrimination complaints generally are also applicable to sexual harassment complaints. That is, at a minimum, the employer should provide a prompt and thorough investigation followed by a response to the employee who made the complaint, together with effective corrective action, if appropriate. However, employers are likely to deal with certain scenarios in sexual harassment cases that do not normally arise in other discrimination claims.

First, the complainant may be objecting to the conduct of fellow employees or even of third parties rather than of management. While sexual harassment usually involves conduct or statements by a supervisor toward a subordinate, it may also be offensive behavior by co-workers. This may present special problems when it comes to investigating the claim since co-workers may be reluctant to confirm complaints against their peers. Union members, for example, may be subject to more or less subtle pressure not to bear witness against fellow union members. Harassment by third parties includes such varied circumstances as the office supply salesman pursuing the purchasing agent's secretary or a taxpayer harassing a tax collector. Employers have a responsibility to take corrective action in any such circumstances.

Another problem that tends to be unique to sexual harassment cases is that victims often say they don't want the perpetrator punished; they only want him (or her) to stop. Victims may even say that they don't want the harasser to know they have complained. It is generally unwise, however, for an employer to agree to be bound by such a request. Nothing prevents the victim from later changing his or her mind and claiming the employer should have done something in response to the complaint. Further, if the harassment involves serious misconduct, the employer may be exposed to liability from other complainants, even if the original complainant never raises the issue again. If the same person harasses other employees, those employees may claim that the employer was aware of the problem and, regardless of the preferences of the original complainant, should have done something to protect others against the same conduct.

Although other forms of harassment in the workplace may not receive as much attention and notoriety as sexual harassment, they can present legal issues that are just as serious. Many employers who have policies prohibiting sexual harassment also prohibit harassment based on race, religion, national origin, and so on. Complaints about such types of harassment should be dealt with in the same manner as complaints about sexual harassment.

The Supreme Court has specified under Title VII the responsibilities of employee complainants and employers in sexual harassment cases. Although employers are vicariously liable for sexual harassment by supervisors, an employer may escape liability if two conditions are satisfied. First, the employer has to demonstrate that it exercised reasonable care to prevent and promptly correct any sexually harassing behavior. Second, the employer must demonstrate that the complainant unreasonably failed to use preventive or corrective measures offered by the employer, or failed in other ways to avoid harm. The second test will normally be satisfied if the employee unreasonably fails to use the employer's procedure for registering complaints.[24]

The Court has held that when sexual harassment results in a victim's dismissal, demotion, or other tangible job impact, the employer is automatically liable. If a supervisor, however, makes harassing threats but does not carry them out, the employer may not be liable if the jurisdiction can show that it made reasonable efforts to prevent and correct the harassment and that, as above, the victim unreasonably failed to pursue the publicized and available procedures for registering complaints.[25]

Jurisdictions should adopt and widely disseminate policy statements condemning sexual harassment. Complaint procedures must be available, prompt, and effective, and jurisdictions should ensure that the procedures do

Red Flag

▶ Even if a victim states initially that he or she does not want the perpetrator punished, failure to pursue disciplinary action in harassment cases can result in liability later.

not require the victim to file the complaint directly with the harasser. Training programs for employees and supervisors about policies and procedures can help insulate jurisdictions from liability for harassment.

Wrongful Discharge, Defamation, Negligent or Intentional Infliction of Emotional Distress, and Other State Law Tort or Contract Claims

As courts broaden traditional causes of action to apply to new issues, employees may also bring an increasing number of claims under state law. A single set of circumstances—for example, events leading up to dismissal of an employee—may give rise to a variety of related claims. In general, if the employer can prove just cause to dismiss the employee, it will have a defense for most of these claims. However, it is useful to understand what types of claims may arise so as to avoid unintentionally couching a legitimate personnel action in language that might trigger a claim.

Wrongful discharge is a tort or contract claim under state law that arises when the employer dismisses an employee in retaliation for some conduct that is protected by an important public policy. For example, an employer generally may not fire an employee for filing a workers' compensation claim since this would discourage employees with legitimate claims from pursuing them and would defeat the purposes of workers' compensation laws. Similarly, an employee who reports violations of state and federal law may be protected from dismissal under this doctrine, even if there is no applicable whistle-blower statute.

Addressing Sexual Harassment

If an employee complains of sexual harassment, the employer must take these steps:

Investigate Promptly

Carefully choose the investigator. Generally, employers use their human resources personnel, but the employer should make sure that an unbiased person decides each complaint. Never have the person accused of harassment conduct the investigation! Make sure the investigator is thorough, takes good notes, and is trusted by employees.

Be discreet. Make sure that the investigation is kept confidential. This will help avoid employer liability for defaming the alleged harasser.

Gather evidence. The victim and accused harasser should both be interviewed, but separately. Ask each for witnesses and also interview those witnesses separately. Ask open-ended questions and be careful not to pressure employees into giving a desired answer. Find out the nature of the relationship between the victim and the alleged harasser, including whether any sexual relationship is or has been consensual. Determine whether the accused harasser has previously been accused of sexual harassment.

Determine whether sexual harassment occurred. Consider (1) whether physical contact occurred, (2) whether any verbal comments are offensive to a reasonable person, (3) whether the harasser has been disciplined for sexual harassment in the past, (4) whether the victim consented to the behavior, and (5) how many incidents occurred. One isolated incident may not constitute sexual harassment. However, if it was severe, if it involved physical touching, if it involved conduct by a supervisor, or if the harasser has been disciplined for harassment in the past, it probably is sexual harassment.

Take Appropriate Action

Inform both employees separately of the determination. Have your sexual harassment policy handy to help answer questions that arise in these interviews. If no harassment is found to have occurred, make sure the alleged victim understands that a thorough investigation has been conducted.

Make sure the penalty fits the crime. Employers must carefully balance the rights of both employees. Appropriate discipline may include a verbal reprimand, written reprimand, order to stay away from the victim, transfer, demotion, pay cut, suspension, or termination. A meeting with both the victim and the harasser at which the harasser is merely reminded to behave is probably not sufficient; however, not all conduct warrants termination. If no sexual harassment has occurred, do not punish the accused.

Do not punish the victim. Although an employer may offer the victim a chance to transfer, the victim should not be transferred against his or her will.

Do not retaliate against the complaining employee. Even if the employer finds that no harassment occurred, neither the alleged harasser nor any other employees should be permitted to retaliate against the employee. Be aware of whether the complaining employee is disciplined, demoted, or denied benefits, and thoroughly document the reasons for any necessary action.

Source: John A. DiNome and Saundra M. Yaklin, with assistance from Caroline A. O'Connell.

An employee may claim defamation if an employer publicly criticizes his or her performance or states the reasons for dismissal to a third party without the employee's consent. An employee may claim that the employer's conduct in carrying out the dismissal was egregious and abusive, and, either negligently or intentionally, caused emotional distress. In general, an employee will bring these claims in state court in a civil lawsuit seeking damages.[26]

Free Speech and Other First Amendment Issues

While some states have adopted legislation establishing free speech rights for public (and in a few cases private) employees, free speech rights for governmental workers generally emanate from the First Amendment to the U.S. Constitution.

Free Speech. Some employees may challenge adverse employment decisions by alleging that a manager violated their First Amendment free speech rights. This is more likely to occur when a manager has relied on an employee's expressive actions as a factor in discipline. The First Amendment guarantees free speech, which public employers must respect, but in the public workplace, this right is qualified in several ways. Governments may have sound reasons for wanting to limit an employee's speech, and courts have been sympathetic to several arguments. (For more on employees' rights to free speech, see Chapter 5.)

Freedom of Association. As with free speech, a government employer must have valid employment-related reasons for limiting freedom of association. Generally, public employers cannot ask prospective employees what organizations they hold memberships in or who their friends and acquaintances are. Nor can the government base an adverse action against a current employee on the personal ties or associations of that employee. Membership in a subversive group is not in itself grounds for dismissal.

Instead, the individual employee must have engaged in or supported some subversive or otherwise illegal action.[27] (For more on employees' right to freedom of association, see Chapter 5.)

Freedom of association may be an issue when an employee alleges that a public employer took a personnel action on grounds of political patronage rather than performance. The Supreme Court has held that party affiliation and support are unconstitutional bases for almost all public personnel actions, including dismissal, transfer, promotion, or recall.[28] However, employees in high-level policy positions and "confidential" employees are not protected.

Whether a person is occupying an exempted policy-making or confidential position is a question of law for the court, which will not determine the answer solely by the job's official designation. At least one federal appeals court has said that the judicial inquiry should be based on whether the "policymaking position authorizes either directly or indirectly meaningful input into governmental decision making on issues where there is room for disagreement on goal formulation or implementation."[29] Whether an employee is judged to be a confidential employee depends on whether he or she acted as a confidential advisor and helped "formulate plans for the implementation of broad goals" or whether the employee had "limited responsibility."[30]

Privacy Issues

Searches of public employees at the workplace will be judged by Fourth Amendment standards. To determine the extent of Fourth Amendment protection, courts must establish the boundaries of the workplace and determine whether the employee had a reasonable expectation of privacy. These issues are decided on a case-by-case basis. A balancing test weighs the employee's legitimate expectations of privacy against the government's need for supervision and control. (For more on employees' Fourth Amendment rights, see Chapter 5.)

Complaints about Employees by Third Parties

Challenge

- Taking citizens' complaints against employees seriously and conducting a thorough investigation, while protecting the employees' legal rights and preserving organizational effectiveness.

Most employment-related complaints are made by employees, but government employers also have to deal with complaints about employees by taxpayers, people with whom the city or county does business, and other third parties. Examples range from allegations of police misconduct made by people who are questioned or arrested, to claims that an inspector has solicited a bribe, to complaints that a town employee has been rude or abusive to a taxpayer.

As with complaints of discrimination or other mistreatment made by employees, a municipality should react to third-party complaints by conducting a prompt and thorough investigation and following up with a response to the complainant, which should include remedial action if appropriate. However, many municipal collective bargaining agreements and some municipal ordinances, personnel rules, or procedures contain specific requirements to be followed in the investigation of and response to complaints by third parties.

A good example of such employee protections is the "police bill of rights" championed by many police unions; this contains such provisions as mandatory notification of the employee who is the subject of the complaint and a prohibition against taking action solely on the basis of an anonymous complaint. Obviously a public employer should take whatever steps are necessary to comply with such requirements without jeopardizing the effectiveness of the investigation or response. Of course, if the complaint alleges criminal misconduct and the jurisdiction elects to press

criminal charges, then all the usual constitutional protections apply. However, as discussed above, the employer should draw a distinction between criminal prosecution and employee discipline; the latter need not necessarily wait for or depend upon the former.

Supervisory personnel should understand, however, that under certain circumstances, employee conduct can give rise to suits by citizens that can result in liability, not only for the employee but also for the jurisdiction and the supervisor. In addition, federal criminal civil rights statutes, which can affect the employment context, apply to municipal or county employees.

On the civil side, under the federal statute 42 U.S.C. 1983, citizens may sue local government employees in federal court for violations of federal constitutional or statutory rights and seek compensatory money damages and/or injunctive and declaratory relief. Citizens may also pursue declaratory and injunctive relief directly from local governments. In addition, compensatory money damages may be sought from a local government because of the actions of its employee if the violation by that employee is found by the court to be pursuant to an "official policy" or "governmental custom."[31]

The fact that jurisdictions can be held liable for compensatory monetary damages for the actions of their employees provides an added incentive to promptly investigate charges of abuse by public employees. Failure to take corrective action in response to such charges can be introduced by subsequent plaintiffs as proof of toleration of such practices, thereby constituting a "governmental custom" justifying the payment of damages.[32] And, even if the employee involved is excused from the suit by virtue of being judged by the court as having acted in "good faith" under the doctrine of qualified immunity, the local government will not be excused from liability. In addition, public employers may be held liable for failure to adequately train employees under some circumstances.[33] Further, a city or county may be held liable for violating a citizen's constitutional rights on the basis of a failure to train, even if no individual employee is found individually liable.[34]

With respect to finding the jurisdiction liable because the employee acted pursuant to an official policy, policy is made when a decision maker who possesses the final authority to establish public policy with respect to the action issues an official proclamation, policy, or edict.[35] Courts seek to identify which city officials speak with final policy-making authority, and the definition of the officials' functions under relevant state law drives the inquiry.[36]

Supervisors also may be held liable for the actions of a subordinate employee judged to have violated a citizen's rights. Supervisor liability may be found when the plaintiff demonstrates an "affirmative causal link" between the supervisor's inaction and harm suffered by the plaintiff.[37] Evidence of failure to investigate or address the propensities of employees to violate citizens' rights can result in supervisor liability.

Under some circumstances, local government employees can be prosecuted for criminal violation of a citizen's civil rights in federal court under 42 U.S.C. 1982. In the event of an official indictment, if the public employer decides there is merit to the charges, it can take action to suspend the employee. The employer is not required to hold a pre-determination hearing in such an event, as long as the suspended employee receives a sufficiently prompt post-suspension hearing.[38]

Contested Cases in the Labor and Employment Arena

General Principles

- It is important to determine insurance coverage immediately when an employment-related lawsuit or administrative proceeding threatens.
- The choice between an all-out defense and pursuit of a settlement should be made early in the proceedings.

- Employers should take administrative complaints seriously and defend them as thoroughly as they would if the claims had been filed in court.

With increasing frequency, workplace problems tend to spill over into administrative and judicial forums. In both the public and private sectors, employment litigation has mushroomed over the past few decades. Newly created statutory rights and protections, common-law developments in many states, and the creativity of plaintiffs' lawyers have all combined to foster a more litigious atmosphere. As noted above, this new environment has even spawned a new type of insurance, which specifically addresses liability resulting from employment decisions.

Regardless of whether a municipality has purchased an EPLI policy, it is wise to notify both the carrier and the broker or agent for any insurance that might possibly apply to an employment-related lawsuit or administrative proceeding. Many such claims are complex in nature and involve a variety of different causes of action or "counts." Insurance protection may not apply for some counts but may be available for others. If a jurisdiction commences its own defense without notifying the appropriate carrier, coverage may well be lost.

Defending Lawsuits in State or Federal Court

If it is determined that no defense will be provided by the jurisdiction's insurance carriers, the next step is to retain competent and experienced counsel. Employment defense work is now recognized as a separate specialty in the legal profession, and a city or county should not count on its corporation counsel or a general practitioner to have this expertise. In larger cities, there may even be attorneys specializing in defending against the particular type of claim involved.

Most defense lawyers will urge that a thorough investigation of the plaintiff's claims be done promptly and that an objective evaluation of the prospects for a successful defense be conducted as early as possible. Litigation is extremely expensive and time-consuming, and it is wise to make an early determination as to whether it is more appropriate to mount an all-out defense or to pursue the possibility of settlement. Once the parties are heavily invested in the outcome of the litigation, it becomes much more difficult to find a mutually acceptable compromise.

Although the steps followed in the defense of an employment-related lawsuit will vary from case to case, they usually include obtaining statements from all potential witnesses and reviewing all available documents and files for relevant evidence. Each side engages in this process initially with respect to its own witnesses and documents. However, the judicial system establishes a formal process for gaining access to the other side's witnesses and documents; this is known as "discovery." In most cases, discovery includes depositions of the other side's witnesses, interrogatories requesting answers to questions addressed to the opposing party, and requests for the production of documents and other relevant information in the possession of the opposing party.

Upon completion of discovery, and after disposal of any pretrial motions, there is usually another opportunity to consider settlement before going to trial. In most cases, the trial is the most expensive part of the litigation process, and of course it involves the greatest risk to both sides. Most lawsuits are settled before trial, and employment litigation is no exception. Public employers may be particularly well advised to consider settling cases in which a jury is involved since jurors (who are generally employees themselves) tend to be sympathetic to the employee's point of view and often think of government as having deep pockets.

If a trial cannot be avoided, the conduct of that proceeding is, of course, in the hands of the jurisdiction's attorney. However, the county or city should insist on being consulted with respect to significant strategy issues since it, of course, has the greatest stake in the outcome of the case.

Responding to Complaints by or through Administrative Agencies

A wide array of employment-related cases arises in the context of an administrative proceeding, rather than in response to (or prior to) court litigation. Examples include wage and hour problems, health and safety issues, workers' compensation claims, and, in many states, employment discrimination claims. Each state or federal agency has different substantive and procedural rules, which vary too widely to permit a meaningful survey within the confines of this chapter. However, a few general principles are worth noting.

First, employers make a mistake when they fail to take administrative complaints seriously or fail to defend them as thoroughly as they would if the claim had been filed in court. In many situations, the decision of an administrative agency carries significant weight in any judicial appeal, and if the agency decision goes against the employer, it may be very difficult to obtain a reversal in court.

Further, administrative complaints tend to be much less expensive to defend than lawsuits. If it is possible to resolve a matter at the administrative level with either a favorable decision or a reasonable settlement, the jurisdiction is generally much better served by doing so. Usually, there are more and better opportunities in an administrative proceeding to discuss the matter informally, explore the merits of both parties' positions, and structure a creative resolution that serves the interests of all concerned.

However, since many claims initiated in an administrative forum later end up in court, it is a good idea to obtain legal advice before responding to an administrative complaint. Often admissions, statements, or other evidence used in one setting can come back to haunt an employer in another. Also, a lawyer may help to ensure that all the legal issues within the jurisdiction of the administrative agency are adequately addressed. It is wise to understand these principles, and to explore their application to the particular dispute at hand, before taking steps that cannot be retraced.

Handling Labor Relations Matters

Union-management relationships tend to be adversarial by their nature, and much of the labor relations process consists of resolving disputes and settling differences. The principles of public sector labor relations are explored in Chapter 4. This chapter focuses only on a few specific types of contested cases in the labor relations arena.

Grievances and Arbitration. Most union contracts contain a procedure for resolving disputes about interpretation or application of the contract's terms, as well as for appealing disciplinary decisions and other management actions. Contractual grievance procedures generally contain several steps, starting with the lowest level of management and usually culminating in binding arbitration by an outside agency. Obviously, it is wise to resolve grievances at the lowest possible level in order to minimize the expenditure of resources and disruption of harmonious working relations between labor and management.

If a dispute ends up before an arbitrator (or panel of arbitrators), the jurisdiction should treat it just as seriously, and focus just as much energy and attention, as it would if the case had arisen in an administrative forum. Many grievances involve potential consequences that may include thousands of dollars in back pay or a major erosion of management's right to operate in the manner it sees fit. Decisions of grievance arbitrators are generally subject to only limited review, and therefore a negative decision in arbitration may be difficult or impossible to reverse in court.[39]

Red Flags

- A local government can lose its insurance coverage if it begins litigation without properly notifying the relevant insurance carrier.
- Admissions or statements by an employer in an administrative setting may later be used in a judicial setting.

Unfair Labor Practice Charges. Most states that have public sector collective bargaining laws include in those statutes a list of practices in which employers are prohibited from engaging. Examples of conduct commonly prohibited by such statutes are failure or refusal to negotiate in good faith over mandatory subjects of bargaining; discrimination against individual employees based on union status or preference; and interference, restraint, or coercion of employees engaged in protected activities, such as forming, joining, or assisting a union. When an employee or a union claims that one or more of these prohibitions have been violated, the applicable statute usually provides a board of labor relations or other agency to which a claim of unfair labor practices can be submitted. A public employer's response to such claims should follow the same procedures and principles as outlined above in the discussion of complaints to administrative agencies.

Alternative Dispute Resolution: Ways to Handle Things That Go Wrong—Without Litigation

Guiding Principle

- Mediation, facilitation, conciliation, early neutral evaluation, arbitration, and other alternative dispute resolution methods can save the local government time and money.

Increasingly, employers use many forms of alternative dispute resolution to resolve disputes when things go wrong in the work-place. Alternative dispute resolution includes processes such as mediation, facilitation, conciliation, early neutral evaluation, arbitration, and minitrials.

Mediation, facilitation, and conciliation are all consensual forms of assisted negotiation or settlement in which a third-party neutral helps the parties reach a mutually agreeable settlement; they differ in how actively the neutral tries to bring the parties together. For example, in mediation, the parties generally meet together across a table to exchange their perspectives on the dispute directly, before the mediator breaks them into separate rooms for individual confidential sessions called "caucuses." Facilitation tends to involve large numbers of parties and consists of the neutral trying to foster orderly discussion in a group meeting. Conciliation is used for discrimination cases under Title VII and may be done with the parties individually through telephone conversations. In all three processes, the neutral has no power to impose a settlement or outcome upon the parties; only the parties themselves may do that if they reach agreement.[40]

Early neutral evaluation and arbitration are adjudicatory proceedings in which the parties to a dispute hire a private judge to decide the case for them. Like advisory arbitration, early neutral evaluation provides a nonbinding decision. Binding arbitration, common in labor relations contracts but finding increasing use in the nonunion sector, involves a private judge rendering a final and legally enforceable decision on the dispute.[41]

Employers interested in using alternative dispute resolution have a wide range of choices and resources. There are government and private providers of alternative dispute resolution services, for example, the Federal Mediation and Conciliation Service and the American Arbitration Association. These third-party providers will supply lists of mediators, arbitrators, fact finders, or other neutral evaluators upon request. In addition, many states have state boards of mediation and arbitration with panels of mediators, arbitrators, and fact finders. Sometimes these panels are empowered to hear disputes regarding particular categories of public employees, such as state employees, municipal employees, or teachers. There are also numerous mediators and arbitrators in private practice. Listings are available from the Association for Conflict Resolution, or from the ABA Section for Dispute Resolution, the fastest growing section of the bar. Both are headquartered in Washington, D.C. Many communities also have community mediation centers that will provide free or low-cost mediation services for employment disputes.

Many nonunion employers are adopting binding arbitration for all employment disputes as a means of avoiding the uncertain outcome of a jury verdict.[42] *In Gilmer v. Interstate/Johnson Lane Corporation,*[43] the Supreme Court held that it would enforce a pre-dispute agreement to arbitrate an age discrimination claim. Arbitration can provide a timely and cost-effective means of resolving employee claims arising out of discipline or dismissal. However, dispute resolution plans should contain certain procedural safeguards for employees if public employers expect them to be enforceable in court. These safeguards include a right to counsel, reasonable discovery, and participation in selecting the arbitrator, and are described in detail in "A Due Process Protocol for Mediation and Arbitration of Statutory Disputes Arising out of the Employment Relationship."[44] This document does not have the force of law, but it is an effort by the dispute resolution profession to regulate itself, and in 1997, a federal court of appeals noted that it would examine employers' plans for these safeguards in considering whether to enforce the arbitration agreement.[45]

Even if an employer does not have a dispute resolution plan in place before things go wrong, the municipality or its counsel may wish to suggest one or more means of dispute resolution before proceeding to litigate a dispute.[46] However, increasingly, employers are designing conflict management systems to handle the wide variety of employment disputes before they turn into formal complaints or litigation. These systems are most effective if they provide for early intervention and multiple points of access, and if they progress from the most informal, cost-effective alternative dispute resolution methods that concentrate on disputants' interests to the more formal, quasi-adjudicatory processes to determine disputants' rights.

Civil Service Commissions or Appeals Boards

General Principle

- Public employees have the right to a hearing and to appeal any adverse personnel decision.

As part of their due process rights, public employees have the right to a hearing and to appeal any adverse personnel decision. In jurisdictions where few grievances arise, an appeals board can be appointed on an ad hoc basis; on the other hand, a city or county with a steady stream of complaints may want to have a permanent appeals board. To ensure political balance on the board, management and labor usually receive the same number of positions to fill while one person has to be acceptable to both sides. For instance, two members of a five-member board may be appointed by management and two members by labor, while the fifth person is jointly appointed by management and the union. In appointing commission members, officials should aim for balance in expertise, appointing some members with a legal background and others with a background in human resource management.

[1] For a more detailed guide to preventing specific kinds of lawsuits, including checklists, sample forms, and policies, see James G. Frierson, *Preventing Employment Lawsuits: An Employer's Guide to Hiring, Discipline, and Discharge* (Edison, N.J.: BNA Books, 1994).

[2] 391 U.S. 563, 20 L.Ed.2d 811, 88 S. Ct. 1731 (1968).

[3] 511 U.S. 661, 128 L.Ed.2d 686, 114 S. Ct. 1878 (1994).

[4] Jonathan Tompkins, *Human Resource Management in Government* (New York: HarperCollins, 1995), 311–312.

[5] Enterprise Wire Co. 46 *Labor Arbitration Reports* 359 (1966): 362–365. See also Adolph M. Koven and Susan L. Smith, *Just Cause: The Seven Tests* (Edison, N.J.: BNA Books, 1992) and Marvin Hill, Jr., and Anthony V. Sinicropi, *Remedies in Arbitration*, 2nd ed. (Washington, D.C.: Bureau of National Affairs): 139–141; 522–556.

[6] 470 U.S. 532 (1985).

[7] *NLRB v. Weingarten, Inc.,* 420 U.S. 251 (1975); *Epilepsy Foundation of Northeast Ohio v. NLRB,* 268 F. 2d 1095 (2001).

[8] For a detailed discussion of different bases for discipline and discharge and ways arbitrators treat them, see Norman Brand, ed., *Discipline and Discharge in Arbitration* (Edison, N.J.: BNA Books, 1998).

[9] For more complete information on this issue, see Frank Elkouri and Edna Asper Elkouri, *Resolving Drug Issues* (Edison, N.J.: BNA Books, 1993); and on disability discrimination claims more generally, see Burgdorf (1996); James G. Frierson, *Employer's Guide to the Americans with Disabilities Act* (Edison, N.J.: BNA Books (1995); and Tia Schneider Denenberg and Richard V. Denenberg, *Alcohol and Other Drugs: Issues in Arbitration* (Edison, N.J.: BNA Books, 1991).

[10] Section 501 of the Rehabilitation Act of 1973, 29 U.S.C. §791.

[11] Americans with Disabilities Act, 42 U.S.C. § 12101, et seq.

[12] 42 U.S.C. §4551 et seq.

[13] Federal Personnel Manual Supplement 792-2, Alcohol and Drug Abuse Programs, 1980, 7. This manual provides an extensive statement of reasonable accommodation duties to alcoholic employees.

[14] See *Maddox v. University of Tennessee*, 62 F.3d 843 (6th Cir. 1995).

[15] Jonathan R. Mook and Erin E. Powell, "Substance Abuse and the ADA: What Every Employer Should Know," *Employee Relations Law Journal* 22 (Autumn 1996): 57–78.

[16] Family and Medical Leave Act, 29 U.S.C. §2601, *et seq.*

[17] *Ibid.,* 65.

[18] Tia Schneider Denenberg and Richard V. Denenberg, "Workplace Violence and Dispute Resolution," *Dispute Resolution Journal* 51 (January–March 1996): 6–16.

[19] *Mack v. Otis Elevator Co.*, 326 F.3d 116 (2d Cir. 2003), cert. den. *Otis Elevator v. Mack,* 2003 U.S. LEXIS 8366 (U.S., Nov. 17, 2003).

[20] "Thirty States Have Job Reference Immunity Laws," *IPMA News* (November 1997): 6.

[21] For a primer on equal employment opportunity law, see Nancy Sedmak and Chrissy Vidas, *Primer on Equal Employment Opportunity*, 6th ed. (Edison, N.J.: BNA Books, 1994), and for more comprehensive material on employment discrimination law, see Barbara Lindemann and Paul Gross-

man, *Employment Discrimination Law*, 3rd ed. (Edison, N.J.: BNA Books, 2002).

[22] For a sexual harassment primer that is good for supervisory training and reference, see Barbara Lindemann and David D. Kadue, *Primer on Sexual Harassment* (Edison, N.J.: BNA Books, 1992), and for a more detailed analysis of the developing law of sexual harassment, see Barbara Lindemann and David D. Kadue, *Sexual Harassment in Employment Law* (Edison, N.J.: BNA Books, 1992), and Barbara Lindemann and Paul Grossman, *Employment Discrimination Law,* 3rd ed. (Edison, N.J.: BNA Books, 2002).

[23] *Oncale v. Sundowner Offshore Services*, 523 U.S. 75, 140 L. Ed. 2d 201, 118 S. Ct. 998 (1998).

[24] *Faragher v. Boca Raton*, 524 U.S. 775, 141 L. Ed. 2d 662, 118 S. Ct. 2275 (1998).

[25] *Burlington Industries, Inc. v. Ellerth,* 524 U.S. 742, 141 L. Ed. 2d 633, 118 S. Ct. 2257 (1998).

[26] For more information on these and related claims, see Ronald M. Green and Richard J. Reibstein, *Employer's Guide to Workplace Torts: Negligent Hiring, Fraud, Defamation, and Other Emerging Areas of Employer Liability* (Edison, N.J.: BNA Books, 1992), and Frierson, *Preventing Employment Lawsuits*.

[27] *Scales v. United States*, 367 U.S. 203 (1961).

[28] *Rutan v. Republican Party*, 497 U.S. 62, 111 L. Ed. 2d 52, 110 S. Ct. 2729 (1990).

[29] *Lohorn v. Michal*, 913 F.2d 327 (7th Cir. 1990); *Nekolny v. Painter,* 653 F.2d 1164 (7th Cir. 1981).

[30] *Elrod v. Burns*, 427 U.S. 347, 368, 49 L. Ed. 2d 547, 96 S. Ct. 2673 (1976).

[31] See, for example, *Pembaur v. City of Cincinnati*, 475 U.S. 469, 89 L. Ed. 2d 452, 106 S. Ct. 1292 (1986).

[32] *Monell v. Department of Social Services*, 436 U.S. 658, 56 L. Ed. 2d 611, 98 S. Ct. 2018 (1978).

[33] *City of Canton, Ohio v. Harris*, 489 U.S. 378, 103 L. Ed. 2d 412, 109 S. Ct. 1197 (1989).

[34] *Fagan v. City of Vineland*, 22 F.3d 1283 (3d Cir. 1994).

[35] *Jett v. Dallas Independent School District*, 491 U.S. 701, 105 L. Ed. 2d 598, 109 S. Ct. 2702 (1989).

[36] *McMillan v. Monroe County, Alabama*, 520 U.S. 781, 138 L. Ed. 2d 1, 117 S.Ct. 1734 (1997).

[37] *Shaw v. Stroud*, 13 F.3d 791 (4th Cir. 1994).

[38] *Gilbert v. Homar*, 520 U.S. 924, 138 L. Ed. 2d 120, 117 S.Ct. 1807 (1997).

[39] For a comprehensive reference on arbitration, see Edward P. Goggin and Marlin M. Volz, co-editors, *Elkouri and Elkouri's How Arbitration Works*, 6th ed. (Edison, N.J.: BNA Books, 2003).

[40] For a more detailed discussion of mediation, see Christopher Moore, *The Mediation Process: Practical Strategies for Resolving Conflict*, 3rd ed. (San Francisco, Calif.: Jossey-Bass Publishers, 2003).

[41] For a more detailed discussion of mediation and arbitration of nonunion employment disputes, see Jack T. Dunlop and Arnold M. Zack, *The Mediation and Arbitration of Employment Disputes* (San Francisco, Calif.: Jossey-Bass Publishers, 1997).

[42] *Ibid.*

[43] 500 U.S. 20, 114 L. Ed. 2d 26, 111 S. Ct. 1647 (1991).

[44] American Arbitration Association, "A Due Process Protocol for Mediation and Arbitration of Statutory Disputes Arising out of the Employment Relationship," in *Guide for Employment Arbitration*, Publication No. AAA219-10M-8/96: 19–24.

[45] *Cole v. Burns International Security Services*, 105 F.3d 1465 (D.C. Cir. 1997).

[46] For more information on designing a conflict management program for employment disputes, see David B. Lipsky, Ronald L. Seeber, and Richard D. Fincher, *Emerging Systems for Managing Workplace Conflict: Lessons from American Corporations for Managers and Dispute Resolution Professionals* (San Francisco, Calif.: Jossey-Bass, 2003); and Cathy A. Costantino and Christina Sickles Merchant, *Designing Conflict Management Systems* (San Francisco, Calif.: Jossey-Bass, 1996).

CHAPTER 9

Products and Services for Human Resource Management in Local Government

SIEGRUN FOX FREYSS

Although various resources are available to help the local government executive deal with the increased complexity of public personnel administration, it is important to emphasize that none of the resources can be singled out as the best one. Rather, there are several competing products, services, and vendors, each with strengths and weaknesses. It is also useful to remember at the outset that state and local laws can affect human resource policies, so national vendors may offer less suitable models than regional or local vendors.

The city manager, county administrator, or department head has a choice among three different approaches, or combinations thereof, for obtaining human resource management products or technical assistance:

- Contracting with an outside human resource management consultant
- Purchasing off-the-shelf or standardized packages
- Training for in-house provision of human resource functions.

These services and products are provided by for-profit human resource management consulting firms, nonprofit organizations, the federal government, state agencies, some larger municipalities, and councils of governments. Universities offering graduate degrees in public administration can also be considered. Some public administration faculty work as consultants, or they seek real-life projects for class assignments. Each of these options brings with it certain benefits but also some drawbacks.

Contracting with human resource management consultants can mean a more customized service and may require less of the manager's time than purchase of standardized services or training. On the downside, however, outsourcing tends to be expensive and the administrator may lose control of an important management function.

The use of public administration faculty and students is tempting when their consulting services or internships are offered for free or at a nominal cost. However, service recipients have to subordinate their organizational needs to the research needs of the academician and educational needs of the students. If a personnel procedure is developed de novo as a class project, its validity and reliability have not been tested. Moreover, service continuity is unlikely when the class disbands at the end of the semester or the students graduate.

Of a more permanent nature are university institutes or centers, such as the Institute of Government at the University of Virginia and the Municipal Technical Advisory Service at the University of Tennessee. Their mission is to provide technical assistance to local governments. For information on universities and centers in your area, go to the Web site of the National Association of Schools of Public Affairs and Administration (NASPAA) at www.naspaa.org, which has a searchable database of most graduate public administration programs in the country.

Often the entities supplying human resource consultants also sell ready-to-use, standardized, or adjustable packages dealing with such major personnel functions as creating new classification systems, testing job applicants, and evaluating employee performance. The package may include manuals, diskettes, CDs, and videotapes. In selecting off-the-shelf testing material or performance appraisal forms, managers have to make sure that the products have been tested for their validity and are defensible in case of court challenges. Personnel experts advise that boilerplate human resource policies and forms be checked by the jurisdiction's legal counsel to make sure that they comply with all applicable laws—federal laws and regulations, state statutes, and local ordinances. It is also recommended that the policies and forms be acquired on disk so that they can be readily adapted to comply with local ordinances. Job descriptions vary among local governments for even such common positions as police officer and firefighter. Another consideration is copy-

Tips for Successful Purchasing of Human Resource Products and Services

❏ Compare local providers with regional and national vendors. Local providers may be more knowledgeable about your local ordinances and state laws.

❏ Have legal counsel carefully review any standardized human resource policy or form to ensure compliance with all applicable laws—federal, state, and local.

❏ Purchase human resource policies or forms that are in e-files and can be adapted to local ordinances.

❏ Find out whether examination material and performance appraisal techniques have been tested for validity.

❏ Check copyright protection of human resource products.

right protection: before purchasing a prepared package, the jurisdiction must confirm that all internal entities that need a copy will be entitled to get one.

The providers that offer consulting services or products may also hold training workshops, where managers learn how to implement the purchased products or develop their own personnel tools. Manuals, computer programs on diskettes, and videotapes may supplement or be used in lieu of human trainers. An important drawback of enrolling in such training programs is the time commitment on the part of the manager. An important benefit, however, is that the official can exercise greater control over the implementation of the personnel policy than he or she can under the other options.

Important criteria to look for in selecting a vendor are

- Scope of service
- Track record
- Continuity

- Quality
- Price
- Flexibility or adaptability to the needs of the jurisdiction
- Knowledge of federal, state, and local laws.

Scope refers to the variety of human resource management services offered by one consulting firm. Some vendors specialize in a few functions while others present themselves as comprehensive providers. However, at this stage it appears that one-stop shopping is not yet available, and that may be beneficial in increasing the competition. On the other hand, managers like to limit the number of consultants to a few who know the jurisdiction and whose track record is known. Track record is important to gauge the vendor's professionalism, and continuity is needed to ensure the vendor's availability in subsequent years for follow-up work.

Another term for professionalism is quality of service. In the case of a consulting firm, the local official can inquire whether the staff members complement each other with different expertise, since some questions require knowledge of employment law while other personnel procedures (e.g., testing and performance appraisals), to be valid and reliable, require competence in social science research methods and psychometric analysis. To gauge the quality of vendors, it is advisable to ask the vendor for his or her credentials and professional background and to listen to the vendor's approach. Good consultants will be up-front with their qualifications and the ability of their products to withstand court challenges.

State municipal leagues may offer technical assistance themselves and may also have names of regional or local human resource suppliers on file, including lists of woman- or minority-owned businesses. National for-profit and nonprofit human resource consulting firms advertise their products and services in such publications as *Public Management*, published by the International City/County Management Association; *IPMA News*, published by the International Public Management Association for Human Resources; and *HR Magazine*, published by the Society for Human Resource Management. Major vendors are also on-line. Nonprofit and public technical assistance providers are described below, while all three types of contractors—public, nonprofit, and for-profit—are listed in the subsequent Index of Web Sites Salient for Human Resource Management (see pages 231–232).

The next section describes major nonprofit and governmental technical assistance providers; these are followed by a comprehensive list of HR-related service organizations. In addition to the technical services, many of the HR support organizations also maintain electronic bulletin boards where job openings can be posted.

Nonprofit and Governmental Technical Assistance Providers

Nonprofits

American Society for Public Administration (ASPA)

Established in 1939, the society provides a forum for practitioners and academicians in public administration to exchange theoretical and practical knowledge. The exchange is primarily achieved through conferences, publications, and workshops. The society also has more than 110 local chapters covering the various regions around the country and 20 sections representing the major public administration subfields.

American Society for Public Administration
1120 G Street, NW, Suite 700
Washington, DC 20005
Tel.: 202/393-7878
Fax: 202/638-4952
E-mail: info@aspanet.org
Web site: www.aspanet.org

CPS Human Resource Services

This service, originally founded in 1935 by the California State Personnel Board, has offered comprehensive personnel management solutions for public agencies nationwide since 1985. It presents itself as a cost-effective service for any size agency but especially for small ones with limited resources. Although CPS is a public agency, it is self-supporting and therefore charges a fee for its services. It is based in Sacramento, California, with regional offices in Washington, D.C., and Madison, Wisconsin.

CPS Human Resource Services
241 Lathrop Way
Sacramento, CA 95815
Tel.: 916/263-3600
Fax: 916/263-3613
E-mail: info@cps.ca.gov
Web site: www.cps.ca.gov

International City/County Management Association (ICMA)

Since 1914, ICMA has served local government administrators by offering them services and products strengthening their management capacity. For a list of ICMA training resources, see the Professional Development and Training section of bookstore.icma.org.

International City/County Management
Association (ICMA)
777 North Capitol Street, NE, Suite 500
Washington, DC 20002-4201
Tel.: 202/289-4262
Fax: 202/962-3500
Web site: http://icma.org

International Public Management Association for Human Resources (IPMA-HR)

IPMA-HR was created in 1973 by combining the Public Personnel Association, founded in 1906, and the Society for Personnel Administration, established in 1937. The mission of IPMA-HR is to optimize the performance of government at the federal, state, and local levels by providing HR leadership, professional development, information, and services.

International Public Management Association
for Human Resources
1617 Duke Street
Alexandria, VA 22314
Tel.: 703/549-7100
Fax: 703/684-0948
E-mail: ipma@ipma-hr.org
Web site: www.ipma-hr.org

Local Government Institute (LGI)

Established in Seattle, Washington, in 1988, the institute provides wide-ranging services to local governments in all 50 states and English-speaking foreign countries. One of its special foci is human resource management, for which it offers technical assistance, how-to manuals, reference books, and software.

Local Government Institute
1231 Farallone Ave.
Tacoma, WA 98466-6718
Tel.: 253/565-6253
Tel.: 800/277-6253 (USA only)
Fax: 253/565-2575
E-mail: info@lgi.org
Web site: www.lgi.org

National Academy of Public Administration (NAPA)

NAPA was chartered by Congress in 1984 as an independent, nonpartisan organization to assist governments at the federal, state, and local levels in improving their managerial effectiveness, efficiency, and accountability. Much of its work is done through five standing panels, one of which focuses on the public service, including public personnel management, development and training, and other human resource issues.

National Academy of Public Administration
1100 New York Ave., NW, Suite 1090 East
Washington, DC 20005

Tel.: 202/347-3190
Fax: 202/393-0993
E-mail: academy@napawash.org
Web site: www.napawash.org

National Association of Counties (NACo)
NACo was founded in 1935 to strengthen the national voice of counties. Currently, it offers an extensive line of services including legislative, research, technical, and public affairs assistance, as well as enterprise services to its members, while continuing to represent the counties in Washington, D.C.

National Association of Counties
440 First Street, NW, Suite 800
Washington, DC 20001
Tel.: 202/393-6226
Fax: 202/393-2630
Web site: www.naco.org

National Association of Towns and Townships (NATaT)
NATaT was founded in 1976 with the objective to strengthen the effectiveness of town and township government. An important function is educating lawmakers and public policy officials about how small-town governments operate and advocating policies on their behalf in Washington, D.C. The National Center for Small Communities (NCSC) used to be the training and technical assistance division of NATaT, but NCSC was incorporated separately in 1997.

National Association of Towns and Townships
444 North Capitol Street, NW, Suite 397
Washington, DC 20001-1202
Tel.: 202/624-3550
Fax: 202/624-3554
E-mail: natat@sso.org
Web site: www.natat.org

National Center for Small Communities (NCSC)
Until 1997, NCSC was part of NATaT. The mission of the center is to provide public officials

in small jurisdictions with the tools and skills they need to govern effectively, to expand local economies, to protect natural resources, and to preserve the community's character.

National Center for Small Communities
444 North Capitol Street, NW, Suite 397
Washington, DC 20001-1202
Tel.: 202/624-3550
Fax: 202/624-3554
E-mail: ncsc@sso.org
Web site: www.natat.org/ncsc/

National League of Cities (NLC)
NLC, founded in 1924 as the American Municipal Association, includes among its direct members 49 state municipal leagues and 1,700 communities of all sizes. Indirect members are the 18,000 municipalities belonging to the state municipal leagues. NLC's mission is to strengthen and promote cities as centers of opportunity, leadership, and governance. It provides a network for information sharing and for speaking on behalf of America's cities in Washington, D.C., and state capitols.

National League of Cities
1301 Pennsylvania Avenue, NW
Washington, DC 20004-1763
Tel.: 202/626-3000
Fax: 202/626-3043
E-mail: inet@nlc.org
Web site: www.nlc.org

Society for Human Resource Management (SHRM)
Founded in 1948, SHRM currently has more than 500 affiliated chapters within the United States and members in more than 100 countries, representing more than 180,000 individuals. Its mission is to serve the needs of HR professionals by providing the most essential and comprehensive resources available. The society primarily serves private sector HR professionals, but its extensive on-line

library/bookstore is also useful for public administrators.

Society for Human Resource Management
1800 Duke Street
Alexandria, VA 22314
Tel.: 703/548-3440
Fax: 703/535-6490
E-mail: shrm@shrm.org
Web site: www.shrm.org

Federal Agencies

National Committee for Employer Support of the Guard and Reserve (ESGR)

ESGR is an agency within the office of the Assistant Secretary of Defense for Reserve Affairs. Its mission is to promote cooperation and understanding between Reserve component members and their civilian employers and to assist in the resolution of conflicts arising from an employee's military commitment.

Employer Support of the Guard and Reserve (ESGR)
1555 Wilson Boulevard
Suite 200
Arlington, VA 22209
Tel.: 800/336-4590
Web site: www.esgr.com

U.S. Department of Agriculture (USDA) Graduate School

Originally founded in 1921 to serve USDA employees, the graduate school has expanded to train personnel at all levels of government in the United States and abroad. Its mission is to improve the performance of government and to provide opportunities for individual life-long learning through education, training, and related services. The school is self-supporting and charges tuition fees. Its many and wide-ranging programs are offered in the Washington, D.C., area, at regional training centers, in cities throughout the nation, in other countries, and through distance education.

Customer Service Center/Registrar's Office
Graduate School
U.S. Department of Agriculture
600 Maryland Ave., SW, Suite 120
Washington, DC 20024-2520
Tel.: 202/314-3300
Fax: 866/329-4723
E-mail: customerservicecenter@grad.usda.gov
Web site: www.grad.usda.gov

U.S. Department of Labor (DOL)

DOL enforces labor laws, collects labor statistics, and administers a variety of programs. In partnership with state-operated employment services, DOL maintains America's Job Bank, which is a free employment service for both job seekers and employers wishing to post job vacancies.

U.S. Department of Labor
200 Constitution Avenue, NW
Washington, DC 20210
Tel.: 1-866-4-USA-DOL
Web site: www.dol.gov

U.S. Equal Employment Opportunity Commission (EEOC)

EEOC offers a variety of technical assistance and training programs at locations throughout the country. The purpose of these seminars, which are geared to public and private employers, is to encourage voluntary compliance with federal laws prohibiting job discrimination based on race, color, religion, national origin, sex, age, or disability. A fee is charged to cover the costs of the training. More information about the seminars can be obtained at www.eeotraining.eeoc.gov/.

U.S. Equal Employment Opportunity Commission
1801 L Street, NW
Washington, DC 20507
Tel.: 202/663-4900
For automatic connection with nearest EEOC field office: 1-800/669-4000
Web site: www.eeoc.gov

U.S. Office of Personnel Management (OPM)

Some of the services and products developed by OPM are offered for a fee to local governments. But many handbooks and other publications can be downloaded directly from its Web site, since federal documents are not protected by copyright laws.

U.S. Office of Personnel Management
1900 E Street, NW
Washington, DC 20415-1000
Tel.: 202/606-1800
E-mail: general@opm.gov
Web site: www.opm.gov
Web site: www.opm.gov/hr/employ/main.htm (describes products OPM offers to other jurisdictions, including local governments)

State-Sponsored Human Resource–Related Programs

In addition to professional organizations and the federal government, state governments can be sources of information on HR issues. Employment and labor laws vary by states, and the state HR department may offer training material and coordinate courses on state-specific regulations in various localities as well as on-line. Links on the state government portal tend to direct users to appropriate sites.

Academic Resources

National Association of Schools of Public Affairs and Administration (NASPAA)

This organization provides accreditation services for master of public administration programs in the United States. Its Web site lists all NASPAA-affiliated schools and programs broken down by states. Local government managers can access this list to find a nearby university program that might offer services related to human resource management.

National Association of Schools of Public Affairs and Administration
1120 G Street, NW, Suite 730
Washington, DC 20005
Tel.: 202/628-8965
Fax: 202/626-4978
E-mail: naspaa@naspaa.org
Web site: www.naspaa.org

Cornell University, School of Industrial and Labor Relations

Government managers who would like to learn more about public and private sector labor relations may find the products and services offered by Cornell University's School of Industrial and Labor Relations useful. The school maintains a gateway to workplace-oriented Web sites at www.workindex.com.

School of Industrial and Labor Relations
Cornell University
Ives Hall
Ithaca, NY 14853-3901
Tel.: 607/255-2222
E-mail: ilrlib@cornell.edu
Web site: www.ilr.cornell.edu/school.html

Index of Web Sites Salient for Human Resource Management

American Arbitration Association
www.adr.org
American Society for Public Administration
www.aspanet.org
Bureau of National Affairs, Inc.
www.bna.com
Bureau of Labor Statistics
www.stats.bls.gov
CPS Human Resource Services
www.cps.ca.gov
Families and Work Institute
www.familiesandwork.org
Government Jobs
www.govtjobs.com
HR World
www.hrworld.com

Industrial/Organizational Solutions, LLC
   www.iosolutions.org

International City/County Management
Association (ICMA)
   http://icma.org

International Institute of Municipal Clerks
(IIMC)
   www.iimc.com

International Public Management Association
for Human Resources (IPMA-HR)
   www.ipma-hr.org

Job Center Employment Services
   www.jobcenter.com

Jobs, domestic and international
   www.monster.com

JAMS (Alternative Dispute Resolution Service)
   www.jamsadr.com/

Local Government Institute
   http://lgi.org

National Academy of Public Administration
   www.napawash.org

National Association of Counties
   www.naco.org

National Association of Government Archives
and Records Administrators (NAGARA)
   www.nagara.org

National Association of Schools of Public
Affairs and Administration (NASPAA)
   www.naspaa.org

National Association of Towns and Townships
(NATaT)
   www.natat.org

National Center for Small Communities
(NCSC)
   www.natat.org/ncsc/

National Civic League
   www.ncl.org

National League of Cities
   www.nlc.org

National Public Employer Labor Relations
Association
   http//www.npelra.org

Professional Association for Compensation,
Benefits and Total Rewards
   www.worldatwork.org

Public Technology, Inc.
   www.pti.org

Society for Human Resource Management
   www.shrm.org

Training and Seminar Locators
   www.tasl.com

U.S. Bureau of the Census, census of federal,
state, and local governments
   www.census.gov/govs/www/index.html

U.S. Conference of Mayors
   www.usmayors.org

U.S. Department of Agriculture, Graduate
School
   www.grad.usda.gov

U.S. Department of Labor
   www.dol.gov

U.S. DOL, Occupational Safety and Health
Administration
   www.osha.gov

U.S. Equal Employment Opportunity
Commission
   www.eeoc.gov

U.S. gateway site of federal information for
state and local governments
   www.firstgov.gov/Government/State_
   Local.shtml

U.S. Library of Congress, links to state and
local government resources
   http://lcweb.loc.gov/global/state/
   stategov.html

U.S. Merit Systems Protection Board
   www.mspb.gov

U.S. National Labor Relations Board
   www.nlrb.gov

U.S. Office of Personnel Management
   www.opm.gov

Work Index
   www.workindex.com

WorldatWork (formerly the American
Compensation Association)
   www.worldatwork.org/

Selected Bibliography

Preface

Cohen, Steven, and William Eimicke. *Tools for Innovators: Creative Strategies for Managing Public Sector Organizations.* San Francisco: Jossey-Bass, 1998.

Freyss, Siegrun Fox. "Local Government Operations and Human Resource Policies: Trends and Transformations." In *The Municipal Year Book 2004,* pages 17–25. Washington, D.C.: ICMA, 2004.

Gill, Robert P. "Essentials of Workforce Planning." *IPMA-HR News* (February 2004).

ICMA. *Local Government Online: Putting the Internet to Work.* Special Report. Washington, D.C.: ICMA, 2000.

IPMA. *Workforce Planning Resource Guide for Public Sector Human Resource Professionals.* Alexandria, Va.: IPMA, 2002.

James, Kay Coles. "The HR Paradigm Shift and the Federal Human Capital Opportunity." *Public Manager* 30, no. 4 (Winter 2001–02): 13–16.

Kaplan, Robert S., and David P. Norton. *The Balanced Scorecard: Translating Strategy into Action.* Boston: Harvard Business School Press, 1996.

Moulder, Evelina. *Recruiting and Selecting Local Government Employees: Programs and Practices,* Special Data Issue no. 5 (2000). Washington, D.C.: ICMA, 2001.

———. *Compensation and Benefits for Local Government Employees: Programs and Practices.* Special Data Issue no. 6 (2000). Washington, D.C.: ICMA, 2001.

Osborne, David, and Ted Gaebler. *Reinventing Government: How the Entrepreneurial Spirit Is Transforming the Public Sector.* Reading, Mass.: Addison-Wesley, 1992.

Rothwell, William J. "Knowledge Transfer: 12 Strategies for Succession Management." *IPMA-HR News* (February 2004): 10–11.

Smith, Russell L. "The 'Electronic Village': Local Governments and E-Government at the Dawn of a New Millennium." In *The Municipal Year Book 2002,* pages 34–41. Washington, D.C.: ICMA, 2002.

Wilson, Barbara J. *E-Government: Managing for the Future.* Fort Worth, Tex.: City of Fort Worth, 2003.

Chapter 1   Planning and Paying for Work Done

Abosch, Kenan S., and Janice S. Hand. *Broadbanding Design: Approaches and Practices.* Scottsdale, Ariz.: American Compensation Association, 1994.

Beyerlein, Michael M., et al. *Beyond Teams: Building the Collaborative Organization.* San Francisco: Jossey-Bass/Pfeiffer, 2003.

Brown, Preston "Tim," and Susan K. Cavanaugh. *Building Successful Organizations: A Guide to Strategic Workforce Planning.* Washington, D.C.: National Academy of Public Administration, 2000.

Bryson, John M. *Strategic Planning for Public and Nonprofit Organizations: A Guide to Strengthening and Sustaining Organizational Achievement.* San Francisco: Jossey-Bass, 1995.

Bryson, John M., and Farnum K. Alston. *Creating and Implementing Your Strategic Plan: A Workbook for Public and Nonprofit Organizations.* San Francisco: Jossey-Bass, 1996.

Cavanaugh, Susan Knighton. *The Case for Transforming Public Sector Human Resource*

Management. Washington, D.C.: National Academy of Public Administration, 2000.

Condrey, Stephen E., ed. *Handbook of Human Resource Management in Government.* San Francisco: Jossey-Bass, 1998.

Gordon, Gerald L. *Strategic Planning for Local Government.* Washington, D.C.: ICMA, 1993.

Harris, Patricia A. *Total Quality Management: Strategies for Local Government.* Washington, D.C.: ICMA, 1993.

ICMA. *Compensation 2004: An Annual Report on Local Government Executive Salaries and Fringe Benefits.* Washington, D.C.: ICMA, 2004.

ICMA. *Salaries 2004.* CD-ROM. Washington, D.C.: ICMA, 2004.

Johnston, William B., et al. *Civil Service 2000.* Washington, D.C.: Hudson Institute for the U.S. Office of Personnel Management, 1988.

Judy, Richard W., and Carol D'Amico. *Workforce 2020: Work and Workers in the 21st Century.* Indianapolis, Ind.: Hudson Institute, 1997.

Kawecki, Charles, Kristi Cameron, and Joan Jorgenson. *Revisiting Civil Service 2000: New Policy Direction Needed.* Washington, D.C.: U.S. Office of Personnel Management, 1993.

Klingner, Donald E., and John Nalbandian. *Public Personnel Management: Contexts and Strategies,* 4th ed. Upper Saddle River, N.J.: Prentice-Hall, 1998.

Lawler, Edward E., III. *Rewarding Excellence: Pay Strategies for the New Economy,* 2nd ed. San Francisco: Jossey-Bass, 2000.

Mears, Peter. *Organizational Teams.* Delray Beach, Fla.: St. Lucre Press, 1994.

Mohrman, Susan Albers, Susan G. Cohen, and Allan M. Mohrman Jr. *Designing Team-Based Organizations: New Forms for Knowledge Work.* San Francisco: Jossey-Bass, 1995.

Moulder, Evelina. "Police and Fire Personnel, Salaries, and Expenditures for 2003." In *The Municipal Year Book 2004,* pages 123–176. Washington, D.C.: ICMA, 2004.

NAPA. *Modernizing Federal Classification: An Opportunity for Excellence.* Washington, D.C.: National Academy of Public Administration (NAPA), 1991.

National Commission on the State and Local Public Service. *Hard Truths/Tough Choices: An Agenda for State and Local Reform.* Albany, N.Y.: Nelson A. Rockefeller Institute of Government, 1993.

Nutt, Paul C., and Robert W. Backoff. *Strategic Management of Public and Third Sector Organizations: A Handbook for Leaders.* San Francisco: Jossey-Bass, 1992.

Pierce, Jon L., John W. Newstrom, Randall B. Dunham, and Alison E. Barber. *Alternative Work Schedules.* Boston: Allyn and Bacon, 1989.

Pynes, Joan E. *Human Resources Management for Public and Nonprofit Organizations,* 2nd ed. San Francisco: Jossey-Bass, 2004.

Risher, Howard. "The New Compensation Model." *IQ Service Report.* Washington, D.C.: ICMA, December 1998.

Risher, Howard, Charles H. Fay, and Associates. *New Strategies for Public Pay: Rethinking Government Compensation Programs.* San Francisco: Jossey-Bass, 1997.

Sumser, Ray. *Broadband Pay Experience in the Public Sector.* Washington, D.C.: NAPA, 2003.

Tompkins, Jonathan. "Strategic Human Resources Management in Government." *Public Personnel Management* 31 (Spring 2002): 95–109.

Chapter 2   Recruiting for a High-Performance Workforce

Arthur, Diane. *The Employee Recruitment and Retention Handbook.* New York: AMACOM, 2001.

Brice, Maurice. *Diversity: A New Direction.* Washington, D.C.: NAPA, 2002.

Buford, James A., Jr. *Personnel Management and Human Resources in Local Government.* Auburn, Ala.: Auburn University Press, 1991.

Equal Employment Opportunity Commission. "Uniform Guidelines on Employee Selection

Procedures." 29 *Code of Federal Regulations* § 1607 (1997).

Fisher, Cynthia D., Lyle E Schoenfeldt, and James B. Shaw. *Human Resource Management,* 5th ed. Boston: Houghton Mifflin, 2003.

Heneman, Herbert G., and Timothy A. Judge. *Staffing Organizations,* 4th ed. Boston: McGraw-Hill, 2003.

Lord, J. Scott. "Internal and External Recruitment." In *Human Resource Planning, Employment, and Practice,* ed. Wayne F. Cascio, 73–102. Washington, D.C.: Bureau of National Affairs, 1989.

Schmidt, Frank L., and Deniz S. Ones. "Personnel Selection." *Annual Review of Psychology* 43 (1992): 627–670.

Chapter 3   Maintaining a High-Performance Workforce

Aamodt, Michael C. *Applied Industrial/ Organizational Psychology,* 4th ed. Belmont, Calif.: Thomson/Wadsworth, 2004.

Ammons, David N. *Municipal Benchmarks: Assessing Local Performance and Establishing Community Standards,* 2nd ed. Thousand Oaks, Calif.: Sage, 2001.

Carnevale, David G. "Human Capital and High Performance in Public Organizations." In *Public Personnel Administration: Problems and Prospects,* 3rd ed., ed. Steven W. Hays and Richard C. Kearney. Upper Saddle River, N.J.: Prentice Hall, 1995.

———. *Trustworthy Government: Leadership and Management Strategies for Building Trust and High Performance.* San Francisco, Calif.: Jossey-Bass, 1995.

deLeon, Linda, and Ann J. Ewen. "Multi-Source Performance Appraisals: Employee Perceptions of Fairness." *Review of Public Personnel Administration* 17 (1997): 22–36.

Denhardt, Robert B. *The Pursuit of Significance: Strategies for Managerial Success in Public Organizations.* Belmont, Calif.: Wadsworth, 1993.

Ferris, Gerald R., Sherman D. Rosen, and Darold T. Barnum. *Handbook of Human Management.* Cambridge, Mass.: Blackwell, 1995.

Glaser, M. "Tailoring Performance Management to Fit the Organization: From Generid to Germane." *Public Productivity and Management Review* 14 (1991): 303–319.

Goleman, Daniel. *Emotional Intelligence.* New York: Bantam Books, 1994.

Gore, Al. *From Red Tape to Results: Creating a Government That Works Better and Costs Less: Reinventing Human Resource Management.* Vice President's Report, National Performance Review. Washington, D.C.: U.S. Government Printing Office, 1993.

Holzer, Marc, and Kathe Callahan. *Government at Work: Best Practices and Model Programs.* Thousand Oaks, Calif.: Sage, 1998.

ICMA. *Employee Performance: Appraisal and Management Training Package.* Washington, D.C.: ICMA, 1997.

———. *Performance Appraisals for Local Government Employees: Programs and Practices.* Washington, D.C.: ICMA, 2001.

Ingraham, Patricia W., James R. Thompson, and Ronald P. Sanders, eds. *Transforming Government: Lessons from the Reinvention Laboratories.* San Francisco: Jossey-Bass, 1998.

Klagge, Jay. "360-Degree Sociometric Feedback for Individual and Organizational Change." *Public Administration Quarterly* 19 (1995): 366.

Kleinbeck, Uwe, Hans-Henning Quast, Henk Thierry, and Hartmut Hacker, eds. *Work Motivation.* Hillsdale, N.J.: Lawrence Erlbaum, 1990.

Lawler, Edward E., III. *Treat People Right: How Organizations and Employees Can Propel Each Other into a Virtual Spiral of Success.* San Francisco: Jossey-Bass, 2003.

Lovrich, Nicholas P. "Assessing the Performance of the Individual on the Job." In *Handbook on Public Personnel Administration and Labor Relations,* ed. Jack Rabin,

Thomas Vocino, W. Bartley Hildreth, and Gerald J. Miller. New York: Marcel Dekker, 1983.

———. "Performance Appraisal: Seeking Accountability and Efficiency through Individual Effort, Commitment, and Accomplishment." In *Public Personnel Administration: Problems and Prospects,* 3rd ed., ed. Steven W. Hays and Richard C. Kearney. Upper Saddle River, N.J.: Prentice Hall, 1995.

Meyer, Herbert H., Emanuel Kay, and John R. P. French. "Split Roles in Performance Appraisal." *Harvard Business Review* (January–February 1965): 123–129.

Mohrman, Allan M., Susan M. Resnick-West, and Edward E. Lawler III. *Designing Performance Appraisal Systems: Aligning Appraisals and Organizational Realities.* San Francisco: Jossey-Bass, 1989.

Nalbandian, John. "Performance Appraisal: If Only People Were Not Involved." *Public Administration Review* 41 (1981): 392–396.

Noe, Raymond A. *Employee Training and Development,* 2nd ed. Boston: McGraw-Hill/Irwin, 2002.

Perry, James L. "Compensation, Merit Pay, and Motivation." In *Public Personnel Administration: Problems and Prospects,* 3rd ed., ed. Steven W. Hays and Richard C. Kearney. Upper Saddle River, N.J.: Prentice Hall, 1995.

Risher, Howard, Charles H. Fay, and Associates. *New Strategies for Public Pay: Rethinking Government Compensation Programs.* San Francisco: Jossey-Bass, 1997.

Roberts, Gary E. "Developmental Performance Appraisal in Municipal Government: An Antidote for a Deadly Disease?" *Review of Public Personnel Administration* 15, no. 3 (1995): 17–43.

———. "Linkages between Performance Appraisal System Effectiveness and Rater and Ratee Acceptance: Evidence from a Survey of Municipal Personnel Administrators." *Review of Public Personnel Administration* 12, no. 3 (1992): 19–41.

———. "Maximizing Performance Appraisal System Acceptance: Perspectives from Municipal Government Personnel Administrators." *Public Personnel Management* 23 (1994): 525–549.

Roberts, Gary E., and Tammy Reed. "Performance Appraisal Participation, Goal Setting and Feedback: The Influence of Supervisory Style." *Review of Public Personnel Administration* 16, no. 4 (1996): 29–60.

Shareef, Reginald. "Skill-Based Pay in the Public." *Review of Public Personnel Administration* 14, no. 3 (1994): 60–74.

Smith, Sharon L., and Ronald J. Stupak. "Public Sector Downsizing Decision-Making in the 1990s: Moving beyond the Mixed Scanning Model." *Public Administration Quarterly* 18 (1994): 359–379.

Waldman, David A., Leanne E. Atwater, and David Antonioni. "Has 360-Degree Feedback Gone Amok?" *Academy of Management Executive* 12 (May 1998): 86–94.

Yammarino, Francis J., and Leanne E. Atwater. "Implications of Self-Other Rating Agreement for Human Resources Management." *Organizational Dynamics* (Spring 1997).

Chapter 4   Labor-Management Relations

Bogue, Bonnie G., Carol Vendrillo, and Liz Joffe. *Pocket Guide to Workplace Rights of Public Employees,* 2nd ed. Berkeley, Calif.: Institute of Industrial Relations, University of California, 1998.

Coleman, Charles J. *Managing Labor Relations in the Public Sector.* San Francisco: Jossey-Bass, 1990.

Coulson, Robert. *Labor Arbitration: What You Need to Know,* 5th ed. New York: American Arbitration Association, 2000.

Cozzetto, Don A., Theodore B. Pedeliski, and Terence J. Tipple. *Public Personnel Administration: Confronting the Challenges of Change.* Upper Saddle River, N.J.: Prentice Hall, 1996.

Fisher, Roger, William Ury, and Bruce Patton. *Getting to Yes: Negotiating Agreement without Giving In,* 2nd ed. New York: Penguin Books, 1991.

Keane, William G. *Win! Win or Else: Collective Bargaining in an Age of Public Discontent.* Thousand Oaks, Calif.: Corwin Press, 1996.

Kearney, Richard C., with David G. Carnevale. *Labor Relations in the Public Sector,* 3rd ed. New York: Marcel Dekker, 2001.

Smith, Ralph R. *Practical Guide to Interest-Based Bargaining,* 2nd ed. Huntsville, Ala.: FPMI Communications, 2000.

Chapter 5   Employee Rights: Avoiding Legal Liability

Center for Personnel Research. *Employee Handbook Toolkit.* Alexandria, Va.: International Public Management Association for Human Resources (IPMA-HR, formerly International Personnel Management Association), 2003.

———. *Employee Handbooks.* Alexandria, Va.: IPMA-HR, 1998.

Condrey, Stephen E., ed. *Handbook of Human Resource Management in Government.* San Francisco: Jossey-Bass, 1998.

Miceli, Marcia, and Janet P. Near. *Blowing the Whistle: The Organizational and Legal Implications for Companies and Employees.* New York: Lexington Books, 1992.

National Center for HIV, STD, and TB Prevention, CDC. "Updated U.S. Public Health Guidelines for the Management of Occupational Exposures to HBV, HCV and HIV and Recommendations for Postexposure Prophylaxis." Atlanta, Ga.: Centers for Disease Control and Prevention (CDC), 2001.

Occupational Safety & Health Administration. *Guidelines for Preventing Workplace Violence for Health Care and Social Service Workers.* Document no. OSHA 3148-01R. Washington, D.C.: OSHA, 2004.

Roberts, Robert. *White House Ethics: The History of the Politics of Conflict of Interest Regulation.* Lanham, Md.: Rowman & Littlefield, 1998.

Rosenbloom, David. "Constitutional Problems for the New Public Management in the United States." In *Current Public Policy Issues: The 1998 Annals,* ed. Khi Thai and Rosalyn Carter. Boca Raton, Fla.: Academic Press, 1998.

Rosenbloom, David, and James Carroll. "Public Personnel Administration and Law." In *Handbook of Public Personnel Administration,* ed. Jack Rabin et al. New York: Marcel Dekker, 1994.

Rosenbloom, David, and Rosemary O'Leary. *Public Administration and Law,* 2nd ed. New York: Marcel Dekker, 1997.

Steingold, Fred S., Amy Delpo, and Lisa Guerin, eds. *The Employer's Legal Handbook,* 5th ed. Berkeley, Calif.: Nolo Press, 2003.

Chapter 6   Employee Benefits: Creating an Environment for Excellence

Beam, Burton T., Jr., and John J. McFadden. *Employee Benefits,* 6th ed. Chicago: Real Estate Education, 2001.

Black, Ann. *New Era of Benefits Communication,* 2nd ed. Brookfield, Wis.: International Foundation of Employee Benefit Plans, 2000.

Bureau of Labor Statistics, U.S. Department of Labor. *Employee Benefits in State and Local Governments, 1998.* Bulletin 2531. Washington, D.C.: Bureau of Labor Statistics, 2000.

"Defined Contribution Retirement Plans." *MIS Report.* Washington, D.C.: ICMA, October 1996.

EBRI. *EBRI Databook on Employee Benefits,* 4th ed. Washington, D.C.: Employee Benefit Research Institute, 1997.

———. *Fundamentals of Employee Benefit Programs,* 5th ed. Washington, D.C.: Employee Benefit Research Institute, 1996.

Harker, Carlton. *Self-Funding of Health Care Benefits,* 5th ed. Brookfield, Wis.: International Foundation of Employee Benefit Plans, 2003.

Harris, Jennifer D. *2001 Survey of State and Local Government Employee Retirement Systems.* Chicago: Public Pension Coordinating Council, 2002.

Johnson, Richard E. *Flexible Benefits: A How-To Guide,* 6th ed. Brookfield, Wis.: International Foundation of Employee Benefit Plans, 2002.

Krass, Stephen J. *The Pension Answer Book.* Brookfield, Wis.: International Foundation of Employee Benefit Plans, 2004.

McKay, Robert J. *Canadian Handbook of Flexible Benefits,* 2nd ed. New York: Wiley, 1996.

Moulder, Evelina. *Compensation and Benefits for Local Government Employees: Programs and Practices.* Special Data Issue no. 6 (2000). Washington, D.C.: ICMA, 2001.

———. *Local Government Health Benefits: Responses to Costs and Customers.* Special Data Issue no. 2 (2003). Washington, D.C.: ICMA, 2003.

Pacelli, Jane D. *Benefit Design in Public Employee Retirement Systems.* Chicago: Government Finance Officers Association, 1994.

Rosenbloom, Jerry S. *The Handbook of Employee Benefits: Design, Funding, and Administration,* 5th ed. New York: McGraw-Hill, 2001.

Chapter 7   Employee Responsibilities: Setting Expectations

Goleman, Daniel. *Emotional Intelligence.* New York: Bantam Books, 1995.

Howie, Robert M., and Laurence A. Shapiro. "How Long Is Enough? Leaves of Absence as Reasonable Accommodation under ADA." *Employee Relations Law Journal* 29 (Fall 2003): 33–49.

Johnson, Pamela, and Julie Indvik. "Rudeness at Work: Impulse over Restraint." *Public Personnel Management* 30 (Winter 2001): 457–465.

Schaner, Dean L. "Romance in the Workplace: Should Employers Act as Chaperons?"

Employee Relations Law Journal 20 (Summer 1994): 47–71.

Silbergeld, Arthur F., and Stacie S. Polashuk. "Chronic Serious Health Impairments and Worker Absences under Federal Employment Law." *Labor Lawyer* 14 (Summer 1998): 1–22.

Starkman, Paul E. "Answering the Tough Questions about Alcoholism and Substance Abuse under the ADA and FMLA." *Employee Relations Law Journal* 25 (Spring 2000): 43–77.

Chapter 8   When Things Go Wrong

American Arbitration Association. "A Due Process Protocol for Mediation and Arbitration of Statutory Disputes Arising out of the Employment Relationship." In *Guide for Employment Arbitrators,* pages 19–24. Publication AAA219-1OM-8/96. New York: American Arbitration Association, 1996.

Anderson, Jonathan B, and Lisa B. Bingham. "Upstream Effects from Mediation of Workplace Disputes: Some Preliminary Evidence from the USPS." *Labor Law Journal* 48 (1997): 601–615.

Bingham, Lisa B. "Mediating Employment Disputes: Perceptions of REDRESS at the United States Postal Service." *Review of Public Personnel Administration* 17 (1997): 20–30.

Brand, Norman, ed. *Discipline and Discharge in Arbitration.* Washington, D.C.: Bureau of National Affairs, 1998.

Denenberg, Tia Schneider, and Richard V. Denenberg. *Alcohol and Other Drugs: Issues in Arbitration.* Washington, D.C.: BNA Books, 1991.

———. "Workplace Violence and Dispute Resolution." *Dispute Resolution Journal* 51 (January–March 1996): 6–16.

Dunlop, Jack T., and Arnold M. Zack. *The Mediation and Arbitration of Employment Disputes.* San Francisco: Jossey-Bass, 1997.

Elkouri, Frank, and Edna Asper Elkouri. *Resolving Drug Issues.* Washington, D.C.: Bureau of National Affairs, 1993.

Frierson, James G. *Employer's Guide to the Americans with Disabilities Act,* 2nd ed. Washington, D.C.: Bureau of National Affairs, 1995.

———. *Preventing Employment Lawsuits: An Employer's Guide to Hiring, Discipline, and Discharge.* Washington, D.C.: Bureau of National Affairs, 1994.

Green, Ronald M., and Richard J. Reibstein. *Employer's Guide to Workplace Torts: Negligent Hiring, Fraud, Defamation, and Other Emerging Areas of Employer Liability.* Washington, D.C.: BNA Books, 1992.

Hill, Marvin F., Jr., and Anthony V. Sinicropi. *Remedies in Arbitration,* 2nd ed. Washington, D.C.: BNA Books, 1991.

Koven, Adolph M., and Susan L. Smith. *Just Cause: The Seven Tests,* 2nd ed. Washington, D.C.: Bureau of National Affairs, 1992.

Lindemann, Barbara, and Paul Grossman. *Employment Discrimination Law,* 3rd ed. Washington, D.C.: Bureau of National Affairs, 1996.

Lindemann, Barbara, and David D. Kadue. *Primer on Sexual Harassment.* Washington, D.C.: Bureau of National Affairs, 1992.

———. *Sexual Harassment in Employment Law.* Washington, D.C.: Bureau of National Affairs, 1992.

Moore, Christopher W. *The Mediation Process: Practical Strategies for Resolving Conflict,* 3rd ed. San Francisco: Jossey-Bass, 2003.

Ruben, Alan Miles, ed. *Elkouri and Elkouri: How Arbitration Works,* 6th ed. Washington, D.C.: BNA Books, 2003.

Sedmak, Nancy J., and Chrissie Vidas. *Primer on Equal Employment Opportunity,* 6th ed. Washington, D.C.: Bureau of National Affairs, 1994.

Chapter 9   Products and Services for Human Resource Management in Local Government

Ban, Carolyn, and Norma M. Riccucci, eds. *Public Personnel Management: Current Concerns, Future Challenges,* 3rd ed. New York: Longman, 2002.

Berman, Evan M., James S. Bowman, Jonathan P. West, and Montgomery Van Wart. *Human Resource Management in Public Service: Paradoxes, Processes, and Problems.* Thousand Oaks, Calif.: Sage, 2001.

Daley, Dennis M. *Strategic Human Resource Management: People and Performance Management in the Public Sector.* Upper Saddle River, N.J.: Prentice Hall, 2002.

Nigro, Felix A., and Lloyd G. Nigro. *The New Public Personnel Administration.* Itasca, Ill.: F. E. Peacock, 2000.

Shafritz, Jay M., et al. *Personnel Management in Government: Politics and Process,* 5th ed. New York: Marcel Dekker, 2001.

Wilson, Barbara J. *E-Government: Managing for the Future.* Fort Worth, Tex.: City of Fort Worth, 2003.

List of Contributors

Siegrun Fox Freyss (editor, Preface, and Chapter 9) teaches in the master of science in public administration program at the California State University, Los Angeles. Her publications have appeared in *The Municipal Year Book*, the *Review of Public Personnel Administration*, the *Public Administration Review*, the *Journal of Urban Affairs* and as chapters in several books. She has also been a research consultant and technical assistance provider to various public agencies and private, nonprofit organizations. She has an M.A. in city planning and holds a Ph.D. in government from the Claremont Graduate University.

Lisa B. Bingham (Chapter 8) practiced labor and employment law for ten years and was a partner in the Hartford, Connecticut, law firm of Shipman & Goodwin before joining the faculty of the Indiana University School of Law as a lecturer in law. She became a member of the faculty at IU's School of Public and Environmental Affairs in 1992. In 1997, she cofounded the Indiana Conflict Resolution Institute, a national theory center for evaluating dispute resolution programs in organizations. She directs the evaluation of the U.S. Postal Service's mediation program for employment disputes and has served as a consultant to the U.S. Department of the Air Force and National Institutes of Health. A mediator and arbitrator, Bingham is a member of the American Arbitration Association's National Employment ADR Task Force. She has published more than twenty articles. She earned her J.D. with high honors from the University of Connecticut School of Law.

N. Joseph Cayer (Chapter 6) is a professor of public affairs at Arizona State University. He specializes in human resource management and labor relations. He is the author or co-author of six books in the field of public administration and public policy, including *Public Personnel Administration in the United States*. His articles have appeared in journals such as *Public Administration Review, Review of Public Personnel Administration, Public Personnel Management, and Employee Assistance Quarterly*. He taught at Lamar University, the University of Maine, and Texas Tech University before joining the Arizona State University faculty in 1980.

Brian Clemow (Chapter 8) is a partner in the labor and employment law department of Shipman and Goodwin, LLP, in Hartford, Connecticut. He has taught public sector labor law at the University of Connecticut Law School and has chaired the Labor and Employment Law Section of the Connecticut Bar Association. He serves as labor counsel to both the executive and judicial branches of the government of the state of Connecticut.

Don A. Cozzetto (Chapter 7) is a professor and the dean of the College of Professional Studies, at Florida Gulf Coast University, the nation's newest university. He has written extensively in the areas of personnel administration and personnel law. His recent book, *Public Personnel Administration: Confronting the Challenges of Change*, is used in graduate programs across the country. He also has extensive experience as a practitioner in state and local governments. His Ph.D. is in public administration and public policy.

John A. DiNome (Chapter 5) represents a variety of regional and national employers in collective bargaining, labor arbitration, and employment-related litigation and is also labor counsel for a number of municipalities. He is a frequent author and lecturer on several national education programs in the field of labor and employee relations and has lectured extensively on all facets of public sector labor and employment law on behalf of numerous organizations, including the Pennsylvania Department of Community Affairs, the Pennsylvania State Association of Boroughs, the Pennsylvania State Association of Township Supervisors, the International City/County Management Association, and the National League of Cities. He received his J.D. with honors from the Rutgers University School of Law, where he served as president of the student body.

Barry M. Feldman (Chapter 4) has been the city manager of West Hartford, Connecticut, since 1985. Before 1985, he served as city manager in Sterling Heights, Michigan, and Portsmouth, Ohio. He has published in *PAR, The Municipal Year Book,* and *Public Budgeting and Finance.* He served as a member of a six-member committee appointed by the Connecticut state legislature charged with recommending ways to reorganize the Connecticut state government and is an adjunct professor at the University of Connecticut and Trinity College. He holds a Ph.D. from the University of Connecticut.

Richard C. Kearney (Chapter 4) is a professor and chair of the Department of Political Science at East Carolina University in Greenville, North Carolina. He has also taught at the University of Connecticut, University of South Carolina, and University of Northern Iowa. His research and teaching specialties are human resource management, labor relations, and state and local politics. He has published widely in professional journals, and his most recent books include *Labor Relations in the Public Sector* (3rd ed.), and, as coauthor, *State and Local Government* (5th ed.), and *Public Personnel Administration: Problems and Prospects* (4th ed.).

Nicholas P. Lovrich (Chapter 3) is a professor of political science and director of the Division of Governmental Studies and Services at Washington State University. The division provides applied research services to federal, state, and local government agencies and assists with faculty and graduate student research. His research has been published in *Journal of Politics, State and Local Government Review, Public Administration Review, American Journal of Public Administration, Public Administration Quarterly, Social Science Quarterly, American Behavioral Scientist, Urban Affairs Quarterly,* and *Public Personnel Management.* He has been editor in chief of the *Review of Public Personnel Administration* since 1990. He holds a B.A. from Stanford, and M.A. and Ph.D. degrees in political science from the University of California at Los Angeles.

Arthur H. McCurdy (Chapter 3) has twenty years' experience as a human resource practitioner in both the public and private sectors. His experience includes thirteen years with the State of Montana, where he became the governor's designee for collective bargaining and chief of the Labor Relations and Employee Benefits Bureau. His research has been published in *Review of Public Personnel Administration.* He is also a certified employee benefit specialist. Currently he is an assistant professor in the Division of Governmental Studies and Services at Washington State University. He holds a B.A. from the University of Washington, an M.A. from Western Washington University, and a Ph.D. from Washington State University, all in political science.

Saranne P. Murray (Chapter 8) is a partner in the labor and employment law department of Shipman and Goodwin, LLP, in Hartford, Connecticut. She is co-counsel to the National Public Employer Labor Relations Association and has served as the principal labor relations specialist for the state of Connecticut.

W. David Patton (Chapter 2) is the director of the Center for Public Policy and Administration, University of Utah. He has been a labor negotiator representing both unions and local government, a training director, a management recruiter, and a personnel consultant for state and local governments. He teaches human resource management and organizational leadership in the department of political science at the University of Utah. He has published the text, *Human Resource Management: The Public Service Perspective,* and articles in several journals in the fields of public personnel administration and labor relations. He earned an M.P.A. from Brigham Young University and a Ph.D. from the University of Utah.

Theodore B. Pedeliski (Chapter 7) is a professor in the Division of Economics and Public Affairs at the University of North Dakota, where he has taught administrative law and personnel law in a masters of public administration program for twenty years. He is a coauthor with Don A. Cozzetto of *Public Personnel Administration: Confronting the Challenges of Change* and has also coauthored articles on privacy in the workplace in *Review of Public Personnel Administration* and *Public Personnel Management.* He received his Ph.D. from the University of Minnesota in 1972 in political science and public law.

David H. Rosenbloom (Chapter 5) is Distinguished Professor of Public Administration at American University in Washington, D.C. Among his books on the legal-constitutional aspects of American public administration are *Federal Service and the Constitution* and *Public Administration and Law,* 2nd edition (with Rosemary O'Leary). He was appointed to the 1992 Clinton-Gore presidential transition team with responsibilities for the Office of Personnel Management. In 1993, he appeared as an expert witness before the Senate Committee on Governmental Affairs with regard to Hatch Act reform. He holds a Ph.D. in political sci-

ence from the University of Chicago, and in 1994 he was awarded an honorary doctor of laws degree from Marietta College, in Ohio, from which he earned his B.A.

Aleksandra Stapczynski (Chapter 1) manages her own personnel management consulting practice, Human Resources Services, Inc., in Massachusetts. She has fifteen years of experience providing technical assistance to cities and towns in all areas of municipal personnel management. She has provided consulting services to more than 250 Massachusetts municipalities, delivering work products that include studies concerning classification and compensation, salary and benefits surveys, personnel bylaws, personnel policies and procedures, performance appraisal and merit systems, job descriptions, personnel system improvements, staffing studies, and general personnel management studies. She is a former employee of the Massachusetts Municipal Association and the Commonwealth of Massachusetts Department of Revenue. She holds a bachelor's degree in government and a master's degree in public administration from Suffolk University, Boston.

Jonathan Tompkins (Chapters 1 and 7) is currently director of the master of public administration program at the University of Montana. His teaching responsibilities include courses in human resource management, organization theory, and research methods. He has published several articles relating to personnel administration, as well as a book, *Human Resource Management in Government.* He has also served as a consultant to several state and local government agencies. He received his Ph.D. in political science from the University of Washington in 1981.

Will Volk (Chapter 6) is the employee relations director for Dakota County, Minnesota. His experience during more than twenty-five years in the human resources field in manufacturing, retailing, banking, and government includes a number of specialist assignments in the compensation, benefits, and staffing functions as well as management and senior management positions. Mr. Volk was an early adopter and developer of a successful 501(c) (9) trust-based medical plan. He has also developed and implemented full merit compensation systems in both nonunion and union environments, including Dakota County, Minnesota, which has nearly 1,600 employees represented by 18 bargaining units. Mr. Volk holds a bachelor's degree from the University of St. Thomas in St. Paul, Minnesota.

Charles R. Wise (Chapter 8) is professor of public affairs at Indiana University. He is the immediate past president of the National Association of Schools of Public Affairs and Administration, which accredits master of public administration programs in the United States. He has served as managing editor of *Public Administration Review*, on the National Council of the American Society for Public Administration, as director of intergovernmental affairs for the U.S. Department of Justice, and as associate dean of the School of Public and Environmental Affairs at Indiana University. He is currently the project director of the parliamentary development project for Ukraine. He is the author of numerous articles and books on public law and administration, public organizations, legislative organizations and processes, and comparative administration. He has three times been awarded the William E. Mosher and Fredrick C.

Mosher Award for best academic article to appear in *Public Administration Review* in a year. He holds master's and doctoral degrees from Indiana University.

Stephanie L. Witt (Chapter 2) is an associate professor and chair of the Department of Political Science at Boise State University. She is currently the book review editor of *Review of Public Personnel Administration*. Her most recent book is *Anti-Gay Rights: Assessing Voter Initiatives*. She is the author of *The Urban West* and *The Pursuit of Race and Gender Equity*. Her research has appeared in journals such as *Review of Public Personnel Administration*, *Public Administration Review*, *Social Science Journal*, *State and Local Government Review*, and *American Politics Quarterly*. She received her Ph.D. from Washington State University.

Saundra M. Yaklin (Chapter 5) is a practicing attorney with Reed Smith Shaw & McClay, LLP. She handles a wide range of employment and labor matters in both the public and private sectors, but she focuses primarily on equal employment opportunity litigation. She has coauthored articles on the Fair Labor Standards Act and has also written extensively on the Americans with Disabilities Act, sexual harassment, and other fair-employment issues. Ms. Yaklin graduated from Western Michigan University in 1987 and received her J.D. degree from the University of Pennsylvania. She is admitted to the Pennsylvania and New Jersey bars.

Index

Absenteeism. *See* Attendance
Acknowledgment forms, in employee handbooks, 111
Administrative agencies, 220–221
Advancement. *See* Employee advancement
Advertisements, recruitment, 37–39, 57
Affirmative action, 34, 149
Affirmative discipline, 204. *See also* Employee discipline
Age Discrimination in Employment Act of 1967 (ADEA)
    compliance with, 34
    employee record retention and, 117
    enforcement of, 123
    prohibitions of, 121, 123
    protections of, 121–123
Agency for Healthcare Research and Quality, 155
Alcohol abuse, 182, 206–207
Alternative dispute resolution, 221–223
American Arbitration Association, 104, 222
American Association of Retired Persons (AARP), 175
American Bar Association, 222
American Federation of State, County, and Municipal
    Employees (AFSCME), 96, 101
American Nurses Association, 96
American Society for Public Administration (ASPA), 227
Americans with Disabilities Act (ADA)
    employee record retainment and, 116
    employee termination and, 139
    enforcement of, 122
    job descriptions and, 25
    medical examinations and, 54, 115
    prohibitions of, 119, 120, 122
    provisions of, 34, 115, 120, 154, 181
    substance abuse issues and, 182, 206, 207
Appeals boards, 223
Arbitration
    explanation of, 104
    methods for handling, 221, 222
Assessment centers, 49, 51–52
Association for Conflict Resolution, 222
Associations
    constitutional rights and, 145
    membership in state and local employee, 97
    unions vs., 96
At-will employment, 109–110
Attendance
    alcoholism and, 206
    discipline related to, 205–206, 209
    expectations of, 179–181
    family obligations and, 159
    special considerations regarding, 205–206
Award programs, 160–161
Awards, 86

Background investigations, 52–53
Bargaining in good faith, 98, 99
Bargaining unit, 96–98. *See also* Collective bargaining

Behaviorally anchored rating scales (BARS), 66, 68
Benefits. *See* Employee benefits
Bereavement leave, 158
Bidding process, 171
Bloodborne pathogens, 141
Bonuses, 85
Broadbanding
    explanation of, 21–22, 83
    framework for, 23
    traditional classification vs., 83
Budgeting
    challenges of, 4–5
    guiding principles of, 4
    strategies for, 5–6

Cafeteria benefit plans. *See* Flexible benefit plans
Career service, 7
Career tracks, 81–82
Caucuses, 222
Centers for Disease Control and Prevention (CDC), 141
Child labor laws, 40
Cigarette smoking, 140, 141
Civil Rights Act Amendments of 1972, 34, 61
Civil Rights Act of 1866, 119, 120
Civil Rights Act of 1871, 118–120
Civil Rights Act of 1991, 118, 119
Civil Rights Act of 1964 -Title VII
    compliance with, 24, 34, 61
    employee record retainment and, 116
    enforcement of, 119
    prohibitions of, 120
    protections of, 118, 120, 215, 222
    sexual harassment and, 126
Civil Service Act of 1883, 7
Civil service commissions, 223
Civil Service Reform Act of 1978, 8, 94
Civil service system
    downsizing and, 90
    explanation of, 7
    job advancement and, 82, 84
    structural characteristics of, 7–8
Classification and compensation system. *See also* Pay
    challenges for, 8–9
    functions of, 9–10
    guiding principles of, 8
    tips for developing successful, 22
Classification and pay plans. *See also* Pay
    alternative approaches to, 20–22
    benefits and, 26
    contract employees and, 28
    cost-of-living adjustments and, 24
    example of, 19
    guiding principles of, 10
    implementation of, 22–23
    interns and, 26

job analysis and, 10–13
job descriptions and, 11, 14–17, 25
job sharing and, 27
legislation and, 24, 26
part-time employees and, 26–27
position classifications and, 11, 18
red-circled positions and, 23–24
salary/wage surveys and, 19–20
temporary employees and, 27–28
union issues and, 24
Cleveland Board of Education v. Loudermill, 205, 207, 210
Code of Conduct, 192
Cohabitation, 184
Collective bargaining. *See also* Labor-management relations;
    Labor unions
  arbitration and, 104
  bargaining unit representatives and, 97–98
  contract negotiation and, 98–99, 101–102
  determining bargaining unit and, 96–97
  elected officials and, 100
  employee discipline and, 204
  fact finding and, 103–104
  guiding principles of, 96, 102
  historical and legal background of, 93–96
  mediation and, 103
  private vs. public sector, 94
  state list for, 95
  strikes and, 102–103
Communication
  of benefit plans, 172–173
  of expectations and responsibilities of employees, 194–198
Compensation. *See also* Classification and compensation
    system; Classification and pay plans; Employee benefits;
    Pay
  collecting and analyzing data to determine, 19
  competency-based, 80–81
  example of, 19
  performance-based, 78–81
  salary range-based, 21
  skill-based, 80–81
  step-based, 20
Competency-based pay, 80–81
Complaints. *See* Employee complaints
Comprehensive Alcohol Abuse and Alcohol Prevention
    Treatment and Rehabilitation Act Amendments of 1979,
    206
Comprehensive Alcohol Abuse and Alcohol Prevention
    Treatment and Rehabilitation Act of 1970, 206
Computer use, 186–189
Conciliation, 222
Concurrent validity, 47
Cone method for interviews, 51
Confidentiality. *See also* Privacy
  ethical obligations for, 189
  of personnel records, 114–115
Consent decrees, 90
Consolidated Omnibus Budget Reconciliation Act (COBRA),
    156
Constitutional rights
  ambiguous laws and, 141–142
  due process and, 147–149, 205
  equal protection, 149–150
  First Amendment, 112–113, 143–146, 202
  guiding principles of, 141
  privacy, 146–147

public service model for analyzing, 142–143
  tips for avoiding problems related to, 142
Construct validity, 47
Consultants, benefit plan, 171, 172
Content validity, 47
Contract employees, 28
Contracts
  administration of, 105–107
  at-will employment and, 109–110
  explanation of, 55
  implied, 110
  negotiation of, 98–99, 101–102
  oral, 110
  oral and implied, 110
  personnel policies as, 110
  post-termination, 211
Cornell University, School of Industrial and Labor Relations,
    231
Cost of living adjustments (COLAs), 24
Court orders, 90
CPS Human Resource Services, 228
Criminal History and Driving Record Form, 45
Criminal misconduct, 208
Criterion validity, 47
Critical incident assessment, 66

Dakota County, Minnesota, 164–167
Dating, 183–184
Daugherty standards, 205
Defamation claims, 139, 217
Defined benefit plans, 160, 162
Defined contribution plans, 160–162
Department of Commerce, 155
Department of Justice, 122
Department of Labor
  certification of health care provider form, 130
  employee record retention requirements, 117
  information about, 230
  notification of rights under FMLA, 134
Disability insurance, 156
Discharge. *See* Employee termination
Disclaimers, in employee handbooks, 110–111
Discretionary leave, 180
Discrimination
  EEOC charges related to, 124–126
  employee complaints related to, 213–214
  employee rights related to, 115, 118
  legislation related to, 118–124
  retaliation claims and, 124
  third-party complaints about, 218
Dispute resolution, 221–223
Domestic partners, 174
Downsizing, 88–90
Driving under the influence (DUI), 206
Drug abuse, 182–183, 206–207
Drug testing, 54, 182–183
Due process
  constitutional rights and, 205
  procedural, 147–148
  substantive, 148–149

E-mail
  freedom of speech issues and, 144, 187
  guidelines for use of, 187, 188

EEOC. *See* Equal Employment Opportunity Commission (EEOC)
Elder care, 175
Employee advancement
    constraints on linking performance to, 82, 84
    elements of system for, 81–82
    linking performance to, 81–82, 84
Employee assistance programs (EAPs), 78, 159, 175
Employee benefit plans
    administrative issues for, 170
    communication of, 172–173
    defined benefit, 160, 162
    defined contribution, 160–162
    evaluation of, 173–177
    flexible, 163–169 (*See also* Flexible benefit plans)
    guiding principles of, 161, 163
    insured vs. self-insured arrangements for, 165, 170
    open enrollment for, 173
    purchase and design considerations for, 171–172
    strategies to reshape, 175–178
Employee benefits
    awards, 160
    bereavement, 158
    challenges related to, 153
    disability insurance, 156
    employee assistance/wellness programs, 159
    employee development, 157–159
    explanation of, 26
    family and medical leave, 154
    flexible schedules/telecommuting, 159, 160
    guiding principles of, 153
    health care, 155–156
    holiday, vacation, sick, and family care leave, 156–157
    housing and moving incentives, 160
    legal insurance, 156
    mandated, 153–154
    optional, 154–161
    retirement pensions, 160–161
    Social Security, 154
    unemployment compensation, 154
    uniforms, 160
    workers' compensation, 154
Employee Benefits Survey, 176–177
Employee complaints
    administrative agencies handling, 220–221
    challenges of, 212
    defamation, 139
    of defamation, 139, 217
    defending lawsuits related to, 219–220
    of discrimination, 213–214
    of free speech restrictions, 217
    of freedom of association restrictions, 217
    guiding principles for handling, 212
    of harassment, 214–216
    of privacy restrictions, 217
    of wrongful discharge, 215
Employee development. *See also* Training
    employee performance and, 78
    opportunities for, 157–159
Employee discipline. *See also* Employee termination
    affirmative, 204
    alcohol and drug abuse and, 206–207
    appeal rights and, 204–205
    criminal misconduct and, 208
    freedom of speech issues and, 143–144, 202

    guiding principles for, 201
    investigation and documentation of misconduct and, 202–203
    liability claims and, 211–212
    off-duty misconduct and, 208–209
    progressive, 203–204
    sick leave abuse and other attendance problems and, 205–206, 209
    steps to take prior to, 203
    of supervisors and managers, 209–210
    threats and violent behavior and, 138–139, 207–208
    tips for successfully handling, 211
    for violent behavior, 138–139
Employee handbooks. *See* Personnel policy manuals
Employee misconduct
    investigating and documenting, 202–203
    off-duty, 208–209
    policy for criminal, 208
Employee performance
    advancement or desirable assignments based on, 81–84
    compensation based on, 78–81
    downsizing and, 88–90
    goal setting to improve, 76–78
    individual development plans for, 78
    motivators for, 84–86
    during organizational change, 86–88
Employee performance evaluation
    challenges of, 60
    choosing method for, 62–63
    comparing employees against average employee, 63–66
    comparing employees against each other, 67–73
    court challenges to, 61
    criticism in, 74
    employee response and appeals to, 74–75
    guiding principles for, 59–60
    implementation of program for, 73–76
    labor unions and, 62
    program implementation for, 73–76
    termination and, 75–76
    timing of, 74
    tips for, 75
    top-level support for, 61–62
    validity and reliability issues in, 60–61
Employee performance evaluation methods
    to avoid, 73
    behaviorally anchored rating scales, 66, 68
    critical incident assessment, 66, 67
    forced-choice rating, 65
    forced distribution of employees, 67, 69
    narrative essay, 63–64
    objective, 64
    paired employee comparisons, 67, 68
    participatory techniques for, 70, 71
    pass-fail, 72
    peer rating, 69–70
    self-rating, 68
    360-degree feedback, 70–72
    upward feedback, 70
    using evaluators other than supervisors, 67–68
    weighted checklist, 65–66
Employee records. *See* Personnel records
Employee recruitment
    advertising and, 37–39, 57
    challenges of, 34
    external, 37

guiding principles of, 33–34
hiring process and, 53–56
internal, 35, 37
job announcements and, 35, 36
overview of, 33
responsibility for, 34–35
selection process and, 39–53 (*See also* Employee selection)
tips for successful, 39
Employee responsibilities
for attendance, 179–181
changing policies for, 198–199
communicating expectations and responsibilities for, 194–198
for computer and Internet use, 186–189
for confidentiality, 189
for interpersonal relationships, 183–186
for off-duty activities, 190–193
for political activity, 143, 189–190
for residency, 193
for workplace conduct, 181–183
Employee Retirement Income Security Act (ERISA), 117
Employee rights
employee contracts and, 55, 109–110
equal employment opportunity and harassment policies and, 111–112 (*See also* Sexual harassment)
First Amendment rights and, 112–113
leaves of absence and, 113 (*See also* Family and Medical Leave Act (FMLA)
personnel policy manual and, 110–114
political patronage and, 111
workplace violence and, 113
Employee selection
application forms and resumes for, 41, 42–44, 50
assessment centers and, 49, 51–52
background investigations and, 52–53
challenges of, 39
criminal history and, 45
eligibility lists and, 41, 46
guiding principles for, 39
interviews and, 46, 48–51
methods for, 40–41
minimum qualifications and, 40
performance tests and, 46
responsibility for, 39–40
written tests and, 46, 47
Employee termination
for discipline problems, 201
methods for handing, 210–212
performance evaluation and, 75–76
procedural issues and, 205
violent behavior and, 139
Employee violence, 138–139, 207–208
Employees
at-will, 109–110
communicating expectations and responsibilities of, 194–198
contract, 28
criminal misconduct by, 208
drug testing for, 54, 182–183
engaged in outside employment, 191–192
identification of potentially violent, 208
identity and eligibility proof for, 53–54
medical examinations for, 54, 115
negligent retention of, 140
part-time, 26–27

probationary period for, 54–55
temporary, 27–28
third-party complaints about, 218–219
threats by, 207–208
Employment Practices Liability Insurance (EPLI), 212, 219
Equal Employment Opportunity Act of 1972, 34
Equal Employment Opportunity Commission (EEOC)
charges under, 124–126
enforcement of discrimination legislation by, 118, 122–124
explanation of, 34, 230
substance abuse issues and, 207
Equal employment opportunity (EEO), 34, 111
Equal Pay Act of 1963, 28
compliance with, 24
employee record retention and, 116
enforcement of, 124
prohibitions in, 123
Equal protection rights, 149–150
Essential functions, 25
Ethics codes, 192
External recruiting, 37
External strategic planning, 2

Facilitation, 222
Fact finding, 103–104
Fact-finding conferences, 125
Fair Labor Standards Act (FLSA), 24, 116, 154, 159
Family and Medical Leave Act (FMLA)
bereavement leave and, 158
Department of Labor notification of rights under, 134
employee record retention and, 117
medical certification and, 130–131, 138
notification requirements of, 132–134, 136–137
provisions of, 113, 124, 129, 132, 154, 180–181
substance abuse treatment and, 207
Family care leave, 156–157
Family-friendly workplace, 159
Federal Mediation and Conciliation Service, 103, 222
Fifth Amendment, 147–149
First Amendment rights
employee handbook statements on, 112–113
free speech and, 186, 187, 217
freedom of association and, 144–145
general speech on matters of public concern, 143–144
oaths and, 146
to organize, 94
partisan speech and activity and, 143
religion and, 145–146
whistle-blower protections and, 146
Fisher, Roger, 99
FlexComp Plan (Dakota County, Minnesota), 164–165
Flexible benefit plans. *See also* Employee benefit plans
administrative issues regarding, 170
demographic change and, 174
flexible spending, 163
insured vs. self-insured, 165, 170
paid time off, 163–167
questions and answers for, 168–169
tradable, 163
Flexible schedules, 159, 160
Flexible spending plans, 163
Flexible work schedules, 86
FMLA. *See* Family and Medical Leave Act (FMLA)
Forced-choice rating, 65

Forced distribution of employees' ratings appraisal technique, 67, 69
Formalization, in merit system, 7–8
Fourteenth Amendment, 147–149
Fourth Amendment rights, 146–147, 217
Fraternal Order of Police, 96
Free speech issues
    e-mail and, 144, 187
    employee complaints related to, 217
    employee discipline and, 143–144, 202
    Supreme Court and, 202
Freedom of association, 144–145, 217

Gainsharing programs, 101
Gender-based classifications, 150
Getting to Yes: Negotiating Agreement Without Giving In (Fisher & Ury), 99
Gifts, 86
Gilmer v. Interstate/Johnson Lane Corporation, 222
Goal setting, 76–78
Government Performance and Results Act of 1993, 5
Grievances
    explanation of, 105–106
    methods for handling, 221
Griggs v. Duke Power Company, 47

Harassment
    employee complaints related to, 214–215
    employee handbook statements on, 111–112
    nonsexual forms of, 129
    sexual, 126–129
Hatch Act, 189
Hatch Act Reform Amendments, 189
Health care plans
    COBRA coverage and, 156
    overview of, 155–156
    statistics regarding, 154, 155
Health care reimbursement funds, 177
Health issues
    infectious diseases as, 141
    medical leave and (*See* Family and Medical Leave Act (FMLA))
    smoking as, 140, 141
Health maintenance organizations (HMOs), 155, 156
Heart and Lung Act (Pennsylvania), 140
Hepatitis, 141
Hiring. *See also* Employee recruitment; Employee selection; Job interviews
    conditional job offers and, 53–54
    guiding principle for, 53
    negligent, 139
    orientation and, 55–56
    probationary period and, 54–55
HIV/AIDS, 141
Holiday leave, 156–157
Hostile work environment, 127. *See also* Sexual harassment
Housing allowances, 160
HR Manager web site, 10
Human capacity building strategies, 3
Human resource management products/services
    academic organizations providing, 231
    criteria for selection of, 226–227
    federal agencies providing, 230–231
    nonprofits supplying, 227–230
    overview of, 225–226
    tips for purchasing, 226
    Web sites for, 231–232

Immigration and Control Act, 117
Infectious diseases, 141
Interest-based bargaining, 99, 101
Internal recruiting, 35, 37
Internal Revenue Code (IRC), 161
Internal strategic planning, 2. *See also* Strategic planning
International Association of Fire Fighters, 96
International Brotherhood of Teamsters, 96
International City/County Management Association (ICMA), 228
International Personnel Management Association, 157
International Public Management Association for Human Resources (IPMA-HR), 46, 228
Internet
    accessing benefit plan information on, 173
    guidelines for use of, 186–189
    human resource management sites on, 231–232
Internet resources
    HR Manager, 10
    for job announcements, 35
Interns, 26
Interpersonal relationships, 183–186
Interviews
    EEOC, 125
    job, 46, 48–51, 197–198
Iowa Association of School Boards, 101

Job analysis
    advancement systems and, 81
    Americans with Disabilities Act and, 25
    explanation of, 10–11, 34
    performance evaluation using, 63
    position analysis questionnaire for, 12–13
Job announcements, 35, 36
Job application forms
    criminal history and driving record, 45
    example of, 42–44
    explanation of, 41
Job Description Sample Form, 14–15
Job descriptions
    Americans with Disabilities Act and, 25
    example of, 14–15
    example of essential functions for, 16–17
    explanation of, 11
    performance evaluation using, 62–63
Job interviews
    communication of policies during, 197–198
    cone method for, 51
    errors made during, 48, 49
    explanation of, 46, 48–49
    illegal questions for, 48–50
    tips for successful, 49
Job orientation sessions, 197–198
Job rating scales, 11, 18
Job sharing, 26–27
Jurisdictions, job sharing between, 27
Just cause, 204

Knowledge, skills, and abilities (KSAs)
    employee performance and, 76, 77, 81
    job advancement and, 82
    job analysis and, 10, 45

rating scale for, 18
  selection methods and, 41
  strategic planning and, 1, 3

Labor-management committees, 107
Labor-management relations
  arbitration and, 104, 221, 222
  best practices for reinventing, 103
  challenges in local government, 107–108
  collective bargaining and, 95–102 (*See also* Collective
    bargaining)
  contract administration and, 105–107
  fact finding and, 103–104
  grievances and, 105–106, 221
  legislation affecting, 94
  mediation and, 103
  private vs. public sector, 94
  strikes and, 102–103
  tips for maintaining good, 99
  unfair labor practice charges and, 221
Labor strikes, 102–103
Labor unions. *See also* Collective bargaining
  background of, 93–94
  challenges in relationships between management and,
    107–108
  classification and pay structures and, 24
  downsizing decisions and, 89–90
  freedom of association and, 145
  job advancement and, 82
  performance evaluations and, 62
  work teams and, 32
Landrum-Griffin Act, 93, 94
Lawsuits, in state or federal court, 219–220
Layoffs, 88–89
Leave
  bereavement, 158
  discretionary, 180
  employee handbook statements on, 113
  family and medical, 132, 154, 156–157
  holiday, 156–157
  maternity, 157
  military, 157
  personal, 156–157, 175
  sick, 156–157
  vacation, 156–157
Legal insurance, 156
Liberty, 148
Local Government Institute (LGI), 228
Long-term care insurance, 175, 176
Long Term Care Security Act, 176
Loudermill decision, 205, 207, 210

Market-based pay, 22
Maternity leave, 157
Mediation, 103, 222
Medical examinations, 54, 115
Medical issues. *See* Health issues
Merit pay. *See* Pay for performance
Merit system
  constraints of, 6–7
  explanation of, 7
  structural characteristics of, 7–8
Military leave, 157
Minimum qualifications, 40
Misconduct. *See* Employee misconduct

Mission statements, 2
Moving allowances, 160

Narrative essays, for performance evaluation, 63–64
National Academy of Public Administration (NAPA), 228–229
National Association of Counties (NACo), 229
National Association of Schools of Public Affairs and
    Administration (NASPAA), 231
National Association of Towns and Townships (NATaT), 229
National Center for Small Communities (NCSC), 229
National Committee for Employee Support of the Guard and
    Reserve (ESGR), 230
National Education Association (NEA), 96
National Labor Relations Act (NLRA), 93, 94, 97, 102
National League of Cities (NLC), 229
Negligent hiring, 139
Negligent retention, 139
Nepotism rules, 184–185
No Electronic Theft Act, 186–187
No smoking policy, 140, 141
Nonsuspect classifications, 149–150

Oaths, 146
Objective method of performance evaluation, 64
Occupational Safety and Health Act, 137
Occupational Safety and Health Administration (OSHA)
  workplace health and, 141
  workplace violence and, 138, 139
Off-duty activities, 190–193
Office of Personnel Management (OPM), 231
Older Workers' Benefit and Protection Act, 123
Organizational change, 86–88
Organizational charts, 6
Orientation sessions, 197–198
Overtime pay, 26

Paid time-off (PTO) arrangements
  example of, 166–167
  explanation of, 157, 163–165
  questions and answers for, 168–169
Paired employee comparisons, 67, 68
Part-time employees, 26–27
Participatory performance evaluation methods, 70, 71
Partisan speech, 146
Pay. *See also* Classification and compensation system;
    Classification and pay plans; Compensation
  broadbanding and, 21–23
  collecting and analyzing data to determine, 19
  competency-based, 80–81
  cost-of-living adjustments to, 24
  determining appropriate levels of, 9
  legislation and, 24, 26
  market-based, 22
  rating scales for compensable factors to determine, 11, 18
  for red-circled employees, 23–24
  skill-based, 80–81
  union issues and, 24
Pay for performance, 22, 79–80
Pensions. *See* Retirement benefits
Performance. *See* Employee performance; Employee
    performance evaluation; Employee performance
    evaluation methods
Performance budgeting, 5
Performance standards, 76. *See also* Employee performance
    evaluation

Performance tests, 46
Personal leave programs, 156–157, 175
Personnel policies, 110
Personnel policy manuals
    acknowledgment forms and, 111
    contents of, 195
    disclaimers and, 110–111
    equal employment opportunity policies and, 111
    First Amendment rights and, 112–113
    function of, 194–197
    guiding principles of, 110
    harassment policies and, 111–112
    leaves of absence and, 113
    political patronage and, 111
    workplace violence and, 113
Personnel records
    confidentiality of, 114–115
    contents of, 115
    guiding principles on, 114
    retention of, 114, 116–117
    right to inspect, 115
    tips for maintaining, 115
Personnel system
    budgeting and, 4–6
    choosing best approach for, 8
    civil service system and, 7–8
    classification and compensation system and, 8–28 (*See also*
        Classification and compensation system)
    executive personnel office and, 8
    guiding principle of, 6
    objectives of, 6–7
    strategic planning and, 1–4
    structure of, 6
Pickering v. Board of Education, 202
Police bill of rights, 218
Policy Statement on Affirmative Action Programs for State
        and Local Agencies (Equal Employment Opportunity
        Commission), 34
Political activity, 143, 189–190
Political patronage, 111
Position Analysis Information Sheet, 12–13
Position classification
    explanation of, 11, 18
    function of, 19
Post-termination contracts, 211
Predictive validity, 47
Preferred provider organizations (PPOs), 155, 156
Pretax savings plans, 177
Privacy. *See also* Confidentiality
    constitution protections for, 146–147
    employee complaints about restrictions of, 217
Probationary period, 54–55
Problem-solving teams, 29
Procedural due process, 147–148
Professional associations, 62, 227–230
Progressive discipline, 203–204. *See also* Employee termination
Public property use, 186–189
Public service model, 142–143

Quality of work life (QWL) programs, 107
Quid pro quo sexual harassment, 127

Reagan, Ronald, 141
Recruitment. *See* Employee recruitment
Recruitment interviews. *See* Job interviews
Reference checks, 52–53

Rehabilitation Act of 1973
    enforcement of, 122
    prohibitions of, 120, 122
    protections of, 120
    substance abuse programs and, 206
Relationship-by-objectives (RBO) program, 102
Reliability
    performance evaluation system, 60–61
    test, 47
Religion, 145–146
Request for proposal, 171
Request for quotation, 171
Residency requirements, 193
Responsibility. *See* Employee responsibilities
Resumes, 41
Retaliation claims, 124
Retirement benefits, 160–161
Rewards, 85–86
Romantic relationships, 183–184

Safety, 138
Salaries. *See* Classification and compensation system;
        Classification and pay plans; Pay
Salary range-based compensation plan, 19, 21
Search and seizure, 146–147
Self-directed work teams, 29–30, 107
Self-insured arrangements, 165, 170
Separation agreements, 210
Service Employees International Union, 96
Sexual harassment
    approaches and solutions to, 128
    challenges related to, 126
    employee complaints related to, 214–216
    employee handbook statements on, 111–112 .
    guiding principles related to, 126
    legislation related to, 126–127
    tips for avoiding problems with, 129
    types of, 127
Sick leave
    abuse of, 205–206
    provisions for, 156–157
Skill-based compensation, 80–81
Skill-based pay, 80–81
Smoking, 140, 141
Social Security, 154
Society for Human Resource Management (SHRM),
        229–230
Special-purpose teams, 29
State Employees Association of North Carolina, 96
State Occupational Safety and Health Administration
        (OSHA) laws, 117
Step-based compensation plan, 19, 20
Strategic planning
    elements of, 2–4
    explanation of, 1–2
    external, 2
    guiding principles of, 1
    internal, 2
    tips for successful, 4
Strategic plans, 2
Strikes, 102–103
Substance abuse. *See* Alcohol abuse; Drug abuse
Substantive due process, 148–149
Succession planning, 82
Sunshine bargaining, 98. *See also* Collective bargaining

Supervisors
    change in, 87–88
    communicating expectations to employees by, 198
Supreme Court, U.S.
    affirmative action and, 149
    dispute resolution and, 222
    due process and, 148
    employee discipline and, 205
    family and medical leave and, 132
    First Amendment rights and, 112
    free speech issues and, 202
    freedom of association issues and, 217
    job selection criteria and, 47
    nonsuspect or gender classifications and, 150
    political activities of public employees and, 143
    sexual harassment and, 215
    whistle-blower protections and, 146
Suspect classifications, 149

Taft-Hartley Act, 93, 94
Teamwork. *See* Work teams
Telecommuting, 159
Temporary employees, 27–28
Termination. *See* Employee termination
Tests
    drug, 54, 182–183
    function of, 7
    performance, 46
    validity and reliability of, 47
    written, 46
Texas Public Employees Association, 96
Threats, 207–208
360-degree feedback performance evaluation, 70–72
Time off, 85–86
Title VII. *See* Civil Rights Act of 1964 - Title VII
Total quality management (TQM) programs, 107
Tradable plans, 163
Training. *See also* Employee development
    employee development and, 157–159
    orientation, 55–56
    performance evaluation, 62, 73
    as performance reward, 85
    safety and health, 138
    sexual harassment awareness, 128
Tuberculosis, 141

Unemployment compensation, 154
Unfair labor practice charges, 221
Uniform allowances, 160
Uniform Guidelines on Employee Selection Procedures
    (Equal Employment Opportunity Commission),
    34, 47
Uniform Services Employment and Reemployment Rights
    Act of 1994 (USERRA), 121, 124
Unions. *See* Labor unions
Upward feedback performance evaluation, 70
Ury, William, 99

U.S. Department of Agriculture (USDA) Graduate School, 230

Vacation leave, 156–157
Validity
    performance evaluation system, 60–61
    test, 47
Veterans' Employment and Training Service (VETS), 124
Violence. *See* Workplace violence

Wages. *See* Classification and compensation system;
    Classification and pay plans; Pay
Wagner Act. *See* National Labor Relations Act (NLRA)
Wards Cove v. Antonio, 47
Waters v. Churchill, 202
Weighted checklist, 65–66
Weingarten rights, 90
Wellness programs, 159
Whistle-blowers, 146
Work rules
    change in, 199
    communication of, 194, 196
Work teams
    challenges for, 28
    effective vs. ineffective, 31
    explanation of, 29
    guiding principles for, 28
    methods for rewarding, 85
    problem-solving, 29
    self-directed, 29–30, 107
    special-purpose, 29
    strategies for effective, 30–32
Workers' compensation
    cost control and, 135
    disability statutes and, 135
    explanation of, 154
    guiding principles of, 133, 135
    investigation of claims under, 135
    physician access and, 135
    reforming trends and, 136–137
Workplace
    alcohol abuse in, 182
    computer and Internet use in, 186–189
    confidentiality issues in, 189
    drug abuse in, 182–183
    family-friendly, 159
    personal relationships and, 183–186
    safety in, 138
Workplace violence
    employee discipline and, 138–139, 207–208
    employee handbook statements on, 113
    guiding principles related to, 137
    prevention of, 138, 140
    victims of, 139–140
Wrongful discharge, 215

Zero-tolerance policies, 207

Human Resource Management in Local Government,
Second Edition

Design: Will Kemp
Composition: Barton Matheson Willse & Worthington
Printing and binding: Cenveo, Atlanta, Georgia